THE A TO Z
OF MICROWAVE COOKING

THE A TO Z
OF MICROWAVE COOKING

Marty Klinzman and Shirley Guy
Photography by Peter Brooks

NEW
HOLLAND

New Holland (Publishers) Ltd
37 Connaught Street
London W2 2AZ

First published in the United Kingdom 1988

© New Holland (Publishers) Ltd

Edited by Marje Hemp
Sketches by Anne Westoby
Typeset by McManus Bros Ltd
Lithographic reproduction of colourplates by Hirt & Carter Ltd
Printed and bound by Printpak Books

ISBN 1 85368 011 7

Foreword

For our newest cookery book we chose to adopt a fresh approach to microwave cooking, which, we hope, will make life a great deal easier and more fun for microwave users. Putting ourselves in your place, we listed all the foods you might possibly want to microwave and set about finding out more about them and testing recipes. The result is the most comprehensive microwave book yet written, with over 400 entries all arranged alphabetically and more than 600 recipes covering all your favourite foods.

As well as supplying recipes for almost every occasion, we have included basic cooking instructions and microwave techniques for the novice, and given a wealth of hints and ideas on how to use your microwave to best advantage, making this book of great practical value in the kitchen.

Like any appliance, a microwave oven has certain limitations as not all foods can be microwaved successfully. These limitations, highlighted in the text for your convenience, are relatively few and are more than compensated by the many undeniable advantages microwaving has over conventional cooking. Looking through the pages of this book you will be amazed at the incredible variety of meals and dishes this electronic wonder can help you create and how versatile and efficient it can be.

Marty Klinsman   *Shirley Guy*

Happy microwaving!

How to use this book

VARIABLE POWER LEVELS
All recipes in this book have been tested using microwave ovens with variable power levels. Each level serves a definite purpose and recommended power levels should be used where possible. If your oven does not have the recommended settings, you may not achieve the same results. Microwave ovens achieve lower power settings by automatically cycling energy on and off so foods may be microwaved at a higher power than recommended as long as additional attention is given to stirring, turning or rotating them. Foods that need to be simmered slowly or delicate dishes should not be attempted at higher power levels. The following are power levels used in recipes in this book:

Full Power (100%) is used to cook foods at a high temperature in a short time. The Full Power setting is used in many of the recipes given.

High (70%) is used for foods that require more attention than those cooked at Full Power.

Medium (50%) is used for slower cooking, such as when microwaving some sauces and meats.

Defrost (30%) is used not only to defrost foods, but also to cook delicate foods or dishes that need long, slow simmering.

Low (15%) is used for extremely gentle cooking and for keeping foods warm before serving.

Note: Some microwave ovens have multiple power levels to give greater flexibility in cooking a wide range of foods. Check the instruction book for levels that correspond to the above. Where settings are numbered, the numbers often correspond to the percentage power. For example, 5 corresponds to medium (50%).

COOKING TIMES
The cooking times given for all recipes in this book are intended merely as a guide, since the amount of microwave energy required will differ according to the make of oven used, the size and type of container, the quantity of food, the temperature of food before cooking, the depth of food in the container, and personal preferences where such foods as meats, poultry and casseroles are concerned. The time indicated above each recipe is a guide to the length of microwaving time and *not* the total preparation time.

ADAPTING RECIPE TIMES
All the recipes in this book have been tested in microwaves with an output of 600 to 650 watts. Household current sometimes varies during periods of peak use such as early evening or in very cold weather.

As a general rule, if you have a 500 watt microwave oven, add approximately 15 – 20 seconds to each minute of cooking time. If you have a 700 watt microwave, decrease the cooking time by about 15 seconds per minute.

Note: Always check food at the minimum cooking time to see whether it is done, then add more time if necessary.

HOW TO CHECK TIMING
If you are uncertain about the household current, or if you wish to use the recipes in this book with microwave ovens of different wattage, you can check the timing and make adjustments to the recipe. To check timing, pour 250 ml (8 fl oz) iced water into a glass measuring jug. Place in the microwave and microwave on Full Power until the water reaches a good boil. Time the action carefully. If your oven takes 3¼-3¾ minutes, the recipes in this book should be correct for you. If your microwave oven takes considerably longer, add extra time to the cooking period, and if the water boils in less time, decrease the cooking time.

INGREDIENTS
In microwave cooking as in conventional cooking, the exact quantity of ingredients is necessary to ensure a dish is perfectly prepared.

☐ All measurements in this book are given in both standard metric and imperial units. It is essential to follow one set of measurements as they are not interchangeable. The ingredients are listed in the order in which they are used in the method.

☐ Avoid substituting key ingredients unless alternatives are given and avoid doubling or halving recipes as the timing will need critical adjustment. Unlike a conventional oven, the more food you have in the microwave oven the longer it will take to cook.

☐ Seasonings and spices can be varied according to personal taste but take care not to overdo it. Microwave cooking takes place so quickly that herbs and spices have little time to develop fully. Vegetables, too, retain all their natural flavour and require very little salt.

GENERAL MICROWAVE HINTS
When using Full Power, foods cook in about a quarter to a third of the time required for conventional cooking. Microwave ovens vary in speed and evenness of cooking, so always underestimate the cooking item and test whether foods are ready at the minimum time. Remember foods continue to cook after removal from the microwave, so allow for standing time.

☐ Watch the cooking process closely and check the food often. If the food seems to be cooking unevenly, then stir, rearrange or rotate it.

☐ Reduce the amount of herbs and spices used, especially strongly flavoured ones, as they keep their flavouring power in the microwave. For many casseroles and meat dishes the seasoning can be added near the end of the cooking time.

☐ Select bowls and other containers that are larger than those used in conventional recipes and fill one-third to one-half full, as foods tend to rise higher and increase in volume in the microwave (*see also* Equipment).

□ As a general rule, use less liquid when cooking vegetables, stews and casseroles. Watch the dish and add a little more liquid if necessary during the cooking time.

□ Ingredients should be of a uniform shape and size so they cook more evenly. Small pieces cook more rapidly than large ones.

ADVANTAGES OF MICROWAVING

There are many advantages to cooking in a microwave, as you will discover as you continue to use yours. The microwave is useful in busy households where family members cannot always be together at meal times or when quick meals are needed, while anyone living alone will find it ideal for cooking small quantities. Here are some of the more obvious advantages:

Speed: This is one of the greatest advantages, as microwaving takes about one-third to one-quarter of conventional cooking time.

Economy: Not only do microwave ovens use less power than conventional ovens (650 watts as opposed to the 2,200 watts of one element in a conventional oven), but they are used for a shorter time. Moreover, there is no need to preheat the microwave, as heat is generated instantly in the food when it is switched on. It also switches off at the end of the set cooking time, so no power is wasted.

Mobility: Microwaves use a standard 13 amp plug and household current, so they can be used almost anywhere where there

is a stable surface. Although they can be placed in any area of the kitchen, a work surface is usually the most convenient. Some people like to place the microwave on a sturdy trolley, so that it can be wheeled from kitchen to dining-room or patio.

Safe and easy to use: Microwaves are simple to operate and most dishes remain cool enough to handle easily. This means they can be used safely by the young, the elderly and the disabled, with little danger of burning.

Defrosting: There is no need to panic if you have forgotten to take a roast or casserole from the freezer. The microwave will defrost foods quickly and effectively without affecting the flavour or texture of the food.

Flavour and nutrition: Many foods cook in their own juices, or with the addition of very little liquid, thus retaining their natural flavour and most vitamins and nutrients. Many foods can be cooked in the microwave without the addition of oil or butter, making it useful for people on slimming diets or for those who are avoiding cholesterol.

Reheating: The microwave will reheat foods, such as casseroles, soups or individual plates of food, with no added moisture and no change in texture or flavour. Leftovers are just as appetizing as the first time they were served, and a plate of food saved for a latecomer will look and taste as fresh as newly cooked.

Cooler cooking: The microwave itself does not get hot, so even during long cooking periods, or when the temperature inside the oven is extremely high, the kitchen will stay cool. This is a great help with processes like preserving fruits and vegetables in the middle of summer.

Easy cleaning: The microwave is easier to clean than a conventional oven as foods do not often boil over and do not burn onto the oven surfaces. If spills occur, the metal or acrylic surfaces inside are easy to wipe clean.

Saves washing up: Food can often be cooked and served in the same container, so there is less washing up to do after cooking in the microwave. Food does not burn easily in the microwave, and containers heat only from contact with hot food, so there will be fewer sticky or crusty pans to wash.

* Asterisks denote recipes found elsewhere in this book.

PROCEDURE IN CASE OF FIRE

If a fire starts in your microwave, press the stop pad and leave the door closed. Then turn off the power at the switch and pull out the plug.

Newspaper and brown bags are made of recycled paper which contain impurities. These may cause arcing which will damage the appliance and could set it alight. Never dry clothes or paper in the oven or they may catch fire.

A

ADVOCAAT

A Dutch liqueur made from brandy, egg yolks and sugar. It is bottled and drunk alone or with other drinks. Whip a little advocaat into cream and use in trifles and other desserts.

Advocaat

Defrost (30%)
6 minutes

6 eggs
200 g (7 oz) caster sugar
200 mℓ (6½ fl oz) brandy
few drops of vanilla extract

Beat eggs well and set aside. Combine sugar and brandy in a jug and microwave on Defrost (30%) for 5-6 minutes, stirring every minute until sugar dissolves. Let mixture cool, then add to the eggs, beating constantly. Add vanilla extract and mix well. Pour into bottles and store in a cool dry place for 1 week before serving.
Makes about 750 ml (1¼ pints)

AGAR-AGAR

A gelatinous product obtained from certain seaweeds. It is also known by the name of Japanese or vegetable gelatine and is available either as a powder or in shredded form. Agar-agar melts and sets at a far higher temperature than gelatine, but does not have the same easy melt-in-the-mouth texture. It is, however, extremely useful in Kosher cooking.
See also Gelatine.

ALCOHOL

Alcohol adds a wonderful finishing touch to many home cooked dishes, often adding richness and always improving the flavour.

Wine, sherry, port and beer are frequently used when preparing savoury dishes, while liqueurs are slightly sweeter and enhance the flavour of many fruits and desserts.

It is perfectly safe to use all types of alcohol in the microwave. Wine may be reduced to use in a sauce, or meat may be simmered slowly in wine. Wine marinades may be warmed before being used. Brandy, whisky or other spirits may be heated in the microwave to be used to flambé, but on no account should the food be flambéed in the microwave oven.

To flambé, pour 45 mℓ (3 tablespoons) brandy into a small ovenproof glass jug and microwave on Full Power for 15 seconds. Pour over warmed food and ignite.

ALMOND

Sweet almonds are one of the most popular nuts worldwide. Bitter almonds are not eaten raw, but an essence is distilled from them and used as a flavouring. Sweet almonds are used whole, flaked or chopped for baking, cooking and confectionery. On their own, they are easily toasted or fried in the microwave. Serve toasted almonds as appetizers with drinks, use as garnishes for pilaus or combine with fish or poultry. Ground into a paste, almonds are used for nut butters, pralines, marzipan, tarts, fillings and sweets.

To blanch almonds, microwave 250 ml (8 fl oz) water for about 2½ minutes on Full Power, until it is boiling. Add the almonds and microwave for 30 seconds. Drain, then slip off the skins.
To toast almonds, place the flaked or blanched nuts in a browning dish and microwave on Full Power for 4-5 minutes, stirring every minute.

Almond vegetable medley

Full Power
12 minutes

1 small onion, chopped
15 g (½ oz) butter or margarine
300 g (11 oz) frozen peas
400 g (14 oz) canned cream of mushroom soup
275 g (10 oz) canned mushrooms, drained
5 mℓ (1 teaspoon) lemon juice
2.5 mℓ (½ teaspoon) caster sugar
45 g (1½ oz) potato crisps, coarsely crushed
60 g (2 oz) toasted almonds*

Combine chopped onion and butter and microwave on Full Power for 1-2 minutes or until onion is tender. Add peas, soup, mushrooms, lemon juice, sugar and microwave for 10-13 minutes, or until peas are tender, stirring once during cooking. Sprinkle crushed crisps and almonds on top and microwave for 1 minute more.
Serves 6

Almond bark

High (70%)
3 minutes

500 g (18 oz) white chocolate, broken up
100 g (3½ oz) blanched, toasted almonds*

Line a baking sheet with waxed paper and set aside. Microwave chocolate in a large glass bowl on High (70%) until just softened, 2-3 minutes. Do not overcook or chocolate will become grainy. Stir in almonds and mix well. Spread mixture on to the baking sheet and refrigerate until set. To serve, break into pieces. Store, tightly covered, in a cool place.
Makes about 600 g (1 lb 5 oz)

Almond ice cream

Full Power, High (70%)
14 minutes

100 g (3½ oz) caster sugar
75 mℓ (2½ fl oz) water
440 mℓ (14 fl oz) milk
345 mℓ (11 fl oz) single cream
6 egg yolks
3 egg whites
30 mℓ (2 tablespoons) caster sugar
60 g (2 oz) toasted almonds, chopped*
45 mℓ (3 tablespoons) Amaretto liqueur

Place sugar and water in a large bowl, microwave on Full Power for 2 minutes, stirring every 30 seconds. Brush sides of bowl with water to remove sugar crystals. Microwave for 6 minutes, or until deep caramel colour. Very carefully add the milk and cream, stir, then microwave for 3 minutes. Beat yolks and caster sugar very well. Pour on the hot milk mixture, beat again. Microwave on High (70%) for 3 minutes. Stir well, cool, then freeze until firm. Beat egg whites until stiff. Cut frozen ice cream into chunks, process about a third at a time in a food processor until smooth. Add about a third of the egg white to each batch, process until combined. Place ice cream in a large bowl, add nuts and liqueur, stirring well. Pour into freezer trays or one large container. Freeze until firm.
Serves 6-8

Praline

Full Power
10 minutes

150 g (5 oz) caster sugar
100 mℓ (3½ fl oz) water
pinch of cream of tartar
60 g (2 oz) unblanched almonds

Mix sugar and water together in a medium-sized bowl. Microwave on Full Power for 2 minutes. Add cream of tartar and stir. Microwave on Full Power for a further 8-10 minutes, until a deep golden colour. Place nuts on a well-greased baking sheet and pour caramel over. Allow to cool completely. Remove praline from the baking sheet, and break into pieces. To crush, drop a few pieces at a time on to moving blades of a food processor. Process until finely chopped and use as required. Praline may be stored in an airtight container for several weeks.
Makes about 250 g (9 oz)

ALUMINIUM
A metal used for making a wide range of household utensils and kitchen foil. Normally it is a good conductor of heat, but like all metals it reflects microwaves. Aluminium saucepans and other utensils should not be used in the microwave as they may cause arcing, which looks and sounds like lightning or sparks inside the oven and could damage the appliance. Also, aluminium has a shielding effect on

the food, so food does not become hot. If possible, avoid reheating frozen dishes packed in shallow aluminium trays. Transfer the food to a casserole dish, cover and microwave. (*See* Convenience Foods.)

Aluminium foil
Because of the shielding effect metal has on food in the microwave, small pieces of aluminium foil may be used to cover sensitive areas, such as the breast bone of chicken, wing tips or ends of legs, to keep these from becoming overcooked. Small pieces of foil may also be used to shield the corners of square or rectangular baking dishes to keep those areas from becoming overcooked during microwaving. Take care not to let it touch the sides of the oven or arcing may occur.

Aluminium foil has another use in microwave cookery. When meat is cooked it should be covered with foil or 'tented', shiny side of the foil inwards, to deflect heat back onto the meat and finish the cooking process. Cover loosely to allow the steam to escape, or the food will lose its crisp, roasted look and taste steamed.

ANCHOVY
Canned anchovies are fillets of small marine fish, salted and preserved in brine or oil. They are used mainly for salads and savory dishes, or for garnishing pizzas, stuffed eggs and other foods. Anchovy essence and anchovy paste are used in sauces and fillings. Anchovy butter is made by pounding anchovies with butter and is used on toast or in other savoury dishes. Use canned anchovies sparingly in microwave cooking as the flavour is strong. If you prefer a milder anchovy flavour, soak the fillets in milk for 30 minutes before using.

Anchovy and potato bake

Full Power
22 minutes

4 – 5 potatoes, sliced
30 g (1 oz) butter
30 mℓ (1 fl oz) oil
2 onions, thinly sliced
60 g (2 oz) canned anchovies, drained and chopped
black pepper
125 mℓ (4 fl oz) single cream
100 mℓ (3½ fl oz) milk
15 g (½ oz) dried breadcrumbs
2.5 mℓ (½ teaspoon) paprika
15 g (½ oz) butter

Soak potato slices in cold water for 10 minutes, drain. Place butter and oil in a 20 – 25-cm (8 – 10-inch) shallow casserole, microwave at Full Power for 1 minute. Add onions and stir to coat with the butter. Microwave for 4 minutes, stirring at least twice, remove onions from casserole. In the same casserole, arrange half the potatoes, then half the onions and half the anchovies. Repeat the layers. Sprinkle with black pepper.

Combine cream and milk in a jug, microwave for 1 minute, pour over the potatoes. Mix the breadcrumbs and the paprika, sprinkle over the potatoes and dot with butter. Cover casserole with a lid. Microwave for 16 – 18 minutes.
Serves 4 as a light meal

ANGEL CAKE
A light-textured American cake baked in a high-sided tube tin. The large number of beaten egg whites in this type of cake, makes it unsuitable for microwave cooking.

ANGELICA
A tall aromatic plant, pale green in colour with celery-like stems and leaves. It has white flowers and a distinctive musky smell. Most of the plant can be used in some way, including the seeds which give an oil that is used to flavour liqueurs such as Benedictine. The roots may be used in casseroles, and the leaves in salads. Crystallized angelica is perhaps best known as a decoration for cakes, desserts and sweets. It is quickly and easily made in the microwave.

Crystallized angelica

Full Power
18 minutes

3 – 4 stalks fresh angelica
water
salt
250 g (9 oz) caster sugar
280 mℓ (9 fl oz) water
green food colouring

Cut angelica stalks into 10-cm (4-inch) lengths. Place in a bowl, cover with water and add a little salt. Drain and rinse well. Place caster sugar and water in a large bowl, microwave on Full Power for 8 – 10 minutes, stirring at least twice. Add angelica and a few drops of green colouring, microwave for about 10 minutes, until stems are glossy. Allow stems to drain on a rack. Sprinkle with a little extra caster sugar and allow to dry. Store in an air-tight container.

APPETIZER
Something to soothe and at the same time excite the palate. Like the trailer of a top-rated film, it should prepare one for greater things to come. Many appetizers, such as meat balls or stuffed vegetables, can be precooked and reheated shortly before serving. With the microwave you can serve a large selection of tempting hot appetizers with a minimum amount of fuss

and effort. Do most of the preparation ahead of time and a minute or two after your guests arrive, offer them piping hot snacks.

Creamy stuffed mushrooms

Full Power
7 minutes

8 large flat mushrooms
15 g (½ oz) butter
½ onion, chopped
3 spring onions, including tops, chopped
1 garlic clove, crushed
250 g (9 oz) cream cheese
30 mℓ (2 tablespoons) chopped parsley
2.5 mℓ (½ teaspoon) oregano
1 egg yolk
salt and black pepper
30 g (1 oz) Cheddar cheese, grated
15 g (½ oz) Parmesan cheese
15 g (½ oz) soft white breadcrumbs
extra butter
parsley sprigs

Wipe mushrooms. Cut off stems and chop. Microwave butter in a small bowl on Full Power for 45 seconds. Add onion, spring onion and garlic, stir so as to coat the vegetables with the butter. Microwave for 1 minute, add mushroom stems and microwave 1 minute more. Beat cream cheese, parsley, oregano, egg yolk and seasonings. Add onion mixture. Divide mixture between upturned mushroom caps. Combine cheeses and breadcrumbs, and sprinkle over mushrooms. Dot with a little butter. Arrange mushrooms in a circle in a shallow dish. Cover with vented plastic wrap and microwave for 4 – 5 minutes until the cheese has melted and the mushrooms are piping hot. Garnish with a little parsley and serve immediately. Smaller mushrooms will be done more quickly.
Serves 6 – 8

Bacon-wrapped snacks

Full Power
3 minutes

250 g (9 oz) streaky bacon rashers

Choose any of the following fillings:
400 g (14 oz) canned mussels or oysters, drained
pineapple chunks
stuffed olives
stoned prunes
glacé cherries
frankfurter chunks

Remove rind from bacon and cut each rasher into three. Select the filling of your choice. Wrap a piece of bacon around filling and secure with a wooden cocktail stick. Arrange twelve of the snacks on a grill rack, cover with a piece of greaseproof paper. Microwave on Full Power for 3 minutes. Turn each snack over, microwave for 2 – 3 minutes more, until bacon is crisp. Serve immediately.

Baked oysters

Full Power, Medium (50%)
6 minutes

8 freshly opened oysters, drained
30 mℓ (2 tablespoons) melted butter
15 mℓ (1 tablespoon) lemon juice

Stuffing
30 g (1 oz) soft breadcrumbs
5 mℓ (1 teaspoon) mixed herbs
60 g (2 oz) Cheddar cheese, grated
45 mℓ (3 tablespoons) chopped parsley
30 mℓ (2 tablespoons) finely chopped onion
20 mℓ (4 teaspoons) finely chopped green pepper
½ chicken stock cube
45 mℓ (3 tablespoons) water

First make the stuffing. Combine breadcrumbs, herbs, cheese, parsley, onion and green pepper, mixing well. Dissolve stock cube in water and microwave on Full Power for 30 seconds. Add to the breadcrumb mixture and toss to mix.

Pierce oysters with a large fork to break the membrane and prevent oysters from bursting during microwaving. Mix melted butter with lemon juice and dip oysters in the mixture. Place oysters either in small shell dishes or rinsed oyster shells. Top oysters with prepared stuffing and drizzle with any remaining butter mixture. Arrange in a circle on a plate and microwave on Medium (50%) for 4 – 5 minutes. Stand for 1 minute before serving.
Serves 4

Salami pizza bites

Full Power
3 minutes

125 g (4 oz) salami, finely chopped
175 g (6 oz) Cheddar cheese, grated
2.5 mℓ (½ teaspoon) oregano
60 mℓ (4 tablespoons) chilli sauce
36 round savoury biscuits

Mix together salami, cheese, oregano and chilli sauce. Place about 5 ml (1 teaspoon) of the mixture on each biscuit. Arrange twelve biscuits in a circle on a flat plate and microwave on Full Power for 1 minute, or until cheese has melted. Repeat with remaining biscuits.
Makes 36 appetizers

Smoked salmon rounds

Full Power, Defrost (30%)
5 minutes

100 g (3½ oz) butter
75 mℓ (2½ fl oz) single cream
20 mℓ (4 teaspoons) lemon juice
Tabasco
salt and black pepper
3 egg yolks
7.5-cm (3-inch) length of cucumber
2 thick slices fresh pineapple
125 g (4 oz) peeled and cooked prawns
60 g (2 oz) smoked salmon trimmings
8 slices of bread, toasted
butter
paprika
parsley

Place butter in a large jug, microwave on Full Power for 1 minute. Add cream, lemon juice, seasonings and yolks, whisk well. Microwave on Defrost (30%) for about 4 minutes, whisking every 30 seconds during cooking. Beat very well as the sauce will continue to cook. Cover with a piece of greaseproof paper and set aside. Dice cucumber and place in a sieve to drain. Dice pineapple and place in a bowl. Add prawns, salmon, cucumber and sauce. Butter toast and, using a 7.5-cm (3-inch) cutter, cut into rounds. Reheat salmon mixture for 1 – 2 minutes, if necessary. Spoon on to toast rounds, sprinkle with a little paprika and garnish with a parsley sprig. Serve hot or cold. *Makes 8*

APPLE

The apple, one of the world's most important and versatile fruits, has been cultivated for at least 3 000 years. Although there are many different varieties, apples can generally be divided into two categories: those for eating and those for cooking. However, in most cases they overlap and cook equally well in the microwave oven. Apples are used in a wide variety of dishes ranging from pies, tarts and sauces to cakes and strudels. They can also be successfully canned, dried or turned into jams and jellies. Fresh apples keep well thanks to modern refrigerated storage, and are available all year round. When using raw apples, as in fruit salads, brush with a little lemon juice to keep the flesh from turning brown. The microwave oven is a great help in baking, stewing and preserving apples and in reconstituting dehydrated apple rings (*see Dried Fruit*).

To bake apples, core and stuff 4 apples with raisins, dates, mincemeat or the filling of your choice. Top with a little sugar and sprinkle with cinnamon or mixed spice. Arrange apples in a circle in a flat casserole and microwave on Full Power for 7 – 8 minutes.
To stew apples, peel, core and slice 450 g (1 lb) apples. Add sugar and cinnamon to taste. Microwave, covered, on Full Power for 5 minutes.

Apple sauce

Full Power
8 minutes

500 g (18 oz) cooking apples, peeled, cored
   and sliced
45 mℓ (3 tablespoons) water
2 whole cloves
30 g (1 oz) caster sugar
pinch of salt

Place apples, water and cloves in a bowl and
cover with a lid or vented plastic wrap.
Microwave on Full Power for 8 minutes. Remove
from the microwave, take out cloves and mash
apples. Stir in sugar and salt. Serve warm or
cold.
Serves 4 – 6

Honey apple cake

Full Power
8 minutes
Bake 160 °C/325 °F/gas 3
35 minutes

6 large Granny Smith apples
90 g (3 oz) honey
30 g (1 oz) butter
pinch of cinnamon
5 mℓ (1 teaspoon) grated lemon rind
30 mℓ (2 tablespoons) lemon juice
15 mℓ (1 tablespoon) brandy

Topping
100 g (3½ oz) butter
90 g (3 oz) caster sugar
2 eggs
100 g (3½ oz) ground almonds
2 drops of almond essence
15 g (½ oz) plain flour

Peel, core and slice apples thickly and set aside.
Put honey and butter into a 22.5-cm (9-inch) pie
dish. Microwave for 2 minutes on Full Power.
Stir well and add cinnamon, lemon rind and
juice. Microwave for 2 minutes. Stir in brandy
and apples. Microwave, covered, for 4 – 5
minutes.
   Meanwhile make the topping. Cream butter
and sugar very well, add eggs one at a time,
beating well after each addition. Carefully fold
in ground almonds, almond essence and sifted
flour. Spread on top of apples. Bake in a
conventional oven at 160 °C/325 °F/gas 3 for 35
– 40 minutes. Serve warm with plenty of
whipped cream.
Makes 1 x 22.5-cm (9-inch) pie

Honey baked apples

Defrost (30%)
12 minutes

4 large cooking apples
water
30 mℓ (2 tablespoons) honey
5 mℓ (1 teaspoon) ground ginger
2.5 mℓ (½ teaspoon) cinnamon
pinch of ground cloves
30 mℓ (2 tablespoons) medium-sweet sherry

Cut a slice from each apple and put aside. Trim
just enough off the bottom of the apples to allow
them to stand. Core the apples and stand in a
shallow dish and replace lids. Add a little water
and microwave on Defrost (30%) for 10 – 12
minutes, or until apple is just soft enough to
scoop out flesh with a spoon. Mix the cooked
apple with the remaining ingredients and spoon
back into the apple shells. Replace lids and
reheat if necessary.
Serves 4

Apple raisin meringue

Full Power, High (70%)
14 minutes

1 kg (2¼ lb) apples
15 mℓ (1 tablespoon) water
60 g (2 oz) seedless raisins
2 egg yolks
soft brown sugar
2.5 mℓ (½ teaspoon) cinnamon
30 mℓ (2 tablespoons) brandy

Topping
2 egg whites
90 g (3 oz) caster sugar

Peel, core and slice apples. Place in a bowl
with water. Cover and microwave on Full Power
for 4 – 5 minutes. Cool, then purée. Add raisins,
egg yolks, sugar, cinnamon and brandy. Spoon
into a deep microwave dish.
   For the topping, beat egg whites until stiff,
then beat in half the sugar, a little at a time.
Gently fold in the remaining sugar and spoon
the mixture over the apples in the dish.
Microwave on High (70%) for 7 – 9 minutes or

until meringue is set. Serve warm or cold.
Serves 4

Spiced apple ring

Full Power
11 minutes

90 g (3 oz) butter or margarine, softened
30 mℓ (2 tablespoons) treacle
30 mℓ (2 tablespoons) golden syrup
5 mℓ (1 teaspoon) ground ginger
2.5 mℓ (½ teaspoon) cinnamon
2.5 mℓ (½ teaspoon) mixed spice
175 g (6 oz) plain flour
60 g (2 oz) caster sugar
5 mℓ (1 teaspoon) bicarbonate of soda
pinch of salt
1 egg, beaten
175 g (6 oz) canned apple slices, drained
90 mℓ (3 fl oz) light sugar syrup*

In a large microwave jug, place butter, treacle,
syrup, ginger, cinnamon and mixed spice.
Microwave on Full Power for 2 minutes. Sift
flour, sugar, bicarbonate of soda and salt into a
mixing bowl. Stir in the melted mixture, beaten
egg and sugar syrup. Beat well. Arrange apple
slices in the bottom of a greased 22.5-cm (9-
inch) microwave ring pan. Spoon spice mixture
over and microwave on Full Power for 7 – 9
minutes. Stand for 5 minutes before turning out.
Serve with cream or custard.
Serves 6

Apple and sausage bake

Full Power
22 minutes

250 g (9 oz) dried apple rings
30 mℓ (2 tablespoons) oil
30 g (1 oz) butter
2 onions, sliced
4 – 6 potatoes, sliced thickly
salt and black pepper
5 mℓ (1 teaspoon) dry mustard
5 mℓ (1 teaspoon) caraway seeds
about 250 mℓ (8 fl oz) stock
500 g (18 oz) frankfurters

Garnish
parsley or paprika

Soak apple rings in water for 1 hour, drain off
excess liquid, set aside. Using a shallow
casserole, microwave oil and butter on Full
Power for 1 minute. Add onions and toss to coat
with the oil. Microwave for 4 – 5 minutes, stirring
every minute. Add potatoes, apples,
seasonings, mustard and caraway seeds, stir
to combine. Pour on enough stock to come just
a little more than halfway up the sides of the
casserole. Cover, microwave for 13 minutes.
Cut the frankfurters into 1-cm (½-inch) thick
slices, add to the casserole and stir in carefully.
Cover and microwave for 4 – 5 minutes more,
until the potatoes are cooked. Sprinkle liberally
with paprika or parsley before serving.
Serves 4 – 6

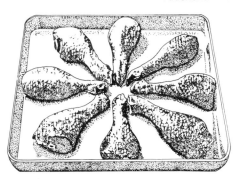

APRICOT

A small golden-coloured fruit which, when fully ripe and freshly picked, has a memorable smell and a delicious taste. Fresh apricots travel badly and do not keep for long periods, so it makes sense to bottle them, dry them, or turn them into jam or chutney. Dried apricots are often used in fruit compotes, baked goods and meat or poultry dishes. Canned apricots are useful for desserts and puddings and apricot jam is widely used in confectionery for fillings and glazes. The microwave can be used for a variety of apricot dishes, for reconstituting dried apricots (*see* Dried Fruit) and for warming jam for glazing.

To stew apricots, take 500 g (18 oz) ripe apricots, cut in half and remove stones. Place in a casserole or bowl, sprinkle with 15 ml (1 tablespoon) water and microwave, covered, on Full Power for 7 – 9 minutes, stirring once or twice during cooking. Add sugar to taste and stir to dissolve.

Apricot pecan bread

High (70%)
10 minutes

100 g (3½ oz) pecan nuts, finely chopped
150 g (5 oz) wholewheat flour
125 mℓ (4 fl oz) milk
60 g (2 oz) dried apricots, chopped
75 mℓ (2½ fl oz) oil
60 g (2 oz) caster sugar
90 g (3 oz) honey
1 egg
10 mℓ (2 teaspoons) grated orange peel
2.5 mℓ (½ teaspoon) cinnamon
10 mℓ (2 teaspoons) baking powder
2.5 mℓ (½ teaspoon) salt

Grease a 1.5-litre (2¾-pint) glass ring dish and coat with half the chopped nuts. Combine the remaining ingredients and mix well. Spoon mixture into prepared dish and microwave on High (70%) for 8 – 10 minutes, or until a wooden cocktail stick inserted near the centre comes out clean. Stand in the dish for about 8 minutes before turning out on a wire rack to cool. Cool completely before slicing.
Makes 1 round ring loaf (12 – 15 slices)

Spiced apricot halves

High (70%)
5 minutes

400 g (14 oz) canned apricot halves
250 mℓ (8 fl oz) syrup from the apricots
pinch of ground cloves
1 small piece of cinnamon stick
10 mℓ (2 teaspoons) red wine vinegar
2.5 mℓ (½ teaspoon) ground ginger
2.5 mℓ (½ teaspoon) dry mustard
glacé cherries

Arrange apricot halves hollow side downwards in a shallow dish. Add all remaining ingredients, except cherries, and cover. Microwave on High (70%) for 5 minutes. Cool apricots in syrup. Drain and place a glacé cherry in the hollow of each apricot half. Arrange as a tasty garnish around ham, gammon or a bacon joint.
Serves 6

Dried apricot chutney

Full Power
27 minutes

500 g (18 oz) dried apricots, chopped
1 onion, chopped
1 garlic clove, crushed
1 green chilli, chopped
375 mℓ (12 fl oz) vinegar
150 g (5 oz) raisins
5 mℓ (1 teaspoon) salt
2.5 mℓ (½ teaspoon) cayenne
15 mℓ (1 tablespoon) ground ginger
10 mℓ (2 teaspoons) dry mustard

Place apricots, onion, garlic and chilli in a large bowl. Add vinegar and stir well. Cover with vented plastic wrap. Microwave on Full Power for about 9 minutes or until ingredients have softened. Stir at least twice during cooking time. Add remaining ingredients and stir well. Re-cover, and microwave for 18 – 20 minutes or until the mixture thickens. Cool slightly, then pour into clean dry bottles.
Makes about 500 g (18 oz)

ARCING

Arcing occurs when microwaves are reflected from metal equipment or utensils used in the microwave oven, or when such containers or utensils come into contact with the oven wall or another container. This reflection of microwaves from metal shows up as sparks inside the oven and may be harmful to the power source. Silver or gold trim on tableware may also cause arcing inside the oven. Frequent exposure to microwaves will burn away the trim.

The limited use of aluminium foil in microwaves has been approved by some manufacturers, and will not cause arcing if properly handled. Strips of foil, used to shield corners of baking dishes or protruding bones of poultry or meat, and shallow aluminium foil containers are usually safe to use, as long as no foil touches the sides of the oven. Check with the manufacturer's instructions before using any metal in your microwave oven.

ARRANGEMENT OF FOOD

The arrangement of food in the microwave is an extremely important factor for even cooking because microwaves are not uniformly distributed in the oven cavity, nor do they penetrate foods evenly.

For more even cooking
☐ Always place the thicker or larger portions of food towards the outside of the container because microwaves penetrate the outer edges of the food first. For example, chicken legs or fish steaks should have the thinner part towards the centre of the dish.
☐ Foods of equal size should be arranged in a circular pattern. For example, potatoes to be baked, meat balls or individual portions of custard or eggs should be placed in a ring pattern or circle in the microwave.
☐ Where possible, do not place foods directly in the centre of the microwave or too close to the sides as these are areas of minimal microwave activity.
☐ Foods should also be arranged to a uniform depth. Vegetables should be spread out in a shallow casserole rather than heaped in the middle.
☐ When reheating a meal, keep foods to an even depth and arrange denser or thicker foods towards the outside of the plate.
☐ Rearranging food during cooking will help it cook more evenly. Move foods from the centre to the outside, or from the outside towards the centre to give a more even absorption of microwaves. This will also help shorten the cooking time.

ARROWROOT

Arrowroot is a thickener used for cream sauces and clear, delicate glazes. It cooks in the same way as cornflour, but is superior in clarity, appearance and absence of any taste of its own. Substitute 5 ml (1 teaspoon) arrowroot for every 15 g (½ oz) flour called for as a thickening agent, or for 7 g (¼ oz) cornflour.

ARTICHOKE, GLOBE

This unusual vegetable is related to the thistle. The edible part is the young flower bud, most of which is tough and only the small fleshy part at the base of the scales is eaten. Once the scales and hairy 'choke' have been removed the 'heart' or succulent flower base and top of the stalk are revealed and make wonderful eating.

Globe artichokes

Full Power, High (70%)
18 minutes

4 medium-sized globe artichokes
100 mℓ (3½ fl oz) water
45 mℓ (3 tablespoons) white wine
generous pinch of salt
1 lemon slice
1 garlic clove, peeled
black peppercorns
5 mℓ (1 teaspoon) oil

Wash artichokes and trim away stalk, lower leaves and tips. Place in a cooking bag or covered casserole. Combine all the remaining ingredients and pour over the artichokes. Microwave on Full Power for 18 – 20 minutes. Rearrange the artichokes halfway through cooking time. To test if the artichokes are cooked, remove one of the lower leaves. The leaf should peel off easily. Drain upside down and cool. Carefully lift out the middle portion and set aside. Using the handle end of a teaspoon, scrape away the hairy choke. Replace leaves and level the base so that artichoke can stand upright. Serve hot with melted butter, hollandaise* or Béarnaise* sauce or serve cold with French dressing*. To reheat, arrange in a circle in a dish, cover and microwave on High (70%) for 4 – 5 minutes.
Serves 4

Artichokes vinaigrette

Defrost (30%)
3 minutes

4 globe artichokes, cooked* and trimmed
15 mℓ (1 tablespoon) chopped parsley
15 mℓ (1 tablespoon) chopped dill pickle
1 hard-boiled egg, mashed
10 mℓ (2 teaspoons) finely chopped chives
15 mℓ (1 tablespoon) chopped green pepper
salt and black pepper
15 mℓ (1 tablespoon) tarragon vinegar
30 mℓ (2 tablespoons) cider vinegar
90 mℓ (3 fl oz) oil
generous pinch of paprika
lettuce leaves

To garnish
lemon wedges
parsley sprigs

Combine all the ingredients, except artichokes, in a small bowl. Microwave on Defrost (30%) for 3 minutes. Stir well. Spoon a little sauce into the centre of each artichoke before replacing the middle leaves and chill well. Serve the remaining sauce in a sauce boat. Place each artichoke on a plate lined with a lettuce leaf, garnish with a lemon wedge and a parsley sprig.
Serves 4

ARTICHOKE, JERUSALEM

This curious vegetable is a tuber about the size of a small potato. Its creamy, slightly smoked flavour certainly makes up for its beige, knobbly appearance. Jerusalem artichokes discolour easily when peeled or cut, and if not used immediately, should be covered with cold water to which a squeeze of lemon juice has been added.

Jerusalem artichokes

Full Power
8 minutes

500 g (18 oz) Jerusalem artichokes
60 mℓ (4 tablespoons) water
pinch of salt
15 g (½ oz) butter
10 mℓ (2 teaspoons) lemon juice
black pepper

Scrub artichokes well. If they are very big, peel them. Cut into 5-mm (¼-inch) thick slices. Place artichokes, water and salt in a 1-litre (1¾-pint) casserole and cover. Microwave on Full Power for 5 minutes, stir once. Cover again and microwave for a further 3 – 5 minutes until tender. Stir and add butter, lemon juice and black pepper. Stand for 5 minutes before serving.
Serves 4 – 6

Artichoke and prawn starter

Full Power, High (70%)
17 minutes

These individual portions can be made ahead and be reheated at the last minute.

250 g (9 oz) Jerusalem artichokes
60 mℓ (4 tablespoons) milk
60 mℓ (4 tablespoons) single cream
200 g (8 oz) prawns, peeled and deveined
15 g (½ oz) butter
15 g (½ oz) plain flour
15 mℓ (1 tablespoon) Parmesan cheese, grated
salt and black pepper
15 g (½ oz) butter
15 g (½ oz) fresh white breadcrumbs

Scrub artichokes well, cut into 5-mm (¼-inch) thick slices. Place artichokes, milk and cream in a deep bowl. Cover with vented plastic wrap. Microwave on Full Power for 3 minutes, stir and cover. Microwave on High (70%) for 5 – 7 minutes until tender. Remove artichokes from the liquid and set aside. Add prawns to liquid, and replace cover. Microwave on Full Power for 3 minutes, remove prawns and combine with artichokes. Combine butter and flour, work about half into the liquid and stir well. Microwave for 45 seconds and stir again. Add more flour mixture if necessary and microwave to thicken. Add artichokes, prawns and Parmesan. Season to taste. Divide mixture between four scallop shells. Heat a browning dish on Full Power for 4 minutes. Add butter and crumbs and stir to combine. Microwave for

1 – 3 minutes, stirring every 30 seconds. Sprinkle on top of prawns and artichokes. To reheat, microwave for a few minutes on Medium (50%).
Serves 4

ASPARAGUS

Asparagus is a member of the lily family that grows wild in parts of Europe and Russia and is also cultivated commercially. The shoots are harvested for a short season only, generally during late spring. Green asparagus shoots are cut when the slender tips are clear of the soil while white asparagus shoots are grown under a mound of earth and have never seen the light of day. They are usually thick-stemmed, pale in colour and only a short part of the length is tender enough to eat. Whether green or white, serve fresh asparagus spears hot with butter or sauce, or cooked and chilled with a vinaigrette dressing. Asparagus can also be used in soups, quiches, or for appetizers and garnishes.

To microwave asparagus

Trim ends of 250 g (9 oz) fresh asparagus and place in a casserole dish with 45 ml (3 tablespoons) water. Cover and microwave on Full Power for 6 – 8 minutes for green asparagus, and 8 – 10 minutes for white asparagus. Stand for 3 – 4 minutes before serving. If serving cold, rinse immediately in cold water.

Serving suggestions

☐ Serve cold with mayonnaise combined with a little lemon juice and seasoned with fresh dill and freshly ground black pepper.
☐ Serve with hollandaise sauce* and chopped parsley.
☐ Serve with melted butter and lemon juice (*see* Butter).

Asparagus with creamy lemon sauce

Medium (50%)
4 minutes

750 g (1¾ lb) cooked green asparagus*
3 large egg yolks
45 g (1½ oz) butter
250 mℓ (8 fl oz) whipping cream
white pepper
pinch of salt
45 mℓ (3 tablespoons) low-fat soft cheese
45 mℓ (3 tablespoons) fresh lemon juice

Refresh cooked asparagus under cold water, drain and chill. Combine egg yolks, butter, 125 mℓ (4 fl oz) of the cream, pepper and salt in a large jug and microwave on Medium (50%) for 3 – 4 minutes, stirring every minute until mixture is pale and thick. Do not let the mixture boil. Remove from the oven and beat in the

Great starters: Avocado Ring Mould and Avocado Soup (page 17)

cheese and lemon juice. Let mixture cool. Beat remaining cream to stiff peaks and gently fold into egg mixture. Arrange asparagus on a platter or on individual serving plates and spoon sauce over. Any leftover sauce will keep, covered, in the refrigerator for 2 – 3 days.
Serves 4

Seafood asparagus casserole

Full Power, High (70%)
7 minutes

double quantity hollandaise sauce*
125 ml (4 fl oz) soured cream
few drops of Tabasco
250 g (9 oz) cooked green asparagus*
15 g (½ oz) butter
30 g (1 oz) soft breadcrumbs
paprika
200 g (7 oz) canned tuna, drained and flaked
100 g (3½ oz) shrimps, drained
1 hard-boiled egg, sliced

To garnish
parsley sprigs

Mix hollandaise sauce with soured cream and Tabasco and set aside. Drain asparagus well. Microwave butter on Full Power for 30 seconds, then add breadcrumbs and paprika and toss to coat. Arrange cooked asparagus in a casserole and sprinkle tuna and shrimps on top. Cover with hollandaise sauce. Microwave on High (70%) for 5 – 6 minutes, until hot. Arrange egg slices on top and sprinkle with buttered crumbs. Microwave for 30 seconds more. Garnish with parsley sprigs. *Serves 6*

ASPIC

This is a light, crystal-clear savoury jelly in which cold eggs, fish, poultry, meat or vegetables are served. Aspic is sometimes chopped as a garnish, used as a transparent glaze or combined with mayonnaise or white sauce to coat cold foods. When used as the basis for layered savoury moulds, aspic jelly provides an exotic centre piece for a cold buffet. Like all jellies, aspic is easily made in the microwave. Egg white and egg shell are added to the basic gelatine mixture in order to clarify it.

To chop aspic, take the required amount of aspic out of the refrigerator. Put it into a piece of wet greaseproof paper. Use a wet knife to chop up the jelly. Chop the jelly quickly and carefully, as it will lose its sparkle if overchopped.

Chaud-froid sauce

A creamy aspic used for coating cold fish, meats, poultry or hard-boiled eggs.

300 ml (½ pint) béchamel sauce*
150 ml (5 fl oz) aspic jelly*
30 ml (2 tablespoons) single cream
salt and white pepper

Combine the warm béchamel sauce with liquid aspic jelly. Season to taste. Add the cream and strain through a fine sieve. Stand over a bowl of ice to thicken. Use when starting to thicken. If the sauce becomes too thick to use, place in the microwave on Defrost (30%) for 1 – 2 minutes.
Makes 500 ml (16 fl oz)

Oeufs chaud-froid

6 hard-boiled eggs
mayonnaise
salt and pepper
5 ml (1 teaspoon) Worcestershire sauce
generous pinch of dried tarragon
450 ml (14½ fl oz) chaud-froid sauce*
150 ml (5 fl oz) aspic jelly*

Garnish
cucumber skin
carrot slices
mushroom slices
red pimento strips
stuffed olives
pickled walnuts
chopped aspic jelly*

Cut the hard-boiled eggs in half lengthways. Remove the yolks and place in the bowl of a food processor. Add a little mayonnaise to moisten. Season with salt, pepper, Worcestershire sauce and tarragon, process until smooth. Use the filling to stuff the egg white halves, carefully sandwich them together again. Wipe clean with paper towel. Place on a wire cooling rack. Coat with a layer of chaud-froid sauce. Remember that it is better to use two or three thin layers of chaud-froid than one thick layer. Garnish neatly with small, decorative vegetable shapes. Dip each garnish into a little melted aspic jelly before placing on the egg, this will 'fix' it in position. Allow to set. Carefully spoon a little clear aspic jelly over eggs. Refrigerate for at least 15 minutes before serving. Serve on a bed of chopped aspic.
Makes 6

Aspic jelly

Full Power
10 minutes

450 ml (14½ fl oz) water
1 stock cube, beef or chicken
60 ml (4 tablespoons) dry sherry
30 ml (1 tablespoon) wine vinegar
30 ml (1 tablespoon) cider vinegar
grated rind and juice of ½ lemon
1 small carrot, roughly chopped
1 celery stick, roughly chopped
1 thick onion slice
1 egg white
1 egg shell
pinch of salt
45 ml (3 tablespoons) powdered gelatine
2.5 ml (½ teaspoon) caster sugar
black peppercorns

Mix all the ingredients in a large bowl. Microwave on Full Power for 5 minutes, whisking with a balloon whisk every minute. Whisk briskly until a good 'head' of foam has formed. Continue to microwave for a further 5 minutes, opening the door every 30 – 40 seconds as the mixture boils up. Do not allow the liquid to boil up through the 'head'. Allow to settle for 5 minutes. Tie a jelly bag or suitable cloth on to a stand, and pour boiling water through the cloth to scald it. Strain jelly through the warmed cloth. The mixture should be clear. Re-strain if necessary.
Makes about 500 ml (16 fl oz)

AUBERGINES

Aubergines, also known as eggplants, are members of the tomato family. The glossy, purple fruits have a spongy white flesh which is slightly bitter in flavour. To reduce the bitterness, it is a good idea to salt them before cooking. Aubergines can be boiled, baked or fried and are an important ingredient in dishes such as Ratatouille (page 185) and Moussaka (page 152). *See also* Aubergine caviar (page 84).

To microwave aubergines
Slice 2 medium aubergines, sprinkle with salt and stand for 30 minutes. Rinse and pat dry. Place in a casserole dish with 45 ml (3 tablespoons) water, cover and microwave on Full Power for 8 – 10 minutes.

Note: There is no need to peel aubergines before cooking.

AU GRATIN

A French word for a cooked dish, covered with breadcrumbs or cheese and browned under a grill. It is not possible to brown food in a microwave without a special browning unit, but the basic dish can be cooked in the microwave and then placed under a preheated conventional grill for a few minutes to brown.

AVOCADO

There are several varieties of these subtropical fruits, ranging from small finger-shaped ones to the larger rounded or pear-shaped ones. When buying avocados choose those that are firm and unblemished. To ripen avocados, wrap in newspaper and store at room temperature, preferably in a dark place. When ripe the flesh feels soft if pressed gently. Cut the ripened avocados in half, twist open and find a creamy fruit.

Avocados are extremely versatile. Not only can they be sliced and served in salads or simply eaten as they are, but they can be used for soups, stuffed and served hot or cold, added to meat dishes or even puréed and folded into ice cream. Baked avocados are becoming increasingly popular and they respond particularly well to microwave cooking.

Mexican meat balls

Full Power
8 minutes

1 avocado, peeled and stone removed
lemon juice
1 small green chilli, seeded and chopped
1 egg, beaten
15 mℓ (1 tablespoon) chopped onion
10 mℓ (2 teaspoons) lemon juice
1 garlic clove, finely chopped
salt and pepper
500 g (18 oz) lean minced beef
45 g (1½ oz) Cheddar cheese, grated

Slice half the avocado and sprinkle with lemon juice, then set aside. Mash or process the remaining avocado in a processor. Add chilli, egg, onion, lemon juice, garlic and salt and pepper. Mix well. Add beef and mix thoroughly. Shape mixture into about 36 balls. Place half the balls in a circle on a flat microwave platter and microwave on Full Power for 3½ – 4 minutes or until done to taste. Repeat with remaining balls. Chop remaining avocado slices and sprinkle over hot meat balls. Serve with chilli sauce, if desired.
Serves 12 as an appetizer

Avocado and veal

Full Power, High (70%)
25 minutes

6 – 8 veal schnitzels
salt and black pepper
75 g (2½ oz) butter
1 bunch of spring onions, chopped
200 g (7 oz) mushrooms, finely chopped
2.5 mℓ (½ teaspoon) dried tarragon
1 large avocado, peeled and diced
15 mℓ (1 tablespoon) lemon juice
30 g (1 oz) soft breadcrumbs

Sherry sauce
15 g (½ oz) butter
15 g (½ oz) flour
75 mℓ (2½ fl oz) dry sherry
150 mℓ (5 fl oz) chicken stock
generous pinch of paprika
100 mℓ (3½ fl oz) single cream

Lay schnitzels on a board, and pound gently with a meat mallet to flatten if they are too thick. Season with salt and black pepper. Place 30 g (1 oz) butter in a small bowl, microwave on Full Power for 1 minute. Add spring onions and stir to coat with butter, microwave for 3 minutes until soft. Add mushrooms, tarragon, avocado, lemon juice and breadcrumbs. Season well with salt and pepper. Divide filling between schnitzels, spread out fairly evenly. Roll up each schnitzel and secure with a wooden cocktail stick. Heat a browning dish on Full Power for 6 minutes. Add 45 g (1½ oz) butter and allow to foam. Place rolled schnitzels in heated browning dish, microwave for 4 minutes, turning the veal every minute. Remove from dish and set aside.

For the sauce, place the butter in a jug, microwave for 45 seconds, stir in the flour. Add the sherry, stock and paprika, and stir well. Microwave for 2 minutes, stirring every 30 seconds. Add the cream. Arrange schnitzels in a shallow casserole, pour sauce over and cover. Microwave on High (70%) for 8 – 10 minutes. Remove cocktail sticks before serving.
Serves 6

Baked stuffed avocados

Full Power
6 minutes

100 g (3½ oz) canned salmon, drained
½ small onion, finely chopped
60 g (2 oz) soft breadcrumbs
2 ripe avocados
15 ml (1 tablespoon) lemon juice
salt and pepper
60 g (2 oz) Cheddar cheese, grated
paprika

Mash salmon and mix with chopped onion and breadcrumbs. Cut avocados in half and scoop out flesh. Mix with lemon juice, and mash flesh. Add to salmon mixture, mixing well. Season to taste. Spoon mixture into avocado shells and sprinkle with grated cheese and paprika. Arrange on a large plate with narrow ends of avocados towards the centre. Microwave on Full Power for 6 – 8 minutes, or until heated through.
Serves 4

Avocado ring mould

Full Power
2 minutes

250 mℓ (8 fl oz) water
90 g (3 oz) packet lemon jelly
1 avocado, peeled and stone removed
200 mℓ (6½ fl oz) mayonnaise
1 small garlic clove
5 mℓ (1 teaspoon) chopped onion
salt and pepper
2.5 mℓ (½ teaspoon) Worcestershire sauce
15 mℓ (1 tablespoon) finely chopped chives

To garnish
shredded lettuce
tomato slices
parsley sprigs

Pour water into a bowl and microwave on Full Power for about 2 minutes, until the water is boiling. Add jelly and stir to dissolve.
Set aside and allow jelly to thicken. Put jelly

and remaining ingredients in a blender goblet, blend until smooth. Rinse a ring mould with water and pour in slightly thickened liquid. Place in the refrigerator and leave until set. To remove from mould, dip mould into hot water for a few seconds, and loosen the edge a little. Turn out on to a plate lined with shredded lettuce. Garnish with tomato slices and parsley sprigs.
Serves 6

Avocado wholewheat American muffins

High (70%)
10 minutes

1 small avocado, peeled and stone removed
1 egg
30 g (1 oz) caster sugar
90 g (3 oz) wheatgerm
125 g (4 oz) wholewheat flour
15 mℓ (1 tablespoon) baking powder
2.5 mℓ (½ teaspoon) salt
250 mℓ (8 fl oz) milk

Roughly chop the avocado and beat with the egg until the mixture is smooth. Mix together the dry ingredients and add to the avocado mixture along with the milk. Stir until just combined. Pour half the batter into six large paper cases. Arrange in a circle in the oven and microwave on High (70%) for 3 – 5 minutes. Remove muffins and repeat process with remaining mixture.
Makes 12

Avocado soup

Full Power
9 minutes

7 g (¼ oz) butter
5 spring onions, chopped
3 avocados, peeled and stones removed
750 mℓ (1¼ pints) chicken stock
black pepper
15 mℓ (1 tablespoon) lemon juice
Tabasco
250 mℓ (8 fl oz) single cream
30 mℓ (2 tablespoons) chopped parsley

Microwave butter on Full Power for 30 seconds. Add spring onion, microwave for 1 minute, then set aside. Set aside half an avocado for garnishing and chop the remainder roughly. Place chicken stock in microwave and microwave on Full Power for 3 minutes. In a blender, combine spring onion, avocado, chicken stock, black pepper, lemon juice and Tabasco. Blend until smooth. Pour into a large bowl and add cream. Microwave for 4 – 5 minutes until piping hot. Stir two or three times during the cooking time. Carefully dice remaining avocado, add to the soup. Sprinkle with parsley and serve with plenty of crispy croûtons*. This soup may also be served cold.
Serves 6

Overleaf left: Almond Ice Cream (page 10)
Overleaf right: Almond Bark (page 9)

B

BABY FOODS

The microwave is ideal for heating baby foods to just the right temperature. If prepared baby food comes in a wide mouth jar, it can be heated in the container, thus saving time and effort in washing up. Even the baby's bottle can be heated in the microwave. Invert the nipple, then microwave on Full Power for 1 minute. Be sure that no metal lids are used and do not heat narrow-necked glass bottles in the microwave as pressure may build up in the lower part of the bottle, causing it to shatter.

If you have a blender or food processor and a microwave, you can prepare delicious, nutritious baby foods at home. Vegetables are quickly cooked in the microwave and chicken and fish poach to perfection. Purée cooked foods with a little milk or plain stock and refrigerate for later. Reheat in the microwave just before serving. Desserts, such as custards and milk puddings, or fruit purées are easy to make and cook quickly (*see* individual entries). Here are some more ideas for baby foods:

Apple purée

Peel, core and slice a medium-sized apple. Place in a bowl, sprinkle with 15 ml

(1 tablespoon) water and cover with vented plastic. Microwave on Full Power for 3 minutes until soft, stirring once or twice during cooking. Mash or purée with a little honey or fruit juice.

Prune purée

See Dried Fruit for instructions for stewing prunes, then purée in a blender or food processor and strain.

Baked banana purée

Peel and slice a ripe banana and place with a little honey in a covered container in the microwave. Microwave on Full Power for about 1 minute, or until soft, then purée with a little orange juice.

Puréed vegetables

See Cooking Chart for Vegetables (page 224). Purée cooked vegetables in a blender or food processor with a little milk, plain stock or water.

BACON

Bacon is prepared from a salted or smoked side of pork. Centuries ago, it was discovered meat could be kept for long periods if it was cured this way. Today we have a choice of smoked or unsmoked bacon, and a variety of different cuts. These react slightly differently in the microwave, depending on the amount and distribution of the fat.

Streaky bacon

This bacon comes from the belly of the pig, with alternating streaks of fat and lean. It is sold in strips, known as rashers. Streaky bacon microwaves particularly well because the fat is evenly distributed.

Back bacon

Sometimes referred to as 'prime', this bacon is also sold as rashers. The lean flesh is edged with fat, and a little care must be taken when microwaving back bacon as the fat portion is inclined to burn if over-

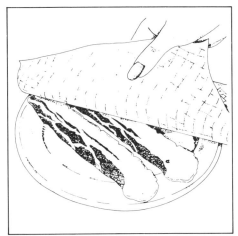

Place waxed paper over bacon while it is cooking to prevent fat from spattering the walls of the microwave.

cooked. Some back bacon rashers have a tail of streaky bacon.

Shoulder bacon

As the name implies, this meat is taken from the shoulder. The slices are shorter, thicker and more uneven in shape than the other cuts. Shoulder bacon microwaves well although it is fairly lean.

To microwave bacon

There is less mess and shrinkage if bacon is cooked in the microwave than if fried conventionally. A special microwave bacon rack is ideal for cooking bacon, as it allows the fat to drain off automatically. However, any flat shallow dish will do.

Arrange 4 – 6 rashers of bacon, with or without rinds, on the rack. Cover with waxed paper or parchment paper. Microwave on Full Power for about 5 minutes until cooked, turning and rearranging bacon on the rack to ensure even cooking. Drain bacon on kitchen paper before serving. Microwave slightly longer for very crisp bacon.

To defrost bacon
Place a 250 g (9 oz) packet of bacon on a plate. Microwave on Defrost (30%) for 3 – 4 minutes. Turn the packet over after half the cooking time. Stand for 5 minutes before using.

Warning: Do not defrost bacon in foil-lined packets.

Spaghetti with egg and bacon

Full Power, High (70%), Medium (50%)
13 minutes

60 g (2 oz) butter
2 eggs
2 egg yolks
90 g (3 oz) Parmesan cheese, grated
8 bacon rashers, rinds removed
7.5 mℓ (1 teaspoon) paprika
pinch of cayenne
125 mℓ (4 fl oz) single cream
black pepper
300 g (11 oz) cooked spaghetti*

Place butter in a bowl, microwave on Medium (50%) for 1 – 2 minutes until soft, set aside. Beat eggs and yolks well, stir in half the Parmesan cheese, set aside. Arrange bacon on a rack, cover with waxed paper, microwave on Full Power for 6 – 8 minutes, until crisp. Cut bacon into small pieces. Pour about half the bacon fat into a bowl. Stir in paprika, cayenne and cream. Microwave on High (70%) for 3 minutes. Mix well and add bacon.

Place piping hot spaghetti in a shallow casserole, stir in soft butter and the bacon mixture. Add egg and cheese mixture, stirring well. Cover and microwave on Medium (50%) for 3 – 5 minutes. Serve with the extra cheese.
Serves 4

Blue cheese bacon sticks

Full Power
12 minutes

10 streaky bacon rashers, rinds removed
about 60 g (2 oz) blue cheese, grated
20 grissini (Italian breadsticks)

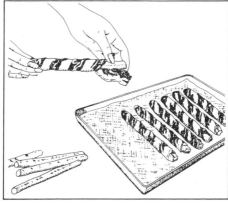

Wind each bacon strip diagonally around a grissini or breadstick and place on a plate or microwave baking tray.

Cut bacon rashers in half lengthwise. Sprinkle cheese on top and press down. Wrap one strip in a spiral around each breadstick. Place waxed paper on each of three paper plates and divide breadsticks among plates. Cover with waxed paper. Microwave each plate on Full Power for 3 – 4 minutes, or until bacon is cooked.
Makes 20 bacon sticks.

Bacon joint with ginger

Full Power, High (70%), Medium (50%)
1 hour 45 minutes

1 – 1.5 kg (2¼ – 3lb) bacon joint
water
60 mℓ (4 tablespoons) ginger ale concentrate
1 onion, quartered
1 carrot, roughly chopped
1 celery stick, roughly chopped
peppercorns

Glaze
45 mℓ (3 tablespoons) orange marmalade
60 mℓ (4 tablespoons) orange juice
5 mℓ (1 teaspoon) soy sauce
pinch of ground ginger

Place bacon joint in a 3-litre (5-pint) casserole, cover with water and soak for at least 6 hours, drain off water. Cover once again with water, add ginger ale concentrate, vegetables and peppercorns. Microwave on Full Power for 25 minutes, reduce power level to High (70%), microwave for about 1 hour, until joint is tender. Drain. Combine glaze ingredients, spoon over joint. Return joint to covered casserole, microwave on Medium (50%) for 15 minutes. Serve hot or cold.
Serves 6

BAIN-MARIE
A bain-marie is a water bath for keeping sauces or other dishes hot without drying out. Dishes that need gentle cooking, such as baked custard, caramel custard or pâtés, can be cooked in a bain-marie or in a conventional oven in a baking pan partially filled with hot water. In microwave cooking, there is no need for a water bath as foods do not dry out.

BAKE BLIND
To bake blind is to bake a pie or pastry shell without its final filling. The unbaked pastry shell should be pricked all over with a fork, covered with waxed or greaseproof paper and then filled with dried beans or rice to prevent the base of the pastry from rising. Microwave the pastry shell as directed in recipe, but remove the paper and beans toward the end of cooking time.
See also Pastry.

BAKING
Many cakes, breads and desserts can be baked in the microwave with great saving of time and excellent results. Some can be microwaved in less time than it takes to

prepare them. Items which cannot be successfully baked in a microwave include puff or flaky pastry, choux pastry, Yorkshire pudding, classic meringues, and chiffon cakes.
See also Cakes, Breads, Quick Breads, Biscuits and Pastry.

BAKING POWDER
Baking powder is a leavening agent composed of sodium bicarbonate plus various acids or acid salts. When water or liquid is added to baking powder, carbon dioxide is given off and the mixture to which the baking powder has been added is aerated. Too much baking powder can spoil the texture and flavour of a cake or quick bread, so it is important to use only the amount called for in the recipe. Cakes containing baking powder rise to greater volume in the microwave, giving an airy, fluffy texture. For some baked goods that take only a few minutes to microwave, try letting the mixture stand for 3-4 minutes before microwaving in order to start the reaction between the baking powder and the liquid.

BANANA
This tropical fruit bruises easily and should be handled carefully. Ripen at room temperature and never store in the refrigerator. When fully ripe, the banana is high in natural sugars and is easily digested. It also contains vitamins A, B and C, potassium, and other mineral salts. Sliced or chopped bananas should be sprinkled with lemon juice to prevent discoloration.

With the help of the microwave, bananas can be turned into instant desserts, or they may be added to sauces for meat or fish dishes. Take great care when microwaving bananas as they can become very hot as a result of their high sugar and moisture content. Do not attempt to microwave bananas in their skins without first slitting them as they are likely to explode.

Baked bananas

Full Power
4 minutes

4 medium bananas
30 g (1 oz) caster sugar
60 mℓ (4 tablespoons) fruit juice

Peel and slice bananas, sprinkle with sugar and fruit juice. Cover and microwave on Full Power for 4 minutes. Stand for 3 – 4 minutes, then mash to serve as baby food, or serve with cream for pudding.
Serves 2 – 4

Overleaf left: from top to bottom, Bacon-Wrapped Snacks (page 11), Mexican Meat Balls (page 17), Salami Pizza Bites (page 11)
Overleaf right: from top to bottom, Lemon Bars, Chocolate and Coconut Biscuits, Chocolate-topped Peanut Butter Bars (pages 34 and 35)

Caramelized bananas

Full Power
17 minutes

75 g (2½ oz) butter
6-8 bananas
75 g (2½ oz) caster sugar
250 mℓ (8 fl oz) orange juice
30 mℓ (2 tablespoons) lemon juice
15 g (½ oz) toasted almonds*
ice cream

Place butter in a large shallow casserole, and
microwave on Full Power for 3 minutes until very
hot. Add bananas, turn to coat with butter,
microwave for 2 minutes, turn and microwave
for 2 minutes more. Remove bananas, set
aside. Add sugar to butter, microwave for 3 – 4
minutes, until beginning to brown. Stir every
minute. Add orange and lemon juice and stir.
The mixture may caramelize slightly.
Microwave for 5 minutes. Add bananas, cover
and microwave for 2 minutes more. Sprinkle
with nuts and serve with ice cream.
Serves 4 – 6

BARLEY
Barley, like wheat, is a cereal crop and one
of the earliest cultivated grains. Originally
barley was used to make bread, but its low
gluten content resulted in a heavy texture.
Barley does, however, make a tasty and
nutritious addition to soups and casseroles.
Pearl barley, the polished grain, is the most
widely available barley today and is traditionally used in the making of Scotch
broth. With the focus on high-fibre whole
grain products, barley is increasing in popularity. Barley normally requires long slow
cooking but the microwave reduces this
cooking time considerably.

Barley water

Full Power, Medium (50%)
1 hour 10 minutes

A refreshing, nutritious drink, often given to
invalids.

100 g (3½ oz) pearl barley
1.25 litreś (2¼ pints) water
thinly pared rind and juice of 3 lemons
caster sugar to taste, about 75 g (2½ oz)

Place barley, water, lemon rind and sugar in a
large bowl. Cover with vented plastic wrap.

Microwave on Full Power for 10 minutes. Stir to
dissolve sugar. Cover again, and microwave on
Medium (50%) for 1 hour. Strain and add lemon
juice. Refrigerate and serve well chilled.
Makes 1.25 litres (2¼ pints)

Lamb with wholewheat topping

Full Power, Medium (50%)
1 hour 22 minutes

750 g (1¾ lb) boneless lamb, cut in cubes
15 g (½ oz) plain flour
salt and black pepper
15 mℓ (1 tablespoon) oil
2 onions, chopped
1 garlic clove, crushed
375 mℓ (12 fl oz) stock, beef and chicken
   combined
60 g (2 oz) pearl barley
4 carrots, thickly sliced
2.5 mℓ (½ teaspoon) thyme
60 mℓ (4 tablespoons) tomato purée
175 g (6 oz) frozen peas

Topping
250 g (9 oz) wholewheat flour
15 mℓ (1 tablespoon) baking powder
salt
2.5 mℓ (½ teaspoon) thyme
60 mℓ (4 tablespoons) oil
1 egg
5 mℓ (1 teaspoon) vinegar
milk and water

Paprika wash
15 g (½ oz) butter, melted
pinch of paprika

Toss meat in flour, salt and pepper. Place oil in
a large casserole, microwave on Full Power for
2 minutes. Add meat, onion and garlic,
combine well. Microwave for 5 minutes, turning
every minute. Now add the stock, pearl barley,
carrots, thyme and tomato purée. Cover and
microwave for 10 minutes. Stir well, microwave
on Medium (50%) for 1 hour, stirring from time
to time.
   Meanwhile make the topping. Place the dry
ingredients in a bowl. In a measuring jug,
combine the oil, egg and vinegar. Add
sufficient milk and water to the oil and egg
mixture to make the liquid measure 250 mℓ
(8 fl oz). Pour into dry ingredients and mix to
form a stiff dough. Form into small balls and
flatten slightly. Stir peas into meat and arrange
the topping around the edge of the casserole.
Combine butter and paprika, brush onto the
topping. Microwave on Full Power for 5 – 6
minutes. Serve immediately.
Serves 4 – 6

BASTING
Basting is a process of spooning fat or
liquids over food while it is cooking to keep
it moist. Most foods do not dry out as much
during microwaving as they would during
conventional cooking, nevertheless foods
such as meat, fish or poultry may still need
some basting during microwave cooking.

BATTERS
Batter recipes such as pancakes and
Yorkshire puddings need conventional
cooking to form a crust and become crisp,
and therefore cannot be cooked in the
microwave. Pancakes will, however, reheat perfectly in the microwave and can be
used in combination with other filling and
sauce ingredients.

BEAN SPROUTS
Almost any whole grains or large seeds can
be sprouted in your kitchen. They can also
be purchased fresh or canned from many
supermarkets. Mung beans are perhaps the
best known of the sprouting beans, but
other interesting varieties include lentils,
lucerne, cress, fenugreek, Japanese radish,
mustard and sunflower. All sprouts are
rich in vitamin C and to preserve their nu-
tritional value, cook them for a short time
in the microwave and always serve them
crisp.

Chicken and sprouts

Full Power, High (70%)
27 minutes

3-4 boneless chicken breasts
salt and black pepper
30 mℓ (2 tablespoons) oil
450 g (1 lb) cooked rice
300 g (11 oz) canned or 100 g (3½ oz) fresh
   bean sprouts
60 g (2 oz) Japanese radish sprouts (optional)
150 mℓ (5 fl oz) chicken stock
30 mℓ (2 tablespoons) soy sauce
2.5 mℓ (½ teaspoon) grated lemon rind
5 mℓ (1 teaspoon) dried basil, or 10 mℓ
   (2 teaspoons) fresh basil

Arrange chicken breasts in a large shallow
casserole, season lightly. Cover and
microwave on High (70%) for 13 – 15 minutes,
remove from the casserole, stand for 5 minutes,
then cut into slivers. Set aside. Add oil to the
casserole, microwave on Full Power for 2
minutes. Add rice and sprouts, toss to coat with
oil. Microwave uncovered for 4 minutes, stirring
twice during the cooking time. Add stock and
remaining ingredients, toss to combine.
Microwave on High (70%) for 8 minutes, stirring
every 2 minutes. Serve immediately.
Serves 4

Peas and sprouts

Full Power
8 minutes

30 g (1 oz) butter
½ onion, chopped
250 g (9oz) frozen peas
generous pinch of caster sugar
150 g (5 oz) bean sprouts
salt and black pepper
5 mℓ (1 teaspoon) chopped mint

Place butter in a shallow casserole, microwave on Full Power for 1 minute. Add onion, toss to coat with butter and microwave for 2 minutes. Stir in the peas, sugar, sprouts, salt and pepper. Cover and microwave for 5 – 6 minutes, stirring once during the cooking time. Stir in the chopped mint and serve.
Serves 4 – 6

BEANS, CANNED

Canned green beans make a handy addition to the store cupboard. For extra flavour and added bulk stir the contents of a can into a quick casserole supper for 1.

To reheat a 400 g (14-oz) can of green beans, pour beans and liquid into a bowl, and cover. Microwave for about 2 minutes, drain, add a knob of butter and use as required.

Tuna casserole

Full Power, Medium (50%)
13 minutes

60 g (2 oz) margarine
1 small onion, sliced
30 g (1½ oz) plain flour
250 mℓ (8 fl oz) chicken stock
pinch of nutmeg
200 g (7 oz) canned tuna, drained
salt and black pepper
400 g (14 oz) canned sliced green beans, drained
45 g (1½ oz) stuffed olives, chopped
100 g (3½ oz) Cheddar cheese, grated
60 g (2 oz) fresh brown breadcrumbs, toasted
5 mℓ (1 teaspoon) paprika
15 mℓ (1 tablespoon) chopped parsley

Place the margarine in a shallow casserole, microwave on Full Power for 2 minutes. Add onion, stir to coat with margarine and microwave for 2 minutes. Stir in flour, microwave for 10 seconds. Pour in chicken stock, stir well. Microwave for 2 minutes, stirring every 30 seconds. Add nutmeg, tuna, seasonings, beans, olives and half the cheese, stir well. Combine breadcrumbs, remaining cheese, paprika and parsley. Sprinkle on top of the casserole. Microwave on High (70%) for 7 – 9 minutes until bubbling. *Serves 4*

BEANS, DRIED

Dried beans absorb plenty of liquid so it is not necessary to reduce the amount of water used when cooking these vegetables in the microwave. Dried beans also take time to become tender, so you may find that the microwave cooking time is almost the same as for conventional cooking. Microwaved beans are more attractive, as they keep their shape and are not broken up by frequent stirring, although the texture is firmer than in conventional cooking, and may not appeal to those who are used to very soft or mushy baked beans.

Cooked dried beans

Full Power, Medium (50%)
2 hours

350 g (12 oz) dried beans, rinsed
1.5 litres (2¾ pints) water
1 small onion
½ carrot
½ celery stick
4 streaky bacon rashers, cooked* and crumbled
10 mℓ (2 teaspoons) salt
generous pinch of pepper

Place beans, water, onion, carrot, celery, bacon, salt and pepper in a large casserole. Cover and microwave on Full Power for 20 minutes. Stir. Microwave, covered, on Medium (50%) for 1 hour 30 minutes to 1 hour 40 minutes, or until beans are tender, stirring every 45 minutes. Stand for 10 minutes before using in the dish of your choice.
Makes 8 – 10 servings

Maple baked beans

Defrost (30%)
1 hour 15 minutes

1 quantity cooked dried beans*
8 bacon rashers, cooked* and crumbled
100 g (3½ oz) soft brown sugar
125 mℓ (4 fl oz) maple-flavoured syrup
45 mℓ (3 tablespoons) finely chopped onion
15 mℓ (1 tablespoon) Worcestershire sauce
5 mℓ (1 teaspoon) cinnamon
salt and pepper

Drain beans, reserving the liquid. Stir bacon, brown sugar, syrup, onion, Worcestershire sauce, cinnamon and salt and pepper into the beans. Add 375 mℓ (12 fl oz) of the reserved liquid to the bean mixture. Cover and microwave on Defrost (30%) for 1¼ – 1½ hours, or until beans are very tender and the flavours have blended. Stir occasionally as the mixture bakes, and add more reserved cooking liquid from the beans if necessary. Stand for at least 10 minutes before serving. *Serves 8 – 10*

Savoury baked beans in tomato sauce

Full Power, High (70%)
1 hour 15 minutes

1 quantity cooked dried beans*
3 onions, chopped
2 garlic cloves, finely chopped
60 g (2 oz) butter or margarine
45 mℓ (3 tablespoons) plain flour
375 mℓ (12 fl oz) hot water
1 chicken stock cube
90 mℓ (3 fl oz) tomato paste
salt and pepper
Tabasco (optional)

Drain the beans, reserving the liquid. In a large casserole, microwave the onions, garlic and butter on Full Power for 4 – 7 minutes, or until onion is tender. Stir in the flour and add the water, chicken stock, tomato paste and salt and pepper. Mix well, then microwave on Full Power for 10 – 15 minutes, or until the sauce has thickened, stirring at least twice. Place beans in a large casserole and add the sauce. Cover and microwave on High (70%) for 50 – 60 minutes or until beans are very soft. Add reserved bean liquid as needed during microwaving and stir 3 – 4 times. Add a few drops of Tabasco during the last 15 minutes of cooking time if desired. Stand for at least 10 minutes before serving. *Serves 8*

BEANS, GREEN

Fresh green beans are tasty, versatile and economical. Young beans need only to be 'topped and tailed' before cooking. For variety, slice diagonally or chop.

To microwave fresh green beans

Top and tail 500 g (18 oz) beans. Place in a bowl or casserole, add 45 ml (3 tablespoons) water and salt. Cover and microwave on Full Power for 12 – 14 minutes until beans are just tender, drain and serve.

Serving suggestions

☐ Add a little butter and freshly ground black pepper.
☐ Sprinkle beans with toasted almonds*.
☐ Top with crumbled cooked bacon*.
☐ Add a little garlic to butter, and add to cooked beans.

Overleaf left: Apple Cream Gingerbread Cake served with a mixture of whipped cream and smooth apple sauce (page 45)
Overleaf right: Lemon-glazed Pound Cake (page 44), Chocolate Walnut Cake (page 45)

Venetian green beans

Full Power, High (70%)
22 minutes

500 g (18 oz) small green beans
3 – 4 tomatoes
30 g (1 oz) butter
10 mℓ (2 teaspoons) Italian olive oil
1 small onion, chopped
1 garlic clove, chopped
1 bay leaf
pinch of dried marjoram
salt and black pepper

Wash beans, top and tail them and remove strings, but leave beans whole. Place tomatoes in microwave for a few seconds on Full Power, then remove skins and chop. Place butter and oil in a large shallow casserole, microwave 1 minute, add onion and garlic, toss to coat with butter mixture. Microwave for 2 minutes. Add tomato, bay leaf, marjoram and seasonings, cover and microwave for 7 minutes, stirring from time to time. Now add beans, stir to combine, cover and microwave on High (70%) for 12 – 14 minutes. Add a little boiling water if the tomato becomes too dry. Remove bay leaf before serving.
Serves 6

Green beans with soured cream and dill

Full Power, Medium (50%)
11 minutes

500 g (18 oz) green beans
10 mℓ (2 teaspoons) fresh or 5 mℓ (1 teaspoon) dried dill
salt
45 mℓ (3 tablespoons) water
125 mℓ (4 fl oz) soured cream

To Garnish
dill sprigs

Top and tail beans, string and cut diagonally. Place beans in a bowl, combine dill, salt and water, pour over beans, cover. Microwave on Full Power for 9 – 10 minutes, stir once during cooking time. Drain and place in a serving dish. Microwave soured cream on Medium (50%) for 1½ minutes, pour over beans. Garnish with dill sprigs.
Serves 6

BEEF

Many cuts of beef can be cocked in the microwave to juicy tenderness in a third to half the time it takes conventionally. Also, there are fewer preparation dishes and no baked-on mess to clean up. Some meats are microwaved on Full Power, but for many, a lower power setting allows the meat to cook with less care and attention. Several cuts of beef are discussed in this section, and each will have instructions on how it can be microwaved to best advantage. The Beef Chart opposite gives general information at a glance.

See also Casseroles, Hamburgers, Meat balls, Meat loaf, Mince and individual names of beef dishes.

BEEF POT ROASTS

Pot roasts and less tender, large cuts of meat, such as silverside and aitch-bone need different techniques from tender roasts. They are generally microwaved covered, with a little liquid added for moisture. Use Full Power for a short time, then lower the power level so that the meat is slowly steamed and simmered to break down the tough fibres and promote tenderness. Pot roasts will not have a crisp surface since the cooking method requires moist heat. Acid ingredients such as tomatoes, pineapple, vinegar or wine will also help tenderize the meat, and gravies and sauces made from the cooking liquid add flavour and improve the finished appearance. Pot roasts may be cooked in a roasting bag but remember to tie the bag loosely with string or pierce it with a knife to allow the steam to escape. Do not use metal twist ties as they may cause arcing or cause the roasting bag to melt.

Marinated pot roast

Full Power, Medium (50%)
45 minutes – 1 hour 30 minutes

250 mℓ (8 fl oz) tomato sauce (as served with pasta)
75 g (2½ oz) soft brown sugar
15 mℓ (1 tablespoon) Worcestershire sauce
15 mℓ (1 tablespoon) vinegar
5 mℓ (1 teaspoon) dry mustard
pinch of chilli powder
pinch of salt
pinch of allspice
1 – 1.5 kg (2¼ – 3 lb) pot roast

Mix together the tomato sauce, brown sugar, Worcestershire sauce, vinegar, mustard, chilli

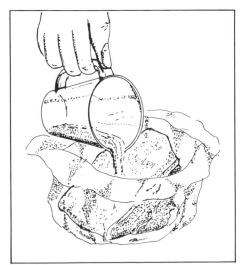

Place the pot roast in a roasting bag in the baking dish. Pour required liquid or marinade over the roast and close the bag loosely or pierce with a knife.

powder, salt and allspice. Pierce the roast with a skewer on all sides and place in a roasting bag. Place in a shallow casserole. Pour tomato mixture over meat and tie the bag loosely. Refrigerate for 12 hours or overnight, turning the bag over occasionally to ensure the meat is evenly marinated.

Place the casserole containing the roast and marinade ingredients in the microwave. Microwave on Full Power for 5 minutes. Reduce power to Medium (50%) and continue microwaving for 20 – 30 minutes per 500 g (18 oz), or until meat is tender. After half the cooking time, turn entire bag over. At end of cooking time, stand for 10 minutes before carving. Skim fat from the sauce and thicken if desired. Serve sauce with the meat.
Serves 6

Baked spiced brisket

Full Power, High (70%), Medium (50%)
3 hours

2 kg (4¼ lb) salted brisket
water
15 mℓ (1 tablespoon) pickling spice
2 carrots, sliced
1 large onion, sliced
2 potatoes, sliced
whole cloves

Topping
90 g (3 oz) soft brown sugar
100 mℓ (3½ fl oz) tomato sauce (as served with pasta)
25 mℓ (5 teaspoons) dry mustard
30 mℓ (2 tablespoons) wine vinegar
15 mℓ (1 tablespoon) cornflour
30 mℓ (2 tablespoons) water

Place brisket in a 4.5-litre (8-pint) casserole, add sufficient water to cover meat. Cover and microwave for 10 minutes on Full Power. Pour the water off and repeat this process twice more to reduce saltiness. Cover brisket again with water, add pickling spice and vegetables. Cover meat and microwave for 15 minutes. Reduce power level to High (70%) and microwave for 1½ hours more, or until the brisket is just tender. Stand meat in liquid for 10 minutes after completion of cooking time. Remove meat, score fat on top of brisket in a diamond pattern and stud with cloves. Drain vegetables and set aside. Pour liquid into a jug, leaving 250 mℓ (8 fl oz) in the casserole and add meat. Combine all ingredients for topping, pour over meat and cover. Microwave for 10 minutes on Full Power, reduce power level to High (70%) for 10 minutes. Now reduce power level to Medium (50%) for 20 minutes. The top of the meat will be a deep reddish brown colour. Remove meat, place on a carving board and keep warm. Combine cornflour and water, stir into liquid in the casserole. Microwave on Full Power for 2 minutes, stirring well. Add vegetables, microwave for 2 minutes more and pour into a serving bowl. Carve thinly, spoon a little of the vegetable sauce on to each serving.
Serves 8

BEEF CHART

BEEF CUT	DEFROST TIME Per 500 g (18 oz) (on Defrost 30%)	COOKING TIME Per 500 g (18 oz) (Full Power)	METHOD
Steak	3 – 4 minutes, stand 5 – 10 minutes	3 – 5 minutes, stand 1 minute	Separate pieces as soon as possible. Microwave in browning dish.
Boned and rolled roast	8 – 12 minutes, stand 1 hour	*rare* 8 – 10 minutes *medium* 9 – 12 minutes *well done* 10 – 13 minutes	Defrost wrapped for half the time. Unwrap, shield warm sections, and lie meat on its side.
Large joints on the bone	10 – 14 minutes, stand 1 hour	*rare* 8 – 10 minutes *medium* 9 – 12 minutes *well done* 10 – 13 minutes, stand 10 minutes	Defrost wrapped for half the time, then shield bone. Turn meat over after half the defrosting time, then again after half the cooking time.
Minced beef	9 – 12 minutes, stand 5 minutes	use as required	Break up during defrosting. Remove thawed pieces.
Stewing beef	10 – 12 minutes, stand 15 minutes	use as required	Separate pieces during defrosting. Remove thawed sections.

BEEF ROASTS

Tender cuts of beef, such as rolled or standing ribs, are ideal for microwaving. Even if a lower power setting is used, the meat will roast more quickly than conventional cooking and will require less attention during cooking time.

Boneless, compact roasts with a uniform shape and weighing between 1 and 2 kg (2¼ and 4¼ lb) are best for microwaving. A roast which is thinner at one end will be done first in that area. Long, thin roasts will cook faster than short, thick ones.

To roast tender cuts
Select a high quality piece of beef. Place it on a rack deep enough to keep the meat above the juices. It is not necessary to add water, but the meat may be brushed with a browning agent* (page 39) to enhance the colour and add flavour. Cover loosely so the meat will not be steamed and use a Medium (50%) setting to prevent shrinkage and retain juiciness, tenderness and flavour. (See chart right for cooking times.)

If the roast is to be done evenly, it should be turned over after half the microwave cooking time has elapsed. Start the roast fat side down if it is to be turned over during cooking. Standing time is very important after roasting meat as it allows the temperature to equalize. Allow 10 – 20 minutes standing time and cover meat with a 'tent' of aluminium foil, shiny side in, to retain heat.

BEEF STEAKS

Tender cuts of steak such as minute steak, T-bones and fillet can be microwaved in a browning dish and will remain juicy and full of flavour. The chart above right is for microwaving steaks on Full Power in a browning dish, and gives medium-rare results. Cut steaks 2.5-cm (1-inch) thick and

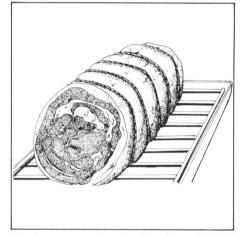

Boneless, compact roasts with uniform shape are best for microwave cooking.

preheat browning dish according to the manufacturer's instructions. To test, cut with a knife tip from the edge towards the centre. The area closest to the bone is the last to cook. Adjust timing if necessary. For well-browned steaks butter both sides before microwaving, using about 15 g (½ oz) butter per steak. Drain juice after cooking the first side of steak.

Braised steak
Less tender steaks may be microwaved in liquid on Medium (50%). Gentle simmering helps to soften the meat and if such liquids as tomato juice or wine are used, the slight acidity assists the tenderization process. Marinating meat also helps to tenderize and flavour steak. Pounding beef steak with a meat mallet or the edge of a saucer partially breaks down tough fibres, though steaks tenderized this way often lack flavour and are best served with a tasty sauce.

Swiss steak

Medium (50%)
1 hour 15 minutes

750 g (1¾ lb) tenderized steak
30 g (1 oz) plain flour
7.5 mℓ (1½ teaspoons) salt
2.5 mℓ (½ teaspoon) black pepper
1 large onion, thinly sliced
400 g (14 oz) canned whole tomatoes

Cut meat into six pieces. Dredge steaks with a mixture of flour, salt and pepper. Place in a large casserole and cover with sliced onion. Chop the tomatoes and add to the casserole with the liquid from the can. Cover and microwave on Medium (50%) for 70 – 80 minutes, or until meat is tender. Rearrange meat after half the microwaving time. If a thicker sauce is desired, stir in 15 g (½ oz) plain flour for every 250 mℓ (8 fl oz) liquid and microwave for 2 – 3 minutes more.
Serves 6

BEEF STEWS

Less tender cuts of beef can be microwaved with liquids and vegetables to make tasty stews. The cooking time will depend on the type and amount of meat used, and on the quantity of vegetables added to the dish. Cut the meat and vegetables into smaller pieces than you would for conventional cooking, and make them more or less uniform in size. Simmering gently on a lower power setting, such as Medium (50%), and adding an acid ingredient, such as vinegar, pineapple, tomato juice or wine, will help to tenderize the meat and will give the stew added flavour. The temperature probe cannot be used with stews as there is no uniform substance, like a large piece of meat, to give an accurate temperature reading. Remember, too, microwaved

stews do not evaporate as much as conventional ones, so reduce the liquid by up to one third.

Beef bourguignonne

Full Power, Defrost (30%)
55 minutes

2 onions
3 streaky bacon rashers, rinds removed
200 g (7 oz) mushrooms, sliced
750 g (1¾ lb) beef topside, cut into cubes
15 g (½ oz) plain flour
250 mℓ (8 fl oz) red wine
60 mℓ (4 tablespoons) beef stock
1 – 2 cloves garlic, finely chopped
2.5 mℓ (½ teaspoon) dried thyme
2.5 mℓ (½ teaspoon) dried oregano
15 mℓ (1 tablespoon) freshly chopped parsley
salt and pepper

Chop onions and dice bacon. Place in a bowl, cover and microwave on Full Power for 5 minutes. Stir in mushrooms and beef. Microwave, covered, for 5 minutes, stirring after 3 minutes. Mix in the flour, red wine, stock, garlic and herbs. Season to taste with salt and pepper. Microwave, covered, for 2 minutes. Stir well, then reduce power to Defrost (30%) and microwave, covered, for 40 – 45 minutes, or until meat is tender. Stand for 10 minutes before serving. Serve with rice or noodles.
Serves 6

Spicy Malaysian beef

Full Power, High (70%), Medium (50%)
1 hour 15 minutes

175 g (6 oz) desiccated coconut
625 mℓ (1 pint) water
15 mℓ (1 tablespoon) tamarind pulp
60 mℓ (4 tablespoons) hot water
750 g (1¾ lb) stewing steak, cubed
30 g (½ oz) plain flour
salt and black pepper
45 mℓ (3 tablespoons) oil
1 onion, quartered
2 garlic cloves
1 small piece of fresh ginger
5 mℓ (1 teaspoon) turmeric
2.5 mℓ (½ teaspoon) cayenne
45 g (¾ oz) blanched almonds
5 mℓ (1 teaspoon) ground coriander
5 mℓ (1 teaspoon) caraway seeds
grated rind of 1 lemon
1 green pepper, seeds removed

Combine coconut and water in a large jug. Microwave on Full Power for 2 minutes and stand for 30 minutes. Strain and set aside. Infuse tamarind pulp in hot water for 15 minutes. Strain and add to coconut milk. Place cubes of stewing steak in a bowl. Add flour, salt and pepper, and toss well. Heat a browning

From left to right: Hot Buttered Lemonade (page 34), Hot Tomato Cocktail (page 33), Mulled Red Wine (page 33)

ROASTING CHART FOR TENDER BEEF CUTS

BEEF CUT	COOKING TIME minutes per 500 g (18 oz) Medium (50%)	COOKING TIME minutes per 500 g (18 oz) Full Power
Boned and rolled roast	*rare:* 11 – 13 minutes *medium:* 13 – 14 minutes *well done:* 15 – 16 minutes	*rare:* 8 – 10 minutes *medium:* 9 – 12 minutes *well done:* 10 – 13 minutes
Large joints on the bone	*rare:* 11 – 13 minutes *medium:* 13 – 14 minutes *well done:* 15 – 16 minutes	*rare:* 8 – 10 minutes *medium:* 9 – 12 minutes *well done:* 10 – 13 minutes

STEAK COOKING CHART

TYPE	NUMBER	1st SIDE (Full Power)	2nd SIDE (Full Power)
Minute steaks	1 – 2	1 minute	1 – 1½ minutes
	4	2 minutes	2 – 2½ minutes
Sirloin or rump	1 – 2	2 minutes	2 – 2½ minutes
	3	5 minutes	3 – 3½ minutes
T-Bone	1	3 minutes	2 minutes
Fillet	1 – 4	2 minutes	2 – 2½ minutes

dish for 5 minutes, add the oil and heat for 1 minute. Now add the meat and stir every 30 seconds for 2 minutes. Microwave for 2 minutes more, stirring at least twice. Place remaining ingredients in the work bowl of a food processor, process to a paste. Add to the meat and stir well. Pour in the coconut milk, stir then cover. Microwave on High (70%) for 40 minutes, stirring from time to time. Reduce power to Medium (50%) for a further 25 minutes, or until meat is tender. Serve with boiled rice and a selection of sambals.
Serves 4

Note: If tamarind pulp is unavailable, use 45 mℓ (3 tablespoons) brown vinegar instead.

Beef olives with soured cream

Full Power, Medium (50%)
50 minutes

750 g (1¾ lb) beef topside, thinly sliced
30 g (1 oz) plain cake flour

Stuffing
30 mℓ (2 tablespoons) oil
2 bacon rashers, chopped
1 onion, chopped
60 g (2 oz) soft breadcrumbs
45 mℓ (3 tablespoons) chopped parsley
30 mℓ (2 tablespoons) tomato paste
generous pinch of dried thyme
salt and black pepper

Sauce
30 mℓ (2 tablespoons) oil
2 celery sticks, chopped
300 mℓ (½ pint) beef stock
45 mℓ (3 tablespoons) sherry
5 mℓ (1 teaspoon) caraway seeds
1 bay leaf
150 mℓ (5 fl oz) soured cream

To make the stuffing, place oil in a bowl and microwave on Full Power for 1 minute. Add bacon and onion, toss to combine. Microwave for 4 minutes. Add breadcrumbs, parsley, tomato paste and thyme. Season well with salt and pepper and mix to combine. Place a little filling on each slice of beef, roll up and secure with a toothpick. Toss in flour. Heat a browning dish for 5 minutes. Carefully add the oil and microwave for 1 minute. Place beef olives in the browning dish and microwave for 1 minute. Turn the meat and microwave for 1 minute more. Repeat once more if necessary. Remove meat from browning dish and place in a shallow casserole. To the residue in the browning dish, add the celery, beef stock, sherry, caraway seeds and bay leaf, stirring to combine. Pour over the meat. Cover and microwave for 4 minutes. Turn the meat over, cover and microwave on Medium (50%) for 30 – 35 minutes, stirring at least twice during the cooking time. Stir in the soured cream and microwave for 4 minutes. Sprinkle with chopped parsley before serving. Serve with rice or noodles.
Serves 6

Beef stroganoff

Full Power, High (70%), Medium (50%)
17 minutes

15 g (½ oz) plain flour
2.5 mℓ (½ teaspoon) salt
500 g (18 oz) sirloin or rump steak, cut in thin strips
45 g (1½ oz) butter
1 large onion, peeled and chopped
125 g (4 oz) mushrooms, sliced
1 garlic clove, crushed (optional)
30 g (1 oz) butter
45 g (1½ oz) plain flour
20 mℓ (4 teaspoons) tomato paste
250 mℓ (8 fl oz) beef stock
250 mℓ (8 fl oz) soured cream
45 mℓ (3 tablespoons) medium cream sherry
15 mℓ (1 tablespoon) paprika

Mix flour with salt and use to dredge beef. Heat a browning dish on Full Power for 5 minutes, then remove from the microwave. Add butter followed by the beef and onion. Cover and microwave on High (70%) for 3 minutes. Stir, add mushrooms and garlic, cover and microwave for 3 minutes more. Remove from microwave, drain and keep warm.

In a deep bowl, microwave the butter for 30 seconds. Stir in the flour, tomato paste and stock. Microwave on High (70%) for 1½ minutes. Stir and microwave for 2 minutes more or until sauce is thick. Stir in soured cream and sherry and pour over the meat. Microwave on Medium (50%) for 2 – 3 minutes to heat through. Sprinkle with paprika and serve with noodles or rice.
Serves 4 – 6

Beef goulash

Full Power, Defrost (30%)
1 hour 15 minutes

4 bacon rashers, rinds removed, chopped
1 large onion, sliced
30 g (1 oz) butter or margarine
125 mℓ (4 fl oz) tomato purée or pousada
15 mℓ (1 tablespoon) paprika
15 mℓ (1 tablespoon) caster sugar
3 tomatoes, peeled and chopped
500 g (18 oz) topside of beef, cut in small cubes
salt and pepper
30 g (1 oz) plain flour
250 mℓ (8 fl oz) hot beef stock
60 mℓ (4 tablespoons) red wine
45 mℓ (3 tablespoons) soured cream

Garnish
paprika
chopped parsley

Place bacon in a large casserole, cover and microwave on Full Power for 4 minutes. Add onion and microwave for 2 minutes, then stir in butter, tomato purée, paprika, sugar, tomatoes, beef, salt and pepper to taste. Microwave, covered, for 5 minutes, stirring after 2½

minutes. Stir in the flour, stock and wine. Cover and microwave on Defrost (30%) for 50 – 60 minutes, or until meat is tender. Stir occasionally during cooking. Before serving, stir in soured cream and sprinkle with paprika and chopped parsley. Serve with hot buttered noodles. *Serves 4 – 6*

BEEF TEA
Beef tea is a concentrated beef broth with a flavour so delicious it will tempt even the poorest appetite. It is often used in a convalescent's diet, as even a small portion contains a lot of nourishment. The stock is ideally homemade but a cube may be substituted if necessary.

Beef tea

High (70%)
60 minutes

500 g (18 oz) lean stewing steak
2 carrots
500 mℓ (16 fl oz) stock or water
1 egg white
10 mℓ (2 teaspoons) sherry (optional)

Mince the meat and the carrots, place in a 1-litre (1¾-pint) casserole. Add stock and lightly whisked egg white, stir to combine. Cover and microwave on High (70%) for 1 hour, stirring every 15 minutes. Strain through a piece of muslin, and add the sherry. Reheat in the microwave and serve with toast.
Makes about 750 mℓ (1¼ pints)

BEER
Beer used in cooking adds subtle flavour that livens up soups, stocks, sauces or stews. It also blends well with fish and cheese dishes. As a marinade, beer will penetrate and tenderize meats, and when used in basting, it adds not only flavour, but gives meat an attractive glaze and colour. Beer used in microwave cooking blends well with other flavours. All traces of alcohol disappear during cooking, leaving the slightly bitter taste of hops and the aroma of malt.

Beer and Cheddar fondue

Full Power, Medium (50%)
10 minutes

125 mℓ (4 fl oz) beer
500 g (18 oz) Cheddar cheese, grated
30 g (1 oz) plain flour
5 mℓ (1 teaspoon) dry mustard
pinch of garlic salt
60 mℓ (4 tablespoons) milk
2.5 mℓ (½ teaspoon) Worcestershire sauce

Microwave beer in a deep casserole on Full Power for 45 – 60 seconds. Combine cheese, flour, mustard and garlic salt and add to the hot beer along with milk and Worcestershire sauce. Microwave on Medium (50%) for 7 – 9 minutes or until cheese has melted, stirring every 2

minutes. Place casserole over low heat to keep warm, or reheat as necessary. Serve with chunks of French bread or fresh crisp vegetables. *Serves 4 – 6*

BEESTING CAKE
A rich German yeast cake, filled with a thick custard cream, from which it gets its name. This custard is traditionally made from the thick albuminous milk, called beestings, produced by a newly calved cow. The recipe that follows is not strictly traditional, but is a modern version quickly made in the microwave.

Beesting cake

Full Power, Medium (50%)
7 – 8 minutes
Bake 220 °C/425 °F/gas 7
20 minutes

Cake
60 mℓ (4 tablespoons) water
30 mℓ (2 tablespoons) milk
7 g (¼ oz) fresh yeast
30 g (1 oz) caster sugar
225 g (8 oz) plain flour
pinch of salt
45 g (1½ oz) butter
2.5 mℓ (½ teaspoon) grated lemon rind

Topping
15 g (½ oz) almonds, chopped
45 g (1½ oz) caster sugar
few drops of vanilla extract
15 mℓ (1 tablespoon) honey

Filling
30 g (1 oz) butter
30 g (1 oz) plain flour
150 mℓ (5 fl oz) milk
2 egg yolks
30 mℓ (2 tablespoons) caster sugar
few drops of vanilla extract
100 mℓ (3½ fl oz) whipping cream
1 egg white

Combine water and milk in a small jug, microwave on Full Power for about 45 seconds, until lukewarm. Add yeast and 5 mℓ (1 teaspoon) of the sugar, stir until combined. Sprinkle with 30 g (1 oz) of the flour. Cover with plastic wrap, microwave for 10 seconds on Medium (50%). Rest for 3 minutes, then repeat. A frothy fermentation will start to form. Sift the remaining flour and salt into a bowl, add butter and rub in. Now add remaining sugar and lemon rind, mix to combine. Pour in yeast liquid. Using a large mixer, knead until smooth – about 4 minutes. Add a little extra liquid if necessary.

Place the dough in a greased plastic bag, tie the end loosely with string. Microwave on Full Power for 15 seconds, rest for 10 minutes. Repeat two or three times until the dough has doubled in size. Knock back and roll the dough into a circle about 1.5-cm (¾-inch) thick. Place on a greased baking sheet, and shape into a perfect round. Cover with plastic wrap and allow to rise in a warm place for 15 minutes.

For the topping, place all the ingredients in a small bowl, place in the microwave on Medium (50%) for 3 – 4 minutes, until slightly oily in appearance. Spread this mixture over the risen dough and bake in a conventional oven at 220 °C (425 °F gas 7) for 20 minutes. Remove from the oven and cool. Split the cake in half and fill.

To make the filling, place butter in a large jug, microwave on Full Power for 30 seconds, stir in flour, microwave for 10 seconds. Pour in all the milk at once, beating well with a small wire whisk. Microwave for 1½ – 2 minutes, stirring every 30 seconds. Beat in the egg yolks, sugar and vanilla; the mixture will be very thick at this point. Cover with a piece of greaseproof paper and allow to cool to room temperature. Beat the cream until thick, fold into the custard. Now beat the egg white until soft peaks form, fold into the custard. Use this mixture to fill the cake.
Makes 1 x 20 – 25-cm (8 – 10-inch) round cake

BEETROOT

Beetroot is a crimson-coloured root vegetable used in salads or for making Borscht (*see* Soups). To prepare beetroot for cooking, wash and scrub lightly with a brush. Cut off the tops, about 5 cm (2 inch) from the base. Do not peel beetroot or cut off the root as the vegetable will 'bleed' during cooking and lose colour.

To pickle cooked beetroot, slice 6 beetroot and an onion, place in a suitable container and cover with vinegar. Add 3 – 5 mℓ (3 – 5 teaspoons) caster sugar and a little lemon juice. Cover container and chill.

Beetroot

Full Power
28 minutes

6 medium-sized beetroot
150 mℓ (5 fl oz) water
pinch of salt

Trim beetroot and prick lightly with a skewer to prevent them from bursting . Place in a shallow casserole, add water and salt. Cover and microwave on Full Power for 28 – 32 minutes depending on size. Allow to cool, slip off the skins and use as required.

Beetroot and apple salad

6 cooked beetroot*, peeled and sliced
60 mℓ (4 tablespoons) oil
45 mℓ (3 tablespoons) vinegar
5 mℓ (1 teaspoon) caster sugar
salt and black pepper
2 green apples
1 onion, sliced
30 mℓ (2 tablespoons) chopped parsley

Place the sliced beetroot in a bowl. Combine oil, vinegar, sugar and seasonings. Pour over beetroot and stand for at least 30 minutes. Peel, quarter, core and slice the apple. Add to the beetroot with sliced onion and combine all the ingredients carefully. Turn into a salad bowl and sprinkle with parsley.
Serves 4 – 6

BEURRE BLANC

Beurre blanc, or directly translated, white butter, comes traditionally from the Loire valley in France. The sauce resembles hollandaise, but it is even more delicate as it is made of butter whisked into a reduction of wine, vinegar and shallots. The reduction of liquid is quickly achieved in the microwave and leaves no overpowering odour in the kitchen.

Beurre blanc

Full Power
8 minutes

45 mℓ (3 tablespoons) white wine vinegar
45 mℓ (3 tablespoons) dry white wine
2 shallots, chopped
250 g (9 oz) cold butter, cut up
salt and white pepper

Place the wine vinegar, wine and shallots into a bowl. Microwave on Full Power for 8 – 10 minutes, until the liquid has been reduced to about 20 mℓ (4 teaspoons). Strain the mixture. Stand the bowl with the reduced liquid in a shallow dish, pour near boiling water into the dish to a depth of about 2.5 cm (1 inch). Now whisk in the cold butter a few pieces at a time to make a smooth creamy sauce. If the butter starts to soften too quickly, remove the bowl from the hot water. The butter should soften and thicken the sauce without melting. Season to taste and serve as soon as possible. The sauce may be kept warm on Low (15%) if necessary for a few minutes. Care should be taken as the sauce becomes oily if it is actually heated.
Makes about 250 mℓ (8 fl oz)

BEVERAGES

See also individual entries, such as Coffee, Tea, Eggnog, etc.

The microwave is very popular for heating beverages, as it speeds up and simplifies the preparation. A cup of coffee or tea will be ready in about 1½ minutes, and most other water-based beverages can be heated on Full Power for quick results. Drinks with a high proportion of milk or eggs, such as eggnog, must be heated on a lower power level as they may curdle if heated too rapidly. Milk-based beverages, such as hot chocolate, need to be watched closely as they tend to boil over easily. The temperature probe, set at Medium (50%) and 60 °C (140 °F), can be used to heat milk-based beverages and will help to prevent them from boiling over.

To microwave beverages
When heating more than three individual cups of liquid at a time, arrange them in a circle for even heating. Use a deep 2 – 3 litre (3½ – 5-pint) casserole or jug for large quantities. Do not attempt to defrost or heat beverages in a narrow-necked bottle as pressure builds up in the lower part of the bottle, and may cause it to shatter.

Beverages that are cooked, such as old-fashioned eggnog, cocoa or hot lemonade, need little change of ingredients for microwaving and very little stirring during cooking. Stir liquids before microwaving and do not overfill the cups or mugs as liquid may spill over as it expands. A large heatproof jug, 1- and 2-litre (1¾- and 3½-pint) measuring jugs and heat-proof mugs are all useful for microwaving and serving hot drinks, but avoid any cups or jugs that have a metal trim.

Mulled red wine

High (70%)
10 minutes

150 g (5 oz) caster sugar
1 x 750 mℓ (1¾-pint) bottle good red wine
grated rind of ½ lemon
grated rind of ½ orange
3 cloves
pinch of mace
1 x 4-cm (1½-inch) piece of cinnamon stick
90 g (3 oz) butter
60 g (2 oz) soft brown sugar
125 mℓ (4 fl oz) brandy

Place sugar in a deep casserole or glass bowl. Add wine, stir and stand to dissolve. Stir in lemon and orange rind, cloves, mace and cinnamon. Microwave on High (70%) for 8 – 10 minutes. Cream butter until light and fluffy. Add brown sugar and beat very well. Remove wine from microwave and strain into six goblets. Top each drink with a spoonful of the butter and sugar mixture and add a little brandy.
Serves 6

Hot tomato cocktail

Full Power
6 minutes

750 mℓ (1¼ pints) tomato juice
15 mℓ (1 tablespoon) lemon juice
5 mℓ (1 teaspoon) Worcestershire sauce
5 mℓ (1 teaspoon) dried dill
100 mℓ (3½ fl oz) vodka (optional)

Place tomato juice, lemon juice and Worcestershire sauce in a 1-litre (1¾-pint) jug and microwave on Full Power for 5 – 6 minutes, or until hot. Pour into four mugs or heatproof glasses and sprinkle with dill. Add a splash of vodka to each drink if desired.
Serves 4

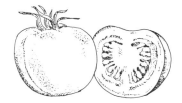

Hot buttered lemonade

Full Power
14 minutes

100 g (3½ oz) caster sugar
500 mℓ (16 fl oz) water
4 x 2.5-cm (1-inch) pieces of cinnamon stick
6 whole allspice
4 whole cloves
125 mℓ (4 fl oz) lemon juice
60 mℓ (4 tablespoons) brandy or rum
15 g (½ oz) butter

Combine sugar and water in a 1-litre (1¾-pint) jug. Loosely tie spices in cheesecloth and add to the sugar mixture. Microwave on Full Power for 6 – 7 minutes, or until boiling. Stand for 30 minutes to infuse, then stir in lemon juice. Microwave for 6 – 7 minutes longer. Remove spices and stir in brandy or rum. Pour into four mugs and top each with a knob of butter. Serve with cinnamon sticks to use as swizzle-sticks if desired.
Serves 4

BICARBONATE OF SODA

Bicarbonate of soda is used as a raising agent with cream of tartar or an acid ingredient, such as dates, treacle or golden syrup, if fresh milk is used in the recipe. It is used alone in recipes using sour milk or buttermilk. In many recipes, bicarbonate of soda is added towards the end of the mixing, as it starts to react immediately upon contact with the liquid. It also helps to darken cakes such as gingerbread and rich fruit cakes.

BISCUITS AND BARS

When using the microwave the best choice for biscuits are those with a stiff, crumbly batter containing more flour than fat. Moulded biscuits or sugar biscuits can also be baked in the microwave, but drop biscuits may tend to become hard and dry. Remember, a full batch of biscuits takes longer to microwave than to bake conventionally as only a few biscuits can be baked at a time. The texture of microwaved biscuits differs somewhat from those baked in a conventional oven, and they do not brown during microwave baking, so choose recipes for those that have natural colour, or are iced.

Bars can also be baked in the microwave, but again the finished product does not brown, so top them with a sugar coating or icing. Although round containers are best for microwave baking, bars typically

CHART FOR HEATING BEVERAGES

TEMPERATURE	BEVERAGE	AMOUNT	POWER	TIME (minutes)
Boiling	water	250 mℓ (8 fl oz)	Full Power	3 – 4
		500 mℓ (16 fl oz)	Full Power	5 – 7
		1 litre (1¾ pints)	Full Power	10 – 12
Scalding	milk	250 mℓ (8 fl oz)	Medium (50%)	3 – 4
		500 mℓ (16 fl oz)	Medium (50%)	5 – 7
Steaming	water	250 mℓ (8 fl oz)	Full Power	1½ – 2
		500 mℓ (16 fl oz)	Full Power	2½ – 3
		1 litre (1¾ pint)	Full Power	4 – 6
	coffee or tea	250 mℓ (8 fl oz)	Full Power	1 – 2
		500 mℓ (16 fl oz)	Full Power	2 – 3
		1 litre (1¾ pints)	Full Power	4 – 5
	milk	250 mℓ (8 fl oz)	Medium (50%)	2 – 3
		500 mℓ (16 fl oz)	Medium (50%)	5 – 7
		1 litre (1¾ pints)	Medium (50%)	8 – 10

are cut into squares or rectangular shapes. Square dishes may be used, but it is wise to shield the corners with a small strip of aluminium foil to prevent them from overcooking before the centre is done. If your microwave does not have a turntable, you may wish to rotate the baking dish a quarter turn halfway through the cooking time.

Chocolate and coconut biscuits

Full Power
23 minutes

250 g (9 oz) margarine
200 g (7 oz) caster sugar
250 g (9 oz) self-raising flour
30 g (1 oz) cocoa powder
pinch of salt
150 g (5 oz) desiccated coconut
125 mℓ (4 fl oz) boiling water
5 mℓ (1 teaspoon) instant coffee powder
100 g (3½ oz) plain chocolate
1 quantity chocolate icing*

Cream margarine and sugar until light and fluffy. Sift dry ingredients into a bowl, and add coconut. Combine water and instant coffee. Add one-third of dry ingredients to margarine mixture, and beat to combine. Now add one-third of the water, and mix. Repeat until all the ingredients have been combined. Line a microwave baking sheet with parchment paper, or grease a plain baking sheet. Roll dough into walnut-sized balls. Arrange on the baking sheet in a circle, leaving 5 cm (2 inch) between each ball. Microwave on Full Power for 4 – 5 minutes. Lift off paper with a spatula and cool on a rack. Repeat until all the dough has been used, about five more batches.

When biscuits are cool, microwave chocolate on Full Power for 2½ – 3 minutes stirring at least once during cooking time. Spread chocolate on the flat side of half the biscuits. Spread icing on the other half, and sandwich one of each together.
Makes about 24 double biscuits.

Almond bars

Medium (50%)
19 minutes

125 g (4 oz) butter, softened
60 g (2 oz) soft brown sugar
150 g (5 oz) plain flour

Topping
2 eggs
200 g (7 oz) soft brown sugar
few drops of vanilla extract
15 g (½ oz) plain flour
5 mℓ (1 teaspoon) baking powder
2.5 mℓ (½ teaspoon) salt
100 g (3½ oz) desiccated coconut
100 g (3½ oz) unblanched flaked almonds

For the base, beat the butter and brown sugar together until light. Add flour and mix to a soft dough. Press evenly in the bottom of a 25-cm (10-inch) microwave baking dish. Microwave on Medium (50%) for 6 minutes, then stand for 5 minutes to set slightly. For the topping, beat together the eggs, brown sugar, vanilla essence, flour, baking powder and salt until well mixed. Add coconut and half the almonds, mixing well. Spread mixture evenly over base and sprinkle with remaining almonds. Microwave on Medium (50%) for 10 – 13 minutes. Allow to cool before cutting.
Makes 24 bars

Crispy fruit bars

Full Power
1½ minutes

60 g (2 oz) rice crispies
45 g (1½ oz) dried apricots, chopped
45 g (1½ oz) glacé cherries, quartered
45 g (1½ oz) sultanas
30 g (1 oz) nuts, such as peanuts or pecans, chopped
30 g (1 oz) butter or margarine
15 large marshmallows

Measure cereal, apricots, cherries, sultanas and nuts into a bowl and set aside. Grease a 22.5-cm (9-inch) square baking dish. Place butter and marshmallows in a large bowl and microwave on Full Power for 1 – 1½ minutes, or until marshmallows have melted. Stir to blend, then quickly stir in reserved ingredients. Press mixture gently into the prepared baking dish and cool completely before cutting into bars.
Makes 16 – 30 bars, depending on size

Chocolate-topped peanut butter bars

Full Power, Medium (50%)
8 minutes

60 g (2 oz) smooth peanut butter
60 g (2 oz) caster sugar
45 g (1½ oz) soft brown sugar
45 g (1½ oz) butter or margarine
1 egg
few drops of vanilla extract
60 g (2 oz) plain flour
45 g (1½ oz) quick-cooking oats
2.5 mℓ (½ teaspoon) bicarbonate of soda
pinch of salt

Topping
30 g (1 oz) smooth peanut butter
90 g (3 oz) plain chocolate, broken in pieces

Beat together peanut butter, sugars, butter, egg and vanilla extract until light and fluffy. Combine dry ingredients and add to peanut butter mixture. Mix well and spread in a 20-cm (8-inch) baking dish. Shield the corners of the dish with aluminium foil and microwave on Full Power for 3 – 5 minutes, or until the top is no longer damp. Cool before spreading with topping.
    To make the topping, place peanut butter and chocolate in a small bowl. Microwave on Medium (50%) for 1½ – 3 minutes, or until melted. Stir, then spread over the baked mixture. Cut into squares to serve.
Makes 15 – 24 bars, depending on size

Lemon bars

Full Power
10 minutes

400 g (14 oz) canned sweetened condensed
    milk
125 mℓ (4 fl oz) lemon juice
5 mℓ (1 teaspoon) grated lemon rind
175 g (6 oz) Marie biscuit crumbs
75 g (2½ oz) soft brown sugar
75 g (2½ oz) butter, melted
45 g (1½ oz) walnuts, chopped

Beat together the condensed milk, lemon juice and lemon rind until thick and smooth, then set aside. Combine crumbs, sugar and butter. Place about two-thirds of the mixture in the bottom of a 20-cm (8-inch) baking dish and press down firmly. Pour lemon mixture over and spread evenly. Sprinkle remaining crumb mixture and nuts over the top and pat down gently. Shield corners of the dish with

aluminium foil. Microwave on Full Power for 8 – 10 minutes. Let cool in the dish, then cut into bars.
Makes 16 – 24 bars, depending on size

BLACK FOREST CAKE
This wickedly rich chocolate cake is a speciality from Germany's Black Forest. Layers of moist chocolate cake are sandwiched together with Kirsch, cherries and cream. The recipe below is ideal for microwave users who are short of time.

Black Forest cake

Defrost (30%), Full Power
11 minutes

1 packet chocolate cake mix
1 packet instant chocolate pudding mix
3 eggs
100 mℓ (3½ fl oz) oil
220 mℓ (7 fl oz) milk
45 g (1½ oz) ground almonds
45 g (1½ oz) finely processed cake crumbs
15 mℓ (1 tablespoon) Kirsch

Filling
60 mℓ (4 tablespoons) Kirsch
425 g (15 oz) canned cherry pie filling
500 mℓ (16 fl oz) whipping cream, stiffly beaten
2 large chocolate flaky bars
5 glacé or maraschino cherries
10 mℓ (2 teaspoons) icing sugar

Line the bases of two 20-cm (8-inch) round baking dishes with greaseproof paper. Place cake mix and pudding mix in a bowl. In a jug, combine the eggs, oil and milk. Pour on to the cake mix and beat with an electric mixer for four minutes. Fold in the ground almonds, cake crumbs and Kirsch. Divide equally between the two dishes. Microwave on Defrost (30%) for 7 minutes. Then microwave on Full Power for 4 – 5 minutes, or until the cake starts to pull away from the sides of the dish. Leave cake to stand for at least 15 minutes before turning out on to a cooling rack.
    When cold, slice each cake horizontally into two. Sprinkle each layer with a little Kirsch. Flavour beaten cream with a little Kirsch. Fit a piping bag with a star nozzle and fill with cream. Pipe a thick circle of cream around the edge of the two layers. Fill the inside of the circles with cherry pie filling.
    To assemble the cake, put a layer with filling on to a board and place a plain layer on top. Spread with cream, cover with the second filled layer and finally the remaining plain layer. Spread more cream over the top of the cake and round the sides. Break a few chunks off the chocolate flaky bar to use as decoration and chop remainder roughly. Press flaky chocolate on to the sides of the cake and sprinkle remainder on top. Pipe generous swirls of cream around the edge of the cake. Place a cherry on top of every alternate swirl, arrange chunks of flaky chocolate on each side of the cherries. Sift icing sugar over the chocolate in the middle. Refrigerate until required.
Makes 1 x 20-cm (8-inch) cake

BLANCHING
Blanching usually refers to dipping vegetables into boiling water for various lengths of time before freezing or using in salads, in order to destroy and inactivate enzymes and to set colours.

To blanch vegetables
Slice or dice vegetables in the usual way and blanch only about 500 g (18 oz) at a time. Do not add salt as it may cause spotty dehydration on the vegetables. Microwave vegetables and boiling water on Full Power in a covered casserole or roasting bag for the time specified for each vegetable. At the end of the microwave time, drain the vegetables and plunge into iced water until chilled. Then drain and freeze, or use as desired.

VEGETABLE BLANCHING CHART

VEGETABLE	AMOUNT	WATER	MINUTES on Full Power
Green Beans	500 g (18 oz)	125 mℓ (4 fl oz)	3½ – 5
Broccoli	500 g (18 oz)	125 mℓ (4 fl oz)	3 – 5
Carrots	500 g (18 oz)	60 mℓ (4 tablespoons)	3½ – 5½
Cauliflower	500 g (18 oz)	125 mℓ (4 fl oz)	3 – 5
Sweetcorn	300 g (11 oz)	60 mℓ (4 tablespoons)	4 – 5
Peas	500 g (18 oz)	60 mℓ (4 tablespoons)	3 – 4
Spinach	500 g (18 oz)	–	2 – 3

BLINTZES
These small pancakes, filled with either a sweet or savoury mixture, are easily reheated in the microwave. Arrange 12 – 15 small blintzes in a shallow casserole, and cover. Microwave on Medium (50%) for about 7 minutes.

Cream cheese blintzes

High (70%)
4 minutes

12 – 14 thick crepes*
500 g (18 oz) cream cheese
few drops of vanilla extract
1 egg
30 g (1 oz) caster sugar
10 mℓ (2 teaspoons) custard powder
30 g (1 oz) caster sugar
5 mℓ (1 teaspoon) cinnamon

Beat cream cheese, vanilla, egg, caster sugar and custard powder together. Spoon about 45 mℓ (3 tablespoons) of the filling on one side of each pancake, fold in the sides, then roll up.

Place each blintz seam-side down in a shallow dish. Cover with vented plastic wrap, and microwave on High (70%) for 4 – 5 minutes, until piping hot. Combine cinnamon and sugar, sprinkle over the blintzes and serve immediately.
Makes 12 to 14

BOBOTIE

Bobotie is a mince dish of Javanese origin, soft-textured with a light curry flavour and a savoury custard topping. With the help of the microwave, the preparation and cooking time of this dish is considerably reduced.

Bobotie

Full Power, High (70%), Medium (50%)
40 minutes

30 mℓ (2 tablespoons) oil
1 onion, chopped
15 mℓ (1 tablespoon) curry powder
1 slice of white bread
200 mℓ (6½ fl oz) milk
500 g (18 oz) minced beef or lamb
10 mℓ (2 teaspoons) apricot jam
15 mℓ (1 tablespoon) lemon juice
30 mℓ (2 tablespoons) seedless raisins
6 dried apricots, roughly chopped
salt and black pepper
2 eggs
30 g (1 oz) slivered almonds
2 bay leaves

Pour oil into a large bowl, and microwave on Full Power for 1 minute. Add onion and curry powder, stirring to combine. Microwave for 5 minutes, stirring once during cooking time. Meanwhile, soak the bread in half the milk for a few minutes, then mash with a fork. Add the bread to the fried mixture, together with the meat, jam, lemon juice, raisins, apricots and seasonings. Mix very well, using a fork to break up the meat.

Cover and microwave on High (70%) for 8 – 10 minutes, stirring at least once during cooking time. Press into a shallow casserole and smooth the top. Combine the remaining milk and eggs, pour over the meat mixture. Spike the top with almonds, and lay the bay leaves in the middle. Microwave on Medium (50%) for 25 – 30 minutes until the egg mixture has set. Serve with yellow rice, fruit chutney, onion and tomato, and desiccated coconut.
Serves 4

BOILING

Boiling foods such as hams, salted beef, potatoes, spaghetti and rice takes almost as long to cook in the microwave as it does on the stove top. The main advantage of cooking these in the microwave is that they require little attention and the kitchen does not become steamy and full of odours.

Always stir liquids before placing them in the microwave to boil or reheat. This will prevent surface tension resulting from the liquid heating under a skin – it may also prevent a minor eruption as the liquid bursts through the skin.

Boiling water for hot drinks in the microwave is simple and quick. For 1 – 2 drinks, boil the water in cups or mugs from which they are to be served. Remember, if you need more than 750 mℓ (1¼ pints) of boiling water it is quicker to use a kettle.

QUANTITY	FULL POWER
200 mℓ (6½ fl oz) water (1 large cup or mug)	1¾ – 2 minutes
400 mℓ (13 fl oz) water (2 large cups or mugs)	2¼ – 2½ minutes

Do not overfill cups or mugs, but leave a space between the surface of the water and the top of the cup to prevent spillage as the water expands. When heating more than two cups at once, arrange them in a circle, with space between each, leaving the centre empty. Add instant coffee, tea, Bovril or soups after the water has boiled.

When heating more than one mug of liquid place the cups or mugs in a circle with space between them and in the centre. Leave sufficient space at the top for the liquid to expand. Milk-based drinks should be watched carefully.

Milk can be brought to the boil very quickly in the microwave. Select a container or jug considerably larger than the volume of milk to be heated. Watch through the door and as boiling starts, open the door to avoid spillage.

QUANTITY	FULL POWER
150 mℓ (5 fl oz) milk	1½ minutes
500 mℓ (16 fl oz) milk	3½ – 4 minutes

Sugar syrups can be made very easily and safely in the microwave but be sure to select a good quality heat-resistant bowl or microwave container as the syrup becomes extremely hot. The bowl should be considerably larger than the volume of syrup being boiled (*see* Sugar Syrups).

BOLOGNESE

Refers to foods which originated in the Italian city of Bologna. Bolognese sauce is a rich tomato and minced beef sauce traditionally served with spaghetti.
See also Pasta.

Bolognese sauce

Full Power
24 minutes

500 g (18 oz) lean minced beef
4 streaky bacon rashers, rinds removed and chopped
1 garlic clove, finely chopped
1 onion, finely chopped
1 celery stick, finely chopped
100 g (3½ oz) button mushrooms, sliced
15 g (½ oz) flour
400 g (14 oz) canned whole tomatoes
salt and pepper
15 mℓ (1 tablespoon) chopped parsley
2.5 mℓ (½ teaspoon) dried mixed herbs
10 mℓ (2 teaspoons) tomato paste
150 mℓ (5 fl oz) dry red wine
150 mℓ (5 fl oz) beef stock

Combine minced beef, bacon, onion, garlic and celery in a large casserole and microwave on Full Power for 8 minutes, stirring occasionally to break up the meat. Add mushrooms and flour and microwave 1 minute. Add tomatoes, seasoning, herbs, tomato paste, wine and stock. Cover and microwave for 15 minutes, stirring occasionally. Stand for 10 minutes before serving with hot cooked spaghetti.
Serves 4

BOUILLON

A plain unclarified broth or stock.
See Stock.

BOUQUET GARNI

Bouquet garni is a bouquet of herbs tied with string, or tied in a small square of muslin. It is used to give flavour to sauces, stews or stocks. The basic ingredients are a bay leaf, thyme sprig and 3 parsley sprigs, but many other ingredients can be used. Marjoram, lemon thyme, basil, tarragon, chillies, cinnamon sticks and orange peel are some of the extras that can be added to the bouquet garni to enhance the flavour of a dish, though it is best to keep the bouquet fairly simple. A bouquet garni can be used in microwave dishes such as stews, casseroles and soups to give added flavour. It is always removed at the end of cooking time.

BRAINS

Calf's or lamb's brains make the best eating. Cook brains as soon as possible after purchasing them as they are extremely perishable. They are usually sold in 'sets', one of which is sufficient for 2 portions.

Fried brains

Full Power, Medium (50%)
23 minutes

2 sets brains
water
vinegar
1 egg
salt and black pepper
generous pinch of paprika
pinch of thyme
30 g (1 oz) plain flour
45 g (1½ oz) butter
lemon wedges

Place the brains in a large bowl, add 1 litre (1¾ pints) water and 10 mℓ (2 teaspoons) vinegar. Soak for 2 – 3 hours, and change the water mixture twice. Drain brains and remove the outer membrane. Rinse off any particles of blood. Rinse bowl and place brains in the bowl. Add 1 litre (1¾ pints) water and 10 mℓ (2 teaspoons) vinegar but do not cover. Microwave on Full Power for 4 minutes. Reduce power to Medium (50%) and microwave for 10 minutes. Allow to stand for a further 10 minutes. Drain and pat dry. Dip brains in lightly beaten egg. Combine seasonings, herbs and flour and use to coat brains. Heat a browning dish on Full Power for 6 minutes, add butter and microwave for 30 seconds. Fry brains for 1 – 2 minutes, until golden brown. Turn over, place in microwave for 1 – 2 minutes more. Drain on kitchen paper and serve immediately. Serve with lemon wedges.
Serves 2 – 4

BRAISING

This is a combination of baking and steaming. When meat is braised, it is usually placed on a bed of chopped vegetables, with flavourings such as onion, herbs and bacon. Just enough liquid is added to moisten the contents of the casserole, which is covered and the meat is slowly cooked. Microwaves with variable power settings make braising easy, as it is possible to cook the ingredients slowly to develop tenderness and flavour.

BRANDY

Brandy, a spirit distilled from grapes, is often used in the kitchen to flavour sauces and desserts, and to flambé foods.

To flambé desserts or meats

Warm 45 ml (3 tablespoons) brandy by microwaving on Full Power for about 15 seconds. Pour over the food and ignite. Do not ignite food while it is still in the microwave.

BRAWN

Brawn is a well-seasoned jellied loaf made of meat and bone slowly simmered in water or stock until the meat softens and the gelatine is extracted from the bone. Extra gelatine may be required for a firmer set. Chill brawn mixture in a loaf dish, then turn out and slice.

Homemade brawn

Full Power, Medium (50%)
1 hour 45 minutes

1 pork knuckle, cut in pieces
750 g (1¾ lb) chuck steak, cubed
250 g (9 oz) soft beef shin, cut in pieces
1 onion, chopped
mace blade
large parsley sprig, chopped
pinch of cloves
few drops of Tabasco
salt and black pepper
30 mℓ (2 tablespoons) vinegar
2 bay leaves
2.5 mℓ (½ teaspoon) curry powder
1 litre (1¾ pints) water
5 mℓ (1 teaspoon) powdered gelatine
½ beef stock cube
15 mℓ (1 tablespoon) water

To garnish
lettuce leaves
2 hard-boiled eggs
gherkins
small tomatoes

Place all ingredients except gelatine, stock cube and 15 mℓ (1 tablespoon) water into a 4-litre (6½-pint) casserole. Cover and microwave on Full Power for 15 minutes. Reduce power to Medium (50%), microwave for 1½ hours. Cool slightly, remove bay leaves and bones from meat. Combine gelatine, stock cube and water, add 100 mℓ (3½ fl oz) of cooking liquid to gelatine, microwave for 1 minute. Add to meat mixture. Cool until liquid begins to thicken. Pour into a lightly oiled 22.5 x 12.5-cm (9 x 5-inch) loaf dish and add sufficient of the liquid to cover meat. Refrigerate until set. To turn out, dip dish into hot water; introduce an air bubble between the brawn and the dish by pulling away from the edge. Invert on to a plate lined with lettuce. Garnish with slices of hard-boiled egg, gherkins and small tomatoes.
Serves 8

BREAD

Bread is a mixture of flour, water and a leavening agent – usually yeast, baking powder or bicarbonate of soda – which has been shaped and baked to a warm, soft texture. Over the years the combinations of ingredients have altered a great deal, resulting in the wonderful variations which are found in the stores and in recipes today: light crispy baguettes from France, flattened pitta breads from the Middle East, tortillas from Mexico and, of course, a wide selection of scones and quick

breads. Although it is not possible to make all these breads in the microwave, a great deal of time may be saved by using the microwave for part of the proving process.

Breads cooked in the microwave will not have a golden crust, but you can brush them with oil or egg and sprinkle with toasted sesame seeds, poppy seeds or sunflower seeds to give them an appetizing appearance.

Quick breads
Most quick breads react well to microwave baking. Coffee cakes, fruit breads, American muffins and yoghurt breads rise well, are light in texture and have a good appearance. Plain scones, however, do not brown, so cut them in half and top with jam and cream before serving. Scone doughs may also be topped with interesting toppings before baking. This not only makes them look appetizing, but adds variety and flavour.
See also Quick Breads.

Yeast breads
Dough for yeast breads can be proved in the microwave in half the normal time by using short bursts of microwave energy with resting periods of about 10 minutes in between. Follow the recipe directions for mixing and proving yeast breads as accurately as possible. Once the dough has risen, it can be shaped and baked conventionally if a crisp brown top is required. Remember you can also use your microwave to scald the milk, to melt the butter and to start the fermentation process.
See also Yeast Cookery.

Toppings for quick and yeast breads
☐ Top savoury breads with cooked, crumbled bacon and cheese before cooking.
☐ Carefully browned onion, paprika or crushed biscuit crumbs also make a good topping.
☐ Brush breads with soy sauce or gravy browning before baking.
☐ Sprinkle with seeds or crushed wheat before baking.
☐ Sprinkle a mixture of brown sugar and nuts, or brown sugar and spices on to sweet breads.

Defrosting and reheating bread and rolls
Take care not to microwave breads and rolls too long when defrosting or reheating as bread toughens and hardens. All breads which have been reheated in the microwave should be eaten immediately.

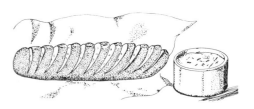

To defrost bread and rolls, place frozen loaf, slices or rolls in the microwave, cover loosely with kitchen paper or waxed paper, and microwave on Defrost (30%) until just soft.

BREAD	TIME ON DEFROST (30%)
1 x 1 kg (2¼ lb) brown or white loaf	7 minutes
1 x 500 g (18 oz) special loaf (milk loaf, currant loaf or special wholewheat)	3 minutes
1 – 2 slices of brown or white bread	30 seconds
1 bread roll	30 seconds

To reheat rolls, buns or muffins, arrange in a circle on a piece of kitchen paper in the microwave. Cover loosely, microwave on Medium (50%).

NUMBER	TIME ON MEDIUM (50%)
1	20 – 30 seconds
2	25 – 35 seconds
3	45 – 60 seconds
4	55 – 70 seconds

To warm garlic bread, place a French loaf filled with garlic, herb or any other flavoured butter in a roasting bag. Tie the open end loosely with string. Microwave on High (70%) for about 2 minutes.

BREAD SAUCE

A mixture of bread and flavoured milk combine to make this sauce, traditionally served with roast chicken or turkey.

Bread sauce

Full Power
7 minutes

6 whole cloves
1 onion, peeled
250 ml (8 fl oz) milk
90 g (3 oz) soft fresh white breadcrumbs
60 g (2 oz) butter, roughly chopped
salt and pepper

Stick cloves into onion and place in a bowl with the milk, breadcrumbs, butter, salt and pepper. Cover and microwave on Full Power for 5 minutes. Leave to stand for 15 minutes, then remove onion and add a little more milk to thin if necessary. Microwave, uncovered, for 2 minutes longer, stirring after 1 minute.
Makes about 400 ml (13 fl oz)

BREADCRUMBS

Breadcrumbs may be dried successfully in the microwave, but they do not brown, so use them only to coat food which will be deep-fried.

To dry breadcrumbs, spread 60 g (2 oz) soft breadcrumbs onto a plate. Microwave for 4 – 5 minutes on Medium (50%), stirring at least once during the cooking time. Allow to cool completely before storing.

BREAKFAST

Breakfast is one of the most important meals of the day. It gets the day off to a good start and provides the energy to get everyone through a busy morning. Whether the breakfast is simple or elaborate, the microwave can play an important part in its preparation. Egg dishes are quickly cooked, beverages are almost instant and cooked cereals or porridge can be prepared in individual portions. There is little cleaning up as most foods can be microwaved in serving dishes.
See also Eggs, Cereals, Bacon, Coffee, Tea and Cocoa.

BROCCOLI

Broccoli is becoming an increasingly popular vegetable and cooked in the microwave, it retains its valuable vitamin C and vitamin A content. When choosing broccoli, look for heads with green sprigs and crisp stems which snap easily in the fingers.

To prepare broccoli for cooking, wash well and divide into even-sized florets. Trim stem ends leaving up to 5 cm (2 inches) of stalk. Because the stalks take longer to cook than the heads, arrange spears in a circle with the stem ends outwards.

To microwave fresh broccoli

Wash 500 g (18 oz) broccoli, divide into spears and trim ends leaving up to 5 cm (2 inches) of stalk. Arrange in a baking dish with stems towards the outside of the dish. Add water and cover with a lid or vented plastic wrap. Microwave on Full Power for 8 – 10 minutes or until tender. Stand, covered, for 2 minutes and drain before serving.

Serving ideas for broccoli

☐ Toss hot, cooked broccoli with melted butter, toasted almonds* and sesame seeds before serving.
☐ Spoon hollandaise sauce* over hot, cooked broccoli and top with a sprinkling of paprika and finely grated lemon peel.
☐ Sprinkle freshly chopped basil and grated Cheddar cheese over hot, cooked broccoli.

Curried broccoli bake

Full Power
9 minutes

30 g (1 oz) butter or margarine
15 g (½ oz) seasoned cornflake crumbs
30 ml (2 tablespoons) chopped parsley
500 g (18 oz) cooked broccoli*
3 hard-boiled eggs, sliced
400 g (14 oz) canned cream of mushroom soup
60 ml (4 tablespoons) dry white wine
60 ml (4 tablespoons) mayonnaise
5 ml (1 teaspoon) curry powder

Microwave butter in a small bowl on Full Power for 30 seconds. Stir in cornflake crumbs and parsley and set aside. Arrange broccoli spears with stems towards the outside of a baking dish and place egg slices on top. Mix together the soup, wine, mayonnaise and curry powder. Cover with vented plastic wrap and microwave on Full Power for 4 minutes, stirring after the second and third minute. Pour sauce over ingredients in the baking dish and cover with waxed paper. Microwave on Full Power for 4 minutes, then sprinkle with buttered cornflake crumbs. Microwave on Full Power for 30 seconds, then stand for 5 minutes before serving.
Serves 4 – 6

Cheesy broccoli

Medium (50%)
30 minutes

300 g (11 oz) freshly cooked broccoli*
150 g (5 oz) herbed croûtons*
250 g (9 oz) Cheddar cheese, grated
30 ml (2 tablespoons) chopped green pepper
45 ml (3 tablespoons) chopped spring onion
125 ml (4 fl oz) tartare sauce
10 ml (2 teaspoons) lemon juice
4 eggs, lightly beaten
400 g (14 oz) canned evaporated milk

Chop broccoli very coarsely. Grease a microwave casserole and place half the croûtons in the bottom. Top with half the cheese. Mix broccoli with green pepper and onion. Stir in tartare sauce and lemon juice. Spoon into the casserole and top with remaining cheese and croûtons. Beat eggs with evaporated milk and pour over ingredients in the casserole. Cover with plastic wrap and refrigerate for at least 2 hours or up to 24 hours. To serve, pierce the plastic wrap and microwave on Medium (50%) for 25 – 30 minutes, or until heated through and bubbly.
Serves 4

BROWNIES

An American flat, nutty cake divided into squares which are rich and chewy, and usually chocolate-flavoured. These family favourites are easy to make in the microwave.

Chocolate pecan brownies

High (70%), Medium (50%)
12 minutes

75 g (2½ oz) butter or margarine
150 g (5 oz) plain chocolate
200 g (7 oz) caster sugar
100 g (3½ oz) plain flour
2.5 mℓ (½ teaspoon) baking powder
2.5 mℓ (½ teaspoon) salt
2 eggs
60 g (2 oz) pecan nuts, finely chopped

Place butter and 60 g (2 oz) plain chocolate in a 20-cm (8-inch) baking dish. Microwave on High (70%) for 1–2 minutes until melted. Mix well, then stir in the sugar, flour, baking powder, salt, eggs and nuts. Mix well. Grate remaining chocolate and fold into batter. Spread batter evenly in the dish. Shield corners of the dish with aluminium foil and microwave on Medium (50%) for 8 – 10 minutes or until a skewer inserted about 2.5 cm (1 inch) from the edge comes out clean. Cool on a heatproof surface and when cold, cut into bars.
Makes 16 – 20 bars

BROWNING FOODS

Foods brown during cooking due to a chemical reaction between food sugars and amino acids. This takes place slowly at low temperatures and more quickly at higher temperatures. During quick microwave cooking, the surface temperature of food does not change enough to bring about natural browning. For this reason most foods do not have the same appearance as when cooked conventionally, unless they have been brushed with a browning agent before being cooked. Large roasts and poultry will brown slightly if they are cooked longer than about 25 minutes because the fats reach a high temperature, causing some change in colour. If you prefer browned foods, experiment with the many ways to overcome this lack of colour:

Cakes, bars and biscuits

Cakes, bars and biscuits do not brown as they do in a conventional oven but they are usually iced before serving, so the difference in appearance is not noticeable. If no icing is used, there are several toppings that improve the appearance. A mixture of cinnamon and sugar, toasted coconut or chopped nuts, or a blend of soft brown sugar and nuts can be sprinkled on top of the cake or loaf before microwaving or af-

ter part of the cooking time. Fruit pie fillings spread on top of a cooked sponge mixture also look and taste good. The simplest of all, sifted icing sugar, can be most effective when sprinkled over a microwaved cake.

Bread

Breads can be brushed with beaten egg, milk or melted butter. Sprinkle with seeds, bran or wheatgerm before microwaving to give a good colour to the finished product. Breads can also be browned under the grill for a few minutes, but be sure the container will withstand the heat. Many of the recipes in the bread section include toppings which add both flavour and colour.

Meat

Meat cooked in small portions does not brown in the microwave because of the rapid cooking time, although larger roasts develop some natural colour when microwaved for longer than about 25 minutes. The appearance of beef, lamb and pork will be improved by brushing with soy or Worcestershire sauce or sprinkling with brown onion soup powder, herbs or crumbled beef stock cubes before microwaving. Microwaved meats basted with a marinade during cooking or served with a sauce also have a better appearance and flavour.

Chicken

Chicken can be brushed with melted butter and sprinkled with herbs, paprika, brown

BROWNING AGENT CHART

AGENT	FOODS	METHOD
Soy sauce	Hamburgers, beef, lamb, pork, poultry and sausages	Brush on to meat or poultry, or add to marinades
Melted butter and paprika	Poultry and fish	Brush food with butter, sprinkle with paprika
Worcestershire sauce	Hamburgers, beef, lamb and pork	Brush or add to marinade
Brown onion soup powder	Hamburgers, beef and lamb	Sprinkle on before microwaving
Barbecue sauce and steak sauce	Hamburgers, beef, lamb, poultry and sausages	Brush on or add to marinade
Bacon strips	Hamburgers, beef, lamb and poultry	Lay over food which browns under bacon as it cooks
Streusel topping	Cakes and puddings	Sprinkle on before microwaving
Biscuit crumbs, cinnamon sugar or nuts	Cakes and puddings	Sprinkle on before microwaving
Wheatgerm, oatmeal, crushed cereal, sesame or poppy seeds	Bread and rolls	Brush food with milk, then roll in topping
Breadcrumbs	Scones and casseroles	Brush scones with melted butter, and sprinkle with crumbs. Combine crumbs with a little butter, sprinkle on to casseroles

onion soup powder or crumbled chicken stock cube before microwaving. Small portions can be coated with egg and crumbs to develop a 'crust' during cooking. Soy sauce, Worcestershire sauce or barbecue sauce are also useful coatings for poultry.

Ham, gammon and poultry

Ham, gammon and poultry can be successfully glazed with fruit preserves, honey or marmalade to add colour and flavour to the dish.

Casseroles

Casseroles can be topped with crushed potato crisps, buttered breadcrumbs, grated cheese or crumbled, cooked bacon to give an attractive finish.

BROWNING DISHES

Because they cook quickly, many microwaved foods do not have the attractive browned appearance associated with conventional cooking. With a special browning dish it is possible to brown foods such as hamburgers, steaks, chops, toasted sandwiches, and to fry eggs so that they have an appetizing appearance. Browning dishes are made of ceramic glass and have a special coating under the base to attract microwave energy. When the dish is preheated at Full Power in the microwave, the bottom of the dish becomes hot. Thus, the surface of the food is seared and browned, while the rest of the food is cooked by microwave energy.

BROWNING DISH CHART

Always use Full Power when using the browning dish. Add butter or oil once the dish has been preheated. Do not use non-stick sprays or coatings as they scorch.

FOOD	PREHEAT TIME	BUTTER OR OIL	1st SIDE	2nd SIDE
100 g (3½ oz) almonds	–	–	4–5 minutes, stir every minute	
4 chicken pieces	5–6 minutes	15 ml (1 tablespoon) oil	6 minutes	4–5 minutes
4 chops, lamb	5–6 minutes	15 ml (1 tablespoon) oil	3 minutes	1–3 minutes
2 eggs (yolks pricked)	2–3 minutes	15 g (½ oz) butter	1½–1¾ minutes	
4 fish portions	4–5 minutes	15 ml (1 tablespoon) oil	2–3 minutes	4–5 minutes
6 fish fingers (frozen)	5–6 minutes	brush food with melted butter or oil	2 minutes	1–2 minutes
2 toasted sandwiches	4–5 minutes	15 g (1 tablespoon) butter	30–40 seconds	15–25 seconds
2 pieces French toast	4–5 minutes	15 g (1 tablespoon) butter	30–40 seconds	15–25 seconds
4 hamburgers	4–5 minutes	–	2 minutes	1–2 minutes
4 sausages	5–6 minutes	15 ml (1 tablespoon)	1½–2 minutes	1½–2 minutes
2 steaks	6–8 minutes	–	3 minutes	2–2½ minutes
2 schnitzels (crumbed)	5–6 minutes	30 g (1 oz) butter	45 seconds	1–1½ minutes

Foods such as steaks, toasted sandwiches or chops are normally turned during the cooking time to brown on both sides. Preheating times will vary according to the size and shape of the dish, as well as the type of food to be cooked, so always follow the manufacturer's and recipe's directions.

Because the browning dish gets hot, wear oven gloves when handling it. Do not place the hot dish directly on the work surface. The bottom of the dish cools as the food browns, so before browning a second batch of food, wipe the dish clean and reheat for about half the original time.

Covering the browning dish with a lid or waxed paper will reduce spattering and splashing that may occur with fatty foods during cooking. Refer to the chart for specific cooking times.

Browning hints

☐ Browning dishes can also be used for ordinary microwave cooking, as the surface does not function as a browner when covered with food.
☐ To increase browning, use a spatula to flatten or press food against the cooking surface for better contact.
☐ Thaw food completely before browning; ice crystals in food prevent browning.
☐ To remove burned-on food, soak the browning dish in hot soapy water, then wash out. Do not use abrasive pads on the surface.

BROWNING ELEMENT

A browning element similar to an electric grill is built into some microwaves in the top of the cooking cavity. It is used to seal food before cooking or to crisp and brown food after microwaving.

BRUSSELS SPROUTS

Brussels sprouts are a popular winter vegetable shaped like small, tightly packed cabbages. Like many leafy vegetables they are very easily overcooked but when microwaved for a few minutes in very little water, they retain their bright green colour, crisp texture and excellent flavour.

To microwave Brussels sprouts

Take 500 g (18 oz) Brussels sprouts, remove outer leaves and trim. Make a small cross on the base of each one. Soak in plenty of salted water for 10 minutes. Drain, but do not dry, and place sprouts in a shallow dish. Cover with vented plastic wrap, and microwave on Full Power for 12 – 15 minutes. Stir once during cooking time. Add a little butter and black pepper before serving.

Brussels sprouts with cream

Full Power, High (70%)
12 minutes

500 g (18 oz) Brussels sprouts
salt and black pepper
pinch of nutmeg
100 ml (3½ fl oz) single cream

Trim the base of the sprouts carefully, remove outer leaves and cut a small cross in the base of each one. Soak in plenty of salted water for 10 minutes. Drain, but do not dry, and place sprouts in a shallow dish. Cover and microwave on Full Power for 4 minutes, stir once during the cooking time. Drain off any liquid from the dish. Add black pepper, nutmeg and cream. Cover and microwave on High (70%) for 8 – 10 minutes, until the Brussels sprouts are just tender, stir carefully. Stand for 5 minutes before serving.
Serves 4 – 6

Lemon and cheese Brussels sprouts

Full Power
13 minutes

500 g (18 oz) Brussels sprouts
water
salt
30 g (1 oz) butter
10 ml (2 teaspoons) lemon juice
2.5 ml (½ teaspoon) grated lemon rind
black pepper
15 ml (1 tablespoon) grated Parmesan cheese

Trim the bases and discard outer leaves. Cut a shallow cross in the base of the Brussels sprouts. Soak in plenty of salted water for 10 minutes. Drain, but do not dry; place sprouts in a shallow dish. Cover and microwave on Full Power for 12 minutes, stirring twice during the cooking time. Drain and stand covered for 3 minutes. Meanwhile make the sauce. Place butter, lemon juice, rind and pepper in a small bowl, microwave for 45 seconds. Stir to combine and pour over sprouts. Sprinkle with Parmesan cheese and serve.
Serves 4 – 6

BUTTER

Butter is a natural fat product churned from cream and is one of the most highly concentrated dairy foods. For eating, and for much of our cooking, butter has no equal as it adds flavour and enriches recipes whenever it is used. A simple melted butter sauce makes all the difference to many dishes, especially fish and vegetables. Softening, melting and clarifying butter can be done in the microwave in just a few seconds. It is also perfect for making herb butters and butter sauces.

Clarified butter, or ghee, is one of the best mediums for frying or sautéing foods because it does not burn as easily as ordinary butter, nor do foods stick to the bottom of the pan.

To soften butter, unwrap butter and place in a small container. Microwave on Low (15%) for the following times:

AMOUNT	TIME ON LOW (15%)
250 g (9 oz)	2 minutes
125 g (4 oz)	1¼ minutes
60 g (2 oz)	45 seconds

To clarify butter, place 125 g (4 oz) butter in a large measuring jug and microwave on High (70%) for 2 minutes or until boiling. The clear layer which floats to the top is clarified butter. Pour off the clear portion and use for frying. The residue need not be wasted as it can be poured over cooked vegetables just before serving.

Dill butter

Full Power
1¼ minutes

125 g (4 oz) butter
30 mℓ (2 tablespoons) lemon juice
2.5 mℓ (½ teaspoon) dried dill or
10 mℓ (2 teaspoons) fresh dill
2.5 mℓ (½ teaspoon) onion salt
2.5 mℓ (½ teaspoon) celery salt
pepper

Place butter in a jug and microwave on Full
Power for 1¼ minutes. Stir in lemon juice, dill,
onion salt, celery salt and pepper. Serve warm
with fish, shellfish or vegetable dishes.
Makes about 125 mℓ (4 fl oz)

Garlic and parsley butter

Low (15%)
45 seconds

125 g (4 oz) butter
15 – 30 g (½ – 1 oz) chopped parsley
10 mℓ (2 teaspoons) lemon juice
10 mℓ (2 teaspoons) chopped onion
2 garlic cloves, finely chopped
2.5 mℓ (½ teaspoon) dry mustard

Place butter in a measuring jug and microwave
on Low (15%) for 45 seconds or until softened.
Add the remaining ingredients and beat with an
electric mixer until light and fluffy.
Makes about 200 mℓ (6½ fl oz)

Variation
Herb butter: Follow the directions for softening
butter above and add 10 mℓ (2 teaspoons)
chopped parsley, 10 mℓ (2 teaspoons) lemon
juice, 2.5 mℓ (½ teaspoon) thyme, or 2.5 mℓ
(½ teaspoon) mixed herbs and salt and pepper
to taste. Beat as above.

Lemon butter sauce

Full Power
1 minute

60 g (2 oz) butter
30 mℓ (2 tablespoons) lemon juice
15 mℓ (1 tablespoon) chopped parsley
pepper

Place butter in a glass jug and microwave on
Full Power for ½ – 1 minute, or until melted. Stir
in lemon juice, parsley and pepper. Keep
warm. Serve with fish, or vegetables such as
asparagus or broccoli.
Makes about 60 mℓ (4 tablespoons)

Almond butter sauce

Full Power
7 minutes

30 g (1 oz) flaked almonds
125 g (4 oz) butter
2.5 mℓ (½ teaspoon) seasoned salt

Place almonds in a glass pie dish and add 15 g
(½ oz) of the butter. Microwave on Full Power
for 5 – 6 minutes, stirring every 2 minutes until
almonds are toasted. Add remaining butter and
microwave for 1 minute. Stir in seasoned salt
and serve warm.
Makes about 125 mℓ (4 fl oz)

BUTTERMILK
Buttermilk, a by-product of butter-
making, is milk with most of the fat and
some milk solids taken out. It differs from
skimmed milk in that it is sour and more
easily digested. In cooking, buttermilk is
often used with bicarbonate of soda as a
leavening agent for scones, cakes and
quick breads.

Buttermilk pecan cake

Full Power
11 minutes

300 g (11 oz) plain flour
150 g (5 oz) caster sugar
200 g (7 oz) soft brown sugar
5 mℓ (1 teaspoon) grated nutmeg
5 mℓ (1 teaspoon) salt
185 mℓ (6 fl oz) oil
2 eggs, beaten
5 mℓ (1 teaspoon) baking powder
250 mℓ (8 fl oz) buttermilk
5 mℓ (1 teaspoon) bicarbonate of soda
60 g (2 oz) pecans or walnuts, chopped
15 mℓ (1 tablespoon) cinnamon
60 g (2 oz) butter, softened
few drops of vanilla extract
125 g (4 oz) icing sugar
15 g (½ oz) instant coffee powder

In a large mixing bowl, combine the flour,
sugar, brown sugar, nutmeg, salt and oil to
make a crumbly mixture. Reserve 100 g (3½
oz) of the mixture. To the remaining mixture,
add eggs, baking powder and buttermilk mixed
with the bicarbonate of soda. Mix until a smooth
batter is formed. Pour the mixture into a
greased 32.5 x 20 x 5-cm (13 x 8 x 2-inch)
baking dish. Sprinkle the reserved crumbs over
the top, followed by pecans and cinnamon.
Microwave on Full Power for 11 – 13 minutes,
rotating the dish half a turn after 5 minutes.
While the cake is in the microwave, mix the
softened butter with vanilla, icing sugar and
coffee.
   When the cake is cooked, stand on a
heatproof surface to cool for 10 minutes. Then
slowly pour the butter-sugar mixture over the
top so that it soaks into the cake. Serve warm or
cool, cut in squares.
Makes 24 squares

BUTTERNUT
Butternut is a winter squash, full of flavour
and offers variety in the vegetable menu.
This vegetable responds particularly well
to microwave cooking; the colour remains
bright and, as very little water is used, the
flesh remains firm and tasty.

To microwave butternut
Cut one butternut in half, remove membranes and seeds. Arrange cut-side down
in a shallow casserole, add 45 mℓ (3 tablespoons) water. Cover with vented plastic.
Microwave on Full Power for 12 – 15 minutes, turn halfway through cooking time.
Add a little butter and black pepper.

Butternut bake

Full Power
21 minutes

2 medium-sized butternuts
30 mℓ (2 tablespoons) water
60 g (2 oz) butter
45 mℓ (3 tablespoons) golden syrup
small pinch of cinnamon
salt
pinch of grated lemon rind

Peel butternuts and cut in half, remove the
seeds and slice into 1-cm (½-inch) thick slices.
Place in a shallow casserole. Combine all the
remaining ingredients in a jug, microwave on
Full Power for 3 minutes. Stir well, pour over
butternut and cover. Microwave for 18 – 20
minutes, until butternut is tender. Stir butternut
very carefully half-way through cooking time.
Serves 4 – 6

Butternut and apple soup

Full Power
25 minutes

1 medium-sized butternut
2 leeks, sliced
1 Granny Smith apple, peeled, cored and diced
1 medium-sized potato, diced
350 mℓ (11 fl oz) chicken stock
350 mℓ (11 fl oz) beef stock
black pepper
pinch of nutmeg
200 mℓ (6½ fl oz) single cream

To garnish
unpeeled apple slices
1 leek, thinly sliced
parsley sprigs

Place all the prepared vegetables in a 3-litre (5-
pint) casserole. Add stocks and seasonings,
stir well. Cover and microwave on Full Power
until the vegetables are tender, about 20
minutes. Pour vegetables and liquid in batches
into a blender or processor, blend until smooth.
Stir in cream and adjust seasonings. Cover and
microwave for 5 minutes, stirring at least once.
Serve piping hot in soup cups. Garnish each
serving with one or two slices of apple, a few
rings of blanched leek and a tiny sprig of
parsley
Serves 6
Note: To blanch leeks, place slices of leek in a
colander, pour a little boiling water over the
slices before using. This will remove the strong,
uncooked flavour and will give them a good
colour.

CABBAGE

Cabbage is usually included among the unimaginative vegetables as all too often it is served soft and tasteless. By reducing the cooking time and serving with a variety of sauces and other accompaniments, it can, however, be extremely versatile and economical. There are many varieties of cabbage, including the better known Savoy, red cabbage and Chinese cabbage. The microwave is ideal for cooking cabbage, as there is no unpleasant odour in the kitchen and the cabbage remains crisp and bright in colour.

When preparing cabbage to cook in the microwave, either shred or cut into wedges. Shredded cabbage is delicious as it requires the minimum of cooking. For variety, microwave wedges and top with a sauce or blanch individual leaves and wrap around a filling.

To microwave cabbage

Shred or chop 500 g (18 oz) cabbage, place in a casserole and sprinkle with 45 mℓ (3 tablespoons) water. Cover and microwave for 7 – 9 minutes, stirring once during cooking time.

Serving suggestions

☐ Top cooked cabbage wedges with cheese sauce (page 195) and sprinkle with cooked crumbled bacon.

☐ Top cooked cabbage wedges with 400 g (14 oz) canned heated celery soup, to which you have added a generous pinch of celery seeds and 5 mℓ (1 teaspoon) dry mustard.

☐ Stir into cooked shredded cabbage, a mixture of 100 g (3½ oz) cream cheese, 1 crushed garlic clove, 30 ml (2 tablespoons) milk, a generous pinch of paprika or nutmeg, salt and black pepper.

☐ Stir into cooked shredded cabbage 60 ml (4 tablespoons) chopped roasted cashew nuts.

Stuffed cabbage leaves

Full Power
27 minutes

8 large cabbage leaves
60 mℓ (4 tablespoons) water
30 mℓ (2 tablespoons) oil
1 onion, chopped
45 g (1½ oz) sultanas
1 garlic clove, crushed
250 g (9 oz) minced beef
125 g (4 oz) cooked rice
15 mℓ (1 tablespoon) chopped parsley
grated rind of ¼ orange
pinch of nutmeg
salt and black pepper

Sauce
15 mℓ (1 tablespoon) oil
15 mℓ (1 tablespoon) plain flour
juice of 1 orange
100 mℓ (3½ fl oz) beef stock
generous pinch of ground ginger
5 mℓ (1 teaspoon) soft brown sugar

Place cabbage leaves in a 3-litre (5-pint) casserole. Add water and microwave, covered, on Full Power for 4 – 5 minutes, until the leaves are soft and pliable. Drain and remove coarse core from each leaf. Rinse leaves in cold water.

Microwave oil in a bowl for 1 minute. Add onion and stir to coat with oil. Microwave for 2 minutes. Add sultanas, garlic and mince. Mix together and microwave uncovered for 3 minutes. Stir in remaining ingredients, mixing well. Divide the mixture between the eight leaves. Roll up each leaf, beginning at the wide end and folding the sides in. Secure with wooden cocktail sticks, place in a shallow casserole and set aside.

To make the sauce, microwave the oil in a large jug for 1 minute. Stir in the flour and then the remaining ingredients, stir well. Microwave

for 1½ – 2 minutes, stirring every 30 seconds. Pour over cabbage rolls, cover and microwave for 14 – 16 minutes. Stand for 5 minutes before serving.
Serves 4

Creamed cabbage

Full Power
8 minutes

½ cabbage, finely shredded
30 mℓ (2 tablespoons) red wine
10 mℓ (2 teaspoons) wine vinegar
10 mℓ (2 teaspoons) oil
pinch of caraway seeds
1 small garlic clove, crushed
salt and black pepper
10 mℓ (2 teaspoons) caster sugar
10 mℓ (2 teaspoons) chopped parsley
75 mℓ (2½ fl oz) single cream

Place cabbage in a large bowl or casserole, add all ingredients except parsley and cream, and stir to combine. Cover, microwave on Full Power for 7 – 9 minutes. The cabbage should still be slightly crisp. Stir in the parsley and cream, microwave for 1 minute. Stand 2 – 3 minutes before serving.
Serves 4 – 6

Cabbage wedges

Full Power
10 minutes

½ cabbage
90 mℓ (3 fl oz) water

Cut cabbage in wedges, removing outer leaves and core. In a casserole dish, place wedges with core end towards the middle. Add water, cover and microwave on Full Power for 10 minutes, or until tender. Turn wedges over halfway through the cooking time. Let stand, covered, 2 minutes then season as desired before serving.
Serves 4

Braised red cabbage

Full Power, High (70%)
20 minutes

45 g (1½ oz) butter
1 small onion, chopped
2 whole cloves
6 juniper or allspice berries
60 mℓ (4 tablespoons) water
30 mℓ (2 tablespoons) red wine
30 mℓ (2 tablespoons) red currant jelly
1 medium-sized red cabbage, finely shredded
2 Granny Smith apples, peeled, cored and
   chopped

Place butter in a large bowl or casserole, microwave on Full Power for 1 minute. Add onion, stir to combine, and microwave for 2 minutes. Now add cloves, berries, water, red wine and red currant jelly. Microwave for 1 minute. Stir in cabbage and seasonings, microwave covered for 4 minutes. Stir, then add apples. Cover and microwave on High (70%) for 12 – 14 minutes, stirring from time to time. Remove cloves and berries before serving.
Serves 4 – 6

CAKES
Cakes baked in the microwave have good volume and an airy light texture. They bake in about one third of the time they take in a conventional oven, but do not brown. However, once the cake is iced or dusted with icing sugar, it is difficult to tell the difference. See the browning agent chart (page 39) for suggestions on improving the appearance of microwaved cakes. Microwaving does not affect flavour, so cakes taste the same as if baked conventionally. Cakes with a dark colour such as chocolate cake, gingerbread and carrot cake, as well as rich, moist cakes, microwave exceptionally well, and look good too. Victoria sponge cakes can be baked in the microwave, but avoid angel cakes and chiffon cakes.

Hints for microwaving cakes
Remember that it is easy to overbake cakes in the microwave as baking times vary with oven models. The recipes here give a range of cooking times so always check the cake after the minimum time and microwave longer if necessary. Overcooking by even 1½ or 2 minutes results in a cake with hard, dry outer edges. For baking success, take note of the following:

□ If your microwave does not have a turntable, you may find that rotating the pan frequently will give more even results. Unlike conventional baking, the cake will not 'flop' if the door is opened momentarily.

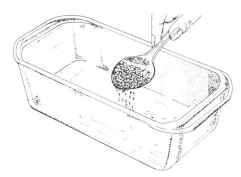
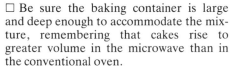

To prevent the cake from sticking to the baking dish, sprinkle lightly with fine biscuit crumbs or chopped nuts before spooning in the batter.

□ Be sure the baking container is large and deep enough to accommodate the mixture, remembering that cakes rise to greater volume in the microwave than in the conventional oven.
□ Do not grease and flour dishes for microwave baking, as this will result in a doughy, sticky coating on the outside of the cake. Prepare dishes by spraying or lightly greasing only. Line cake dishes with waxed paper or kitchen paper and sprinkle greased pans with finely chopped nuts or fine biscuit crumbs so the cake will turn out easily. These cakes will also have an attractive appearance.
□ Ring-shaped cake dishes allow the centre of the cake to bake at the same rate as the outer edges. If you do not have a ring dish, use an ordinary glass casserole and place an upright glass in the centre.
□ The tops of many cakes will still be slightly moist when cooking time is up, but will dry out to some extent during standing time. Standing time is very important when baking cakes in the microwave as cakes continue to cook for some time after microwaving.
□ Always place cakes on a solid heat-resistant surface during standing time so that heat will be retained and the bottom will continue to cook. Do not stand on a wire rack until the cake is turned out to cool.
□ With many cakes, the batter can be left to stand for 3 – 4 minutes before microwaving in order to start the reaction be-

A ring mould, with its empty central area, allows microwaves to penetrate evenly and is the best shape of container for baking cakes in a microwave. Make your own by placing a glass in the centre of a round, shallow dish.

To help the cake cook evenly, place the baking dish on an inverted saucer in the centre of the microwave.

tween the baking powder and the liquid, resulting in better volume.
□ To check the cake is cooked, insert a skewer or wooden cocktail stick near, but not in, the centre. If the skewer comes out clean, the cake is ready to be removed from the microwave.
□ When baking cakes in a square dish, shield the corners with foil to prevent overcooking. Circular dishes will ensure a more evenly baked cake.

Packaged cake mixes
Commercial cake mixes bake very well in the microwave and many manufacturers include microwave instructions on the packet. Where these are not given, use the following directions:
Mix as directed on the packet, using 2 eggs. Grease a deep microwave ring dish and sprinkle with biscuit crumbs, if desired. Pour cake mixture into prepared dish and place on an inverted saucer in the microwave. Microwave on Defrost (30%) for 6 minutes, then microwave on Full Power for 4 minutes or until surface is almost dry. Alternatively, microwave on Full Power only for 6 minutes, or until surface is almost dry. When cooking is complete, stand the dish on a heatproof surface for 10 minutes, then turn cake out on to a wire rack to cool.

Cup cakes or fairy cakes
Cup cakes microwave very quickly and need close attention. Your favourite home-made cake recipe or a packaged cake mix can be baked as cup cakes. For the best shape, spoon mixture into paper-lined microwave muffin dishes, filling them only half full. When microwaving more than two, arrange in a circle and microwave as follows:

NUMBER	TIME ON FULL POWER
1	¼ – ½ minute
2	¾ – 1 minute
3	1 – 1¼ minutes
4	1¼ – 1½ minutes
5	2 – 2¼ minutes
6	2½ – 2¾ minutes

Lemon-glazed pound cake

Full Power, Medium (50%)
28 minutes

60 g (2 oz) Marie biscuit crumbs
500 g (18 oz) caster sugar
300 g (11 oz) butter or margarine
5 eggs
few drops of vanilla extract
few drops of almond essence
2.5 mℓ (½ teaspoon) finely grated lemon rind
350 g (12 oz) plain flour
5 mℓ (1 teaspoon) baking powder
pinch of salt
250 mℓ (8 fl oz) evaporated milk

Lemon glaze
150 g (5 oz) caster sugar
200 mℓ (6½ fl oz) sweet white wine
45 mℓ (3 tablespoons) lemon juice
5 mℓ (1 teaspoon) finely grated lemon rind
100 mℓ (3½ fl oz) orange juice

Grease a large, deep ring dish and sprinkle with biscuit crumbs to coat sides and base evenly. Beat sugar, butter, eggs, vanilla extract, almond essence and lemon rind to combine, then beat until light and fluffy. Sift flour, baking powder and salt, and mix in alternately with the milk. Turn batter into prepared dish and microwave on Medium (50%) for 15 minutes. Increase power level to Full Power and microwave for 5 – 8 minutes, or until top springs back when lightly touched. Stand for 10 minutes, then turn out on a wire rack. With a skewer, make holes over surface of cake so the glaze can soak in.

To make the glaze, mix sugar, wine, lemon juice, orange juice and lemon rind together in a large glass bowl or jug. Microwave on Full Power for 4-5 minutes, stirring at least once. Spoon-glaze over the cake until absorbed. Cool, then sprinkle with icing sugar if desired.
Makes 1 large cake

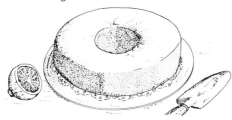

Lemon and cherry upside-down cake

Full Power
18 minutes

400 g (14 oz) canned cherry pie filling
400 g (14 oz) canned peach slices, drained
30 mℓ (2 tablespoons) lemon juice
60 g (4 tablespoons) chopped nuts
45 g (1½ oz) desiccated coconut
1 packet vanilla cake mix
1 packet lemon instant pudding mix
60 mℓ (4 tablespoons) oil

Mix together cherry pie filling, peaches, lemon juice, nuts and coconut. Spread mixture evenly

in two 20-cm (8-inch) well-greased or sprayed microwave cake dishes. Prepare cake mix according to packet directions, adding lemon pudding mix and oil. Pour mixture evenly over the fruit in cake dishes. Microwave, one dish at a time, on Full Power for 6 – 9 minutes, or until cake springs back when touched in the centre. Remove from the oven and loosen edges with a knife. Invert immediately on to a serving dish, leaving cake dish to stand over cake for 2 minutes.

Repeat with remaining layer. Any cherry mixture that sticks to the dish or slides off can be replaced on the cake.
Makes 2 x 20-cm (8-inch) cakes

Mocha cake with almond filling

Full Power
17 minutes

400 g (14 oz) caster sugar
200 g (7 oz) plain flour
75 g (2½ oz) cocoa powder
10 mℓ (2 teaspoons) bicarbonate of soda
5 mℓ (1 teaspoon) baking powder
5 mℓ (1 teaspoon) salt
5 mℓ (1 teaspoon) instant coffee powder
2 eggs
185 mℓ (6 fl oz) strong coffee
185 mℓ (6 fl oz) buttermilk
125 mℓ (4 fl oz) oil
few drops of vanilla extract
few drops of almond essence

Filling
2 eggs
2 egg yolks
200 g (7 oz) caster sugar
250 mℓ (8 fl oz) milk, scalded
30 g (1 oz) plain flour
45 g (1½ oz) butter
60 g (2 oz) toasted almonds*, finely chopped
few drops of vanilla extract
few drops of almond essence
1 quantity chocolate icing*

To make the cake, combine sugar, flour, cocoa, bicarbonate of soda, baking powder, salt and instant coffee powder in a large bowl. Combine eggs, coffee, buttermilk, oil, vanilla extract and almond essence and beat well. Add to dry ingredients and mix well. Pour half the mixture into a greased or sprayed and lined 20-cm (8-inch) cake dish. Microwave on Full Power for 6 – 6½ minutes. Set dish on a rack and cool for 10 minutes. Turn cake out on rack and cool. Repeat with remaining cake mixture.

To make filling, mix together eggs, egg yolks, sugar, milk and flour. Microwave on Full Power for 2 minutes, stirring every 45 seconds. Stir, then continue microwaving for about 2 minutes more, stirring every 30 seconds. The mixture should be thick and smooth. Stir in butter,

almonds, vanilla extract and almond essence, and mix until smooth.

To assemble, cut each cake layer in half horizontally. Place one cake layer on a cake plate and spread with one-third of the filling. Repeat, using all the filling and ending with a final layer of cake. Cover top and sides with chocolate icing. Chill if desired.
Serves 12 – 14

Soured cream spice cake

Full Power
10 minutes

175 g (6 oz) plain flour
300 g (11 oz) soft brown sugar
75 g (2½ oz) butter
250 mℓ (8 fl oz) soured cream
1 egg
2.5 mℓ (½ teaspoon) nutmeg
pinch of ground cloves
2.5 mℓ (½ teaspoon) cinnamon
2.5 mℓ (½ teaspoon) allspice
5 mℓ (1 teaspoon) bicarbonate of soda
30 g (1 oz) hazelnuts, chopped

Combine flour, brown sugar and butter until crumbly. Reserve 100 g (3½ oz) of the mixture and set aside. Mix together soured cream, egg, spices, bicarbonate of soda and stir into remaining crumb mixture until moistened. Spread evenly in a 22.5-cm (9-inch) greased or sprayed round baking dish. Sprinkle with reserved crumb mixture and nuts. Microwave on Full Power for 8 – 10 minutes, or until a wooden cocktail stick inserted near the centre comes out clean. Cool before cutting.
Serves 10

Basic Victoria sponge

Full Power
7 minutes

175 g (6 oz) butter
175 g (6 oz) caster sugar
3 eggs, beaten
175 g (6 oz) plain flour
pinch of salt
10 mℓ (2 teaspoons) baking powder
30 mℓ (2 tablespoons) hot water
few drops of vanilla extract

Beat butter and sugar together until light and fluffy. Add eggs, one at a time, beating well after each. Combine flour, salt and baking powder and fold into butter mixture along with hot water and vanilla extract. Spray or lightly grease a 20-cm (8-inch) cake dish and line with waxed paper or kitchen paper. Turn mixture into prepared dish and microwave on Full Power for 5 – 7 minutes. The cake will be moist on top when cooked, but will continue to cook and dry out during standing time. Check if cake is cooked by inserting a skewer near the centre. The skewer should come out clean. Stand for 5 minutes before turning out to cool. Use as desired.
Makes 1 x 20-cm (8-inch) cake

Apple cream gingerbread cake

High (70%)
13 minutes

oil
cinnamon
125 g (4 oz) margarine
75 g (2½ oz) soft brown sugar
60 g (2 oz) caster sugar
2 eggs
100 g (3½ oz) molasses
15 mℓ (1 tablespoon) grated orange rind
10 mℓ (2 teaspoons) grated fresh ginger
300 g (11 oz) flour
7.5 mℓ (1½ teaspoons) bicarbonate of soda
2.5 mℓ (½ teaspoon) cinnamon
pinch of ground cloves
250 mℓ (8 fl oz) buttermilk
250 mℓ (8fl oz) whipping cream
150 mℓ (5 fl oz) apple sauce*

Lightly oil a 2-litre (3½-pint) ring mould, dust with cinnamon and shake out excess. Cream butter, add sugars and cream until fluffy. Beat in eggs one at a time. Add molasses, orange rind and ginger, beat well. Sift dry ingredients, add one-third to egg mixture, beat well. Add one-third of buttermilk, beat again. Repeat twice more. Pour mixture into prepared dish. Microwave on High (70%) for 13 – 15 minutes. Stand for 20 minutes before turning out onto a rack to cool completely.

To serve, whip cream until thick, add apple sauce and beat to combine. Place cake on serving plate, fill centre with whipped cream mixture. Spoon remaining cream into a bowl and serve separately.
Makes 1 x 25-cm (10-inch) ring cake

Chocolate walnut cake

Full Power, High (70%)
9 minutes

100 g (3½ oz) margarine
200 g (7 oz) caster sugar
3 eggs
few drops of vanilla extract
250 g (9 oz) self-raising flour
60 mℓ (4 tablespoons) cocoa powder
pinch of baking powder
pinch of salt
100 mℓ (3½ fl oz) natural yoghurt
60 g (2 oz) walnuts, chopped
1 quantity chocolate fudge*
whole walnuts

Cream the margarine and sugar until light and fluffy, add eggs and vanilla, beat well. Sift the dry ingredients, add about one third to the creamed mixture and beat well. Then add about one third of the yoghurt, beat. Repeat until dry ingredients and yoghurt have been used up. Stir in the walnuts. Cut a circle of parchment paper large enough to fit the base of a deep 20-cm (8-inch) cake dish or straight sided casserole. Grease or spray the sides of the pan. Pour in the cake mixture, microwave on High (70%) for 7 minutes, then increase the

power level to Full Power, microwave for 2 – 3 minutes. Stand for 10 minutes before removing from the dish. Turn out on to a rack and leave to cool before icing. Pour hot chocolate fudge icing on top of cake, allowing it to drizzle down the sides. Decorate with whole walnuts.
Makes 1 x 20-cm (8-inch) cake

Note: This cake may be microwaved in two shallow 20-cm (8-inch) cake dishes. Microwave cakes one at a time on High (70%) for 4 – 5 minutes, then on Full Power for 1 – 2 minutes.

CANDIED PEEL
Thinly sliced citrus rinds, boiled in a sugar syrup until clear in colour, then dried and tossed in granulated sugar. These dried rinds make delicious eating, especially if the ends have been dipped in melted chocolate. Sugar syrups boil very quickly in the microwave so be sure to check boiling rinds frequently.

Candied peel strips

Full Power
36 minutes

1 orange
1 grapefruit
water
200 g (7 oz) caster sugar
75 mℓ (2½ oz) water
15 mℓ (1 tablespoon) golden syrup
30 mℓ (2 tablespoons) Cointreau
granulated sugar

Cut fruit into quarters, carefully remove flesh. Slice peel thinly into strips either by hand or use a food processor. Place peel in a large bowl and add water to cover. Microwave covered on Full Power for 7 minutes, drain water and repeat twice more, then drain and set aside. In the large bowl, combine sugar, water and syrup. Microwave for 2 minutes, stir well and brush sides of the bowl with water to remove crystals. Microwave for 3 minutes more. Now add peel, microwave for 10 – 12 minutes until peel is glossy. Drain well, then spread on a wire rack overnight. Toss peel in sugar. Store in a sealed container.
Makes about 250 g (9 oz)

CARAMEL
When white or brown sugar is heated to a temperature high enough to turn it to a

deep golden brown colour, it is known as caramel. However, when making caramel in the microwave, water must be added to the sugar before the sugar will react and brown. Caramel is used to colour and flavour cakes, puddings, icings and sauces. It is also the clear, crackly outer coating on friandises and toffee apples. When nuts are added to the caramel, it is known as praline.

Sugar caramel

Full Power
12 minutes

200 g (7 oz) caster sugar
150 mℓ (5 fl oz) water

Mix sugar and water together in a medium-sized bowl. Microwave on Full Power for 2 minutes. Stir, and brush the sides of the bowl with a little water to remove sugar crystals. Microwave for a further 8 – 10 minutes, depending on how dark a caramel is required. Do not allow caramel to become too brown, as cooking continues for some time after microwaving. Use as required.
Makes about 300 mℓ (½ pint)

Hint: To remove hardened caramel quickly and easily from the bowl, fill with hot water and microwave on Full Power for 4 minutes. All the sticky, hard caramel will have softened and the bowl will be easy to wash.

Coffee caramel bombe

Full Power
17 minutes

Caramel layer
450 mℓ (14½ fl oz) single cream
30 g (1 oz) caster sugar
6 egg yolks
100 g (3½ oz) caster sugar
100 mℓ (3½ fl oz) water
15 mℓ (1 tablespoon) instant coffee powder

Mousse filling
100 (3½ oz) caster sugar
125 mℓ (4 fl oz) water
5 egg yolks
15 mℓ (1 tablespoon) rum
300 mℓ (½ pint) whipping cream
2 egg whites
60 g (2 oz) almonds made into praline*

To decorate
100 mℓ (3½ fl oz) whipping cream, stiffly whipped
60 g (2 oz) chocolate caraque*

To make the caramel layer, pour cream into a 1-litre (1¾-pint) jug, microwave to boiling, about 4 minutes. Beat yolks and caster sugar in a food processor until pale in colour. Pour on the boiling cream and process for 1 minute. Set aside. Combine sugar and water in a medium-sized bowl, microwave for 2 minutes, stir to

dissolve sugar. Microwave for 5 – 7 minutes until a deep brown caramel colour. Remove from the microwave and *very carefully* pour in the hot water and coffee powder. Microwave for 1 minute, stir well, then add custard. Pour into a shallow container and freeze until solid. Cut mixture into 3-cm (1¼-inch) cubes, and using a food processor, drop about a third of the chunks on to the moving blades. Process until smooth. Line a 2-litre (3½-inch) chilled pudding basin or bombe mould with this mixture. Freeze until hard.

For the mousse, microwave sugar and water as above, but only cook to the 'thread' stage, about 3 minutes. Whisk yolks with an electric mixer until light and creamy. Pour on the sugar syrup in a steady stream, beating all the time. Continue beating until cool and thick. Flavour with rum. Beat the cream until thick, fold into the mousse mixture. Beat egg whites to stiff peaks. Fold into mixture. Process the praline until fine, fold into mousse. Pour into the lined bombe mould, cover with foil and chill overnight. To unmould, dip mould into hot water for a few seconds, loosen edges carefully with a spatula, turn out on to a platter. Decorate with whipped cream and chocolate caraque*.
Serves 8 – 10

Oeufs à la neige *Floating islands*

Full Power, Medium (50%)
9 minutes

350 mℓ (11 fl oz) milk
1 vanilla pod
3 eggs, separated
pinch of salt
75 g (3 oz) caster sugar
1 quantity sugar caramel*

Microwave milk and vanilla in a shallow casserole on Full Power for 3 minutes. Stand for 5 minutes. Beat egg whites and pinch of salt until stiff, gradually beat in half the sugar. Drop 4 – 5 spoonfuls of the mixture into the milk, microwave until set, about 1 minute. Using a slotted spoon, lift off the egg puffs and drain on kitchen paper. Repeat until all the egg white has been used up, about four batches in all. Strain the milk. Whisk yolks and remaining sugar until thick and pale, add milk and beat to combine. Pour into a jug, microwave on Medium (50%) for 3 – 4 minutes, whisking every 30 seconds. Place a piece of greaseproof paper directly on top of the custard to prevent a skin from forming, then chill. Pour into a shallow serving bowl, float 'islands' on top and drizzle liberally with caramel. Serve as soon as possible.
Serves 6

Caramelized oranges

Full Power
39 minutes

2 oranges, sliced
water
400 g (14 oz) caster sugar
400 mℓ (13 fl oz) water

Place orange slices in a large bowl, and cover with water. Cover bowl with vented plastic wrap and microwave on Full Power for 10 minutes. Drain and set aside. Combine sugar and water, microwave for 4 minutes and stir well. Brush sides of the bowl with water to remove sugar crystals. Microwave for 10 minutes. Add orange slices and microwave for 15 – 20 minutes, until well caramelized. Drain slightly. Store in an airtight container in the refrigerator.
Serves 4

Caramel corn

Full Power
7 minutes

Caramel corn is popcorn coated with a caramelized sugar coating. While it is not suggested that popcorn be popped in the microwave, the syrup can be heated to just the right temperature.

125 g (4 oz) butter
100 g (3½ oz) soft brown sugar
60 mℓ (4 tablespoons) golden syrup
pinch of salt
pinch of bicarbonate of soda
few drops of vanilla extract
125 g (4 oz) popcorn, popped conventionally

Place butter, brown sugar, golden syrup and salt in a 1-litre (1¾-pint) glass jug and microwave on Full Power for 4 minutes, stirring after first and second minutes. Remove from microwave, add bicarbonate of soda and vanilla extract, mixing well. Place popcorn in a large brown paper bag and pour syrup over. Close top of bag tightly and shake well to coat popcorn with syrup. Microwave for 1½ minutes, then shake well. Microwave 1 minute, shake, microwave 30 seconds and shake again. Let mixture cool in bag, then shake well before turning out into a large bowl. Caramel corn keeps well for several days in a sealed air-tight container.
Makes about 350 g (12 oz)

CARE AND CLEANING

As with any other appliance, it is important to read the manufacturer's instruction book on the cleaning and care of your microwave. However, certain guidelines can be followed.

☐ Wipe the inside surface of the microwave with a damp cloth after each use. Also wipe off moisture from the inside of the door.
☐ For thorough cleaning, remove the base, glass shelf or turntable and wash with warm soapy water if necessary. Avoid using harsh abrasive or commercial oven cleaners as these damage the inside surfaces of the microwave and scratches may distort the microwave pattern within the oven.
☐ The interior walls of the microwave remain relatively cool, so splashing and spills should not burn on. However, if spillage occurs, be sure to clean the microwave interior with a quick wipe, as any food particles left adhering to the oven surfaces will attract microwave energy and slow down cooking the next time you use the oven.
☐ Clean any grease or food particles from around the door seal. It is important that a good seal be maintained.
☐ To remove stubborn food particles from the inside surface, place a jug of 250 ml (8 fl oz) water in the microwave and let it boil for a few minutes. The moisture should loosen the pieces of food and they can be wiped away.
☐ To remove unpleasant odours from the microwave, place 250 ml (8 fl oz) water and 60 ml (4 tablespoons) Milton sterilizing solution into a measuring jug. Microwave for 5 minutes. Wipe the inside of the oven with a cloth rinsed in a mixture of warm water and bicarbonate of soda.
☐ The outside of the microwave can be wiped over with a damp cloth. Wipe exterior vents occasionally to remove any condensation, but do not splash water over them.

CARROTS

Carrots, one of our most useful root vegetables, are available all the year round. Carrots can be prepared in a variety of ways and are widely used as a vegetable, in stews, casseroles and soups as well as eaten raw and grated in salads. When microwaving carrots, ensure they are of a similar size or sliced uniformly for even cooking. Carrots have a fairly low moisture content and unless microwaved with a little water, they will toughen. *See also* Blanching.

To microwave carrots
The size and condition of carrots affect the cooking time. Larger carrots will naturally take longer than whole, baby carrots or sliced carrots. The age of the carrot also affects timing, as older carrots will take slightly longer to cook than tender young ones. If carrots are seasoned before cooking, add the salt to the cooking water, as sprinkling salt on the carrots dehydrates them during cooking. Carrots should always be microwaved with water and the dish should be covered to hold in the steam and hasten cooking.
Fresh, whole new carrots. Scrape and trim ends from 500 g (18 oz) carrots. Place in a

Tongue-tingling Tequila Mousse (page 78)

casserole, add 125 ml (4 fl oz) water, cover and microwave for 10 – 12 minutes on Full Power, or until tender. Drain and use as desired.

Fresh, sliced carrots. Scrape and slice 500 g (18 oz) carrots. Place in a casserole, add 45 ml (3 tablespoons) water, cover and microwave for 10 – 12 minutes on Full Power, or until tender. Drain and use as desired.

Frozen, sliced carrots. Place 300 g (11 oz) frozen carrots in a casserole, add 30 ml (2 tablespoons) water, cover and microwave on Full Power for 8 – 10 minutes. Drain and use as desired.

Baked carrot ring

Full Power, High (70%)
30 minutes

125 ml (4 fl oz) water
2.5 ml (½ teaspoon) salt
1 kg (2¼ lb) carrots, peeled and sliced
60 g (2 oz) butter, softened
2 egg yolks
30 g (1 oz) soft brown sugar
5 ml (1 teaspoon) salt
pepper
½ chicken stock cube
hot cooked peas*, for the centre

To garnish
chopped parsley
cooked, crumbled bacon

Place water, salt and carrots in a 3-litre (5-pint) casserole. Cover and microwave on Full Power for 15 – 18 minutes, or until tender. Drain and press carrots through a coarse sieve or make a coarse purée in a food processor. Add butter, egg yolks, brown sugar, salt, pepper and chicken stock cube, mixing well. Spoon mixture into a greased glass ring dish, packing it in firmly. Cover with vented plastic wrap and microwave on High (70%) for 8 – 12 minutes until hot. Stand for 5 minutes to set, then invert onto a serving plate. Fill centre with hot cooked peas. Garnish with chopped parsley and cooked, crumbled bacon.
Serves 4 – 6

Carrot relish

Full Power
19 minutes

Serve at barbecues or with meat dishes.

1 kg (2¼ lb) carrots, sliced diagonally, 1-cm (½-inch) thick
125 ml (4 fl oz) water
2 small onions, sliced
2 small green peppers, sliced into rings
400 g (14 oz) canned tomato soup
10 ml (2 teaspoons) Worcestershire sauce
10 ml (2 teaspoons) prepared mustard
few drops of Tabasco
250 ml (8 fl oz) vinaigrette salad dressing*
chopped parsley

Combine carrots and water in a deep 3-litre (5-pint) casserole. Cover and microwave on Full Power for 12 – 15 minutes, or until just tender, stirring occasionally. Drain well, then add onions and pepper rings. Beat together soup, Worcestershire sauce, mustard, Tabasco and dressing. Microwave for 4 minutes. Stir marinade and pour over vegetables. Toss gently, then cover and chill. To serve, drain off marinade and sprinkle with chopped parsley.
Serves 8 – 10

Carrots with orange sauce

Full Power
14 minutes

8 carrots, thinly sliced
75 ml (2½ fl oz) water
15 ml (1 tablespoon) soft brown sugar
7.5 ml (1½ teaspoons) cornflour
150 ml (5 fl oz) orange juice
15 g (½ oz) butter
salt
pinch of ground ginger
pinch of ground cloves

Place carrots and water in a 1-litre (1¾-pint) casserole and microwave on Full Power for 9 – 10 minutes, or until tender. Drain well. Mix brown sugar and cornflour, stir in orange juice, butter, salt, ginger and cloves. Pour mixture over carrots and toss gently to coat. Microwave for 2 minutes, stir, then microwave 1 – 1½ minutes longer.
Serves 4

Carrot and pineapple cake

Full Power
6 minutes

125 ml (4 fl oz) oil
150 g (5 oz) soft brown sugar
2 eggs
2.5 ml (½ teaspoon) bicarbonate of soda
few drops of vanilla extract
150 g (5 oz) self-raising flour
5 ml (1 teaspoon) mixed spice
5 ml (1 teaspoon) cinnamon
generous pinch of ginger
60 g (2 oz) brazil nuts, chopped
4 medium carrots, grated
2 – 3 slices of fresh pineapple
icing sugar or cream cheese icing*

Beat oil, sugar and eggs well, add bicarbonate of soda and vanilla extract and beat again. Sift

dry ingredients and beat into the mixture about one-third at a time. Add nuts, carrot and pineapple. Beat to combine, the mixture will be very thick. Pour into a sprayed or greased 25-cm (10-inch) ring mould. Microwave on Full Power for 6 – 7 minutes. Leave to cool in the mould for 10 minutes before turning out on to a rack. Dust with sifted icing sugar, or cover with cream cheese icing before serving.
Makes 1 x 25-cm (10-inch) ring cake

CASSEROLES

Casseroles are usually meal-in-one combinations of two or more ingredients, baked and served in the same dish. Casseroles usually contain rice or pasta; meat, fish or poultry; vegetables and seasonings, as well as a sauce or gravy. Slow cooking is advised to allow the flavours of the various ingredients to blend, and many casseroles improve if served the following day. Microwaves with variable power levels have the ability to simmer casseroles for long periods of time, with particularly tasty results. Reheating is usually done without any added liquid so the texture of the dish remains unchanged.

Round or oval containers are best for microwaving, as there are no square corners which tend to overcook. Materials to use include earthenware, clay, heatproof glassware or microwave plastic. If you are in doubt about whether a dish is suitable for microwave use, see how to test for microwave safety on page 89.

Casserole hints and tips

For quick and easy casseroles, select recipes with cooked ingredients. For example, in recipes calling for pasta or rice, these ingredients should be cooked before adding other ingredients. When making casseroles, bear in mind the following:

□ Casseroles containing mayonnaise or soured cream need careful attention as they tend to curdle. Microwave these casseroles to heat through. Do not overcook.

□ Layered casseroles cannot be stirred during cooking, so microwave the dish on a lower power, for example High (70%) or Medium (50%), so the centre can be heated through without the edges overcooking.

□ Cover casseroles for even cooking and to keep food moist.

□ Casseroles layered with a large amount of bread do not bake well in the microwave because the bread absorbs a lot of the moisture and becomes soggy, while the other ingredients become dry.

□ Crumb toppings are excellent for improving the appearance of casseroles. For a quick cheesy crumb topping try melting 60 g (2 oz) butter on Full Power for 1 minute, stir in 60 g (2 oz) dried breadcrumbs, 60 ml (4 tablespoons) Parmesan cheese and 2.5 ml (½ teaspoon) paprika. Sprinkle the mixture over the casserole dish and microwave for 1 minute.

Chicken à la king

Full Power, High (70%)
24 minutes

90 g (3 oz) butter
60 g (2 oz) plain flour
500 mℓ (16 fl oz) single cream
250 mℓ (8 fl oz) chicken stock
30 g (1 oz) butter
1 small red or green pepper, thinly sliced
½ onion, thinly sliced
100 g (3½ oz) mushrooms, sliced
1 x 1.5 kg (3 lb) chicken, cooked* and
   shredded
30 mℓ (2 tablespoons) dry sherry
salt and pepper

To garnish
toasted almonds*
chopped parsley

Place butter in a deep 2-litre (3½-pint) casserole and microwave on Full Power for 1 minute. Stir in flour and gradually mix in the cream and chicken stock. Microwave for 8 – 9 minutes stirring after 4 minutes and thereafter every minute until sauce is thick and smooth. Microwave butter in a large glass jug for 30 seconds. Add green pepper and onions, stirring to coat. Microwave for 2½ minutes then add mushrooms and microwave for a further 1 minute. Drain, and add to the sauce with chicken, sherry, salt and pepper. Microwave on High (70%) for 7 – 10 minutes, stirring after 5 minutes. Stand for 5 – 10 minutes before serving. Garnish with toasted almonds and chopped parsley before serving. *Serves 4 – 6*

Cheesy brunch casserole

Full Power, High (70%)
32 minutes

Make this casserole the night before to serve for a special brunch.

30 g (1 oz) butter
15 g (½ oz) plain flour
300 mℓ (½ pint) milk
125 g (4 oz) cream cheese
250 g (9 oz) pork or beef sausage-meat
1 garlic clove, finely chopped
60 mℓ (4 tablespoons) chopped spring onions
60 mℓ (4 tablespoons) chopped stuffed olives
2.5 mℓ (½ teaspoon) mixed herbs
200 g (7 oz) cooked sweetcorn kernels
10 eggs, lightly beaten
60 g (2 oz) Cheddar cheese, grated
tomato wedges
chopped parsley

Place butter in a 1-litre (1¾-pint) glass measuring jug and microwave on Full Power for 45 seconds. Stir in flour and microwave for 30 seconds. Gradually stir in milk and microwave for 3 – 4 minutes, stirring every minute, until thickened and bubbly. Stir in cream cheese and microwave for 1 minute. Stir until cheese melts and mixture is smooth. Set aside.

In a large casserole combine sausage-meat, garlic and spring onion. Microwave for 5 minutes, stirring twice until meat is cooked. Drain well. Stir in olives, herbs, sweetcorn and eggs. Cover with vented plastic wrap and microwave on High (70%) for 8 minutes, or until eggs are just set, stirring several times. Fold in cheese sauce and cover with plastic wrap. Refrigerate overnight.

To heat, pierce the plastic wrap and microwave on High (70%) for 8 – 10 minutes or until heated through. Stir gently once or twice. Sprinkle cheese over casserole and microwave for 2 minutes. Top with tomato wedges and sprinkle with chopped parsley to serve. *Serves 8*

CAULIFLOWER

Cauliflower, a member of the cabbage family, has a large, compact, edible flower head. Divided into florets, it can be used raw in salads and with dips, or be cooked and used in soups, or served as a vegetable. Cauliflower cooks very well in the microwave, keeping its texture, shape and colour. If it is to be cooked whole, it should be turned upside-down halfway through cooking time so that the florets do not overcook.

Whole cauliflower. Take 1 medium cauliflower, trim leaves and stem and place stem down in a large casserole. Add 45 ml (3 tablespoons) water, cover and microwave on Full Power for 9 – 13 minutes, or until tender. Turn half-way through cooking time.
Cauliflower florets. Divide 1 medium-sized cauliflower into florets, place in a large casserole and add 45 ml (3 tablespoons) water. Cover and microwave on Full Power for 7 – 9 minutes, or until tender.
Frozen cauliflower. Place 300 g (11 oz) frozen cauliflower in a casserole and add 90 ml (3 fl oz) water. Cover and microwave on Full Power for 7 – 9 minutes.

Cauliflower salad in spring onion marinade

Full Power
9 minutes

1 medium-sized cauliflower
60 mℓ (4 tablespoons) water
200 mℓ (6½ fl oz) oil
125 mℓ (4 fl oz) white vinegar
60 mℓ (4 tablespoons) chopped spring onion
30 mℓ (2 tablespoons) lemon juice
1 garlic clove, finely chopped
2.5 mℓ (½ teaspoon) caster sugar
5 mℓ (1 teaspoon) salt
pinch of pepper
lettuce leaves
10 mℓ (2 teaspoons) chopped parsley

Break cauliflower into florets of similar size and place in a large baking dish. Add water, cover and microwave on Full Power for 7 – 9 minutes, or until tender. Leave to cool, then drain well. Combine remaining ingredients except lettuce.

Add to the cauliflower and stir to coat. Cover and refrigerate overnight, stirring once or twice. Before serving, drain cauliflower and reserve marinade. Place cauliflower on lettuce-lined plates and sprinkle with parsley. Reserved marinade can be used as a salad dressing. *Serves 6*

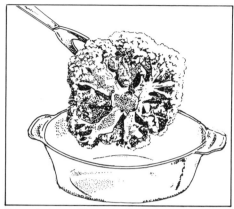

Turn whole cauliflower halfway through cooking.

Cauliflower cheese soup

Full Power, High (70%)
10 minutes

200 g (7 oz) small cauliflower florets
30 g (1 oz) butter
250 mℓ (8 fl oz) hot water
1 chicken stock cube
125 mℓ (4 fl oz) single cream
175 g (6 oz) processed cheese
pinch of nutmeg
pinch of allspice
60 mℓ (4 tablespoons) dry white wine
45 mℓ (3 tablespoons) finely chopped green or
   red pepper
paprika

Place cauliflower and butter in a 2-litre (3½-pint) casserole. Cover and microwave on Full Power for 3 minutes. Stir in water, crumbled chicken stock cube and cream and microwave, covered, on High (70%) for 4 minutes. Purée mixture in a food processor, then stir in cheese, nutmeg, allspice and wine. Stir to melt cheese, then microwave for 2 – 3 minutes to heat through. Sprinkle chopped pepper and paprika over the soup to serve. *Serves 4*

CELERY

The leaves and thin green stems of celery are used for flavouring soups and stuffings, and the thick stems and heart are usually eaten raw in salads, as crudités, or as a snack stuffed with cheese. Celery can also be braised in the microwave to make a good main vegetable dish as well.

Overleaf left: from top to bottom, Chicken and Sprouts (page 24), Tuna Supper Casserole (page 25). *Overleaf right:* Roast Beef (page 29), Beef Olives with Soured Cream (page 31)

To microwave celery

Slice 9 celery sticks into 2.5-cm (1-inch) slices. Place 125 ml (4 fl oz) water and a pinch of salt in a 2-litre (3½-pint) casserole. Add celery, cover and microwave on Full Power for 11 – 13 minutes, stirring after 6 minutes. Celery is crisp yet tender after this amount of time.

Braised celery and peas

Full Power
14 minutes

5 celery sticks, sliced
½ small onion, chopped
30 g (1 oz) butter
30 ml (2 tablespoons) water
2.5 ml (1 teaspoon) salt
300 g (11 oz) frozen peas

Place celery, onion, butter, water and salt in a 2-litre (3½-pint) casserole. Cover and microwave on Full Power for 6 minutes. Stir and add peas. Cover and microwave for 6 – 8 minutes, stirring after 4 minutes.
Serves 6

Celery and blue cheese soup

Full Power
12 minutes

45 g (1½ oz) butter
175 g (6 oz) celery sticks, finely chopped
30 g (1 oz) plain flour
500 ml (16 fl oz) chicken stock
125 ml (4 fl oz) dry white wine
250 g (9 oz) blue cheese, crumbled
15 ml (1 tablespoon) chopped parsley
pepper

Place butter in a 2-litre (3½-pint) casserole and microwave on Full Power for 1 minute. Add celery, tossing to coat. Cover and microwave for 4 minutes. Stir in flour, and gradually add stock and wine. Microwave for 6 minutes, stirring every 2 minutes until thickened. Add the cheese a little at a time, stirring to melt. Stir in parsley and season with pepper. Microwave for 1 minute to heat through.
Serves 4

CEREAL *See* Porridge

CHEESE

Cheese takes only a short time to cook in the microwave because it has a high fat content. With this in mind, great care should be taken in microwaving cheese and cheese dishes, as the proteins in cheese will toughen and become stringy if overcooked. Processed cheese melts more readily than farmhouse cheese and very finely grated cheese reduces the stirring needed in cheese dishes. The cooking needs to be timed in seconds rather than minutes. Where cheese must be cooked for more than a few moments, layer it between other ingredients and use a lower power level.

When adding cheese to cooked sauces, it is not usually necessary to cook the sauce further. Just stir the cheese into the sauce until it melts.

If a recipe needs a topping of cheese, add it just before the dish is cooked and microwave for ½ – 1 minute. Alternatively, sprinkle a topping of cheese as soon as you take the dish from the microwave. If the food is hot, the cheese melts almost instantly. Because there is no direct heat source, the cheese does not brown in the microwave. If browning is desired, place the cooked dish under a grill for a short time until golden and bubbly.

Cheese fondue

Low (15%)
18 minutes

1 garlic clove, crushed
300 ml (½ pint) dry white wine
15 g (½ oz) cornflour
250 g (9 oz) Gruyère cheese, grated
250 g (9 oz) Emmenthal cheese, grated
pepper to taste
30 ml (2 tablespoons) Kirsch
French bread

Rub the garlic over the inside of a deep 2-litre (3½-pint) glass bowl. Add wine and microwave, covered, on Low (15%) for 10 minutes. Sprinkle cornflour over combined cheeses and toss to mix. Gradually mix cheese into the wine, stirring to combine. Season with pepper. Microwave for 5 – 6 minutes, stirring every minute, until cheese melts. Stir in Kirsch and microwave for 1 – 2 minutes to heat through. Serve with French bread cut into cubes. Keep fondue warm over a burner or return to the microwave if necessary.
Serves 4

Cheese ramekins

High (70%)
5 minutes

4 eggs
125 (4 oz) Cheddar cheese, grated
125 ml (4 fl oz) single cream
salt and pepper
5 ml (1 teaspoon) chopped chives
15 g (½ oz) butter

Mix together the eggs, cheese, cream, salt and pepper and chives. Use the butter to grease four ramekins or individual custard dishes. Divide the egg mixture among the dishes and microwave on High (70%) for 4 – 5 minutes. The sides should be set and the centre soft and creamy.
Serves 4

Cheese puffs with dill

Full Power, High (70%)
4 minutes
Convection 200 °C / 400 °F / gas 6
10 minutes

125 g (4 oz) butter
90 g (3 oz) processed cheese, grated
15 ml (1 tablespoon) milk
5 ml (1 teaspoon) finely grated dried onion
2.5 ml (½ teaspoon) chopped fresh dill or pinch of dried dill
2 egg whites, stiffly beaten
about 20 cubes of French bread

Microwave butter on Full Power for 1½ – 2 minutes until melted. Add cheese, milk, onions and dill and stir well. Microwave on High (70%) for 1½ – 2 minutes to melt cheese. Leave mixture to cool slightly, then beat in egg whites. Dip bread in cheese mixture and place on a greased baking sheet. Bake on convection at 200 °C / 400 °F / gas 6 for 8 – 10 minutes, or until golden brown. Serve hot.
Makes about 20 puffs

Cheese and rice pie

High (70%)
17 minutes

350 g (12 oz) hot cooked rice*
15 ml (1 tablespoon) finely chopped chives
1 egg white
45 ml (3 tablespoons) grated Parmesan cheese
60 g (2 oz) salami, chopped
½ small onion, chopped
100 g (3½ oz) Mozzarella cheese, grated
3 eggs, plus 1 egg yolk
400 g (14 oz) canned evaporated milk
2.5 ml (½ teaspoon) salt
generous pinch of dried sage
few drops of Tabasco
6 tomato slices

To garnish
grated Parmesan cheese
chopped chives

Mix rice with chives and unbeaten egg white and spread evenly over bottom and halfway up sides of a 25-cm (10-inch) pie dish. Sprinkle with 45 ml (3 tablespoons) Parmesan cheese. Microwave on Full Power for 2 minutes. Sprinkle with salami, onion and Mozzarella cheese. Beat the eggs, egg yolk, milk, salt, sage and Tabasco in a 1-litre (1¾-pint) jug. Microwave on High (70%) for 4 minutes, stirring every minute. Pour mixture into the crust. Cover with waxed paper, and microwave on High (70%) for 5 minutes. Check, then microwave until the centre is almost set, about 6 – 8 minutes longer. Top with tomato slices and sprinkle with Parmesan cheese and chives. Cover and stand for 10 minutes before cutting.
Serves 6 – 8

Melted cheese sandwich

Full Power
4 minutes

2 slices of bread
butter
2 slices of processed cheese

Toast the bread lightly in a conventional toaster. Preheat a browning dish on Full Power for 3 minutes. When toast is ready, assemble the sandwich. Butter the outside surfaces and place in the hot browning dish. Microwave for 30 seconds on each side.
Makes 1 sandwich

CHEESECAKE

All cheesecakes, whether cooked or uncooked, are made from cottage, cream, Ricotta or low-fat soft cheese. For a creamier, smoother texture, use cream cheese, but for the more health conscious use cottage, low-fat soft or Ricotta cheese. Uncooked cheesecakes are set with the help of gelatine. Cheesecakes can also be baked in the microwave as long as the recipe is specifically for the microwave. Baked cheesecakes which are most successful are those with a crumb crust or biscuit pastry base.

Triple chocolate cheesecake

Full Power, Medium (50%)
3 minutes

22.5-cm (9-inch) chocolate biscuit crust*
2 eggs
100 g (3½ oz) caster sugar
250 g (9 oz) cream cheese
few drops of vanilla extract
15 mℓ (1 tablespoon) cocoa powder
250 mℓ (8 fl oz) soured cream
20 mℓ (4 teaspoons) rum or brandy
175 g (6 oz) plain chocolate, broken in pieces
30 mℓ (2 tablespoons) water
10 mℓ (2 teaspoons) powdered gelatine

To decorate
60 mℓ (4 tablespoons) whipping cream, whipped
grated chocolate

Beat eggs well, add sugar and beat until light and fluffy. Add cream cheese and beat again. Now add vanilla extract, cocoa, soured cream and rum, beat to combine. Microwave chocolate on Full Power for 2 – 3 minutes, stirring at least once during cooking time. Stir into cream cheese mixture. Combine water and gelatine in a small jug, stand for 2 minutes. Microwave on Medium (50%) for 1 minute, stir well. Stir into cream cheese mixture and pour into prepared shell immediately. Chill for at least 4 hours. Before serving, decorate with swirls of whipped cream and chocolate.
Makes 1 x 22.5-cm (9-inch) pie

Baked pineapple cheesecake

Full Power, High (70%), Medium (50%)
14 minutes

60 g (2 oz) butter
125 g (4 oz) Marie biscuits, crushed
15 mℓ (1 tablespoon) soft brown sugar
5 mℓ (1 teaspoon) cinnamon
250 g (9 oz) low-fat soft cheese
2 eggs
10 mℓ (2 teaspoons) grated lemon rind
30 mℓ (2 tablespoons) lemon juice
60 g (2 oz) caster sugar
400 g (14 oz) canned crushed pineapple
10 mℓ (2 teaspoons) powdered gelatine
30 mℓ (2 tablespoons) water

Microwave butter on Full Power for 1 minute. Stir into biscuit crumbs with brown sugar and cinnamon. Press into a 22.5-cm (9-inch) pie plate and microwave for 1 minute. Cool. Mix together low-fat soft cheese, eggs, lemon rind, lemon juice and sugar. Drain pineapple, reserving juice. Add pineapple to cheese mixture and turn into the crust. Microwave on High (70%) for 9 – 11 minutes, or until just set. Cool.
   Sprinkle gelatine over water and stand for 5 minutes. Microwave on Medium (50%) for 30 – 45 seconds, or until gelatine has dissolved. Add gelatine to the reserved pineapple juice, mix well and cool until almost set. Spread pineapple gelatine over cheesecake and chill to set.
Serves 6 – 8

Variation
In place of pineapple use 400 g (14 oz) canned apricots in natural juice. Purée apricots and juice. Use half in cheesecake mixture and mix remainder with dissolved gelatine for the topping and use as above.

Rich strawberry cheesecake

Full Power
6 minutes

125 g (4 oz) digestive biscuits, crushed
45 mℓ (3 tablespoons) finely chopped pecan nuts
15 mℓ (1 tablespoon) soft brown sugar
2.5 mℓ (½ teaspoon) cinnamon
90 g (3 oz) butter or margarine
60 mℓ (4 tablespoons) strawberry jam

Filling
250 g (9 oz) low-fat soft cheese
75 g (2½ oz) caster sugar
15 mℓ (1 tablespoon) grated lemon rind
10 mℓ (2 teaspoons) grated orange rind
30 mℓ (2 tablespoons) white rum or orange liqueur
2 eggs
250 mℓ (8 oz) whipping cream, whipped
1 punnet strawberries, cleaned

Mix together the biscuit crumbs, nuts, sugar and cinnamon. Microwave butter on Full Power for 1 minute to melt. Add to biscuit mixture, stirring to mix well. Press over base of a 20-cm (8-inch) baking dish. Chill until firm. Spread with jam.
   To make the filling, beat low-fat soft cheese until smooth, then beat in sugar, lemon and orange rind, rum or orange liqueur. Add eggs, one at a time, beating well after each addition. Turn mixture into the crust and microwave on Full Power for 5 minutes. Cool, then chill until set. To serve, spread with whipped cream and decorate with strawberries.
Serves 6 – 8

CHERRIES

Cherries have a short summer season. Eat them fresh, preserve them in brandy or use them for friandises*. Out of season, a large variety of canned cherries is available. Use the microwave and a can of cherries to create luscious toppings for ice cream, slices of cake or cheesecake.

Fresh cherries in brandy

Full Power
7 minutes

500 g (18 oz) cherries, stems removed
1 small piece of cinnamon stick
225 g (8 oz) sugar
125 mℓ (4 fl oz) water
15 mℓ (1 tablespoon) lemon juice
150 mℓ (5 fl oz) brandy

Wash and dry cherries. Pack into a warm, sterilized glass jar together with cinnamon stick. Combine sugar, water and lemon juice in a bowl. Microwave on Full Power for 3 minutes, stirring every minute during cooking time. Now microwave without stirring for 4 minutes. Allow to cool slightly, and add brandy. Pour over cherries, seal, label and store in a dark place. Keep for at least one month before using. Serve cherries with a scoop of ice cream. The liquid may also be strained, and drunk as a liqueur.
Makes about 675 g (1½ lb)

Overleaf left: top left, White Chocolate Mousse with Loganberry Sauce (page 63); top right, French Truffles (page 61); bottom, Working with Chocolate (page 60); Chocolate Leaves and Chocolate Caraque.
Overleaf right: Crêpes with Cherry Sauce (page 72)

Cherries jubilee

Full Power
5 minutes

425 g (15 oz) canned stoned dark cherries
30 mℓ (1 tablespoon) caster sugar
1 small piece of cinnamon stick
100 mℓ (3½ fl oz) orange juice
10 mℓ (2 teaspoons) cornflour
5 mℓ (1 teaspoon) custard powder
60 mℓ (4 tablespoons) cherry brandy
60 mℓ (4 tablespoons) brandy
fine strips of orange rind
1 litre (1¾ pints) vanilla ice cream

Drain cherries and place in a heat-resistant serving bowl. In a jug, combine cherry liquid, sugar, cinnamon stick and orange juice. Spoon out about 30 mℓ (2 tablespoons) of the liquid and mix with cornflour and custard powder to form a smooth paste. Add to liquid in jug and stir well. Microwave on Full Power for 4 – 5 minutes, stirring every minute during cooking time. Pour thickened sauce over cherries, microwave for 2 minutes, stirring at least once. Pour cherry brandy and brandy into a jug, microwave for 45 seconds. Pour over cherries and ignite. Sprinkle with fine strips of orange rind. Spoon over scoops of ice cream.
Serves 4 – 6

CHICK PEAS
(Garbanzo beans)
Chick peas, a type of legume, are very popular in Middle Eastern and Mediterranean cuisine. They must be soaked thoroughly before being boiled as they are almost impossible to cook otherwise. The soaking is best done overnight. Chick peas take nearly as much time to cook in the microwave as they do conventionally, but, as it is almost impossible to overcook them, they can be microwaved for a long period. Canned chick peas are also available and are a great time-saver. Combine cooked chick peas with vinaigrette and parsley for a delicious salad, or purée with a little garlic, lemon juice and olive oil to make hummus, a popular dip in the Middle East.

Chick peas

Full Power, Defrost (30%)
60 minutes

250 g (9 oz) dried chick peas
1 litre (1¾ pints) water
750 mℓ (1¼ pints) water
2.5 mℓ (½ teaspoon) salt

Place peas in a large casserole with 1-litre (1¾ pints) water, cover, and stand overnight. Drain and rinse peas. Return to casserole and add 750 mℓ (1¼ pints) water and salt. Cover and microwave on Full Power for 10 minutes. Stir, cover and microwave on Full Power for 10 minutes. Stir, cover and microwave on Defrost (30%) for 45 – 50 minutes or until peas are tender. Stir occasionally. Stand for 10 minutes before using.
Serves 4

Chick pea salad

Full Power, Medium (50%)
12 minutes

This dish makes an interesting first course and is good to serve with lamb or chicken.

125 mℓ (4 fl oz) oil
1 large onion, finely chopped
1 small red or green pepper, chopped
10 mℓ (2 teaspoons) dried thyme
5 mℓ (1 teaspoon) dried tarragon
90 g (3 oz) seedless raisins
2 x 400 g (14 oz) cans of chick peas, drained
   and rinsed
salt and black pepper
125 mℓ (4 fl oz) white wine vinegar
60 mℓ (4 tablespoons) chopped parsley

Place oil in a casserole dish. Microwave on Full Power for 1 minute. Add onion, pepper and herbs. Microwave, covered, on Medium (50%) for 8 – 10 minutes, or until onions are tender. Add raisins and chick peas and microwave for 3 – 4 minutes, stirring twice. Season with salt and pour in vinegar. Let mixture cool to room temperature, then cover and chill overnight. Before serving, add chopped parsley. Serve sprinkled with plenty of freshly ground black pepper.
Serves 6 – 8

CHICKEN
Chicken is an excellent choice for microwave cooking as the flesh is moist and tender, and it cooks in a third to half the time it would normally take in a conventional oven. Many chicken dishes can be microwaved on Full Power but those containing sauces with eggs or cheese are best microwaved on a lower power level. The skin does not become as crisp or golden brown, but the use of crumb coatings and browning agents will improve the appearance and add flavour to the cooked bird.

Guidelines for microwaving chicken
☐ Microwaving renders a good amount of fat from chicken. The fat should be drained off before adding sauces or other ingredients.
☐ Completely defrost whole chickens for quicker and more even cooking.
☐ To prevent overcooking, the wing tips, bone ends and breast bone may be shielded with small strips of aluminium foil for half the cooking time.
☐ To promote even cooking, truss legs and wings close to the body.
☐ Microwave chicken portions with skin side up, and place the thicker parts towards the outer edge of the container.
☐ Stuffed whole chickens take longer to cook so increase the microwave time by 1½ – 2 minutes per 500 g (18 oz).

☐ Check to see that flesh is cooked by cutting the skin between the inner thigh and breast. There should be no traces of pink and the juices should run clear.
☐ Take standing time into consideration when planning to cook chicken. Remove chicken from the microwave, cover loosely with foil, shiny side in, and stand for 10 – 15 minutes before serving.
Whole chicken. Defrost if necessary and shield drumstick and wings with small strips of foil. Use a browning agent (page 39) if desired. Place chicken in roasting bag or covered casserole and microwave on Full Power for 10 – 12 minutes per 500 g (18 oz). Stand for 10 – 15 minutes after cooking.
Chicken portions. Defrost if necessary and arrange skin-side up, preferably in a circle with the thicker ends towards the outside. Cover and microwave on Full Power for 8 – 10 minutes per 500 g (18 oz). Stand for 3 minutes after cooking. Chicken portions may also be crumbed (page 57).

Chicken Marengo

Full Power
32 minutes

1 chicken, cut into portions
1 egg white
125 g (4 oz) soft breadcrumbs
1 packet spaghetti sauce mix
400 g (14 oz) canned whole tomatoes,
   chopped but not drained
250 mℓ (8 fl oz) dry white wine
75 g (2½ oz) mushrooms, sliced (optional)

Remove skin from chicken and pat portions dry. Brush with egg white. Mix breadcrumbs with the dry sauce mix. Coat each portion of chicken with the mixture. Place portions in a deep casserole. Sprinkle with remaining crumb mixture. Microwave, uncovered, on Full Power for 15 minutes. Add remaining ingredients, mix, then microwave for 10 – 12 minutes. Check chicken is cooked through and cook a few minutes more if necessary. Stand for 5 minutes before serving.
Serves 4 – 6

Chicken and spinach bake

Full Power
20 minutes

1.5 kg (3 lb) cooked chicken*
1 onion, chopped
1 celery stick, finely sliced
30 g (1 oz) butter
300 g (11 oz) spinach, cooked*
400 g (14 oz) canned cream of chicken soup
150 g (5 oz) Cheddar cheese, grated
45 mℓ (3 tablespoons) medium sherry
2.5 mℓ (½ teaspoon) tarragon
pepper
125 g (4 oz) soft breadcrumbs
45 g (1½ oz) butter
paprika
chopped parsley

Remove skin and bones from chicken and coarsely chop flesh. Set aside. Place onion, celery and butter in a glass bowl. Microwave on Full Power for 3 – 4 minutes or until vegetables are tender. Add spinach and toss lightly. Turn mixture into a 25-cm (10-inch) baking dish and top with chopped chicken. In a large bowl mix together soup, cheese, sherry and tarragon and season with pepper. Microwave for 3 – 4 minutes until cheese has melted. Stir well and pour over chicken. Microwave remaining butter for 1 minute to melt, then stir in breadcrumbs. Sprinkle over ingredients in the baking dish. Dust with paprika and microwave for 10 – 12 minutes to heat through. Serve sprinkled with chopped parsley.
Serves 4 – 6

Chicken with pineapple and lychees

Full Power
29 minutes

200 g (7 oz) drained, crushed pineapple
45 mℓ (3 tablespoons) soy sauce
15 mℓ (1 tablespoon) white vinegar
10 mℓ (2 teaspoons) prepared mustard
2.5 mℓ (½ teaspoon) ground ginger
1.5 kg (3 lb) chicken, skinned and cut into portions
250 g (9 oz) mushrooms, sliced
1 green pepper, seeded and diced
3 spring onions, including tops, chopped
150 g (5 oz) fresh, peeled and seeded lychees, or drained, canned lychees
parsley

Mix together the pineapple, soy sauce, vinegar, mustard and ginger. Microwave on Full Power for 3 – 4 minutes, or until mixture comes to the boil. Arrange chicken portions in an oval casserole, with large portions towards the outside. Spoon pineapple mixture over and cover with waxed paper. Microwave for 10 minutes, then turn chicken over and baste with sauce. Add mushrooms and green pepper. Microwave for 10 minutes. Add spring onions and lychees and microwave for 3 – 5 minutes more, or until heated through. Sprinkle with parsley.
Serves 4 – 6

Double chicken casserole

Full Power, High (70%)
20 minutes

1 roast chicken*, cut into portions
15 mℓ (1 tablespoon) oil
1 onion, chopped
400 g (14 oz) canned cream of chicken soup
½ chicken stock cube
2.5 mℓ (½ teaspoon) turmeric
2 tomatoes, skinned and chopped
15 mℓ (1 tablespoon) lemon juice
pinch of thyme
black pepper
300 g (11 oz) mushrooms, sliced

Arrange cooked chicken portions in a shallow casserole, set aside. Microwave oil in a large bowl on Full Power for 1 minute. Add onion and toss to coat with oil. Microwave for 3 minutes. Add all the remaining ingredients, except the mushrooms. Microwave for 8 minutes. Stir in the mushrooms and pour over the chicken. Cover, microwave on High (70%) for 8 minutes.
Serves 6

Chicken in mustard orange marinade

Medium (50%), Full Power
15 minutes

2 baby chickens or poussins, split down the centre of the breast
30 g (1 oz) butter
15 g (½ oz) plain flour
30 mℓ (2 tablespoons) water
45 mℓ (3 tablespoons) single cream

Marinade
grated rind and juice of 1 orange
15 mℓ (1 tablespoon) dry mustard
1 garlic clove, crushed
salt and black pepper
2.5 mℓ (½ teaspoon) dried tarragon
150 mℓ (5 fl oz) chicken stock
45 mℓ (3 tablespoons) white wine

To garnish
1 orange, sliced
cress or parsley

Combine all the ingredients for marinade. Lay split chicken flat in a shallow, ovenproof dish. Pour marinade over chickens, cover and stand for at least 2 hours, drain off half the marinade and set aside. Cover chicken with vented plastic, microwave for 12 minutes on Medium (50%). Remove chicken from dish, dot with butter, grill or barbecue conventionally for 20 minutes.

Blend flour with water, add residue from chicken and drained marinade, mix well. Microwave on Full Power for 3 minutes, stirring every minute. Stir in the cream. Pour into a gravy boat. Garnish chicken with slices of orange and cress.
Serves 2 – 4

Crumbed baked chicken

Full Power
20 minutes

1 kg (2¼ lb) chicken pieces

Coating
100 g (3½ oz) savoury biscuits, crushed
2.5 mℓ (½ teaspoon) paprika
salt and pepper

Dip
1 egg, beaten
15 mℓ (1 tablespoon) milk

Combine coating ingredients. Mix together egg and milk for dip. Pat chicken portions dry, dip into liquid, then into coating. Arrange chicken portions on a low rack or plate, placing thickest sections towards outside. Microwave, uncovered so crumbs do not become soggy, on Full Power for 16 – 20 minutes. It is best not to turn chicken portions over during cooking time as the crumb mixture may come off. The chicken portions are cooked when they are tender and the juices run clear. For more succulent results, reduce power level to Medium (50%) after the first 10 minutes, and microwave for 8 – 12 minutes.
Serves 4

Overleaf left: Christmas Cake (page 63), Christmas Pudding (page 64) with Hard Sauce (page 108) and Fruit Mincemeat (page 63)
Overleaf right: Chicken Curry (page 74) served with Dhall (page 134), Rice (page 185) and Green Mango Chutney (page 64)

Chicken pasta bake

Full Power, Medium (50%)
17 minutes

1 roast chicken*
400 g (14 oz) spiral-shaped noodles, cooked*

Sauce
60 g (2 oz) margarine
1 onion, chopped
2 celery sticks, chopped
30 g (1 oz) plain flour
450 mℓ (14½ fl oz) milk
2 egg yolks
350 mℓ (11 fl oz) single cream
30 mℓ (2 tablespoons) lemon juice
5 mℓ (1 teaspoon) turmeric
175 g (6 oz) Cheddar cheese, grated
salt and black pepper
45 mℓ (3 tablespoons) grated Parmesan
  cheese
45 mℓ (3 tablespoons) dried breadcrumbs

Remove the skin and bones from cooked
chicken and dice. Drain the cooked noodles
and rinse well with cold water. Combine
chicken and noodles in a 2-litre (3½-pint)
casserole, set aside. For the sauce, microwave
margarine in a large bowl on Full Power for
1 minute. Add onion and celery and stir well to
coat with margarine. Microwave for 4 minutes,
stirring once during cooking time. Add flour, stir
and microwave for 30 seconds. Pour in milk
and stir well, microwave for 3 – 4 minutes,
stirring every 30 seconds. Add yolks and
cream, mix well. Then add lemon juice,
turmeric, three-quarters of the Cheddar and
season well. Pour over the chicken mixture and
stir to combine. Combine remaining Cheddar,
Parmesan and breadcrumbs, sprinkle on top of
casserole. Microwave on Medium (50%) for 12
– 15 minutes, until piping hot.
Serves 6

CHICKEN LIVERS

Care should be taken when preparing
chicken livers for cooking in the microwave. The livers are covered with a thin
membrane, which must be pricked several
times with a skewer to prevent them from
'exploding'. Always cover the livers during
cooking to prevent accidental splashing.

Chicken livers with chilli

Full Power, High (70%)
18 minutes

45 mℓ (3 tablespoons) oil (preferably half
  sunflower and half olive oil)
250 g (9 oz) chicken livers, cleaned
1 – 2 garlic cloves, crushed
1 small onion, chopped
chilli powder
salt and black pepper
1 small tomato, skinned and finely chopped
bread or rolls

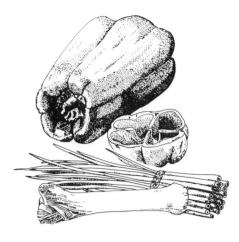

Microwave a browning dish for 7 minutes on
Full Power. Add oil, microwave for 1 minute.
Prick livers very well with a skewer. Add livers to
browning dish, cover and microwave for
1 minute on each side. Drain livers and set
aside. Add remaining ingredients to oil.
Microwave for 4 minutes, stirring at least twice
during cooking time. Add livers, cover and
microwave for 5 – 6 minutes on High (70%).
Serve piping hot with plenty of French bread.
Serves 4 – 6 as a snack

CHILLI CON CARNE

This American dish of beans and beef in a
spicy chilli sauce originated in Texas, but is
now popular all over the world. The beef is
either minced or diced and the amount of
chilli in the sauce is left to the cook. This
microwave version is quick and delicious.

Chilli con carne

Full Power, Defrost (30%)
47 minutes

500 g (18 oz) minced beef
1 onion, chopped
½ green pepper, chopped
400 g (14 oz) canned whole tomatoes, coarsely
  chopped
250 mℓ (8 fl oz) tomato sauce (as served with
  pasta)
5 mℓ (1 teaspoon) dried oregano
1 large bay leaf
5 mℓ (1 teaspoon) chilli powder, or to taste
salt and pepper
400 (14 oz) canned kidney beans, drained
60 g (2 oz) Cheddar cheese, grated

Place beef in a large casserole and break up
with a fork. Add onion and green pepper. Cover
with waxed paper and microwave on Full Power
for 3 – 5 minutes, or until meat loses its pink
colour. Drain, then stir in tomatoes and juice,
tomato sauce, oregano, bay leaf, chilli powder
and salt and pepper. Mix well, then stir in
beans. Cover and microwave for 6 – 7 minutes,
or until the mixture is boiling. Reduce power to
Defrost (30%) and microwave for 30 – 35
minutes or until vegetables are tender. Serve in
individual bowls, sprinkled with grated cheese.
Serves 4 – 6

CHOCOLATE

There is no doubt that chocolate is one of
the world's most popular flavours. Made
from the cocoa bean, chocolate is served as
a drink, used for baking, makes wonderful
desserts and is enjoyed as a confection.
Chocolate responds well to being microwaved, but as it is particularly sensitive to
heat, care must be taken.

Guidelines for microwaving chocolate

□ When making chocolate leaves,
moulded or dipped chocolates, a grey film
sometimes appears on the surface of the
chocolate a day or two after the chocolates
have been made. This is due to overheat-
ing, so it is best to microwave chocolate for
this purpose on Medium (50%).
□ When working with chocolate, the consistency often becomes too thick. Simply
place chocolate in the microwave for a few
seconds to soften.
□ Chocolate is sometimes poured into
paper piping bags and used to decorate
chocolates or cakes. If the chocolate hardens, place the piping bag in the microwave
for a few seconds. This saves a great deal of
time and chocolate.
□ Always chop or break up chocolate before microwaving.
□ When melting chocolate for use in a
cake or dessert, it can be microwaved on
Full Power.
□ White chocolate melts in just under half
the time that milk or plain chocolate takes;
cooking chocolate takes slightly longer.
□ Chocolate taken from the refrigerator
will take longer to melt than chocolate at
room temperature.
□ Remember that chocolate holds its
shape even when melted, so stir often during microwaving time to prevent overheat-
ing.

To melt chocolate for use in baking

Place 100 g (3½ oz) chopped chocolate in a
bowl, microwave on Full Power for 2½ – 3
minutes, stirring every minute. Stir well
and use as required.

To melt chocolate for chocolate-making

Chop 60 g (2 oz) plain chocolate, preferably cooking chocolate, and place in a container. Microwave for 3 – 4 minutes on Medium (50%). Stir well and use as required.

Chocolate caraque

Medium (50%)
4 minutes

75 g (2½ oz) plain chocolate

Break chocolate in pieces and place in a bowl.
Microwave for 4 – 5 minutes on Medium (50%).
Stir well. Using a long straight-edged knife
spread chocolate out thinly on a marble slab or
stainless steel surface. Allow chocolate to just
set. Hold the knife with both hands at an angle
of approximately 45°. Pull knife firmly over

chocolate, forming chocolate curls. Store curls in an air-tight container for up to one week.

Chocolate leaves

Medium (50%)
3 minutes

60 g (2 oz) plain chocolate, preferably cooking chocolate
fresh rose or ivy leaves

Break chocolate in pieces and place in a container. Microwave on Medium (50%) for 3 – 4 minutes. Wash and dry leaves well. If using rose leaves spread chocolate on underside of leaf; if using ivy leaves, spread chocolate on top of leaf. Do not spread chocolate too thinly. Place coated leaves on a piece of foil and refrigerate for a few minutes. Carefully peel leaf away from chocolate. Store until needed in a sealed container. Refrigerate if weather is very hot.
Makes about 30 leaves

Chocolate decorations

Medium (50%)
3 minutes

Heating chocolate to the perfect consistency for piping is extremely difficult. The addition of a few drops of glycerine immediately thickens the chocolate to a manageable consistency.

30 g (1 oz) cooking chocolate, chopped
2 drops of glycerine

Break chocolate in pieces and place in a bowl. Microwave on Medium (50%) for about 3 minutes, stirring once during cooking time. Stir to ensure that the chocolate is completely melted. Add glycerine and stir to combine. Pour mixture into a paper piping bag. Cut off tip. Pipe shapes on to the waxy side of waxed paper. Refrigerate for a few minutes. Peel off and use as a decoration.
Makes 20 – 30

French truffles

Full Power
9 minutes

300 g (11 oz) plain cooking chocolate, chopped
60 mℓ (4 tablespoons) cream
few drops of vanilla extract
toasted almonds*, finely chopped

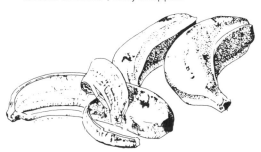

Place chocolate in a bowl, microwave on Full Power for 8 – 10 minutes, stirring every 2 minutes. Microwave cream for 45 seconds, pour into melted chocolate and beat for a few seconds. Add vanilla extract and beat. Refrigerate until firm. Form into small balls, then roll in chopped almonds. Place in paper cases to serve.
Makes about 30

Frozen chocolate bananas

Medium (50%)
6 minutes

6 bananas
12 thin skewers
100 g (3½ oz) plain chocolate, chopped
5 mℓ (1 teaspoon) oil

Peel bananas, halve and insert a skewer into the cut end of each banana. Arrange on a small tray and freeze. Place chocolate in a medium-sized bowl and add oil. Microwave on Medium (50%) for 6 – 7 minutes, stirring at least twice during cooking time. Dip frozen bananas into hot chocolate, allow excess chocolate to drain off. Place carefully on foil, chill in the freezer for 15 minutes. Serve within one day.
Makes 12

Chocolate mousse slice

Full Power
8 minutes

75 mℓ (2½ fl oz) water
75 g (2½ oz) caster sugar
15 g (½ oz) butter to prepare dish
15 g (½ oz) caster sugar to prepare dish
30 g (1 oz) walnuts, chopped
125 g (4 oz) plain cooking chocolate, broken in pieces
125 g (4 oz) butter
30 g (1 oz) cocoa powder
2 egg yolks
4 egg whites
1 quantity Grand Marnier sauce*

Combine water and sugar in a bowl, microwave on Full Power for 2 minutes, stirring well to dissolve sugar crystals. Microwave for 2 minutes more, then cool. Butter a 22.5 x 12.5-cm (9 x 5-inch) loaf dish and sprinkle with sugar. Scatter walnuts on the base. Place chocolate, butter and cocoa powder in a bowl. Microwave on Full Power for 4 – 5 minutes, stirring frequently. Measure 60 mℓ (4 table-spoons) of the sugar syrup and stir into chocolate. Now add yolks and stir to combine. Beat whites to stiff peaks, gently fold into chocolate mixture. Pour into prepared dish and refrigerate for at least 4 hours. To unmould, run a spatula around the edge of the dish, invert mousse on to a platter. To serve, ladle a little Grand Marnier sauce on to a plate, top with a slice of mousse and add a small chocolate decoration*.
Serves 6

Making a Parchment Paper Piping Bag

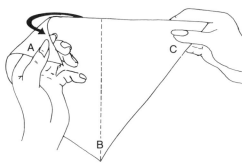

1. Hold triangle as indicated. Bend point A around left hand and pull towards point B. Align inner edge of point A with centre line running through point B.

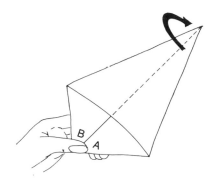

2. Wrap point C around cone already formed, pulling point down to meet at point B.

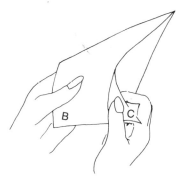

3. Pull ends firmly together at point B until a sharp tip is formed and seams overlap slightly.

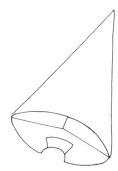

4. To secure the cone, fold the triangle at the top into the cone. Press down firmly. Make two short cuts in the middle, about 2.5-cm (1-inch) apart, and fold over to the inside.

Chocolate orange cones

Medium (50%)
4 minutes

60 g (2 oz) plain cooking chocolate, broken in
  pieces
parchment paper

Filling
125 mℓ (4 fl oz) whipping cream
15 mℓ (1 tablespoon) Van der Hum
10 mℓ (2 teaspoons) pinch of icing sugar
finely grated orange rind

To make the cornet shapes, fold a 25-cm
(10-inch) square of parchment paper in half
diagonally, cut into two with a knife, repeat
twice more, making eight triangles. Fold into
piping bags (see page 61) and staple the three
'tails' together to make the bags firm. Repeat
with another square of paper. Place chocolate
in a small bowl, microwave on Medium (50%)
for 4 – 5 minutes, stir at least once during
cooking time. Brush the inside of the cones with
chocolate, leave to set for a few minutes, brush
a second time to give a good coating.
Refrigerate for 5 minutes, then carefully peel
away the paper. Beat the cream until stiff, stir in
the remaining ingredients. Fill a piping bag
fitted with a medium-sized star nozzle with the
cream. Pipe into the cones. Serve within 2
hours.
Makes 16 cones

Note: To save time, small paper cases can be
painted twice with chocolate before being filled
with orange cream.

White chocolate mousse with loganberry sauce

Full Power
5 minutes

125 g (4 oz) white chocolate, broken in pieces
30 mℓ (2 tablespoons) water
2 egg whites
pinch of cream of tartar
150 mℓ (5 fl oz) whipping cream

Sauce
400 g (14 oz) canned loganberries
30 mℓ (2 tablespoons) caster sugar
10 mℓ (2 teaspoons) lemon juice
30 mℓ (2 tablespoons) Kirsch

To decorate
45 mℓ (3 tablespoons) whipping cream, stiffly
  whipped
loganberries
6 white chocolate leaves*

A wide variety of casseroles, baking dishes,
utensils, microwave plastic, ovenproof glass
jugs and dishes, clay pots and browning dishes
available to microwave users (page 89)

Line the bases of six 7.5-cm (3-inch) ramekins
with a circle of aluminium foil. Place chocolate
and water in a bowl, microwave on Full Power
for 3 minutes, stirring every minute during
cooking time. Leave to cool slightly. Beat the
egg whites and cream of tartar until a firm peak
forms. Stir one-third into the chocolate, then
fold in the remainder. Beat the cream until thick,
then fold into chocolate mixture. Divide mixture
between the ramekins. Chill well, or place in the
freezer until firm. Stand in the refrigerator for 30
minutes before serving. Loosen sides of
mousse with a spatula, turn out on to individual
plates and pour a little sauce around each.
Decorate each mousse with a swirl of cream, a
loganberry and a chocolate leaf.
  To make the sauce, drain off about half the
syrup. Pour loganberries, remaining syrup and
sugar into a jug, microwave on Full Power for
2 minutes. Pour into a blender, add lemon juice
and Kirsch, and blend. Strain through a sieve
and chill before serving. Sauce and mousse will
freeze for up to three weeks.
Makes 6 small servings

CHRISTMAS CAKE

This traditional rich fruit cake is made well
in advance of Christmas. Pour brandy over
the cake from time to time to help it mature. Christmas cake may be served plain,
or decorated with marzipan (see page 144)
and white icing.

Christmas cake

Full Power, Medium (50%)
27 minutes

150 g (5 oz) sultanas
150 g (5 oz) raisins
150 g (5 oz) currants
60 g (2 oz) mixed peel
150 g (5 oz) butter
200 g (7 oz) soft brown sugar
200 mℓ (6½ fl oz) water
5 mℓ (1 teaspoon) bicarbonate of soda
100 g (3½ oz) glacé cherries, chopped
125 g (4 oz) stoned dates, chopped
5 mℓ (1 teaspoon) instant coffee powder
3 eggs, beaten
250 g (9 oz) plain flour
5 mℓ (1 teaspoon) baking powder
2.5 mℓ (½ teaspoon) cinnamon
2.5 mℓ (½ teaspoon) mixed spice
pinch of ground cloves
10 mℓ (2 teaspoons) cocoa powder
125 mℓ (4 fl oz) brandy
45 mℓ (3 tablespoons) chopped preserved
  ginger
2 rings glacé pineapple, chopped
75 g (2½ oz) mixed nuts, chopped
100 mℓ (3½ fl oz) extra brandy

Place sultanas, raisins, currants, peel, butter,
sugar and water in a large bowl. Cover with
vented plastic wrap, microwave on Full Power
for 7 minutes. Stir at least twice during cooking
time. Add bicarbonate of soda, cherries, dates
and instant coffee. Allow to cool completely. Stir

in eggs. Sift dry ingredients and add alternately
with brandy to the fruit mixture until all
ingredients have been combined. Stir in
preserved ginger, glacé pineapple and mixed
nuts. Pour into a deep, lined 17.5-cm (7-inch)
cake dish. If the cake is not going to be iced,
arrange a few almonds attractively on top of the
cake before baking. Cover cake with
greaseproof paper. Microwave on Medium
(50%) for 18 – 20 minutes. Allow cake to cool
before turning out of dish. When cool, slowly
pour brandy over cake. Wrap in aluminium foil
and store until required.
Makes 1 x 17.5-cm (7-inch) cake

Note: In place of the sultanas, raisins, currants
and peel, use 500 g (18 oz) mixed dried fruit.

CHRISTMAS MINCEMEAT

Originally this was a mixture of minced
beef, suet, apples, dried fruit, brandy and
cider used to make mince pies. Today the
meat is omitted and a mixture of the remaining ingredients, in varying propor-
tions, is used. The flavour of mincemeat
improves with keeping, so it should be prepared in advance and refrigerated or kept
in sealed jars.

Fruit mincemeat

Medium (50%), Defrost (30%)
40 minutes

4 apples, grated
grated rind of 1 lemon
150 g (5 oz) seedless raisins
150 g (5 oz) currants
150 g (5 oz) dried figs, chopped
125 g (4 oz) suet, finely chopped or minced
200 g (7 oz) soft brown sugar
30 mℓ (2 tablespoons) golden syrup
15 mℓ (1 tablespoon) mixed spice
5 mℓ (1 teaspoon) ground ginger
2.5 mℓ (½ teaspoon) grated nutmeg
2.5 mℓ (½ teaspoon) salt
45 mℓ (3 tablespoons) brandy
125 mℓ (4 fl oz) cider

Mix the fruit and suet together, then add
remaining ingredients. Place in a large
casserole and microwave on Medium (50%) for
10 minutes. Cover and microwave on Defrost
(30%) for 25 – 30 minutes, until fruit is tender.
Cool and refrigerate in a covered container, or
pack into hot, dry sterilized jars and seal.
Makes about 900 g (2 lb)

CHRISTMAS PUDDING

Rich, fruity Christmas or plum pudding is part of traditional fare. Christmas pudding must be made well in advance to allow it to mature. Not only does the microwave save a great many hours of cooking time, but it may also be used to reheat the pudding before serving. Remember not to include metal charms or coins. Slip these into the pudding after reheating. Usually Christmas pudding is decorated with holly and flamed with brandy.

To reheat Christmas pudding

Sprinkle with a little brandy and cover bowl with vented plastic wrap. Place pudding and bowl (do not reheat a commercial pudding in a metal container) in microwave. Microwave on Medium (50%) for 10 minutes, stand for 3 – 4 minutes before turning out. Turn out on to a heat-resistant plate. Add charms or well-cleaned coins to the pudding and decorate with holly. Warm a little brandy in a jug for 45 seconds on Full Power, pour over and ignite.

Christmas pudding

Medium (50%)
20 minutes

75 g (2½ oz) sultanas
100 g (3½ oz) raisins
75 g (2½ oz) currants
60 g (2 oz) mixed peel
60 g (2 oz) glacé cherries, coarsely chopped
60 g (2 oz) cashew nuts, chopped
1 small carrot, grated
60 g (2 oz) dark brown or muscovado sugar
15 mℓ (1 tablespoon) molasses
1 apple, peeled and grated
60 mℓ (4 tablespoons) brandy
75 mℓ (2½ fl oz) beer
grated rind and juice of ½ lemon
3 eggs, beaten
60 g (2 oz) plain flour
75 g (2½ oz) suet, finely shredded
60 g (2 oz) soft white breadcrumbs
10 mℓ (2 teaspoons) gravy browning
generous pinch of mixed spice
pinch of nutmeg
drop of almond essence

Combine in a large bowl the fruit, nuts, carrot, brown sugar, molasses, apple, brandy, beer, lemon rind and juice. Stand for 1 hour. Add the remaining ingredients and mix very well. Grease or spray a 1-litre (1¾-pint) pudding basin. Place mixture into pudding basin, cover with vented plastic wrap. Microwave on Medium (50%) for 20 – 25 minutes. Stand until cool. Sprinkle with a little extra brandy and cover tightly with aluminium foil. Store until required.
Serves 8

CHUTNEY

Chutney is a tangy Indian pickle or relish traditionally served with curries, but is excellent with cold meats too. These thick, boiled mixtures are usually made from a combination of fruit, vegetables, spices, sugar and vinegar. When made in the microwave, the long tedious cooking time is halved and the strong vinegar smell is kept in the oven cavity.

Apple and tomato chutney

Full Power
42 minutes

400 g (14 oz) ripe tomatoes, skinned and chopped
1 large onion, chopped
2 chillies, chopped
400 g (14 oz) Granny Smith apples, peeled, cored and chopped
15 mℓ (1 tablespoon) pickling spice
5 mℓ (1 teaspoon) mustard seed
250 g (9 oz) raisins
10 mℓ (2 teaspoons) salt
250 g (9 oz) soft brown sugar
2 garlic cloves, crushed
generous pinch of ground ginger
450 mℓ (14½ fl oz) brown vinegar

Place tomatoes, onions, chillies and apples in a large bowl. Cover with vented plastic and microwave on Full Power for 14 minutes, stirring once during cooking time. Place pickling spice and mustard seed in a muslin bag and tie with string. Add all the ingredients to tomato mixture, stirring to combine. Microwave for 28 – 30 minutes, stirring from time to time. Cool, spoon into clean dry jars, seal and label. Store in a cool place until required. Refrigerate once opened.
Makes about 900 g (2 lb)

Banana chutney

Full Power
20 minutes

10 ripe bananas, sliced
410 mℓ (13 fl oz) white vinegar
75 g (2½ oz) seedless raisins
1 onion, finely chopped
150 g (5 oz) soft brown sugar
1 green pepper, seeded and chopped
2.5 mℓ (½ teaspoon) salt
2.5 mℓ (½ teaspoon) ground ginger
pinch of cayenne
2 garlic cloves, crushed
10 mℓ (2 teaspoons) dry mustard

Combine all ingredients in a large heatproof bowl. Cover with vented plastic wrap and microwave on Full Power for 20 minutes. Stir twice during cooking time. Pour into clean, dry jars and cool before sealing. Store in a cool, dry place.
Makes about 900 g (2 lb)

Green mango chutney

Full Power
37 minutes

1 kg (2¼ lb) peeled and chopped, slightly under-ripe mangos
3 – 4 garlic cloves, crushed
150 g (5 oz) sultanas, chopped
125 g (4 oz) dried apricots
400 g (14 oz) soft brown sugar
500 mℓ (16 fl oz) white vinegar
5 mℓ (1 teaspoon) ground ginger
5 mℓ (1 teaspoon) salt
10 mℓ (2 teaspoons) chopped chillies

Combine all ingredients in a very large heatproof bowl. Microwave on Full Power for 5 minutes, stir well. Microwave for a further 32 – 36 minutes, stirring every 5 minutes. The chutney should be syrupy in consistency. Leave to cool before spooning into clean, dry jars. Cover, label and store.
Makes about 1.5 kg (3 lb)

CITRUS FRUIT

To obtain all the juice from fresh citrus fruit, prick the skin lightly and warm fruit in the microwave on Full Power for 15 – 30 seconds. Double the time for fruits taken from the refrigerator.
See also Lemons and Oranges.

CLAMS

A clam is a large bivalve much prized in many parts of the world, especially the United States, which is famous for its clam bakes and clam chowder. Canned clams are more generally available.

Shortcut clam chowder

Full Power
20 minutes

2 x 400 g (14 oz) cans of tomato soup
250 mℓ (8 fl oz) hot water
400 g (14 oz) canned whole tomatoes, roughly chopped
200 g (7 oz) canned clams, minced
400 g (14 oz) canned mixed vegetables
30 mℓ (2 tablespoons) finely chopped onion
90 mℓ (3 fl oz) dry white wine

Combine tomato soup, water, tomatoes and juice and mix well. Stir in clams and liquid, and mixed vegetables with liquid and onion. Cover and microwave on Full Power for 18 – 20 minutes or until hot, stirring twice. Stir in dry white wine and serve.
Serves 6 – 8

COCOA

Cocoa is a product of the cacao bean, which is fermented, roasted, hulled and ground to produce a liquid high in fat content. To make cocoa, a proportion of the fat or cocoa butter is removed and the remaining liquid sets hard. It is then ground into a fine powder.

Cocoa needs to be sweetened before it becomes palatable. To make a hot drink using cocoa, it should be mixed to a paste with a little cold water or milk before adding to the hot liquid or it will become lumpy. Hot cocoa drinks can be quickly made in the microwave in the serving mug. To improve the flavour of cocoa, whisk it to a froth after it has simmered. Instant cocoa or drinking chocolate already contains sugar and mixes into hot milk or water easily. Cocoa powder is also used to flavour cakes, icing, biscuits and desserts. To substitute cocoa powder for melted chocolate in such recipes, use 45 ml (3 tablespoons) cocoa powder and 15 g (½ oz) butter for every 30 g (1 oz) chocolate.

Old-fashioned cocoa

Medium (50%)
3 minutes

60 mℓ (4 tablespoons) water
30 mℓ (2 tablespoons) caster sugar
15 mℓ (1 tablespoon) cocoa powder
185 mℓ (6 fl oz) milk
1 marshmallow

Combine water, sugar and cocoa powder in a large mug. Microwave on Medium (50%) for 2 minutes. Add milk, continue microwaving for 45 – 90 seconds. Top with the marshmallow.
Serves 1

Chocolate marshmallow sauce

Full Power
9 minutes

200 g (7 oz) sugar
185 mℓ (6 fl oz) water
20 large marshmallows
30 g (1 oz) cocoa powder, sifted
few drops of vanilla extract

Combine sugar and water in a large jug. Microwave on Full Power for 7 minutes. Stir through once or twice. Add marshmallows and microwave for 1½ minutes. Stir until completely melted. Add cocoa powder and vanilla extract and mix very well. Microwave for an additional 30 – 40 seconds if necessary. Set aside to cool, then beat sauce until thick, about 5 minutes. Serve warm.
Makes about 500 mℓ (16 fl oz)

COCONUT

The coconut is the fruit of the coconut palm which grows in many tropical and subtropical regions of the world. The shell, which protects the white, sweet, edible flesh, has three 'eyes'. Pierce two of these eyes and the coconut milk will be released. The fresh flesh may be eaten in chunks, or can be grated. Coconut may also be purchased as desiccated or shredded coconut. Small quantities of coconut are quickly toasted in the microwave.

To toast coconut, spread 45 g (1½ oz) desiccated coconut evenly on to a piece of kitchen paper. Microwave on Full Power for 5 – 6 minutes, stirring every minute.

Coconut cream

Full Power
3 minutes

Coconut cream or milk is sometimes needed in recipes especially in Indonesian cookery. Here is a recipe for a good instantly made substitute.

200 g (7 oz) desiccated coconut, or fresh coconut, grated
375 mℓ (12 fl oz) water
125 mℓ (4 fl oz) single cream

Place coconut in the bowl of a food processor, fitted with a metal blade. Combine water and cream in a 1-litre (1¾-pint) jug. Microwave on Full Power for 3 – 4 minutes until just boiling. With the machine running, slowly add boiling liquid to the coconut. Process for 1 minute, then leave mixture to cool for 5 minutes. Strain through a sieve lined with a double layer of cheesecloth. Press the coconut with a wooden spoon to extract the liquid. Then bring the corners of the cloth together and squeeze out any remaining liquid. Keep the liquid covered in the refrigerator and use as required.
Makes about 400 mℓ (13 fl oz)

COFFEE

Different varieties of coffee beans are sold according to the roast. The longer the beans are roasted, the stronger the brew. Coffee is certainly one of the world's favourite beverages and the flavour is widely used in cooking.
To make instant coffee, place 5 ml (1 teaspoon) coffee powder in a cup or mug and add 185 ml (6 fl oz) water. Microwave on Full Power until piping hot.

Filter coffee

Full Power

10 – 15 mℓ (2 – 3 teaspoons) finely ground coffee
185 mℓ (6 fl oz) water

Place coffee in a filter bag. Microwave water on Full Power until boiling. Pour over coffee and allow to filter. To keep warm, microwave cups or jug on Low (15%) for 3 – 5 minutes.
Makes 1 cup

Irish coffee

Full Power
1 minute

150 mℓ (5 fl oz) Irish whiskey
45 mℓ (3 tablespoons) soft brown sugar, or to taste
815 mℓ (26 fl oz) freshly made strong black coffee
150 mℓ (5 fl oz) whipping cream, whipped
cinnamon

Divide Irish whiskey and sugar between four Irish coffee glasses. Arrange glasses in a circle in microwave. Microwave on Full Power for 1 minute. Place a long-handled metal spoon in each glass and pour in hot coffee until glasses are three-quarters full. Stir to dissolve sugar. Carefully pour whipped cream over the back of a spoon so that it floats and does not sink into coffee mixture. Sprinkle with cinnamon and serve immediately. *Serves 4*

Variations
Leave out Irish whiskey and make the following:
Mexican Coffee: Add 150 mℓ (5 fl oz) Kahlua and sprinkle a little grated chocolate on top.
Café Brûlot: Microwave 150 mℓ (5 fl oz) brandy, 1 vanilla bean, 3 whole cloves, 1 small piece of orange rind and a small piece of cinnamon stick on Medium (50%) for 2 minutes, strain and use as above.
Jamaican Coffee: Add 150 mℓ (5 fl oz) Coco Rico or Crème de Cacao and top with a little grated chocolate.
French Coffee: Add 150 mℓ (5 fl oz) orange Curaçao.

Quick cappuccino

Full Power
7 minutes

750 mℓ (1¼ pints) freshly made coffee
125 mℓ (4 fl oz) single cream
cocoa powder

Pour coffee into a large jug. Microwave on Full Power for 6 minutes. Stir in cream. Microwave on Full Power for 1 minute. Pour half the coffee mixture into a blender and blend for 30 seconds or until foamy. Pour into two cups. Repeat the process with remaining coffee. Sprinkle a little cocoa powder on top of each.
Serves 4

Coffee bavarois

Full Power, Medium (50%)
7 minutes

600 mℓ (19 fl oz) milk
6 egg yolks
60 g (2 oz) caster sugar
45 mℓ (3 tablespoons) instant coffee powder
45 mℓ (3 tablespoons) boiling water
45 mℓ (3 tablespoons) coffee cream liqueur
few drops of vanilla extract
100 mℓ (3½ fl oz) water
30 mℓ (2 tablespoons) powdered gelatine
250 mℓ (8 fl oz) whipping cream

To decorate
75 mℓ (2½ fl oz) whipped cream
toasted almonds*

Pour milk into a 1-litre (1¾-pint) jug, microwave on Full Power until very hot, about 5 minutes. Beat yolks and sugar until pale in colour, pour on hot milk and beat to combine. Combine instant coffee and boiling water, stir to dissolve. Add to milk mixture and allow to cool. Then add coffee cream liqueur and vanilla extract. Pour water into a small jug, add gelatine, stir and stand for 3 minutes. Microwave on Medium (50%) for 2 minutes, stir into custard mixture. Beat cream until thick, but not stiff, fold into the thickening custard. Rinse a ring or jelly mould out with cold water, pour in the custard. Refrigerate until set, about 4 hours.

To unmould, dip mould into hot water, introduce an air bubble into the side of the mould using your thumb to pull bavarois away from the mould. Invert on to a glass plate. Decorate with swirls of cream and a few nuts.
Serves 6 – 8

COMPOTE

A simple, but satisfying dessert or breakfast dish of fresh, canned or dried fruit, simmered in a sugar syrup or fruit juice. One kind of fruit only, or a combination of fruits may be used. Serve hot or chilled.

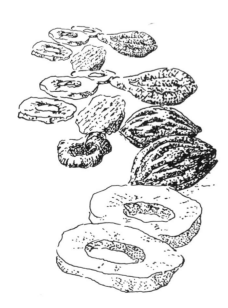

Swedish fruit soup

Full Power, Medium (50%)
42 minutes

1.5 litre (2¾ pints) white grape juice
350 g (12 oz) mixed dried fruit
150 g (5 oz) red currant jelly
45 g (1½ oz) sultanas
1 orange, thinly sliced
5 mℓ (1 teaspoon) finely grated lemon rind
2.5 mℓ (½ teaspoon) whole cloves
2 x 2.5-cm (1-inch) cinnamon sticks
45 g (1½ oz) quick-cooking tapioca
soured cream
soft brown sugar

Presoak a clay cooking pot according to manufacturer's instructions. Combine grape juice, dried fruit, jelly, sultanas, orange slices, lemon rind and spices in the pot. Cover and microwave on Full Power for 10 – 12 minutes. Stand for 10 minutes, then microwave on Medium (50%) for 30 minutes. Stir in tapioca and stand for 5 minutes. Discard cinnamon sticks and cloves if desired. To serve, spoon into individual bowls and top each with a dollop of soured cream and a sprinkling of brown sugar.
Serves 6 – 8

Note: If no clay pot is available, microwave ingredients in a casserole, covered, on High (70%) for 8 – 10 minutes, then stand for 10 minutes and microwave, covered, on Medium (50%) for 20 – 25 minutes before stirring in tapioca. Continue as above.

Apricot and cherry compote

Full Power
4 minutes

400 g (14 oz) canned cherries
12 fresh apricots, halved and stones removed
1 small piece of cinnamon stick
15 mℓ (1 tablespoon) Kirsch

To serve
1 quantity crème pâtissière* or 250 mℓ (8 fl oz) single cream
wafer biscuits

Drain cherries, place liquid in a bowl, add apricots and cinnamon. Cover and microwave on Full Power for 4 – 6 minutes, stirring once during cooking time. Stand for 10 minutes. Add Kirsch and cherries, stir to combine. Chill before serving. Serve plain, with crème anglaise or cream and add a wafer biscuit.
Serves 6

CONDENSED MILK

Caramelizing condensed milk takes only a few minutes in the microwave. Add a few drops of caramel essence and brown colouring to give a good caramel colour.

Caramelized condensed milk

Full Power, High (70%)
8 minutes

400 g (14 oz) canned condensed milk
few drops of caramel essence
few drops of brown colouring

Pour condensed milk into a very deep bowl (if the bowl is too small, the boiling condensed milk will run over the sides). Microwave for 4 minutes on Full Power and 4 minutes on High (70%). Leave to cool.

CONVENIENCE FOODS

Convenience foods take only minutes to prepare in the microwave and are a quick way to serve snacks or meals in a hurry. The chart above is a general guide for defrosting, heating or cooking many frozen or canned foods. As microwave cooking gains in popularity, so many manufacturers are including microwave instructions on convenience foods such as cake and pudding mixes, frozen and pre-cooked foods. For best results with such foods, follow the packet directions.

Tips for microwaving convenience foods

☐ Be sure foods are really heated through before serving. Steam or bubbling around the edges may not mean food is heated through. The centre of the bottom of the container will be warm to the touch when food is completely heated.

☐ Most foods are covered when heating or reheating. Cover appetizers cooked with a sauce or main dishes with waxed paper or vented plastic wrap. Sandwiches to be defrosted and warmed can be covered with kitchen paper. Soups may be covered with waxed paper to prevent spattering.

☐ Do not cover baked foods when thawing or warming as they may become soggy.

☐ For best results, remove casseroles, 'frozen dinners' or baked foods from foil trays before microwaving. Place those foods in a casserole or on a plate.

☐ Some foods, such as sausage rolls or double crust pies and pastries can be defrosted in the microwave, but give much better results if heated in a conventional oven.

COOKING TIMES

Several factors influence the timing and results of foods cooked in the microwave. Understanding these factors and their effects on foods will help you make the most of your appliance.

All recipes in this book have been tested in microwave ovens with an output of 600 to 650 watts. As a general rule, if you have a 500 watt microwave oven, add approximately 20 seconds to each minute of cooking time. If you have a 700 watt microwave, decrease the cooking time by 10 – 15 seconds per minute. Household current

MICROWAVE CHART FOR CONVENIENCE FOODS

	QUANTITY	PREPARATION	DEFROST TIME	COOKING TIME	POWER LEVEL	METHOD
CANNED FOODS						
Soup	400 g (14 oz)	Place in bowl, add liquid as directed	–	5 – 6 minutes	Full Power	Cover, stir frequently
Pasta in sauce	400 g (14 oz)	Place in dish	–	3 – 4 minutes	Full Power	Cover, stir at least once
Baked beans	400 g (14 oz)	Place in dish	–	3 – 4 minutes	Full Power	Cover, stir at least once
Peas or other small vegetables	400 g (14 oz)	Place in dish	–	3 – 4 minutes	Full Power	Cover, stir gently once
Asparagus spears or other large vegetables	400 g (14 oz)	Place in dish	–	4 – 5 minutes	Full Power	Cover, stir once
Meat in sauce	400 g (14 oz)	Place in dish	–	5 – 6 minutes	Full Power	Cover, stir once
Sauces or gravy	400 g (14 oz)	Place in bowl	–	3 – 4 minutes	Full Power	Cover, stir occasionally
Custard or pudding	approx 400 g (14 oz)	Place in bowl	–	3 – 4 minutes	Full Power	Cover, stir once
Fruits, such as fruit cocktail or sliced peaches	400 g (14 oz)	Place in bowl	–	4 – 5 minutes	Full Power	Cover, stir once
FROZEN FOODS						
Individual meat pies	3	Remove foil	1½ – 2 minutes	3 – 3½ minutes	Full Power	Place on kitchen paper, carefully turn over halfway through heating
Sausage rolls or pastry snacks	6 – 8	Place on kitchen paper	2 minutes, stand 3 minutes	2 – 3 minutes	Full Power	Pastry may become soggy so defrost in microwave and heat conventionally for best results
Quiche	20 – 22.5-cm (8 – 9-inch)	Remove from foil, place on plate	5 minutes, stand 5 minutes	6 – 8 minutes	Full Power	Cover with waxed paper
Pizza	approx 225 g (8 oz)	Place on paper plate or kitchen paper	–	4 – 5 minutes	Full Power	Cover with waxed paper to prevent spattering
Meat casserole	approx 500 g (18 oz)	Remove from foil, place in dish	4 minutes, stand 3 minutes, defrost 3 minutes	10 – 12 minutes	Full Power	Cover with waxed paper, stir if possible
'Boil in bag' fish	approx 150 g (5 oz)	Slit top of bag, place in bowl	4 – 6 minutes	2 – 3 minutes	Full Power	Shake contents of bag before serving

sometimes varies during peak periods of use. Always check food at the minimum cooking time to see if it is done, then add more time if necessary. If you are uncertain about the household current, check the timing (see below) and make adjustments to the recipe if necessary.

To check timing, pour 250 ml (8 fl oz) iced water into a glass measuring jug. Place in the microwave and microwave on Full Power until the water reaches a good boil. Time the action and if your oven takes 3¼ – 3¾ minutes, the recipes in this book should be correct for you.

Factors affecting cooking times
☐ **Size of piece** Small pieces of food cook faster than larger ones. When cooking different food together, as in a casserole, pieces should be of similar size so all ingredients will be cooked at the same time.
☐ **Shape of food** When foods are uneven in shape, the thin portions will cook more quickly than the thicker ones. Arrange foods, such as chicken portions, chops or

courgettes with the thicker parts to the outside of the cooking dish.
☐ **Density** Heavy foods, like fruit cake or potatoes, take longer to microwave than light, airy ones. Dense foods also hold heat longer, and standing time is necessary so food can continue cooking after it has been taken out of the microwave.
☐ **Quantity of food** Small amounts cook faster than large ones. When doubling the quantity of food it is necessary to increase the cooking time by a third to a half, but always check if food is ready after the shortest estimated time. When reducing the

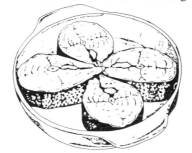

amount of food by half, reduce cooking time by less than half.
☐ **Starting temperature of food** Foods taken directly from the refrigerator take longer to cook than those at room temperature.
☐ **Height of food in oven** Areas of food that are closest to the energy source cook faster, so it is important to turn or shield foods which are higher than 10 – 12.5-cm (4 – 5 inch).
☐ **Composition of food** Foods with a high water, fat or sugar content can be overcooked in the microwave because these substances attract microwave energy. Foods such as cheese, eggs, cream and mushrooms should be cooked for the minimum amount of time and watched closely during cooking.
☐ **Shape of container** Microwaves penetrate foods from the top, bottom and sides, so round containers or ring shapes are best, as they allow food to cook evenly. Containers with square or rectangular shapes allow corners to overcook.

COQUILLES ST JACQUES
The French name for a dish in which scallops are the main ingredient.

Coquilles St Jacques

Full Power, Medium (50%)
14 minutes

30 g (1 oz) unsalted butter
1 onion, finely chopped
500 g (18 oz) scallops
75 mℓ (2½ fl oz) dry white wine
salt and white pepper
30 g (1 oz) plain flour
125 mℓ (4 fl oz) single cream
15 mℓ (1 tablespoon) chopped dill
45 mℓ (3 tablespoons) grated Parmesan
 cheese

To garnish
lemon wedges
fresh dill

Microwave butter in a casserole on Full Power for 45 seconds to melt. Add onion, stir to coat and microwave for 2 minutes. Stir in scallops, wine, salt and pepper. Microwave on Medium (50%) for 6 – 7 minutes, stirring twice until scallops are just done. Drain scallops, reserving liquid, and keep warm. Mix 45 mℓ (3 tablespoons) of the scallop liquid into flour to make a paste, then stir in remaining liquid. Blend in cream and dill. Microwave on Full Power for 3 minutes, or until thickened, stirring after 2 minutes. Stir well until mixture is smooth.

 Divide scallops evenly among individual shells or ramekins. Whisk sauce and spoon over the scallops. Sprinkle with cheese and microwave on Medium (50%) for 1 minute to melt. Garnish with lemon wedges and fresh dill. Serve immediately.
Serves 6

CORNFLOUR
A fine white starch extracted from maize kernels and used chiefly as a thickening agent in Chinese cookery, in custards and other desserts. It is also used to lighten the texture of cakes, biscuits and pastry. Cornflour differs from ordinary flour in that it contains no gluten, making it less likely to form lumps and making it a smoother thickener. A little cornflour added to an egg custard will prevent it from curdling. When mixed into a liquid and heated, cornflour becomes transparent and glossy, so it is an ideal thickener for stewed fruits and for making glazes. Cornflour mixtures need little attention to cook perfectly in the microwave.

 To substitute cornflour as a thickening agent instead of flour, use 7.5 ml (1½ teaspoons) cornflour for every 15 ml (1 tablespoon) plain flour needed in the recipe.

To thicken glazes or sauces
Avoid lumps by mixing the cornflour with sugar or salt before gradually adding the cold liquid. In recipes without sugar, make a paste of cornflour and some of the cold liquid given in the recipe. Introduce this paste gradually into the remaining liquid which has been heated, but is not boiling. When the cornflour is mixed into a cold liquid, microwave on High (70%) for 3 – 4 minutes, or until the mixture is thickened, stirring every minute. For hot liquids, stir mixture very well, then microwave for 1 – 2 minutes, stirring frequently.

COURGETTES
Courgettes, young members of the marrow family, are called 'zucchini' in Italy. They are usually slender, about 10 – 12.5 cm (4 – 5 inch) in length and have a delicate flavour and texture. When cooked, they should have a slightly bitter taste. Most familiar varieties are dark green in colour, but bright yellow ones are also sometimes available. Courgettes cook quickly in the microwave, and in just a few minutes they are ready to serve. Cook them at the last minute and do not keep them waiting as they continue to soften after microwaving. Serve with a sprinkling of herbs such as parsley and basil, and a little cream or butter.

To microwave sliced courgettes
Top and tail 500 g (18 oz) courgettes, slice and place in a casserole. Sprinkle with 30 ml (2 tablespoons) water or stock, cover and microwave on Full Power for 6 – 8 minutes, stirring courgettes halfway through cooking time. A roasting bag could also be used.

To microwave whole courgettes
Top and tail 500 g courgettes and arrange in a round dish so that the thin ends point towards the middle. Cover with vented plastic wrap and microwave on Full Power for 6 – 8 minutes. Stand for 1 – 2 minutes before serving.

Courgette nut bread

High (70%)
10 – 12 minutes

30 g (1 oz) fine Marie biscuit crumbs
150 g (5 oz) cake flour
275 g (10 oz) caster sugar
225 g (8 oz) courgettes, shredded
75 mℓ (2½ fl oz) water
75 g (2½ oz) butter or margarine
2 eggs
few drops of vanilla extract
5 mℓ (1 teaspoon) bicarbonate of soda
2.5 mℓ (½ teaspoon) salt
2.5 mℓ (½ teaspoon) cinnamon
pinch of ground cloves
pinch of baking powder
60 g (2 oz) nuts, such as walnuts or pecans,
 coarsely chopped
30 g (1 oz) raisins

Grease microwave mould and coat with Marie biscuit crumbs. Mix remaining ingredients, except nuts and raisins, and beat until smooth. Add nuts and raisins and turn into the prepared dish. Cover with greased wax paper and microwave on High (70%) for 6 minutes. Check, then microwave for 4 – 6 minutes longer, or until top of bread is dry and springs back to the touch. Cool 10 minutes in the dish, then turn out and cool completely before slicing.
Makes 1 ring loaf

Courgette soup

Full Power
19 minutes

30 g (1 oz) butter
1 onion, chopped
500 g (18 oz) courgettes, peeled and chopped
15 mℓ (1 tablespoon) plain flour
750 mℓ (1¼ pints) chicken stock
salt and black pepper
250 mℓ (8 fl oz) single cream, soured cream or
 yoghurt
15 mℓ (1 tablespoon) dry sherry
10 mℓ (2 teaspoons) chopped fresh dill

To garnish
1 grated courgette
lemon juice
30 mℓ (2 tablespoons) finely chopped chives
dill sprigs

Microwave butter in a large bowl or casserole on Full Power for 1 minute. Add onion and stir to combine. Microwave for 4 minutes, stirring at least once during the cooking time. Add courgettes and flour, stir to combine. Microwave for 2 minutes. Pour in stock and season lightly. Cover and microwave for 12 minutes, stirring occasionaly. Pour soup into a blender, blend until smooth. Stir in cream, sherry and dill.

 To serve hot, microwave for 4 – 6 minutes until piping hot. Ladle into warm soup bowls. Toss grated courgette in a little lemon juice, spoon a little into each bowl, sprinkle with a few chives and add a dill sprig. Serve immediately.
Serves 6

Note: This soup may also be served cold. After blending, chill well, spoon into soup cups and garnish.

Courgettes and tomato sauce

Full Power
18 minutes

6 – 8 courgettes
10 mℓ (2 teaspoons) salt
15 g (½ oz) butter
black pepper

Tomato sauce
15 g (½ oz) butter
1 small onion, roughly chopped
1 garlic clove, roughly chopped
400 g (14 oz) canned tomatoes
salt and black pepper
pinch of sugar
pinch of oregano

Grate courgettes along the length, to have the shreds as long as possible. Place grated courgette and salt in a colander, stand for 20 minutes. Rinse well and dry.

Meanwhile make the sauce. Place all the ingredients in a large bowl and microwave on Full Power for 12 – 14 minutes, stirring at least twice during cooking time. Purée in a blender and strain. Reheat for 3 minutes, stir and keep warm.

To cook the courgettes, microwave butter for 45 seconds in a shallow casserole, add courgettes and toss to combine. Microwave uncovered for 2 – 3 minutes, stirring every 30 seconds. Add a little pepper and stand for 2 – 3 minutes. Turn into a vegetable dish.

To serve, place a spoonful of courgette on to a plate, spoon a little tomato sauce over half the courgette. The crisp courgette blends extremely well with the smooth tomato sauce, and the colour combination is good too.
Serves 4 – 6

COURT BOUILLON
A lightly flavoured combination of white wine, vegetables, herbs and a little lemon juice or vinegar, used for poaching fish and shellfish. Make a court bouillon quickly, without the usual strong smell, in the microwave.

Court bouillon

Full Power, Medium (50%)
11 minutes

1 small onion, quartered
100 mℓ (3½ fl oz) boiling water
750 mℓ (1¼ pints) water
250 mℓ (8 fl oz) white wine
30 mℓ (2 tablespoons) lemon juice
5 mℓ (1 teaspoon) salt
1 small bay leaf
1 carrot, sliced
1 celery stick, roughly chopped
4 parsley sprigs
3 – 4 sprigs of fresh herbs, such as tarragon, thyme, marjoram or dill
12 black peppercorns
small piece of mace
small quantity of fish bones (optional)

Place the onion in a colander and pour boiling water over it to remove the strong flavour. Place onion and all the remaining ingredients into a 2-litre (3½-pint) bowl or microwave dish and cover. Microwave on Full Power for 6 minutes, reduce power level to Medium (50%) and microwave for 5 minutes more. Strain and use.
Makes about 1 litre (1¾ pints)

COUSCOUS
This granular cereal, made from semolina, flour and salt, originates from North Africa. It may be served as an accompaniment to a main dish, as part of a fragrant casserole or combined with fruit, flavouring and cream as a dessert. Traditionally couscous is cooked in a steamer, but this microwave method works well and takes a fraction of the time.

Couscous

Full Power
4 minutes

250 mℓ (8 fl oz) water
45 mℓ (3 tablespoons) oil
2.5 mℓ (½ teaspoon) salt
250 g (9 oz) couscous

Combine water, oil and salt in a large bowl. Microwave on Full Power for 2 – 3 minutes, until boiling. Stir in the couscous, microwave for 1½ minutes, stirring twice during cooking time. Fluff with a fork, cover with plastic wrap and stand for 5 minutes. Use as required.
Makes about 450 g (1 lb)

COVERINGS AND WRAPPINGS
In conventional cooking, many foods are covered to retain moisture and decrease cooking time. The same techniques are used in microwave cooking, but the application may be slightly different. Follow the recipe directions for covering food. If no mention is made of covering, microwave the food uncovered.

Types of coverings
☐ **Plastic wrap or clingfilm** A tight cover of plastic wrap or clingfilm holds in steam as well as heat. Vent the wrap by turning back one corner or making two slits to prevent 'ballooning' during cooking. The lid of a dish can be used instead of plastic wrap when microwaving vegetables, casseroles and meats that require moisture. Take care when removing plastic wrap that you do not get scalded by the steam.
☐ **Waxed or greaseproof paper** A loose cover of waxed or greaseproof paper holds in heat without steaming the food. It also prevents spattering. Use it to cover foods such as fruits, hamburgers, chicken, bacon or roasts where steam is not needed to tenderize the food.

☐ **Roasting bags** hold in steam and help tenderize meat or poultry. Do not use a metal or foil strip to seal the bag as this can cause arcing, and the bag may melt. Fasten with string or an elastic band and make two slashes to prevent 'ballooning' during cooking.
☐ **Kitchen paper** allows steam to escape, promotes even heating and prevents spattering. It also absorbs excess moisture from foods. Use a sheet of paper towels to absorb moisture when drying herbs or freshening chips, pretzels or savoury biscuits. Porous kitchen paper can be used to wrap such foods as hamburgers or hot dogs in rolls, bread rolls or pastries for heating. Use damp kitchen paper to steam fish fillets or scallops, or to soften crêpes in a few seconds.

CRAB
This shellfish is highly valued for its sweet, succulent flesh and though it is often served cold with salads, it is delicious in hot dishes too. Crab is available whole, frozen and canned. Crab sticks are ready-cooked and have a delicious crab flavour, although they are not true crab meat.

To defrost frozen crab
Crab sticks Place 175 g (6 oz) crab sticks in a casserole, cover and microwave on Defrost (30%) for 4 – 5 minutes. Separate during defrosting and allow to stand for 1 – 2 minutes before using.
Crab meat Place 175 g (6 oz) crab meat in a casserole, cover and microwave on Defrost (30%) for 6 – 7 minutes.
Whole crab Place crab in a suitable container, cover and microwave on Defrost (30%) for 12 – 14 minutes per 500 g (18 oz). Stand for 2 – 3 minutes.

To microwave crab
Arrange 500 g (18 oz) thawed crab meat in a round casserole or baking dish. Add 30 ml (2 tablespoons) water or a mixture of water and white wine and cover with vented plastic wrap. Microwave on Full Power for 5 – 6 minutes. The outer flesh should be white and opaque and the centre still translucent. The centre will cook during standing time. Do not overcook, as the flesh will become tough and dry.

Crab and pasta bake

Full Power
14 minutes

90 g (3 oz) butter
1 onion, chopped
45 mℓ (3 tablespoons) plain flour
500 mℓ (16 fl oz) milk
45 mℓ (3 tablespoons) capers, chopped
10 mℓ (2 teaspoons) white vinegar
5 mℓ (1 teaspoon) lemon juice
200 g (7 oz) canned crab meat
salt and black pepper
250 g (9 oz) pasta shapes, cooked
60 mℓ (4 tablespoons) dried breadcrumbs
90 g (3 oz) Gruyère cheese, grated

Microwave butter in a casserole dish for 1½ minutes on Full Power. Add onion and microwave 3 minutes. Stir, then mix in flour and gradually add milk. Microwave 4 – 5 minutes, stirring every minute until smooth and thick. Stir in capers, vinegar, lemon juice and crab. Season well. Fold cooked pasta into crab sauce and place mixture in a deep casserole. Sprinkle with breadcrumbs, then grated cheese. Microwave for 3 – 4 minutes to heat through. If desired, brown under a hot grill before serving.
Serves 4

Savoury crab crêpes

Full Power, Low (15%)
22 minutes

60 g (2 oz) butter
½ onion, chopped
½ green pepper, chopped
1 celery stick, thinly sliced
150 g (5 oz) low-fat soft cheese
250 mℓ (8 fl oz) basic white sauce*
350 g (12 oz) cooked crab* or crab sticks
150 g (5 oz) olives, chopped
250 g (9 oz) water chestnuts, sliced
12 crêpes*

Cheese topping
30 g (1 oz) grated Parmesan cheese
60 mℓ (4 tablespoons) white wine
5 mℓ (1 teaspoon) tarragon
250 mℓ (8 fl oz) basic white sauce*
250 mℓ (8 fl oz) soured cream

To garnish
grated Parmesan cheese
chopped chives

Place butter in a deep 3-litre (5-pint) casserole and microwave on Full Power for 1 minute to melt. Add onion, green pepper and celery and microwave for 4 – 5 minutes, or until vegetables are tender. Add low-fat soft cheese and microwave on Low (15%) for 1½ – 2 minutes to soften. Stir, then mix in white sauce. Add flaked or diced crab meat, olives and water chestnuts. Mix well. Spoon about 75 g (2½ oz) of the mixture down the centre of each crêpe and roll up. Place, seam-side down, in a baking dish. Cover with vented plastic wrap and microwave on Full Power for 8 – 10 minutes or until heated through.

For the topping, mix cheese with wine, tarragon, white sauce and soured cream. Spread over crêpes, cover and microwave for 3 – 4 minutes to heat through. Garnish with Parmesan cheese and chopped chives.
Serves 6 – 8

CRANBERRY SAUCE
A burgundy red, tart sauce traditionally served with turkey, but is excellent with pork and veal as well. For an unusual touch serve this sauce with Crumbed Camembert (page 73).

Cranberry orange sauce

High (70%)
6 minutes

400 g (14 oz) canned cranberry sauce
90 mℓ (3 fl oz) orange juice
45 mℓ (3 tablespoons) vinegar
45 mℓ (3 tablespoons) Crème de Cassis
60 g (2 oz) sultanas
15 mℓ (1 tablespoon) grated orange rind
1 orange, cut in skinless segments
generous pinch of cinnamon
pinch of ground cloves

Combine all ingredients in a deep, 2-litre (3½-pints) casserole. Cover with waxed paper and microwave on High (70%) for 5 – 6 minutes or until heated through. Stir once or twice during cooking. Serve warm or cold.
Makes about 600 mℓ (19 fl oz)

CRAYFISH
Crayfish is a delicacy much sought after around the world. Like all seafoods, crayfish are at their best fresh; however, they may be kept frozen for a few months.

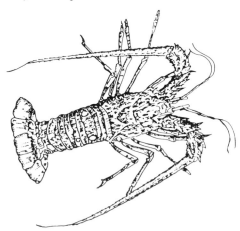

Whole crayfish or crayfish tails microwave particularly well as very little liquid is used, but care must be taken not to overcook them or they will lose their succulence and flavour.

To microwave whole crayfish
Do not try to cook more than two crayfish at a time in the microwave. Cook as for crayfish tails (below) using the same cooking time for two whole crayfish as for four tails.

Crayfish thermidor

Full Power
8 minutes

4 cooked crayfish tails*
30 g (1 oz) butter
1 bunch spring onions, chopped (include some of the green portion)
100 mℓ (3½ fl oz) white wine
300 mℓ (½ pint) Béchamel sauce*
100 mℓ (3½ fl oz) single cream
5 mℓ (1 teaspoon) dry mustard
cayenne
salt and black pepper
90 g (3 oz) Gruyère cheese, grated
30 mℓ (2 tablespoons) grated Parmesan cheese
mashed potato

Place butter in a bowl, microwave on Full Power for 1 minute. Add spring onion, toss to coat with butter and microwave for 2 minutes. Add wine and microwave for 5 minutes to reduce. Pour in Béchamel and cream, beat well to combine, add seasonings and half the Gruyère. Cut crayfish flesh into bite-size pieces, add to sauce. Divide the mixture between the crayfish shells. Pipe four rows of mashed potato on to a large ovenproof serving platter. Stand the crayfish on the potato. Combine remaining Gruyère with Parmesan, sprinkle generously on top of the crayfish mixture. Brown under a conventional grill. Serve immediately.
Serves 4

Steamed crayfish tails

High (70%)
12 minutes

4 crayfish tails, thawed
45 mℓ (3 tablespoons) water
30 mℓ (2 tablespoons) white wine
salt
pinch of thyme

Arrange tails in a circle in a shallow container, add remaining ingredients and cover with vented plastic wrap. Microwave on High (70%) for 12 – 14 minutes, depending on the size of the tails. Flesh should be white in colour and tender. Stand for 2 minutes. Using a pair of scissors cut down both sides of the soft underside and peel away. Starting at the thick end, peel flesh out of shell. Use as required.
Serves 4

Crayfish in cream

Medium (50%)
5 minutes

4 cooked crayfish tails*

Sauce
1 quantity reduced cream*
5 mℓ (1 teaspoon) paprika
black pepper
15 mℓ (1 tablespoon) brandy
10 mℓ (2 teaspoons) lemon juice
parsley sprigs

Whisk the remaining sauce ingredients into reduced cream, microwave on Medium (50%) for 1 – 2 minutes until very hot. Divide sauce between four shallow dishes adding one prepared tail to each. Cover with vented plastic wrap and microwave for 4 minutes. Garnish with sprigs of parsley.
Serves 4 as a starter

CREAM
Cream, the fatty part of fresh milk, is used in a wide variety of dishes to give added richness and smoothness. Cream can be added to sauces and soups, poured over fruits and desserts, whipped for soufflés and puddings, or reduced to make a thick, rich base for a cream sauce.

Reduced cream

Full Power, Medium (50%)
10 minutes

Place 250 mℓ (8 fl oz) cream in a deep 1.5-litre (2¾-pints) casserole. Microwave on Full Power for 2 minutes. Stir and microwave for a further 2 minutes. Stir and reduce power to Medium (50%) and microwave for 6 – 8 minutes, stirring every 2 minutes. Various flavourings can be added to the reduced cream, such as wine, lemon juice, salt and pepper, grated cheese, savoury butter or mustard. This makes a rich, smooth sauce to serve with vegetables, meat or fish, depending on the flavourings.
Makes about 200 mℓ (6½ fl oz)

Orange crème caramel

Full Power, Defrost (30%)
19 minutes

This variation looks exotic, and has an interesting flavour.

½ quantity sugar caramel*
4 eggs
2 egg yolks
30 g (1 oz) caster sugar
15 mℓ (1 tablespoon) Van der Hum or orange Curaçao
2.5 mℓ (½ teaspoon) finely grated orange rind
595 mℓ (19 fl oz) milk
caramelized orange slices*

Pour the hot caramel into a 22.5-cm (9-inch) ring mould, coat base with the caramel and allow to cool. Whisk eggs, egg yolks and sugar lightly, add liqueur and orange rind, whisk again. Pour milk into a 1-litre (1¾-pints) measuring jug, microwave on Full Power for 3 minutes, pour on to egg mixture and whisk to combine. Strain into caramel-lined mould. Cover with vented plastic wrap, stand in a container with 1.5-cm (¾-inch) water, microwave on Defrost (30%) for 16 – 18 minutes. The custard is cooked when the outside is firm and the centre still slightly wobbly. Cool, then chill in the refrigerator for at least 6 hours. To serve, place a plate with a shallow lip on top of the ring mould, invert and the custard will slide out. Arrange caramelized orange slices around the edge of the plate.
Serves 6

Crème brûlée

Full Power, Defrost (30%)
11 minutes

A rich, creamy French dessert with a hard, caramelized sugar topping, literally 'burnt cream'. In the microwave, the custard will cook to a delicate texture without curdling, but you will need a conventional grill to brown the topping.

500 mℓ (16 fl oz) single cream
30 mℓ (2 tablespoons) caster sugar
6 egg yolks
few drops of vanilla extract
3 – 4 bananas, sliced
45 mℓ (3 tablespoons) whisky
100 g (3½ oz) caster white sugar
45 g (1½ oz) soft brown sugar

Pour the cream into a jug and add sugar. Microwave on Full Power for 3 minutes. Stir well to make sure the sugar has dissolved. Beat yolks until fluffy and pale in colour. Add vanilla extract and hot cream. Beat to combine. Arrange a few slices of banana in the bottom of six individual serving dishes, sprinkle with whisky. Divide the hot cream mixture between the six dishes. Cover and arrange in a circle in the microwave. Cook on Defrost (30%) for 7 – 8 minutes. Delicate food such as custard continues to cook for some time after being microwaved. To test that it is ready, shake the custard carefully. The inside should quiver like jelly. Cool, then chill.
Combine the white and brown sugars. Divide between the six dishes and sprinkle evenly on top of each custard. Place custards on a baking sheet and grill conventionally for a few minutes, turning each custard as the top starts to caramelize. When deep golden brown, remove from the oven and chill once more. Decorate with a few slices of banana.
Serves 6

CRÈME PÂTISSIÈRE
This classic creamy custard, used as a filling for cakes and pastries, is quickly made in the microwave. For fruit tartlets,

spoon a thick layer of crème pâtissière into small baked pastry cases. Arrange cooked or canned fruit on top, thicken liquid with cornflour and spoon over fruit to glaze.

Crème Pâtissière

Full Power
2 minutes

45 mℓ (3 tablespoons) plain flour
60 g (2 oz) caster sugar
250 mℓ (8 fl oz) milk
1 vanilla bean or few drops of vanilla extract
3 egg yolks
15 g (½ oz) softened butter
125 mℓ (4 fl oz) whipping cream, whipped

Mix flour and sugar in a 1-litre (1¾-pint) jug, add milk and vanilla, whisk to combine. Microwave on Full Power for 2 – 3 minutes until boiling. Whisk every 30 seconds during cooking time. Remove vanilla bean (if used). Beat yolks well, pour on boiling mixture, whisk until smooth, add butter and whisk again. Cut a piece of greaseproof paper large enough to cover the mixture, place paper directly on top of mixture and allow to cool to room temperature. Fold in whipped cream and use as required. For variation add a little liqueur to flavour or add almond essence instead of vanilla extract.
Makes about 300 mℓ (½ pint)

CRÊPES
Crêpe is the French name for a superb, light pancake made from a thin batter. Although they cannot be cooked in a microwave, frozen crêpes can be succesfully thawed and reheated. Serve crêpes with a sprinkling of cinnamon sugar, or for a main dish, fold or roll them around a savoury filling (*see Savoury Crab Crêpes page 70*). Keep a stack of crêpes handy in the freezer for quick meals and use the microwave to reheat them and to make various fillings or sauces.

To freeze crêpes, stack in groups of ten with waxed paper in between. Wrap well and freeze.
To thaw crêpes, lift off a stack of ten, place on a plate, cover with plastic wrap and microwave on Defrost (30%) for 4 minutes. Use as required.

Basic crêpes

375 mℓ (12 fl oz) milk
3 eggs
200 g (7 oz) plain cake flour
30 g (1 oz) butter or margarine, melted

Place all ingredients in a food processor or blender. Cover and blend for 20 – 30 seconds. Scrape down sides of container and blend 5 seconds more. Chill batter for at least 1 hour, then cook on an electric crêpe pan or in a suitable frying pan.
Makes about 20 crêpes

Note: To make sweet crêpes, add 30 mℓ (2 tablespoons) icing sugar to the basic ingredients.
For thicker crêpes, decrease milk to 325 mℓ (10½ fl oz) and cook in a suitable pan.

Crêpes with cherry sauce

Full Power
11 minutes

250 mℓ (8 fl oz) natural yoghurt
150 g (5 oz) caster sugar
2.5 mℓ (½ teaspoon) cinnamon
12 crêpes*
30 mℓ (2 tablespoons) cornflour
250 mℓ (8 fl oz) loganberry juice
400 g (14 oz) canned red cherries, stoned
5 mℓ (1 teaspoon) grated lemon rind
few drops of vanilla extract
30 mℓ (2 tablespoons) brandy

Combine yoghurt, 100 g (3½ oz) of the sugar and the cinnamon, mixing well. Spread mixture on the crêpes and roll up. Place crêpes in two baking dishes.
　In a deep glass bowl, combine remaining sugar and cornflour. Stir in loganberry juice, cherries with liquid, and lemon rind. Microwave on Full Power until thickened and bubbly, 5 – 7 minutes, stirring after each minute. Stir in vanilla and brandy. Spoon sauce over crêpes in dishes. Microwave, covered for about 3 minutes, or until crêpes are hot. Repeat with remaining dish.
Serves 6

CROISSANTS
These flaky, buttery crescent-shaped rolls are quite unsuitable for cooking or reheating in the microwave as they are too dry and crisp in texture.

CROÛTONS
Croûtons are small cubes of bread that have been crisply fried in oil or butter. They are used to garnish soups, vegetables or salads. Crisp, golden croûtons can be made in the microwave.

Croûtons

Full Power
5 minutes

60 g (2 oz) butter
4 slices of bread, cut into small cubes

Place butter in a large shallow baking dish. Microwave on Full Power for 1 minute. Stir in bread cubes and microwave for 4 – 6 minutes. Stand croûtons for 5 minutes to harden completely before using. Store in an air-tight container.
Makes about 125 g (4 oz)

Variations
Garlic Croûtons: Microwave 1 sliced garlic clove in the melted butter for 45 seconds. Remove garlic before adding bread cubes.

Herbed Croûtons: Add 3 – 5 mℓ (½ – 1 teaspoon) dried herbs along with the bread cubes.
Cheese Croûtons: Add 45 mℓ (3 tablespoons) grated Parmesan cheese immediately after microwaving, but before standing time.

CRUMB CRUSTS
Crumb crusts are excellent for microwave use. Pastry does not brown in the microwave, but biscuit crumbs have a colour of their own and need no further browning. Use precooked fillings or fillings that need little cooking.

Basic crumb crust

Full Power
3 minutes

60 g (2 oz) butter
100 g (3½ oz) Marie biscuits, crumbled
30 mℓ (2 tablespoons) soft brown sugar

Microwave butter in a 22.5-cm (9-inch) pie dish on Full Power for 45 – 60 seconds. Add crumbs and brown sugar and mix well. Gently press mixture into base and sides of the dish and microwave for 1 – 1½ minutes. Cool before using.
Makes 1 x 22.5-cm (9-inch) crust

Variations
Nutty Crust: Proceed as for basic recipe, adding 60 g (2 oz) chopped nuts and 30 mℓ (2 tablespoons) single cream to the crumbs.
Spicy Crust: Use 100 g (3½ oz) ginger biscuit crumbs. Add 2.5 mℓ (½ teaspoon) cinnamon and 30 mℓ (2 tablespoons) single cream. Proceed as for basic recipe.
Chocolate Crust: Use 100 g (3½ oz) crumbled chocolate digestive biscuits, and add 30 mℓ (2 tablespoons) single cream. Proceed as for basic recipe.

Savoury crumb crust

Full Power
1 minute

200 g (7 oz) light savoury biscuits
75 g (2½ oz) butter or margarine

Crush biscuits in a food processor or blender. Place butter in a small jug, microwave on Full Power for 1 – 2 minutes until completely melted. Add biscuit crumbs, stir to combine. Use to line 22.5 – 25-cm (9 – 10-inch) pie plate.
Makes 1 x 22.5 – 25-cm (9 – 10-inch) pie crust

CRUMBED PORTIONS
Crumbed portions of raw or cooked chicken, minced beef and fish make wonderful quick meals in the microwave. As the portions are not fried golden brown, the crumb coating must be made up from interesting, tasty ingredients. These coatings give microwaved food an attractive appearance, flavour and variety.

Crumbed chicken portions

Full Power, Medium (50%)
22 minutes

10 chicken drumsticks or assorted portions

Parmesan crumb coating
60 g (2 oz) dried breadcrumbs
60 mℓ (4 tablespoons) grated Parmesan cheese
10 mℓ (2 teaspoons) very finely chopped chives
generous pinch of chicken seasoning
black pepper
20 mℓ (4 teaspoons) chopped parsley

Dip
1 egg
30 mℓ (2 tablespoons) milk

Dry chicken drumsticks or portions with kitchen paper. Mix the ingredients for coating on a flat plate. Combine ingredients for dip in a shallow bowl. Dip chicken portions into liquid, then into coating. Press coating on to chicken. Arrange chicken on a bacon rack or a round plate, making sure the meatiest sections are towards the outside. Microwave, uncovered, on Full Power for 10 minutes. Turn chicken portions to ensure each one is evenly cooked. Microwave on Medium (50%) for a further 8 – 12 minutes, depending on the thickness of the portions.
Serves 4 – 6

Variations
Savoury biscuit coating
100 g (3½ oz) biscuits, crushed
2.5 mℓ (½ teaspoon) paprika
pinch of thyme
black pepper

Dip
15 mℓ (1 tablespoon) lemon juice
1 egg

Crispy coating
45 – 60 g (1½ – 2 oz) crushed tomato-flavoured potato crisps
30 mℓ (2 tablespoons) grated Parmesan cheese
Dip
45 g (1½ oz) butter, melted

Chicken croquettes

Full Power, High (70%)
11 minutes

60 g (2 oz) margarine
15 mℓ (1 tablespoon) chopped onion
100 g (3½ oz) mushrooms, finely choppped
2 celery sticks, finely chopped
30 g (1 oz) plain flour
150 mℓ (5 fl oz) stock or milk
salt and black pepper
350 g (12 oz) minced cooked chicken

Coating
45 g (2½ oz) margarine
30 g (1 oz) cornflake crumbs
30 mℓ (2 tablespoons) grated Parmesan
  cheese
2.5 mℓ (½ teaspoon) marjoram

Place margarine in a 1-litre (1¾-pint) jug, microwave on Full Power for 45 seconds. Add onion, mushrooms and celery, stir to coat with margarine. Microwave for 2 minutes, stir well. Add flour, stir to combine, add stock or milk and stir again. Microwave for 2 minutes, stirring every 30 seconds. This sauce will be very thick. Add seasoning and chicken, allow to cool. Roll mixture into a sausage shape. Cut into about twelve slices and form each slice into an oval croquette shape.

For the coating, microwave margarine for 45 seconds then brush on to croquettes. On a flat plate, combine crumbs, Parmesan and marjoram. Roll croquettes in this mixture, pat on crumbs to ensure an even coating. Arrange croquettes in a circle on a flat container. Microwave on High (70%) for 5 – 7 minutes, until piping hot. Serve hot or cold.
Makes 12

Crumbed Camembert

Medium (50%)
3 minutes

225 g (8 oz) Camembert cheese (2 halves)
30 g (1 oz) butter
45 g (1½ oz) dried breadcrumbs
15 mℓ (1 tablespoon) chopped parsley

To garnish
4 orange wedges
parsley sprigs
150 mℓ (5 fl oz) cranberry orange sauce*

Place butter in a small bowl and microwave for 45 seconds. Brush Camembert with melted butter. Combine crumbs and parsley, and spread on to a plate. Roll Camembert in crumbs and pat on to ensure an even coating. Arrange both halves on a plate, round sides outwards. Microwave on Medium (50%) for 2 – 3 minutes, until the cheese starts to become soft. Cut each portion in two, serve garnished with an orange wedge, a parsley sprig and about 30 mℓ (2 tablespoons) cranberry orange sauce.
Serves 4

CRYSTALLIZED FRUITS
Whole or sliced fruits are simmered in a thick syrup, then dried until the surface becomes sugary. The whole process takes time, but the results are worthwhile. Using the microwave eliminates having sticky saucepans around for days on end. Fresh or canned fruit, such as pineapples, oranges, lemons and cherries, may be used.

Crystallized pineapple

Full Power
50 minutes

2 x 400 g (14 oz) cans of pineapple rings
500 g (18 oz) caster sugar
30 mℓ (2 tablespoons) Kirsch
caster sugar

Drain fruit, reserving syrup, and arrange in a single layer in a large shallow dish. Sprinkle half the sugar on to fruit, then stand for 12 hours. Drain syrup from fruit. In a large bowl, combine syrup from the fruit, canned syrup and sugar. Microwave on Full Power for 5 minutes, stir well. Microwave for 5 minutes more. Add fruit, making sure it is covered with syrup. Microwave for 5 minutes, stirring once during cooking time. Drain syrup and reserve. Place rings in a shallow dish, sprinkle with Kirsch, cover and stand for 48 hours. Now microwave syrup for 10 minutes, pour over pineapple, stand for 24 hours. Drain off syrup, microwave in a large bowl for 10 minutes. Add pineapple, microwave for 15 – 20 minutes until syrup is honey-coloured, stirring from time to time. Stand for 24 hours. Drain off syrup, cover pineapple with muslin and leave in a sunny place until partly dry. Now sprinkle with caster sugar, turn frequently and leave until thoroughly dry, usually 2 – 3 days is sufficient. Store in an air-tight container.
Makes 8 – 10 rings

CUCUMBER
Although cucumber is generally considered as a salad vegetable or, combined with yoghurt, as a side dish to temper curries, it can also be cooked, pickled, salted and used in soups and sauces. The microwave provides the quick cooking this delicate vegetable needs.

Cucumber sauce

Medium (50%)
3 minutes

125 mℓ (4 fl oz) soured cream
60 g (2 oz) peeled, seeded and chopped
  cucumber
5 mℓ (1 teaspoon) chopped parsley
2.5 mℓ (½ teaspoon) chopped dill
2.5 mℓ (½ teaspoon) chopped chives
5 mℓ (1 teaspoon) lemon juice
pinch of salt

Combine all ingredients and microwave on Medium (50%) for 3 minutes or until warmed through. Serve with poached fish such as salmon.
Makes about 250 mℓ (8 fl oz)

Cucumber and sweetcorn medley

Full Power
5 minutes

1 medium-sized cucumber
400 g (14 oz) canned sweetcorn kernels
salt and pepper
60 g (2 oz) Cheddar cheese, grated

Quarter cucumber lengthwise, then cut crosswise into 1-cm (½-inch) pieces. Mix cucumber with sweetcorn, salt and pepper in a 1-litre (1¾-pint) casserole. Cover tightly and microwave on Full Power for 2 minutes. Stir, cover again and microwave until vegetables are hot, 1 – 3 minutes longer. Sprinkle with grated cheese and stand for 2 minutes before serving.
Serves 4

CUMBERLAND SAUCE
This tangy, full-bodied sauce, flavoured with ginger, cloves, port, red currant jelly and orange and lemon rind, is meant to be served with strongly flavoured meats, such as game, gammon and ham. It is also very good with pickled tongue and roast pork. This microwave recipe is quick and easy to make.

Cumberland sauce

Full Power, Medium (50%)
11 minutes

2.5 mℓ (½ teaspoon) dry mustard
30 mℓ (2 tablespoons) soft brown sugar
pinch of ground ginger
cayenne
generous pinch of salt
250 mℓ (8 fl oz) port
2 whole cloves
15mℓ (1 tablespoon) cornflour
30 mℓ (2 tablespoons) cold water
60 mℓ (4 tablespoons) red currant jelly
5 mℓ (1 teaspoon) finely grated lemon rind
5 mℓ (1 teaspoon) finely grated orange rind
juice of 1 small orange
juice of 1 small lemon

Combine mustard, sugar, ginger, pepper and salt in a large glass jug. Mix to a smooth paste with a little of the port, then stir in remaining port. Add cloves and microwave on Full Power for 2 – 2½ minutes, or until mixture boils, stirring every minute. Reduce power level to Medium (50%) and simmer, covered, for 6 minutes. Mix cornflour to a smooth paste with cold water. Add to sauce and mix well. Microwave on Full Power for 1 – 2 minutes, stirring every 45 seconds, until mixture thickens. Add all remaining ingredients and stir to melt jelly. Check seasoning before serving.

To reheat, microwave on Medium (50%) for 2 – 3 minutes.
Makes about 375 mℓ (12 fl oz)

CURRY

Curries can be made from many different ingredients, including fish, lentils, chicken, meat or vegetables, and are easily and speedily cooked in the microwave. Use less liquid than usual for a more concentrated flavour. No matter the kind of curry you make, serve it with fluffy white or yellow rice and a selection of interesting sambals. Curry should be eaten with a spoon and fork, as a well-cooked curry should not need a knife.

Curry powder is available commercially in many different forms, giving different flavours and strengths to curried dishes. However, a combination of freshly ground spices undoubtedly gives the most interesting results. Commercial curry powder loses flavour with storage, so do not purchase large quantities. Curry paste keeps better. Whole spices, such as coriander, cumin and cardamom, used in freshly ground curry powder have no moisture in them, so it is not possible to 'roast' them in the microwave.

Sambals

Serve 3 – 6 sambals with any curry. Choose from the following:

Chopped tomato and onion, add a chilli for variety
Desiccated or shredded coconut
Diced cucumber with yoghurt and mint
Sliced bananas, tossed in lemon juice
Hot, mild or fruit chutney
Diced pineapple
Poppadums
Roti
Bombay duck
Chopped green pepper
Selection of pickles, such as mangoes, aubergine and kumquat

Chicken curry

Full Power, High (70%), Medium (50%)
50 minutes

1.5 kg (3 lb) chicken, jointed
salt and black pepper
45 g (1¼ oz) plain flour
45 mℓ (3 tablespoons) oil
1 large onion, chopped
10 – 15 mℓ (2 – 3 teaspoons) curry powder
1 green pepper, chopped
1 – 2 garlic cloves, crushed
10 mℓ (2 teaspoons) biriani seeds, crushed
5 mℓ (1 teaspoon) chopped fresh ginger
2 bay leaves
10 mℓ (2 teaspoons) curry leaves
400 g (14 oz) canned tomatoes, liquidized
chicken stock

Season chicken portions and toss in flour. Microwave browning dish on Full Power for 7 minutes. Add oil, microwave for 1 minute. Add chicken, microwave for 2 minutes, turn joints, microwave for 3 minutes more. Remove chicken and place in a 2-litre (3½-pint) casserole. To the browning dish, add onion, curry powder, green pepper and garlic. Microwave for 3 minutes, stirring every minute. Add any remaining flour and pour mixture over chicken. Add remaining ingredients, and mix carefully. Cover and microwave for 10 minutes on High (70%). Reduce power to Medium (50%) for 25 minutes, stirring from time to time. Add a little more chicken stock if necessary. Remove bay leaves and serve.
Serves 4 – 6

Lemon egg curry

Full Power, Medium (50%)
10 minutes

6 hard-boiled eggs, halved
45 g (1½ oz) margarine
2 leeks, sliced
salt and black pepper
2.5 – 5 mℓ (½ – 1 teaspoon) curry paste
400 g (14 oz) canned mushroom soup
30 mℓ (2 tablespoons) sherry
grated rind and juice of 1 lemon

Place margarine in bowl, microwave on Full Power for 1 minute. Add leeks and toss to coat with margarine. Microwave for 3 minutes, stirring once during cooking. Add seasonings and curry paste, stir well. Microwave for 1 minute, then add soup, sherry, lemon rind and juice, stir well. Microwave for 3 minutes. Arrange eggs in a shallow casserole, pour sauce over. Cover and microwave on Medium (50%) for 2 – 3 minutes to heat through. Serve on rice or slices of buttered toast.
Serves 4

Fish curry

Full Power
13 minutes

675 g (1½ lb) haddock, cod or other firm white fish
45 mℓ (3 tablespoons) oil
pinch of black pepper
2.5 mℓ (½ teaspoon) salt
2.5 mℓ (½ teaspoon) turmeric
cayenne
7.5 mℓ (1½ teaspoons) coriander seeds, crushed
generous pinch of aniseed
2 garlic cloves, crushed
1 chilli, chopped
10 mℓ (2 teaspoons) lemon juice
12 curry leaves
1 onion, chopped
15 mℓ (1 tablespoon) tamarind pulp
60 mℓ (4 tablespoons) warm water
15 mℓ (1 tablespoon) plain flour
400 g (14 oz) canned tomatoes
5 mℓ (1 teaspoon) caster sugar
15 mℓ (1 tablespoon) chopped fresh coriander leaves

Cut fish into serving portions, either on or off the bone. Using half the oil, make a paste with the salt, black pepper, turmeric, cayenne, coriander, aniseed, garlic, chilli and lemon juice. Spread over fish and marinate for 2 – 3 hours.

In a large shallow casserole, microwave remaining oil on Full Power for 2 minutes. Add curry leaves and onion, toss to coat with oil. Microwave for 3 minutes. Soak tamarind pulp in warm water for 10 minutes, strain and set aside. Place flour and tomatoes in a blender or processor, blend until smooth. Add strained tamarind liquid and sugar. Add tomato mixture to onion and stir well. Arrange fish in sauce, spooning sauce over each portion. Cover and microwave for 8 – 10 minutes. Stand for 4 minutes before serving. Sprinkle with chopped coriander and serve with rice and a selection of sambals.
Serves 4

CUSTARD

A mixture of milk and eggs, cooked until thickened and set. Because eggs tend to curdle when overheated, a thickener such as cornflour or commercial custard powder, that is slightly sweetened and flavoured, is used for a smoother texture and to bind the mixture. Both baked and stirred custards are easily made in the microwave. Once the process of making custard in the microwave has been mastered, it is possible to be more versatile by changing the flavourings. (*See also* Crème Brûlée and Crème Pâtissière.)

Basic custard

Full Power
7 minutes

500 mℓ (16 fl oz) milk
30 mℓ (2 tablespoons) custard powder
30 g (1 oz) caster sugar

Pour milk into a large jug, reserving a little to mix with the custard powder. Microwave milk, uncovered, on Full Power for 4 minutes. Combine remaining milk with custard powder and sugar, mixing well. Pour a little of the hot milk into custard mixture, mixing well. Pour custard mixture into the jug, mixing constantly. Microwave for a further 3 minutes, stirring after each minute. The custard is ready to use.

To prevent a skin from forming, cover custard with a piece of greaseproof paper. Push paper on to custard so that there is no air trapped on the surface. When custard is required, lift paper off and remove excess custard from the paper with a spatula. The thickness of the custard may be varied by using more or less custard powder.
Makes about 500 mℓ (16 fl oz)

Variation

Chocolate Custard: Add 30 mℓ (2 tablespoons) cocoa powder and an additional 15 mℓ (1 tablespoon) caster sugar to the custard powder and sugar before adding milk. Proceed as above. Stir in 15 g (½ oz) butter just before serving.

Egg custard with apricot sauce

Full Power
15 minutes

500 mℓ (16 fl oz) milk
4 eggs, lightly beaten
60 g (2 oz) caster sugar
30 mℓ (2 tablespoons) orange liqueur (optional)
5 mℓ (1 teaspoon) grated orange rind
pinch of salt
125 mℓ (4 fl oz) hot water

Apricot sauce
400 g (14 oz) canned apricot halves
7.5 mℓ (1½ teaspoons) cornflour
5 mℓ (1 teaspoon) lemon juice

Microwave milk in a 1-litre (1¾-pint) jug on Full Power for 2½ – 4 minutes, or until very hot but

not boiling. Beat eggs with sugar, orange liqueur, orange rind and salt. Gradually beat hot milk into egg mixture. Divide mixture among six custard cups. Place cups in a large round baking dish and pour 125 mℓ (4 fl oz) hot water into the dish. Cover custard with waxed paper. Microwave for 4½ minutes, then shake each cup gently. Remove any that are set but still soft. Rearrange remaining custards and microwave for ½ – 2½ minutes, checking each of the custards every 30 seconds. Stand for 15 minutes to finish cooking.

To prepare sauce, drain apricot halves and reserve syrup. Slice apricots and set aside. Combine 125 mℓ (4 fl oz) reserved syrup, cornflour and lemon juice. Add apricots and

microwave on Full Power for 2 – 4 minutes or until thick, stirring twice. Cool slightly before using. To serve, invert custards on to individual dishes and top each with apricot sauce.
Serves 6

Grand Marnier custard

Full Power, Defrost (30%)
5 minutes

4 egg yolks
30 mℓ (2 tablespoons) caster sugar
150 mℓ (5 fl oz) milk
75 mℓ (2½ fl oz) single cream
30 mℓ (2 tablespoons) Grand Marnier

Beat yolks and sugar until pale. Combine milk and cream in a large jug, microwave on Full Power for 2 – 3 minutes, until very hot. Pour into yolk mixture, beating well. Microwave on defrost (30%) for 3 – 4 minutes, stirring every minute during cooking time. Stir in liqueur, stand over ice to cool quickly. Cover top of custard with a piece of greaseproof paper to prevent a skin from forming. Refrigerate until required.
Serves 4

D

DATES

Dates are rich and nourishing fruits, highly prized in the Middle East. Fresh dates, with smooth brown skins, can sometimes be purchased in large supermarkets, but most dates are available dried. Whole dried dates can be eaten just as they come out of the box, or be stuffed with marzipan, nuts or cherries. Pressed dates, packaged in blocks, are used finely chopped in cooking, baking and sweet making. Date puddings, loaves and cakes microwave well because of their rich moist texture and dark colour.

Date rice pudding

Full Power
7 minutes

175 g (6 oz) cooked rice
90 g (3 oz) packet instant vanilla pudding mix
500 mℓ (16 fl oz) milk
75 g (2½ oz) stoned dates, chopped
5 mℓ (1 teaspoon) grated lemon rind
250 mℓ (8 fl oz) whipping cream
30 mℓ (1 tablespoon) brandy

Combine rice, pudding mix and milk in a 1-litre (1¾-pint) jug and microwave on Full Power for 3 minutes. Stir well. Microwave until mixture bubbles and thickens, 3 – 4 minutes, stirring every minute. Stir in dates and lemon rind and cool to room temperature. Whip cream with brandy and fold into the cooled mixture. Turn into a freezer container, cover and freeze. Remove from freezer 45 minutes before serving, then spoon into individual serving dishes.
Serves 6

Date and orange truffles

Full Power, High (70%)
8 minutes

500 g (18 oz) stoned dates, chopped
125 g (4 oz) butter or margarine
60 g (2 oz) caster sugar
5 mℓ (1 teaspoon) cinnamon
generous pinch of nutmeg
1 egg, well beaten
2.5 mℓ (½ teaspoon) salt
30 mℓ (2 tablespoons) orange juice
10 mℓ (2 teaspoons) grated orange rind
few drops of vanilla extract
60 g (2 oz) pecan nuts, chopped
60 g (2 oz) Marie biscuits, crumbled
100 g (3½ oz) bran flake cereal
finely chopped pecan nuts

Place dates, butter, and sugar in a large bowl. Cover and microwave on Full Power for 4 minutes. Beat in cinnamon, nutmeg, egg and salt and microwave, covered, on High (70%) for 3 – 4 minutes, or until slightly thickened. Add orange juice, orange rind, vanilla, pecan nuts and biscuit crumbs. Cool 10 minutes, then mix in cereal. Shape into 2.5-cm (1-inch) balls and roll in finely chopped nuts. Chill until ready to serve. These truffles can be stored in the refrigerator, tightly covered, for 1 week.
Makes about 50

Chewy date cake

Full Power, High (70%)
13 minutes

150 g (5 oz) raisins
200 g (7 oz) stoned dates, chopped
250 mℓ (8 fl oz) water
30 g (1 oz) butter or margarine
200 g (7 oz) caster sugar
175 g (6 oz) plain flour
2.5 mℓ (½ teaspoon) bicarbonate of soda
5 mℓ (1 teaspoon) cinnamon
2.5 mℓ (½ teaspoon) ground cloves
pinch of salt

Place raisins, dates, water, butter and sugar in a large jug. Microwave on Full Power for 3 – 4 minutes, or until mixture reaches a rapid boil. Cool. Combine dry ingredients and add to cooked mixture. Pour into a greased 20-cm (8-inch) baking dish and microwave on High (70%) for 8 – 9 minutes. Cool in the dish, then cut into squares and serve with whipped cream if desired.
Serves 9 – 12, depending on the size of the squares

Note: For a special date cake, add 45 g (1½ oz) chopped candied peel to the boiled mixture, and 45 g (1½ oz) chopped walnuts or hazelnuts to the dry ingredients.

DEFROSTING

Defrosting food in the microwave is not only quick and convenient, but most of the flavour and moisture is retained, and there is little risk of bacterial growth. When the defrost setting is used, the power is automatically switched on and off in cycles to produce a slow heating process. Frozen food, with the exception of vegetables, should be completely thawed before cooking or reheating which means it should be allowed to stand for approximately the time it has taken to defrost in the microwave. For example, an average-sized cake will take 5 – 7 minutes to defrost and will require the same amount of standing time before serving.

Tips for defrosting
☐ Defrost food slowly so that it does not begin to cook on the outside before it is completely thawed.
☐ When planning a meal take into consideration that large roasts and poultry need to stand for about 30 minutes to 1 hour, the same time it takes to defrost in the microwave.
☐ For best results, be sure that meat and poultry are completely defrosted before microwaving. Ice particles take a long time to melt, but once they become water, they

attract microwave energy and heat quickly. Unless the food is at a uniform temperature, you will find the thawed parts overcooked while the inside is still raw.

□ It is often necessary to reposition or turn foods so they defrost evenly. Shield thin parts with small strips of aluminium foil to prevent them drying out.

□ Place frozen food in a container suitable for microwaving. Be sure the container is large enough to hold the food after thawing, and to allow for stirring if necessary.

□ Foods frozen in foil trays or wrapped in foil should be removed from the container or wrapper and placed in a dish that can be safely used in the microwave.

□ Do not defrost large joints of meat, poultry or bread in sealed plastic bags, as the food tends to 'sweat'. If necessary, leave food in the bags but undo the fastening or puncture the plastic.

□ To speed up defrosting, cover foods and turn. Remove moisture from containers as food defrosts, otherwise microwave energy is wasted heating up this liquid. Remove giblets from poultry as soon as possible.

□ Place baked goods such as breads, cakes or pies on kitchen paper whilst defrosting to absorb excess moisture.

DEFROSTING VEGETABLES

There is no need to thaw frozen vegetables before microwaving, nor to add any extra water. Just place them in a suitable container, even a boilable plastic container or a cooking bag. Before microwaving, frozen vegetables should always be covered and cooking bags or plastic wrap must be pierced to prevent steam from building up. Microwave frozen vegetables for approximately two-thirds of the time required for fresh vegetables.

DEFROSTING CHARTS

See charts on pages 80-81.

DESSERTS

A wide variety of hot and cold desserts can be made with the help of the microwave. Cold desserts such as ice cream and gelatine mixtures are easily made and hot desserts can be made ahead of time and reheated just before serving.

See also individual fruits, Gelatine, Ice Cream, Puddings, Pastry and Pies.

Pecan pudding with lemon sauce

Full Power
13 minutes

90 g (3 oz) butter or margarine
125 g (4 oz) caster sugar
grated rind of ½ lemon
75 mℓ (2½ fl oz) milk
175 g (6 oz) plain flour
15 mℓ (1 tablespoon) baking powder
90 g (3 oz) pecan nuts, toasted* and coarsely
  chopped
3 egg whites

Lemon sauce
juice of 1 lemon
2.5 mℓ (½ teaspoon) cornflour
grated rind of 1 lemon
60 g (2 oz) caster sugar
2 egg yolks

For the pudding, cream butter and sugar with lemon rind until fluffy. Add milk, flour sifted with baking powder and nuts and mix well. Beat egg whites to peaks and fold into the butter mixture. Spoon mixture into six greased and lined baking or custard cups. Microwave on Full Power for 6 – 7 minutes. Stand for 10 minutes, then turn out on individual serving plates.

For the sauce, combine lemon juice with enough water to make 125 mℓ (4 fl oz). Mix in cornflour and lemon rind. Microwave on Full Power for 2 minutes. Stir, then add sugar and beat in egg yolks. Microwave for 4 minutes until sauce has thickened, stirring every minute. Serve hot over warm puddings.
Serves 6

Steamed date and buttermilk pudding

High (70%), Full Power
13 minutes

250 g (9 oz) plain flour
generous pinch of salt
5 mℓ (1 teaspoon) bicarbonate of soda
2.5 mℓ (½ teaspoon) baking powder
5 mℓ (1 teaspoon) cinnamon
generous pinch of nutmeg
5 mℓ (1 teaspoon) mixed spice
3 eggs
250 g (9 oz) soft brown sugar
125 mℓ (4 fl oz) oil
150 g (5 oz) stoned dates, chopped
5 mℓ (1 teaspoon) grated orange rind
250 mℓ (8 fl oz) buttermilk
90 g (3 oz) Brazil nuts, chopped

Sauce
200 g (7 oz) caster sugar
2.5 mℓ (½ teaspoon) bicarbonate of soda
30 mℓ (2 tablespoons) maple syrup
125 mℓ (4 fl oz) buttermilk
125 g (4 oz) margarine

Lightly oil a 2-litre (3½-pint) ring mould. Sift together the dry ingredients. Beat eggs, sugar and oil well, add dates and orange rind, beat again. Add one-third of the dry ingredients, beat well. Now add one-third of the buttermilk, mix well. Repeat twice more. Lastly add nuts and mix. Pour mixture into prepared mould. Microwave on High (70%) for 10 – 12 minutes, then on Full Power for 3 – 4 minutes. Stand for 5 minutes before turning out. Pour some of the sauce over the dessert before serving and serve remaining sauce separately.

To make the sauce, combine all ingredients in a large jug. Microwave on Full Power for 3 – 4 minutes.
Serves 10 – 12

Brandied peach cobbler

Full Power
8 minutes
Convection 180 °C/350 °F/gas 4
35 minutes

90 g (3 oz) cake flour
60 g (2 oz) caster sugar
5 mℓ (1 teaspoon) baking powder
generous pinch of salt
1 egg yolk
125 mℓ (4 fl oz) soured cream
15 g (½ oz) butter, melted
2.5 mℓ (½ teaspoon) finely grated lemon rind
2 x 400-g (14 oz) can sliced peaches
45 mℓ (3 tablespoons) brandy
30 mℓ (2 tablespoons) brown sugar
20 mℓ (4 teaspoons) cornflour
2.5 mℓ (½ teaspoon) mixed spice
60 g (2 oz) butter
15 mℓ (1 tablespoon) lemon juice
few drops of vanilla extract
chopped pecan nuts

Combine flour, caster sugar, baking powder and salt in a mixing bowl. Mix together egg yolk, soured cream and melted butter. Stir in lemon rind. Add liquid to flour mixture and stir to combine. Set batter aside. Drain peaches, reserving 150 mℓ (5 fl oz) of the syrup. In a large casserole, combine brandy, brown sugar, cornflour and mixed spice. Stir in peach slices, reserved syrup and butter. Microwave on Full Power for 6 – 8 minutes, or until thickened and bubbly. Stir every 2 minutes. Mix in lemon juice and vanilla. Drop batter in six mounds on top of hot peach mixture. Bake cobbler on convection at 180 °C/350 °F/gas 4 for about 35 minutes. Sprinkle with chopped pecans.
Serves 6

Baked mocha pudding

Full Power, High (70%)
17 minutes

125 g (4 oz) plain flour
15 mℓ (1 tablespoon) baking powder
salt
30 mℓ (2 tablespoons) cocoa powder
5 mℓ (1 teaspoon) instant coffee powder
45 g (1½ oz) butter
150 g (5 oz) caster sugar
1 egg
few drops of vanilla extract
170 mℓ (5½ fl oz) milk

Syrup
250 mℓ (8 fl oz) water
100 g (3½ oz) soft brown sugar
30 mℓ (2 tablespoons) cocoa powder
2.5 mℓ (½ teaspoon) instant coffee powder

First make syrup: place all ingredients in a 1-litre (1¾-pint) jug, whisk well. Microwave on Full Power for 3 minutes, set aside. Sift dry ingredients. Cream butter and sugar well. Beat in egg and vanilla extract. Add dry ingredients, alternately with milk, into creamed mixture.

Spoon into a greased 20-cm (8-inch) dish. Microwave for 2 minutes, whisk well, then microwave for a further 3 minutes. Carefully pour syrup over the back of a spoon on to the pudding. Microwave on High (70%) for 10 – 12 minutes. cover pudding as soon as it comes out of oven, and stand 3 – 5 minutes. Serve with custard, cream or ice cream.
Serves 4 – 6

Tequila mousse

Medium (50%)
60 seconds

20 mℓ (4 teaspoons) powdered gelatine
75 mℓ (2½ fl oz) cold water
pinch of salt
60 mℓ (2 fl oz) lemon juice
10 mℓ (2 teaspoons) finely grated lemon rind
45 mℓ (3 tablespoons) lime liqueur
45 mℓ (3 tablespoons) Curaçao
75 mℓ (2½ fl oz) tequila
4 eggs, separated
150 g (5 oz) caster sugar
125 mℓ (4 fl oz) whipping cream

Sprinkle gelatine over cold water and stand 5 minutes. Place in microwave on Medium (50%) for 45 seconds, scrape down sides of container and microwave another 5 seconds if necessary to dissolve gelatine completely. Combine gelatine, salt, lemon juice, rind, lime liqueur, Curaçao and tequila, mixing well. Chill until mixture is consistency of unbeaten egg white. Beat egg yolks with 75 g (2½ oz) sugar until very thick. Beat egg yolk mixture into gelatine mixture. Whip cream to soft peaks. Beat egg whites to soft peaks and gradually beat in remaining sugar. Fold cream, then egg whites into the gelatine mixture. Turn into a soufflé dish with a greased, waxed paper collar, or into a large bowl. Chill for about 4 hours, or until firm. To serve, decorate with whipped cream, and sliced fruits such as strawberries or kiwi fruits.
Serves 8

Pineapple sorbet

Full Power
10 minutes

175 g (6 oz) caster sugar
450 mℓ (14½ fl oz) water
2 – 3 pieces of lemon rind
juice of 1 lemon
1 medium pineapple, peeled and chopped
1 egg white

To serve
½ pineapple, grated
30 mℓ (2 tablespoons) Kirsch
6 wafer biscuits

Combine sugar and water in a large bowl. Microwave on Full Power for 5 minutes, stirring once during cooking time. Add lemon juice, rind and chopped pineapple, microwave for 5 minutes. Cool, remove lemon rind and freeze until solid. Remove from freezer, stand for 10

minutes, then cut into 2.5-cm (1-inch) cubes. Beat egg white until peaking consistency. Drop about one-third of the blocks on to the moving blades in a food processor, process until smooth, add one-third of the egg white, process to combine. Remove sorbet from work bowl and place in freezer tray. Repeat twice more. Freeze until firm. To serve, combine grated pineapple and Kirsch. Place 2 – 3 scoops of sorbet into a serving bowl, top with grated pineapple and a wafer biscuit.
Serves 6

Peach Bavarian cream

Full Power, Medium (50%)
13 minutes

75 g (2½ oz) caster sugar
45 g (1½ oz) cornflour
30 mℓ (2 tablespoons) powdered gelatine
pinch of salt
650 mℓ (21 fl oz) milk
2 egg yolks, well beaten
few drops of vanilla extract
2 egg whites
60 g (2 oz) caster sugar
250 mℓ (8 fl oz) whipping cream
90 mℓ (3 fl oz) peach liqueur
3 fresh peaches, sliced
45 g (1½ oz) caster sugar

In a large bowl, mix together sugar, cornflour, gelatine and salt. Gradually stir in milk. Microwave on Full Power for 7 – 9 minutes, stirring every 3 minutes until the mixture is slightly thickened and smooth. Mix a little of the hot mixture into egg yolks, then return to hot pudding and mix well. Microwave on medium (50%) for 2 – 4 minutes, stirring every minute. Chill until the mixture begins to thicken, then add vanilla. Beat egg whites until foamy, gradually add sugar and beat to a soft meringue. Whip the cream and add half the peach liqueur. Fold egg whites and cream into cooled mixture and turn into a 1-litre (1¾-pint) mould. Chill until firm. Unmould and serve with sliced peaches soaked in remaining peach liqueur mixed with sugar.
Serves 6

Trifle

Full Power, Defrost (30%)
6 minutes

1 x 20-cm (8-inch) sponge cake
raspberry jam
150 mℓ (5 fl oz) sweet sherry
400 g (14 oz) canned apricot halves, drained
400 g (14 oz) canned stoned cherries, drained

Custard
300 mℓ (10 fl oz) milk
300 mℓ (10 fl oz) single cream
3 whole eggs
3 egg yolks
15 g (½ oz) plain flour
30 g (1 oz) caster sugar (approximate)
few drops of vanilla extract

Topping
300 mℓ (10 fl oz) whipping cream
100 mℓ (3½ fl oz) sherry
30 mℓ (2 tablespoons) brandy
grated rind and juice of 1 lemon
grated nutmeg
30 g (1 oz) flaked almonds, toasted*
maraschino cherries

Cut cake into fingers to fit the base of a 25-cm (10-inch) deep dessert bowl. Spread one side of the cake with jam, and arrange in bowl, jam side downwards. Saturate with sherry and stand for 2 – 3 hours. Cover with apricots and cherries.

For the custard, pour milk and cream into a 1-litre (1¾-pint) jug, microwave on Full Power for 3 – 4 minutes, until very hot. Beat eggs, egg yolks, flour and sugar very well. Beat in hot milk mixture. Microwave on Defrost (30%) for 3 – 4 minutes whisking every 30 seconds; the cooked custard should coat the back of a spoon. Stir in vanilla. Place a piece of greaseproof paper directly on top of custard and allow to cool to room temperature. Pour over cake and refrigerate.

Just before serving, beat cream until beginning to thicken, slowly add sherry, brandy, lemon rind, lemon juice and a little grated nutmeg. Continue beating until thick. Spread over top of custard. Spike the cream with almonds and decorate with cherries.
Serves 10

DIPS

Dips make attractive, easy-to-serve starters or snacks. Make them in a minute with help from the microwave, or use the microwave to reheat them. Serve dips with an interesting selection of vegetable crudités (see below), savoury biscuits or crisps.

Crudités
Carrot sticks
Celery sticks
Courgette sticks
Cucumber sticks
Cauliflower or broccoli florets
Mangetout
Melon slices
Mushroom caps
Pineapple slices
Radishes
Tomato wedges

Top left: Seafood Artichoke Casserole (page 96)
Top right: Salmon with Lemon and Fruit (page 95)
Bottom left: Turban of Smoked Salmon and Sole (page 97) served with Hollandaise Sauce (page 195)
Bottom right: Rolls of Trout with Mustard Sauce (page 96)

DEFROSTING CHARTS

Meat	QUANTITY	TIME ON DEFROST (30%)	STANDING TIME	METHOD
Beef				
Steak	per 500 g (18 oz)	3 – 4 minutes	5 – 10 minutes	Separate pieces as soon as possible.
Large joints, boned and rolled	per 500 g (18 oz)	8 – 12 minutes	1 hour	Defrost wrapped for half the time. Unwrap, shield warm sections, and lie meat on its side.
Large joints on the bone	per 500 g (18 oz)	10 – 14 minutes	1 hour	Defrost wrapped for half the time, then shield bone. Turn meat over after half the defrosting time.
Minced beef, lamb or pork	per 500 g (18 oz)	9 – 12 minutes	5 minutes	Break up during defrosting. Remove thawed pieces.
Stewing beef, lamb or pork	per 500 g (18 oz)	10 – 12 minutes	15 minutes	Separate pieces during defrosting. Remove thawed sections.
Lamb or Veal				
Leg	per 500 g (18 oz)	8 – 10 minutes	30 minutes	Shield bone-end during defrosting.
Shoulder or loin	per 500 g (18 oz)	7 – 8 minutes	30 minutes	Shield thin portion during defrosting.
Chops	per 500 g (18 oz)	3 – 5 minutes	5 – 10 minutes	Separate chops during defrosting.
Pork				
Leg	per 500 g (18 oz)	8 – 9 minutes	1 – 1½ hours	Select a joint with a uniform shape. Tie into shape if necessary.
Loin	per 500 g (18 oz)	6 – 8 minutes	30 minutes	Shield bone-end during defrosting.
Chops	per 500 g (18 oz)	3 – 5 minutes	10 – 15 minutes	Separate chops during defrosting.
Offal				
Liver and kidney	per 500 g (18 oz)	8 – 10 minutes	5 minutes	Separate pieces during defrosting.
Sausages				
Sausages	per 500 g (18 oz)	6 – 8 minutes	10 minutes	Separate during defrosting.

Poultry				
Chicken (whole)	per 500 g (18 oz)	9 – 10 minutes	30 minutes	Turn over after half the defrosting time. Shield wing tips and breast bone.
Chicken (portions)	per 500 g (18 oz)	6 – 8 minutes	10 minutes	Separate during defrosting.
Duck	per 500 g (18 oz)	10 – 12 minutes	30 minutes	Turn over after half the defrosting time. Shield wing tips and breast bone.
Turkey	per 500 g (18 oz)	10 – 12 minutes	1 hour	Turn several times. Shield wing tips and breast bone.

Fish				
Fillets of hake, cod, sea bass, etc.	per 500 g (18 oz)	5 – 7 minutes	5 minutes	Separate during defrosting.
Haddock	per 500 g (18 oz)	5 minutes	5 minutes	Separate during defrosting.
Steaks (salmon, etc.)	per 500 g (18 oz)	5 minutes	5 minutes	Turn during defrosting.
Trout	2 medium	5 – 7 minutes	5 minutes	Turn during defrosting. Shield tail ends with foil.
Sole	2 large	5 – 6 minutes	5 minutes	Turn during defrosting.
Kipper fillets and 'boil in the bag' fish	per 300 g (11 oz)	3 – 4 minutes	5 minutes	Pierce bag before defrosting.
Prawns, large with shells and heads	per 500 g (18 oz)	7 – 8 minutes	5 minutes	Separate during defrosting.
Prawns, small, peeled and deveined	per 500 g (18 oz)	4 – 5 minutes	5 minutes	Pierce bag if necessary.

Sauces and soups	QUANTITY	TIME ON DEFROST (30%)	STANDING TIME	METHOD
Sauces, sweet and savoury	250 mℓ (8 fl oz)	6 – 8 minutes	5 minutes	Break up and stir as defrosting. Blend until smooth.
Soup	500 mℓ (18 fl oz)	8 – 10 minutes	5 minutes	Break up and stir whilst defrosting. Blend until smooth. Add cream before serving.

Baking

Bread

Bread, whole or sliced	1 kg (2¼ lb)	6 – 8 minutes	5 minutes	Unwrap. Place on kitchen paper. Turn over during defrosting.
Bread	26 x 12 cm	4 – 6 minutes	5 minutes	Unwrap. Place on kitchen paper. Turn over during defrosting.
Bread	1 slice	10 – 15 seconds	1 – 2 minutes	Unwrap. Place on kitchen paper. Time accurately.
Bread rolls	2 4	20 – 25 seconds 30 – 40 seconds	1 – 2 minutes 1 – 2 minutes	Unwrap. Place on kitchen paper.

Cakes

Cupcakes or American muffins	4	1 – 1½ minutes	5 minutes	Unwrap. Place on kitchen paper.
Sponge cake	22.5-cm (9-inch)	2 – 3 minutes	5 minutes	Unwrap. Place on kitchen paper. Turn over after 1 minute.
Doughnuts or sweet buns	4	1½ – 2 minutes	5 minutes	Unwrap. Place on kitchen paper. Turn over after 1 minute.
Loaf cakes or ring cakes	26 x 12 cm or 22-25 cm diameter	5 – 7 minutes	10 minutes	Unwrap. Place on kitchen paper. Turn over after 3 minutes.
Bars	20-22 cm square	4 – 6 minutes	5 – 10 minutes	Unwrap. Place on kitchen paper.
Drop scones	4	25 – 30 seconds	3 – 4 minutes	Unwrap. Place on kitchen paper. Time accurately.
Pancakes or crêpes	10	3 – 4 minutes	–	Unwrap. Place on plate. Cover with plastic wrap.

Pies

Pies or tarts	1 x 20-23 cm	4 – 6 minutes	10 minutes	Unwrap.
Individual pies	1 small 4 small	25 – 30 seconds 2 – 3 minutes	2 minutes 2 minutes	Unwrap. Place upside down on kitchen paper.

Fruit

Fruit, sliced or whole	250 g (9 oz)	5 – 7 minutes	10 minutes	Stir occasionally.
Fruit purée	250 mℓ (8 fl oz)	7 – 8 minutes	5 minutes	Scrape off softened edges whilst thawing.
Fruit packed in syrup	250 g (9 oz)	12 – 15 minutes	10 minutes	Separate during defrosting.

Dairy products

Butter	250 g (9 oz)	2 – 3 minutes	5 minutes	Turn once.
Cheese	–	–	–	Defrost at room temperature, not in microwave.
Cream cheese	250 g (9 oz)	3 – 4 minutes	10 minutes	Remove lid and cover with waxed paper.
Cream	–	–	–	Defrost at room temperature, not in microwave.

Aubergine caviar

Full Power
7 minutes

1 large aubergine, unpeeled and diced
salt
45 mℓ (3 tablespoons) water
60 mℓ (4 tablespoons) chopped parsley
1 garlic clove, crushed
½ onion, chopped
125 mℓ (4 fl oz) mayonnaise
black pepper
2.5 mℓ (½ teaspoon) dried basil
15 mℓ (1 tablespoon) lemon juice

To garnish
1 hard-boiled egg, mashed
parsley sprigs

Sprinkle aubergine with a little salt, stand 15
minutes. Rinse and pat dry. Place aubergine
and water in a bowl, cover with vented plastic
wrap. Microwave on Full Power for 7 – 9
minutes, until tender. Drain and cool. Place all
ingredients into a food processor, process until
smooth. Adjust seasonings. Spoon into a
suitable container, garnish with hard-boiled
egg and parsley. Serve with crudités or
biscuits.
Makes about 400 mℓ (13 fl oz)

Tasty broccoli dip

Full Power, Medium (50%)
11 minutes

150 g (5 oz) frozen broccoli
45 mℓ (3 tablespoons) water
white wine
1 packet mushroom soup
5 mℓ (1 teaspoon) Worcestershire sauce
1 garlic clove, crushed
black pepper
250 mℓ (8 fl oz) soured cream
selection of vegetable crudités

Place broccoli and water in a small bowl and
cover. Microwave on Full Power for 4 minutes.
Drain liquid into a measuring jug, add water
and a little wine to make up to 150 mℓ (5 fl oz) of
liquid. Combine liquid, soup powder,
Worcestershire sauce and garlic in a bowl.
Microwave for 4 – 5 minutes, stirring every 30
seconds. Cool slightly, then purée broccoli and
soup in a blender, until smooth. Add black
pepper and soured cream and blend to
combine. Return to bowl, microwave on
Medium (50%) for 3 minutes. Spoon into a
warmed container, garnish with parsley and
slices of lemon.
Makes about 500 mℓ (16 fl oz)

Previous page left: clockwise, Broccoli, Cheesy
Broccoli and Curried Broccoli (page 38)
Previous page right: from top to bottom,
Cabbage Wedges (page 42) with Tomato
Topping (page 213), with Celery Topping (page
43), with Cheese Sauce (page 195) and crispy
bacon.

DOLMADES
These bite-sized, stuffed vine leaves, a speciality from Greece and Turkey, are
usually served at room temperature as part
of the 'mezze' or hors d'oeuvre, but they
are also sometimes eaten hot with a sauce
as a main course. This dish cooked in the
microwave is particularly moist. Either
fresh or canned vine leaves may be used,
but the fresh ones will require blanching.

To blanch vine leaves, microwave 1 litre
(1¾ pints) water on Full Power for 5 – 6
minutes, until boiling. Add about 15 vine
leaves, push leaves into water, cover with
vented plastic wrap. Microwave for 3 minutes, remove from water and plunge into
cold water. Drain and use.

Dolmades

Full Power, High (70%), Medium (50%)
41 minutes

60 g (2 oz) rice
150 mℓ (5 fl oz) water
75 mℓ (2½ fl oz) oil, half olive and half sunflower
2 medium onions, chopped
300 g (11 oz) minced beef or lamb
30 g (1 oz) pine nuts or flaked almonds
5 mℓ (1 teaspoon) chopped mint
5 mℓ (1 teaspoon) dried dill
45 mℓ (3 tablespoons) chopped parsley
30 mℓ (2 tablespoons) lemon juice
generous pinch of turmeric
½ beef stock cube
salt and black pepper
about 40 blanched vine leaves
45 mℓ (3 tablespoons) water

Garnish
lemon wedges
paprika
fresh vine leaves

Place rice and boiling water in a bowl, cover
with vented plastic wrap. Microwave on Full
Power for 5 minutes. Stand for 5 minutes, then
drain. Pour half the oil into a bowl, microwave
for 2 minutes. Add onion, stir to coat with oil.
Microwave for 3 minutes. Stir well. Add mince,
nuts, mint, dill, parsley, lemon juice, turmeric,
stock cube and seasonings, mix well. Cover,
microwave for 4 minutes, then add rice.
   Use some of the remaining oil to grease a
large shallow casserole. Line casserole with a
third of the vine leaves. If using bottled or
canned vine leaves, wash well. Place remaining
leaves on a board, veined side uppermost.
Place about 20 mℓ (4 teaspoons) of the meat
mixture on the widest part of the leaf, fold

edges inwards and roll up envelope style.
Arrange filled leaves, seams downward and
side by side in a casserole. Microwave
remaining oil and water for 2 minutes, pour over
rolls, cover with a few leaves. Cover casserole,
microwave on High (70%) for 7 minutes, reduce
power to Medium (50%) for a further 20
minutes. Uncover and cool to room
temperature. Serve on a flat platter, garnished
with fresh vine leaves and lemon wedges.
Makes about 26 rolls

DROP SCONES
Drop scones are easily made in the microwave oven, although you will need a
browning dish for this recipe.

Drop scones

Full Power
18 minutes

250 g (9 oz) plain flour
20 mℓ (4 teaspoons) baking powder
2.5 mℓ (½ teaspoon) salt
15 mℓ (1 tablespoon) caster sugar
170 mℓ (5½ fl oz) milk and 170 mℓ (5½ fl oz)
   water, combined
30 mℓ (2 tablespoons) oil

Sift flour, baking powder and salt. Place in a
blender or processor bowl. Add sugar, eggs
and half the milk. Blend until a batter forms,
then add remaining milk and oil. Blend until
smooth. Microwave a browning dish for
6 minutes on Full Power. Wipe with a little oil,
microwave for 30 seconds. Drop 4 – 5
spoonfuls of the mixture on to the browning
dish, turn over almost immediately. Microwave
for 1 minute. Remove and keep warm.
Microwave browning dish for 2 minutes before
using for the next batch. Repeat until all the
mixture has been used up.
Makes about 24 scones

DRIED FRUIT
Dried fruit can be plumped or stewed
quickly and easily in the microwave oven.
To reconstitute or plump dried fruits, heat
250 ml (8 fl oz) water on Full Power for
2 – 3 minutes until boiling. Pour over dried
fruits and stand for a few minutes. Then
drain and use as desired. To infuse dried
fruits with alcohol or liqueur, warm the
liquid for a few seconds in the microwave,
then pour over fruit and stand for several
minutes.

To stew dried fruits

Place 250 g (9 oz) dried fruit such as prunes, apricots, apple rings or mixed dried fruit in a casserole and add about 500 ml (16 fl oz) hot water or to cover. Cover casserole and microwave on Full Power for 4 – 5 minutes, or until boiling. Stir. Microwave, covered, on Defrost (30%) for 9 – 10 minutes or until tender. Add 60 – 90 g (2 – 3 oz) sugar, if desired, and microwave for a further 2 – 3 minutes until sugar dissolves. Add the sugar during the last few minutes of cooking time as adding it early in the stewing process will prevent the fruit from becoming tender.

Dried fruit salad

Full Power
12 – 15 minutes

250 g (9 oz) dried fruits such as apricots,
    apples, peaches, prunes and raisins
grated rind of 1 orange
juice of 1 orange
4-cm (1½-inch) piece of cinnamon stick
500 ml (16 fl oz) apple juice or cider

Place dried fruit in a large bowl, add orange rind, juice, cinnamon and apple juice. Cover and microwave on Full Power for 12 – 15 minutes, stirring twice. Stand at least 5 minutes before serving. Serve warm or cold.
Serves 4 – 6

DRYING BREAD
To dry bread for crumbs or croûtons, place 125 g (4 oz) bread cubes in a shallow dish. Microwave on Full Power for 3½ – 5 minutes, stirring every minute. *See also* Rusks.

DRYING FLOWERS
A novel way to preserve your favourite flowers.

Drying flowers

Full Power
60 seconds

250 ml (8 fl oz) silica gel
flowers such as roses and carnations

Pour the silica gel into a tall cup or glass. Cut flower stems to the length of the cup. Put flowers, one at a time, into the silica gel, ensuring that the stem is completely covered. Microwave on Full Power for 60 seconds. Repeat until all flowers have been microwaved.

DUCK
Duck is not as meaty as chicken, and because of its tendency towards fattiness, it is best roasted. It can also be used to make pâté and the bones are good for soup. Usually available frozen, duck needs to be completely thawed before cooking (*see* Defrosting Chart page 80). When roasting duck in the microwave, place it on a rack so the fat can drain away during cooking, and cover duck with waxed paper to prevent spattering. Start the duck breast side down and turn over during cooking. Glazes give microwaved duck a glossy, colourful finish, and an orange sauce served with the bird will help counteract the richness.

Glazed duck with spicy orange sauce

Full Power
40 minutes

1 duck, about 2 kg (4¼ lb)

Red currant glaze
150 g (5 oz) red currant jelly
30 ml (2 tablespoons) Crème de Cassis
generous pinch of allspice

Spicy orange sauce
225 g (8 oz) orange marmalade
30 ml (2 tablespoons) dry sherry
pinch of ground ginger

Clean the duck and wipe dry. With the tip of a small, sharp knife, pierce skin in several places to allow the fat to escape during cooking. Twist wing tips behind back and pin neck skin to back with a wooden skewer. Tie legs together tightly with string. To prepare red currant glaze, combine jelly, Crème de Cassis and allspice in a large jug. Microwave on Full Power for 2 minutes, or until jelly melts, stirring twice. Brush whole duck with glaze. Arrange duck, breast side down, on a microwave rack placed in a shallow dish. Cover with a tent of greased waxed paper. Microwave on Full Power for 18 minutes. Turn breast side up and drain off fat. Brush again with glaze and microwave, covered with tented waxed paper, for 15 – 18 minutes, or until cooked. Juices should run clear when duck is cooked. Remove from oven, brush again with glaze and cover with foil, shiny side in. Stand for at least 5 minutes.
    To make the orange sauce, combine marmalade, sherry and ginger, mixing well. Microwave on Full Power for 1½ – 2 minutes, or until warm. Stir once. Serve separately with the duck.
Serves 3 – 4

DUMPLINGS
Dumplings should be light in texture and full of flavour. They may be cooked on top of a rich stew, or poached in stock or syrup.

Savoury dumplings

Full Power
6 minutes

250 g (9 oz) plain flour
5 ml (1 teaspoon) salt
15 ml (1 tablespoon) baking powder
125 g (4 oz) suet, finely shredded
about 150 ml (5 fl oz) water

Sift flour, salt and baking powder, add suet. Add sufficient water to give a fairly stiff dough.

Divide into 16 dumplings, about the size of a walnut. Arrange dumplings on top of cooked stew, cover. Microwave on Full Power for 6 minutes. Stand for 3 minutes before serving.
Makes 16 dumplings

Variations
Parsley Dumplings: Add 30 ml (2 tablespoons) chopped parsley to dumpling mixture.
Herb Dumplings: Add 5 ml (1 teaspoon) mixed herbs and 5 ml (1 teaspoon) paprika to dumpling mixture.

DUXELLES
Duxelles, created by a 17th-century French chef, is a mixture of finely chopped mushrooms and onions. Quickly made in the microwave, this delicate mushroom purée is used for stuffings and sauces.

Chicken breasts with duxelles

Full Power, Medium (50%)
25 minutes

4 chicken breasts
100 ml (3½ fl oz) chicken stock
pinch of nutmeg
100 ml (3½ fl oz) single cream

To Garnish
parsley

Duxelles
45 g (1½ oz) butter
6 spring onions
15 ml (1 tablespoon) lemon juice
400 g (14 oz) mushrooms, finely chopped
salt and black pepper
30 ml (2 tablespoons) cream

To make duxelles, microwave butter in a shallow casserole for 1 minute. Add spring onions and mushrooms, stir to coat. Add lemon juice and seasonings, microwave covered for 4 minutes. Drain mushrooms and reserve liquid. Stir cream into mushrooms.
    Arrange lightly seasoned chicken breasts in a shallow casserole, add mushroom liquid, stock and nutmeg. Cover and microwave on Medium (50%) for 14 – 16 minutes. Turn breasts over after half the cooking time. Remove breasts and keep warm. Microwave poaching liquid on Full Power for 4 minutes, whisk in cream and microwave for 2 minutes, whisking every 30 seconds. To serve, spoon mushroom mixture on to a heated platter, arrange chicken on top and coat with sauce. Garnish with parsley.
Serves 4

Overleaf left: Moussaka (page 152) served with a tossed salad
Overleaf right: Cauliflower (page 49) with Cheese Sauce (page 195)

ECLAIRS

Eclairs are made with choux pastry and cannot be baked in the microwave oven.

EGGNOG

Eggnog is a beverage made with eggs, milk and cream, flavoured with nutmeg or cinnamon, and laced with brandy, rum or whisky.

Eggnog almondine

Full Power
6 minutes

1 litre (1¾ pints) milk
60 mℓ (4 tablespoons) whisky
60 g (2 oz) caster sugar
10 mℓ (2 teaspoons) grated orange rind
3 eggs, lightly beaten
90 mℓ (3 fl oz) Amaretto liqueur
5 mℓ (1 teaspoon) grated nutmeg
125 mℓ (4 fl oz) whipping cream
50 mℓ toasted almonds
grated orange rind

Place milk, whisky, sugar and orange rind in a large casserole or jug and microwave on Full Power for 3 minutes. Stir and microwave another 3 minutes. Beat some of the hot milk into the eggs then return this mixture to the hot milk in the jug and mix well. Strain into a serving jug. Stir in Amaretto liqueur and grated nutmeg. Pour into mugs or cups and top with whipped cream, toasted almonds and grated orange rind.
Serves 6

EGGPLANT *See* Aubergine

EGGS

Microwaves with a variable power range make it possible to cook difficult egg dishes such as quiches, custards, omelettes and baked eggs.

When microwaving individual eggs, pay close attention to time and temperature because they are easily overcooked. Egg yolk has a high protein content and absorbs microwave energy more quickly than the white, so it cooks faster. To fry eggs successfully in the microwave, use a browning dish so the egg white will be cooked by direct heat, while the yolk cooks by microwave energy. Cooking eggs in custard cups will force the white up around the sides of the cup so the microwaves pass through it first before reaching the yolk and the white will be cooked when the yolk is ready.

Do not try to microwave an egg in its shell as the tight membrane surrounding the yolk collects microwave energy, causing a build-up of steam. This can result in a small explosion and a messy interior to the microwave. When frying, baking or poaching eggs, lightly puncture the yolk membrane with a skewer or point of a sharp knife to prevent the yolk from bursting.

Eggs continue cooking after being removed from the microwave, so allow for standing time to complete the cooking process. Personal preference will determine exact cooking times, but always check egg recipes at the minimum suggested time. It is easy to microwave the eggs for a few seconds more, but once the egg is overcooked, it becomes tough and rubbery.

Fried eggs

Full Power
4 minutes

A browning dish recipe.

20 g (¾ oz) butter
2 eggs
salt and pepper
chopped parsley (optional)

Preheat a browning dish on Full Power for 2 – 3 minutes. Add butter to dish and allow to melt. Tilt dish to coat evenly with butter. Break eggs into dish and very gently pierce yolks with a thin skewer. Season to taste, cover and microwave for 30 – 60 seconds. Exact timing depends on whether you prefer your eggs lightly cooked or well done. Sprinkle with chopped parsley if desired.
Serves 2

Poached eggs in custard cups

Full Power

For 1 or 2 eggs
60 mℓ (4 tablespoons) hot water per egg
2.5 mℓ (½ teaspoon) white vinegar per egg

Pour water into individual custard cups and add vinegar. Microwave on Full Power for 1 minute or until boiling. Carefully break egg into water and prick egg yolk twice with skewer. Cover with waxed paper and microwave for 30 seconds. Stand in liquid for about 2 minutes. For firmer eggs, stand longer.

For 3 or 4 eggs
Proceed as above with individual custard cups. Timing for boiling water will be 3½ – 4 minutes. Timing for cooking is about 30 seconds per egg.

Poached eggs in a casserole dish

Medium (50%)
8 minutes

3 – 4 eggs
500 mℓ (16 fl oz) water
5 mℓ (1 teaspoon) white vinegar

Heat water and vinegar on Full Power until boiling, about 5 – 6 minutes. Break eggs, one at a time, into a small bowl. Pierce membrane of yolks and tip into boiling water. Cover and microwave on Medium (50%) for 45 seconds per egg. Stand in liquid to become firm, about 2 minutes.

Scrambled eggs

Full Power

For 1 – 3 eggs
7 g (¼ oz) butter per egg
15 mℓ (1 tablespoon) milk per egg
salt and pepper

Melt butter in a measuring jug on Full Power for 30 seconds. Add eggs and milk and beat well. Season to taste with salt and pepper. Microwave for about 45 seconds per egg, stirring after every minute, or after 25 seconds if only 1 egg is cooked. Eggs should be very moist when removed from the oven as they will continue cooking during standing time. Let eggs stand for 1 – 1½ minutes before serving.

For 4 – 8 eggs
Use a larger container and follow above directions, but increase time as follows:
4 eggs   2½ – 3¼ minutes
6 eggs   3½ – 4¼ minutes
8 eggs   4½ – 5¼ minutes

Eggs Florentine

Full Power
2 minutes

300 g (11 oz) spinach, cooked*
125 g (4 oz) low-fat soft cheese
2.5 mℓ (½ teaspoon) freshly ground black
    pepper
2.5 mℓ (½ teaspoon) mixed herbs
salt
4 poached eggs*
4 toasted muffin halves or 4 slices hot toast
4 rolled anchovy fillets

Drain spinach thoroughly. Stir in cheese, pepper, herbs and salt. Microwave on Full Power for 2 minutes or until heated through. Spoon about one-quarter of spinach mixture on each half muffin or piece of toast. Top each with a poached egg and garnish with an anchovy fillet.
Serves 4

Variation
Top eggs and spinach with warm hollandaise sauce*.

Eggs with tuna and cheese

Full Power, Medium (50%)
14 minutes

30 g (1 oz) butter
200 g (7 oz) canned tuna, drained and flaked
9 eggs
125 mℓ (4 fl oz) milk
2.5 mℓ (½ teaspoon) salt
2.5 mℓ (½ teaspoon) dill
2.5 mℓ (½ teaspoon) grated lemon rind
pepper
90 g (3 oz) low-fat soft cheese
buttered breadcrumbs
paprika

Microwave butter in a 20-cm (8-inch) baking dish on Full Power for 30 seconds. Scatter tuna over butter. Mix together eggs, milk, salt, dill, lemon rind and pepper. Pour over tuna and microwave for 5 minutes. Push outer edges to centre and break apart with fork twice during cooking. Spoon cheese over surface of egg mixture and microwave on Medium (50%) for 6 – 8 minutes, or until almost set in the centre. Stand, covered, for 5 minutes, then sprinkle with buttered breadcrumbs and paprika.
Serves 6

Pizza eggs

Full Power
11 minutes

15 g (½ oz) butter
½ small onion, chopped
½ green pepper, chopped
8 eggs, beaten
125 mℓ (4 fl oz) mushrooms, sliced
salt and pepper
generous pinch of oregano
125 mℓ (4 fl oz) well-seasoned tomato sauce
    (as served with pasta)
30 g (1 oz) Mozzarella cheese, grated
3 stuffed olives, sliced

In a 20-cm (8-inch) round baking dish, microwave butter on Full Power for 45 seconds. Add onion and green pepper, stir and microwave for 2 – 3 minutes. Mix eggs, milk, mushrooms, salt and pepper and oregano and pour into baking dish. Microwave for 5 – 6 minutes or until eggs are almost set. Stir gently two or three times during cooking. Pour tomato sauce over eggs, sprinkle with cheese and microwave 1 minute to melt cheese. Garnish with sliced olives. Cut into wedges to serve.
Serves 4 – 6

Puffy omelette

Full Power, Medium (50%)
9 minutes

3 eggs, separated
45 mℓ (3 tablespoons) mayonnaise
30 mℓ (2 tablespoons) water
salt and pepper
30 g (1 oz) butter

Beat egg whites until soft peaks form. Beat egg yolks, mayonnaise, water and seasonings together well. Gently pour mixture over beaten whites and fold in. Place butter in a 20-cm (8-inch) pie dish and microwave on Full Power for 1 minute. Swirl melted butter to coat dish. Gently pour in egg mixture and spread evenly in the dish. Microwave on Medium (50%) for 6 – 8 minutes. Let stand for 30 seconds to 1 minute to set, then run a spatula around sides of dish. Fold one half of the omelette over and gently slide on to a serving plate.
Serves 1 – 2

Variation
Fill omelette with mushrooms, grated cheese, asparagus, green pepper, smoked mussels or oysters.

EQUIPMENT FOR MICROWAVE COOKING
Substances such as glass, pottery, porcelain and paper allow microwave energy to pass through them so containers made of these materials are ideal for microwave use. Containers of aluminium, copper, stainless steel or aluminium foil reflect microwaves and are not suitable for use in the microwave. They may also cause arcing which will damage your appliance.

A range of equipment made of materials that meet the special requirements of microwave cooking is now available. However, there is no need to rush out and buy a complete new set of cookware. Although you will not be using metal saucepans or baking tins, many utensils you already have can be used in the microwave. These include paper plates, paper towels, ovenproof casseroles and glass measuring jugs. It is often possible to cook and serve in the same container, saving not only time, but washing up too.

When purchasing containers for microwave use, remember that round shapes will give more even results than oval or rectangular ones. Larger, shallow bowls are preferable to smaller, deep ones because food with a greater surface area cooks more evenly. However, it is important to have a few deep containers for making sauces, preserves and cream mixtures.

Testing containers for microwave safety
Measure 250 ml (8 fl oz) water in a measuring jug. Place container you wish to test in the microwave and stand the jug in it. Microwave on Full Power for about 1 minute. At the end of that time, the water should be warm and the container cool. If so, the container is ideal for microwave use. If both the water and the container are warm, the container can be used, but the cooking time must be increased, as the

Overleaf left: from top to bottom, Chicken with Pineapple and Lychees (page 57), Chicken Marengo (page 56)
Overleaf right: Dolmades (page 84), vine leaves wrapped around a tasty filling.

container will attract some of the microwave energy away from the food. If the container is warm, but the water is cool, the container has attracted too much microwave energy and is not suitable for microwave cooking.

Materials suitable for microwaving
(*See also* Browning dishes)

Paper may be used with foods that require low heat and short cooking times. Thawing, reheating and some quick cooking methods can make use of paper napkins, towels, cups and plates. Kitchen paper is useful for covering fatty foods, and may also be used to line cake dishes. It absorbs excess moisture and makes turning cakes out easy.

Waxed paper and **greaseproof paper** can be used as a light covering while foods cook, holding in heat but allowing steam to escape. Waxed paper is especially useful for covering such foods as sausages, hamburgers and bacon.

Wax-coated containers should only be used for heating foods for short periods, as high temperatures cause the wax to melt. Paper baking cups are good for microwaving small cakes and crumpets.

Plastic wrap makes an excellent cover for microwave foods as it keeps in both heat and moisture. Be sure to turn back a corner or make two slits in the plastic wrap to prevent it 'ballooning' during cooking.

Roasting bags are convenient for a variety of foods as they promote browning of roasts and poultry while retaining moisture and heat. They are also useful for cooking fruit and vegetables with very little moisture. Do not use metal ties to secure bags; fasten with string or an elastic band. Either make two slits in the bag to allow steam to escape, or tie string loosely around the end.

Plastic containers which are labelled 'dishwasher safe' or 'boilable' can be used for heating or microwaving foods for a short time.

Microwave cookware made of special plastics has been developed for use in both microwave and conventional ovens, and may safely be used to cook any food items in the microwave. Lugs and handles make containers easier to use as they stay cool even though the dish itself may become warm. Most of these carefully designed dishes have slightly rounded corners rather than square corners to prevent food from overcooking at the edges. They also have ridges on the underside of the container to allow microwave penetration from below. The lids of microwave cookware have vents to allow steam to escape. These dishes may be used to store food in the freezer and may be transferred directly to the microwave. Containers such as ring moulds, roasting and loaf dishes, bacon racks, casseroles and baking sheets are available in various styles and colours. Be sure to follow instructions for use and care.

Glass which is ovenproofed, such as Pyrex, and glass ceramic containers, such as Corningware, are ideal for both heating and cooking in the microwave. Clear glass containers allow you to see what is happening to the food. For anyone using the microwave for the first time this is important, especially when checking cakes or puddings to determine when they are cooked. Ordinary glass without any lead content may be used for heating foods for a short time, but do not use for food with a high sugar or fat content, as the glass will crack. A deep glass bowl and two sizes of measuring jugs will be useful additions to your microwave cookware.

Pottery and china without metal trim or content are usually suitable for microwave cooking and can be used in the same way as glassware. Foods can be cooked and served in the same dish, making cleaning up easier. Dark pottery or china slows the microwave cooking process slightly and dishes may become fairly hot to the touch. Avoid containers with a shiny surface or metallic sheen. If you are unsure whether to use a stoneware or pottery container, test it as described on page 89.

Clay pots or Romertopfs may be used for meat casseroles, poultry or joints of meat. Presoak the lid and base according to manufacturer's directions, and test containers as described on page 89. The cooking time is somewhat longer than for an ordinary casserole because the moisture in the pot attracts some of the microwave energy. These pots become hot during cooking, so use gloves when handling them. Do not add cold liquid during the cooking period as the sudden change in temperature may crack the pot.

Natural shells such as scallops make attractive containers for individual servings of seafood and are safe to use in the microwave. Remember cooking time should be reduced for individual servings.

Wooden items contain some moisture that evaporates during microwave cooking and eventually they become so dry that they crack. Use wooden boards or platters for short term heating rather than for actual cooking. Small wooden utensils, such as wooden spoons, are ideal for use in the microwave.

Wicker and straw baskets should be used for short periods only to heat up rolls or bread for a few seconds. Long periods of heating may cause baskets to dry out.

Aluminium foil in small pieces can be used to shield corners of a baking dish, or to prevent chicken legs, wings or meat bone ends from overcooking, without damaging the oven. It is not advisable to reheat frozen foods in aluminium trays. Transfer foods to a glass ceramic container.

Warning: Large sheets of aluminium foil should not be used as a covering or wrapping as this may cause arcing and flashing which may damage your appliance.

Useful extras A spoon rest next to your microwave is a good idea as food is stirred frequently during cooking time. A small metal 'magic' whisk keeps sauces smooth as they cook and a selection of short-handled wooden and plastic spoons is always useful.

Do not use
☐ Plastic freezer containers as they absorb heat from the food during cooking and distort or melt.
☐ Plastic cream or yoghurt cartons or any other lightweight container.
☐ Styrofoam trays for reheating or cooking, but they can be used for defrosting.
☐ Melamine plates and cups as they absorb microwave energy.
☐ Dinnerware with gold or silver trim as it may cause arcing.
☐ Metal pots or bakeware.
☐ Metal thermometers or skewers.
☐ Metal or wire ties for roasting bags.

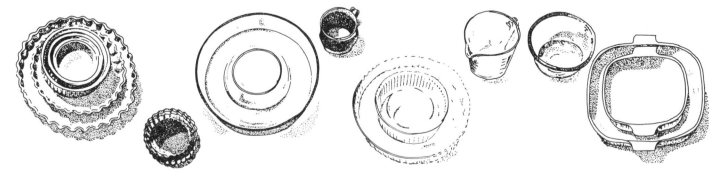

A wide variety of ovenproof ceramic and glass dishes make ideal containers for microwave cookery

FATS

Fats are a concentrated form of body fuel which supplies energy and help in preserving and forming body tissues. Fats used in cookery are both animal and vegetable in origin. Animal fats include butter and lard, which are solid at room temperature and melt at higher temperatures. Vegetable fats include block and soft margarines, as well as oils such as olive, sunflower, maize and other seed and nut oils.

Fats are important ingredients in cooking. They give cakes, breads and pastries a tender texture and provide flavour for sautéed or fried foods. In microwave cooking it is important to remember that foods high in fat content will microwave quickly, as microwaves are strongly attracted to fat molecules. If the fat is unevenly distributed, for example, in back bacon or meat with a large covering of fat on one side, the food will not be uniformly cooked because fat absorbs microwave energy and the meat nearest to it will become overcooked. Always follow instructions for microwaving foods high in fat, and check at the minimum recommended time.

Warning: Do not try to deep-fry with oil in the microwave, as you cannot control the temperature of the oil.

FENNEL

Fennel is a plant with feathery leaves, yellow seeds and a bulbous stem. The flavour of fennel is similar to anise, and the herb is widely used with fish. The leaves can also be used to season pork or chicken dishes. The seeds are popular in sausages and curries, and the bulbous stem can be eaten raw in salads or cooked as a vegetable. When preparing fennel bulbs, wash well and remove outer tough leaf bases.

To microwave whole fennel
Trim and wash 2 medium-sized fennel bulbs. Place in a bowl with 125 ml (4 fl oz) water and a little salt. Cover with vented plastic wrap and microwave on Full Power for about 10 minutes. Drain and use as desired.

Fennel and walnut salad

Full Power
4 minutes

3 small fennel bulbs, cleaned and sliced
125 mℓ (4 fl oz) dry white wine
salt and pepper
1 small bunch of radishes
100 g (3½ oz) walnuts
2 butter head lettuces, washed and patted dry

Dressing
1 egg yolk
30 mℓ (2 tablespoons) lemon juice
15 mℓ (1 tablespoon) French mustard
salt and pepper
125 mℓ (4 fl oz) oil
90 mℓ (3 fl oz) soured cream

Place fennel in a bowl with the wine. Season with salt and pepper and microwave, covered, on Full Power for 3 – 4 minutes, or until just tender. Drain and chill. Grate radishes and coarsely chop walnuts, saving a few whole

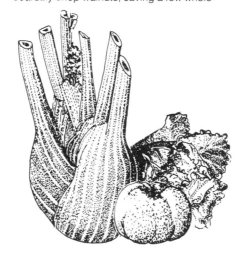

ones for garnishing. To make the dressing, combine egg, lemon juice, mustard and salt and pepper in a blender or food processor and process for a few seconds to mix. With the machine running, gradually pour in oil and blend well. Stir in soured cream and chill well. To serve, arrange lettuce leaves on six individual plates. Top with a little dressing. Add fennel, radishes and nuts. Add a little more dressing and garnish with whole walnuts.
Serves 6

Fennel in creamy wine sauce

Full Power
21 minutes

3 large fennel bulbs, cleaned and thinly sliced
250 mℓ (8 fl oz) water
125 mℓ (4 fl oz) dry white wine
2.5 mℓ (½ teaspoon) salt
60g (2 oz) butter
30 g (1 oz) plain flour
250 mℓ (8 fl oz) single cream
5 mℓ (1 teaspoon) paprika
30 g (1 oz) butter
30 g (1 oz) soft breadcrumbs
60 g (2 oz) Parmesan cheese, grated

Place fennel, water, wine and salt in a large bowl. Cover and microwave on Full Power for about 5 minutes, or until tender. Drain and return cooking liquid to the bowl. Microwave for about 5 minutes, or until reduced to 250 mℓ (8 fl oz). In a large jug, microwave butter for 45 seconds, then stir in flour. Gradually mix in the cooking liquid, cream and paprika. Microwave 3 – 4 minutes, stirring every minute until the sauce is bubbly and thickened. Season to taste with salt. Microwave butter for 30 seconds to melt, stir in breadcrumbs and half the Parmesan cheese.

Divide fennel among four individual baking dishes. Spoon sauce over, sprinkle with breadcrumb mixture and remaining Parmesan cheese. Microwave for 4 – 6 minutes, until bubbly. Stand 2 – 3 minutes before serving.
Serves 4

FIGS

One of the earliest cultivated fruits of which there are more than one hundred varieties. Fresh figs are highly perishable and should be picked and eaten immediately. Green figs make luscious preserves, whilst ripe figs may be eaten as a fruit, served with Parma ham, stewed or turned into jam (*see* Jams). Dried figs are good added to baked desserts, breads, fruit cakes and bars.

Green fig preserve

Full Power
57 minutes

500 g (18 oz) small green figs
1 litre (1¾ pints) cold water
5 mℓ (1 teaspoon) slaked lime (obtainable from chemist)
750 mℓ (1¼ pints) boiling water

Syrup
600 g (1lb 5 oz) preserving sugar
750 mℓ (1¼ pints) boiling water
10 mℓ (2 teaspoons) lemon juice

Wash figs well and remove stems. Cut a small cross in the rounded end. Place figs in a bowl. Combine cold water and slaked lime. Pour over figs and stand 12 hours. Rinse figs very well, then stand in fresh cold water for about 15 minutes. Drain and add boiling water to figs. Cover with vented plastic wrap, microwave on Full Power for 7 minutes. Drain well.

To make the syrup, combine sugar, water and lemon juice in a large bowl. Cover and microwave for 10 minutes, stirring twice during cooking time. Add fruit to boiling syrup. Then microwave, uncovered, for 30 minutes, stirring from time to time during cooking. Drain figs from the syrup. Pack into sterilized jars (see page 116). Microwave syrup, uncovered, for 10 minutes. Pour over figs, cover loosely with lid. When cool, tighten lid and store.
Makes about 450 g (1 lb)

FISH

Fish is one of the best foods for microwave cooking as it retains its subtle flavour and firm texture, and has an excellent appearance too. It is important to remember that fish is a delicate food and is easily overcooked if the timing is not accurate. Always use the minimum time suggested in each recipe, and then test to see if the fish is cooked through. The moment the fish turns opaque, it is done, as it will continue to cook after being taken from the microwave oven. To prepare fish in advance for serving later, undercook it slightly and reheat to complete cooking before serving.

Preserving fruits of the vine, Grape Jelly (page 117)

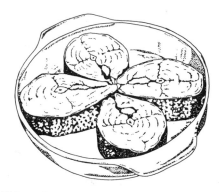

Fish steaks should be arranged with the thicker parts towards the outside of the dish where the microwaves penetrate first.

To poach fish
Poaching is the most frequently used method of cooking fish in the microwave. Arrange pieces of fish with the thin part towards the centre of the dish. Cover loosely with waxed paper and allow about 4 – 6 minutes per 500 g (18 oz) for thick fish steaks and 3 – 4 minutes per 500 g (18 oz) for thinner portions. Change the flavour of the fish by varying the liquid used for poaching. Use white wine, chicken stock or even tomato juice. Add flavouring ingredients such as onion, herbs, peppercorns or lemon slices.

To grill fish
The browning dish provides an excellent means of grilling fish in the microwave, especially for thicker steaks or cutlets. Always turn fish over when juices appear on top and cover with waxed paper.

To steam fish
Cover the container tightly with plastic wrap to hold in as much moisture as possible during cooking. Pierce plastic wrap with a thin skewer or the point of a sharp knife to prevent 'ballooning' during cooking.

Hints for microwaving fish
☐ When microwaving fish coated with breadcrumbs, crushed cornflakes or similar mixtures, use a loose covering of waxed paper or kitchen paper. Steam trapped by an airtight covering will cause the coating to become soggy.
☐ Fold the thin tail section of a whole fish underneath to achieve even cooking, or shield the tail with foil.
☐ Make two or three slashes in the sides of a large whole fish to prevent the skin from bursting and to promote even cooking.
☐ Fish should be fully defrosted before microwaving and pieces should be separated during defrosting time (*See also* Defrosting).
☐ Do not attempt to deep-fry fish in the microwave oven as it is impossible to control the temperature of the oil.

☐ To keep fish from drying out during microwaving, brush with melted butter.
☐ When microwaving 'boil-in-the-bag' fish, remember to pierce the bag before cooking.

Salmon with lemon and fruit

Full Power
11 minutes

6 salmon steaks, about 2.5 cm (1 inch) thick
45 mℓ (3 fl oz) dry white wine
45 g (1½ oz) butter
black pepper
1 lemon, thinly sliced
1 apple, halved, cored and thinly sliced
1 pear, halved, cored and thinly sliced

Arrange salmon steaks in a shallow baking dish with thin ends towards the centre. Sprinkle with wine and set aside. In a large casserole, microwave butter for 1 minute on Full Power. Add lemon, apple and pear slices, toss gently to coat with butter, then microwave, covered, for 1 minute. Gently spoon fruit slices over salmon and add pan juices. Cover with waxed paper and microwave for 4 – 11 minutes, or until fish flakes easily. Stand 5 minutes before serving. Serve fruit with each steak.
Serves 6

Swordfish Provençale

Full Power, High (70%)
20 minutes

750 g (1¾ lb) swordfish or other firm fish, skinned and cubed
60 mℓ (2 fl oz) sweet white wine
60 mℓ (2 fl oz) olive oil
2 celery sticks, thinly sliced
1 leek, finely chopped
2 – 3 garlic cloves, finely chopped
2 x 400-g (14-oz) cans whole tomatoes, with liquid, chopped
10 mℓ (2 teaspoons) lemon juice
1 bay leaf
15 mℓ (1 tablespoon) chopped parsley
5 mℓ (1 teaspoon) oregano
2.5 mℓ (½ teaspoon) basil
2.5 mℓ (½ teaspoon) thyme
salt and pepper

Arrange fish in a shallow baking dish and sprinkle with wine. In a large glass bowl, microwave oil for 45 seconds on Full Power. Add celery, leek and garlic and microwave for 2 – 3 minutes or until vegetables are tender. Add tomatoes and liquid, lemon juice, bay leaf, parsley, oregano, basil and thyme. Season with salt and pepper and microwave for 3 minutes, then reduce power to High (70%) for 5 minutes. Pour sauce over fish and microwave on Full Power for 7 – 9 minutes, or until fish is cooked. Garnish with parsley and lemon slices and serve with hot cooked rice. *Serves 4 – 6*

Elegant fish rolls

Full Power
18 minutes

1 kg (2¼ lb) hake or sole fillets
salt and pepper
½ small onion, chopped
15 g (½ oz) butter
200 g (7 oz) canned salmon, drained
30 mℓ (1 tablespoon) chopped parsley
45 g (1½ oz) butter
30 g (1 oz) plain flour
185 mℓ (6 fl oz) chicken stock
185 mℓ (6 fl oz) milk
100 g (3½ oz) Gruyère cheese, grated
paprika

Skin fillets and thaw if necessary. Sprinkle with salt and set aside. Combine butter and onion and microwave on Full Power for 2 minutes, or until onion is tender. Stir in flaked salmon, parsley and pepper. Mix well, then spread about 45 g (1½ oz) of the filling over each fillet. Roll up and place seam-side down in a baking dish. Microwave butter for about 45 seconds. Blend in flour, stir in stock and milk. Microwave 1 minute, then stir. Microwave until mixture thickens, 3 – 4 minutes, stirring every minute. Pour sauce over fish and microwave for 8 – 9 minutes, or until fish flakes easily. Spoon sauce over fish every 2 minutes. Sprinkle with cheese and paprika and microwave for about 1 minute to melt.
Serves 8 as a starter

Seafood artichoke casserole

Full Power
13 minutes

15 g (½ oz) butter
15 g (½ oz) soft breadcrumbs
45 g (1½ oz) Parmesan cheese, grated
15 mℓ (1 tablespoon) chopped parsley
5 mℓ (1 teaspoon) chopped dill
45 g (1½ oz) butter
30 g (1 oz) plain flour
2.5 mℓ (½ teaspoon) dried thyme or 5 mℓ
  (1 teaspoon) lemon thyme
salt and pepper
250 mℓ (8 fl oz) fish stock (from poaching hake)
125 mℓ (4 fl oz) single cream
10 mℓ (2 teaspoons) lemon juice
400 g (14 oz) hake, poached and cubed
100 g (3½ oz) small peeled shrimps
400 g (14 oz) canned artichoke hearts, drained
  and coarsely chopped
100 g (3½ oz) mushrooms, sliced

Microwave butter in a jug on Full Power for 30 seconds. Stir in breadcrumbs, cheese, parsley and dill. Set aside. Microwave butter in a large jug for 1 minute. Stir in flour, thyme, salt and pepper. Gradually add fish stock and cream. Microwave 3 – 4 minutes, or until thickened, stirring every minute. Stir in lemon juice and add sauce to hake, shrimps, artichoke hearts and mushrooms in a small casserole. Microwave for 6 – 8 minutes until heated through. Just before serving, sprinkle with crumb mixture.
Serves 4 as a main course, 6 as a starter

Mandarin mullet

Full Power
9 minutes

4 red mullet
45 mℓ (3 tablespoons) water
10 mℓ (2 teaspoons) cornflour
10 mℓ (2 teaspoons) chopped parsley
½ chicken stock cube
125 mℓ (4 fl oz) orange juice
30 mℓ (2 tablespoons) dry white wine
15 g (½ oz) butter
300 g (11 oz) canned mandarin oranges,
  drained

To garnish
parsley
grated orange rind

Place fish in a shallow baking dish and sprinkle with water. Cover with vented plastic wrap and microwave on Full Power for 6 – 9 minutes or until fish flakes easily. Stand, covered, while making the sauce.
  Mix cornflour, parsley and chicken stock powder with orange juice and wine and microwave for 2 – 3 minutes until the mixture is thick and bubbly, stirring every minute. Add butter and stir to melt. Stir in orange sections. Drain fish and place on serving plates. Spoon sauce over and garnish with parsley and grated orange rind.
Serves 4

Rolls of trout with mustard sauce

Full Power
17 minutes

2 carrots, cut in julienne
2 – 3 celery sticks, cut in julienne
1 leek, cut in julienne
1 small cucumber, cut in julienne
spring onion tops
45 mℓ (3 tablespoons) water
4 trout, filleted and skinned
salt and black pepper
15 g (½ oz) butter
2 spring onions, chopped
200 mℓ (6½ fl oz) white wine

Mustard sauce
poaching liquid from fish
30 mℓ (2 tablespoons) single cream
5 – 10 mℓ (1 – 2 teaspoons) lemon juice
15 mℓ (1 tablespoon) moutarde de Meaux
  (coarse French mustard)
2.5 mℓ (½ teaspoon) mustard seeds
15 g (½ oz) butter

To garnish
8 lemon slices
parsley or mustard and cress

Take a few julienne strips from each vegetable and carefully tie into a bundle with a spring onion top, making eight bundles. Arrange bundles in a circle in a shallow dish, add water. Cover with vented plastic wrap, microwave on Full Power for 3 – 4 minutes. Vegetables should still be firm.
  Lightly season fish fillets and lay on a board, skin side uppermost. Place a bundle of vegetables on each fillet, roll up and secure with a wooden cocktail stick. Microwave butter in a shallow casserole for 1 minute, add spring onions and microwave 1 minute. Add wine and microwave for a further 2 minutes. Arrange trout rolls in liquid and cover with vented plastic wrap. Microwave for 5 – 7 minutes. Remove fish rolls and keep warm.
  To make the sauce, strain fish cooking liquid and discard solids. Microwave liquid for 4 – 5 minutes to reduce it by about half. Add cream, lemon juice, mustard and mustard seeds. Microwave for 2 minutes, stirring every 30 seconds. Add butter and adjust seasoning if necessary. Remove cocktail sticks from fish, arrange on a serving plate and spoon a little sauce over each of the fillets. Garnish with lemon and parsley or a little mustard and cress.
Serves 4

Skate with baby onions

Full Power
12 minutes

3 – 4 skate wings
10 baby onions
2 bay leaves
400 mℓ (13 fl oz) milk
salt
2.5 mℓ (½ teaspoon) black peppercorns

Sauce
30 mℓ (1 oz) butter
30 mℓ (1 tablespoon) plain flour
45 g (1½ oz) Cheddar cheese, grated
15 mℓ (1 tablespoon) capers

Arrange skate wings in a shallow casserole, with thick parts outwards. Add remaining ingredients and cover with vented plastic wrap. Microwave on Full Power for 9 – 10 minutes. Lift out skate and onions, and keep warm. Strain liquid. In a 1-litre (1¾-pint) jug, microwave butter for 45 seconds. Add flour, stir well and microwave 30 seconds. Add strained liquid and mix well. Microwave for 1½ – 2 minutes, stirring every 30 seconds. Thin sauce with a little extra milk if necessary. Add cheese, stir to melt, then pour sauce over fish. Sprinkle with capers and serve.
Serves 4

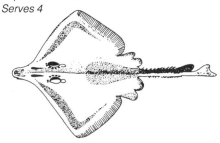

Pickled fish

Full Power, High (70%)
45 minutes

1 kg (2¼ lb) firm white fish
salt and black pepper
1 egg
75 mℓ (2½ fl oz) oil
3 large onions, sliced thickly
7.5 mℓ (1½ teaspoons) turmeric
10 – 15 mℓ (2 – 3 teaspoons) curry paste
75 mℓ (2½ fl oz) wine vinegar
60 g (2 oz) soft brown sugar
15 mℓ (1 tablespoon) apricot jam
100 mℓ (3½ fl oz) tomato sauce (as served with pasta)
100 mℓ (3½ fl oz) water
125 g (4 oz) dried apricots, roughly chopped
1 bay leaf

Cut fish into portions. Season with salt and pepper. Dip fish in egg, drain off excess. Preheat browning dish on Full Power for 8 minutes. Add oil and microwave for 2 minutes. Add fish and microwave for 2 minutes on each side. Drain and set aside. To the oil, add onions, turmeric and curry paste, stir well. Cover and microwave for 8 minutes, stirring twice. Add wine vinegar, microwave for 3 minutes. Add remaining ingredients, microwave for 8 minutes, stirring at least twice during cooking time. Add fish, cover and microwave on High (70%) for 12 minutes, stir carefully twice during cooking time. Cool and refrigerate for at least 24 hours before serving.
Serves 6 – 8

Turban of smoked salmon and sole

Full Power, Medium (50%)
21 minutes

3 soles, filleted
250 g (9 oz) smoked salmon
30 g (1 oz) butter
salt and black pepper

Mousseline
500 g (18 oz) haddock
left-over smoked salmon pieces
2 egg whites
Tabasco
10 – 15 mℓ (2 – 3 teaspoons) lemon juice
25 mℓ (5 teaspoons) chopped parsley
500 mℓ (16 fl oz) single cream, well-chilled
2.5 mℓ (½ teaspoon) dried thyme
pistachio nuts (optional)
1 quantity hollandaise sauce*

To make the mousseline, place fish in work bowl of food processor fitted with metal blade. Season and process until smooth. Add egg whites, Tabasco, lemon juice and parsley, process for a few seconds. With the blades running, slowly add cream, process until well blended. Care must be taken not to overmix at this point. Add thyme and a few pistachio nuts, pulse to combine.

Grease a 25-cm (10-inch) ring mould. Lightly season sole fillets. Arrange fillets crossways in the mould, alternating with smoked salmon and overlapping fish slightly. Allow ends of fish to hang over sides of mould. Pack mousseline into mould. Fold fish ends on to mousseline. Cut a circle of parchment paper slightly larger than mould and cut a few crosses in the centre of paper to allow for expansion. Place paper on top of fish. This dish may be prepared to this stage a few hours in advance. Microwave on Medium (50%) for 20 – 25 minutes. Stand for a few minutes, then drain off any excess liquid. Turn out on to a heated serving platter. Microwave butter on Full Power for 30 seconds, then brush over mould. Serve with hollandaise sauce.
Serves 6

Cod Portugaise

Full Power, High (70%)
26 minutes

2 cod fillets, about 1 kg (2¼ lb)
salt and black pepper
1 lemon, thinly sliced
parsley sprigs

Stuffing
30 mℓ (2 tablespoons) oil
1 large onion, sliced
1 green pepper, chopped
2 celery sticks, chopped
1 – 2 garlic cloves, crushed
45 mℓ (3 tablespoons) chopped parsley
grated rind and juice of ½ lemon
Tabasco
6 crab sticks, sliced
60 g (2 oz) fresh bean sprouts
30 g (1 oz) soft breadcrumbs

Sauce
125 mℓ (4 fl oz) tomato sauce (as served with pasta)
60 mℓ (4 tablespoons) white wine
60 mℓ (4 tablespoons) chicken stock
5 mℓ (1 teaspoon) dried thyme
salt
30 g (1 oz) butter

First make the stuffing. In a medium bowl, combine oil, onion, green pepper, celery and garlic. Microwave on Full Power for 3 minutes, stir well. Add all remaining stuffing ingredients and season well with salt and pepper.

Season fish and place one piece on a lightly oiled baking sheet. Add stuffing and top with second piece of fish, placing it head to tail, to balance thickness. Top with thin lemon slices.

Combine all sauce ingredients in a bowl and microwave for 2 minutes until bubbling and butter has melted. Pour about half the sauce over fish. Cover with vented plastic wrap. Microwave on High (70%) for 18 – 25 minutes, depending on the thickness of the fish. Microwave remaining sauce on Full Power for 3 minutes. Spoon sauce over fish and garnish with parsley.
Serves 4

FISH CAKES

Fish cakes are quickly made in the microwave. They make tasty snacks and are an excellent addition to a lunch box.

Fish cakes

Full Power
29 minutes

500 g (18 oz) hake
300 g (11 oz) smoked haddock
100 mℓ (3½ fl oz) milk
1 bay leaf
salt and pepper
1 onion, chopped
boiling water
½ packet instant mashed potato
generous pinch of thyme
45 mℓ (3 tablespoons) chopped parsley
plain flour
30 mℓ (2 tablespoons) oil

Place fish, milk, bay leaf, seasonings and onion in a large bowl, cover with vented plastic. Microwave on Full Power for 9 – 10 minutes. Drain off liquid and remove bay leaf. Remove skin and bones from fish. Process fish and onion in a food processor until smooth. In a bowl combine instant potato, fish liquid and enough boiling water to form a stiff consistency. Add the mashed potato, thyme and parsley to fish. Process to combine. Shape into fish cakes and sprinkle both sides with a little flour. Preheat browning dish for 8 minutes. Add half the oil and microwave 1 minute. Add half the fish cakes, microwave for 2 minutes, then turn fish cakes and microwave for 2 minutes more. Drain on kitchen paper. Wipe browning dish with kitchen paper. Microwave browning dish for 3 minutes to reheat and repeat cooking procedure with remaining fish cakes. Serve hot or cold.
Makes about 20

FISH FINGERS

Frozen fish fingers microwave very quickly and in a matter of minutes you will have a quick light meal. Serve them with a tasty sauce or dip. When microwaving fish fingers, it is preferable, but not essential, to use a browning dish. Both microwave methods are given here:

To microwave using a browning dish
To thaw, microwave 8 fish fingers on Defrost (30%) for 4 minutes, then stand for 3 minutes. Microwave browning dish on Full Power for 7 minutes. Brush fish fingers with oil, arrange in hot browning dish and

cover loosely with waxed paper. Microwave fish fingers for 1 minute on each side.

To microwave without a browning dish
To thaw, arrange 8 fish fingers in a circle on a plate and loosely cover with waxed paper. Microwave on Defrost (30%) for 4 minutes, then stand for 3 minutes. Brush fish fingers with oil and loosely cover with waxed paper. Microwave on Full Power for 2 – 3 minutes.

FLAMBÉ *See* Alcohol

FLAN
A flan is a round pastry case or pastry shell that is either baked blind, or baked with a sweet or savoury filling. Both the pastry case and filling can be microwaved in a glass pie dish or ceramic flan dish. 'Flan' also sometimes refers to a shallow case made of sponge which has a fruit or other sweet filling.
See also Pastry and Baking Blind.

Tomato and cheese flan

Full Power, Medium (50%)
13 minutes

1 x 22.5-cm (9-inch) shortcrust pastry shell,
   baked blind*
15 g (½ oz) butter
125 g (4 oz) tomatoes, skinned, seeded and
   coarsely chopped
125 g (4 oz) Gruyère cheese, grated
2.5 mℓ (½ teaspoon) basil
4 eggs, beaten
250 mℓ (8 fl oz) single cream
salt and pepper
15 g (½ oz) Parmesan cheese, grated

Microwave butter on Full Power for 30 seconds to melt. Add onion, stir, microwave for 1 minute. Add tomato and spread over the base of the pastry shell. Sprinkle with Gruyère cheese. Mix together the basil, eggs and cream. Season to taste with salt and pepper and pour over the tomato mixture. Microwave on Medium (50%) for 11 – 13 minutes, or until almost set. Sprinkle with Parmesan cheese during last minute of cooking. Allow to stand for 5 minutes before serving
Serves 6 – 8

Gooseberry flan

Full Power, High (70%)
15 minutes

1 x 20-cm (8-inch) shortcrust pastry shell,
   baked blind*
750 g (1¾ lb) gooseberries
90 mℓ (3 fl oz) water
3 large eggs
caster sugar
90 g (3 oz) butter
15 mℓ (1 tablespoon) orange liqueur
whipped cream
grated orange rind

Wash and drain gooseberries and place in a large casserole with water. Cover and microwave on High (70%) for 4 minutes. Increase power to Full Power and microwave for 4 – 5 minutes, or until gooseberries have burst and are soft. Rub gooseberries through a sieve and sweeten to taste with caster sugar. Pour sweetened purée into a casserole dish, add the butter, cut into small pieces, and microwave for 2 – 3 minutes, or until butter melts, stirring every minute. Beat the eggs, add a small amount of the gooseberry purée, then stir egg mixture into the remaining gooseberry purée. Microwave on High (70%) for about 3 minutes, stirring every minute, until the mixture thickens. Cool slightly, then add the orange liqueur. Spoon mixture into the pastry shell and chill until needed. Serve with whipped cream and grated orange rind.
Serves 6 – 8

Note: 1 x 400-g (14-oz) can gooseberries, drained, may be substituted for fresh gooseberries.

FONDANT
A melt-in-the-mouth, flavoured paste of sugar and water used in sweets and icings. The recipe below is rich and smooth.

Fondant

Full Power
20 minutes

600 g (1 lb 5 oz) caster sugar
30 g (1oz) butter
125 mℓ (4 fl oz) milk
pinch of cream of tartar
125 mℓ (4 fl oz) single cream
few drops of vanilla extract
melted chocolate

Place all ingredients, except vanilla extract, in a 4-litre (6½-pint) bowl, stir well. Microwave 10 minutes on Full Power. Wash the sides of the bowl with a brush dipped in cold water to remove all the sugar crystals. Cover with vented plastic, microwave for 2 minutes, then stir well and wash down the sides again. Microwave for 8 – 10 minutes until bubbles appear on the surface (110 °C/230 °F on a sugar thermometer). Cool until the bubbles have subsided. Pour on to a lightly greased marble or stainless steel surface and allow to cool until lukewarm. Knead with a paddle or heavy duty spatula until very smooth. As the mixture cools it begins to crumble; however with kneading, it becomes smooth again. Work in vanilla extract. Cover in plastic wrap and place in an airtight container to 'ripen' for a few days. Stand at room temperature for 1 hour, knead well. Roll out, cut and shape. Allow to dry on a piece of foil or plastic. Dip into melted chocolate.
Makes about 50

FONDUE
Fondue usually refers to a Swiss national dish made from grated cheese gently heated in a casserole or fireproof dish from which it is served. It is eaten communally with guests dipping small cubes of bread into the melted cheese.

Another kind of fondue is fondue bourguignonne. Oil is heated and strips of raw beef and raw vegetables are cooked in the hot oil, then dipped in a selection of tasty sauces.

Chocolate fondue is a melted chocolate sauce used as a dessert. Small pieces of fruit cake or Madeira cake, fresh strawberries, cherries, tangerine segments or banana slices are dipped into the warm chocolate mixture.

Both cheese and chocolate fondue can be made in the microwave oven, but fondue bourguignonne is not suitable for microwave cooking, as it is impossible to control the temperature of the oil.

Swiss cheese fondue

Medium (50%)
6 minutes

1 garlic clove, cut in half
250 mℓ (8 fl oz) white wine
500 g (18 oz) Gruyère cheese, shredded
30 g (1 oz) plain flour
pinch of nutmeg
pinch of pepper
15 – 30 mℓ (1 – 2 tablespoons) brandy
French bread, cut in cubes

Rub a 2-litre (3½-pint) casserole with cut garlic. Add wine and microwave on Medium (50%) for 3 – 4 minutes or until bubbles form. Do not boil. Combine cheese, flour, nutmeg and pepper and toss gently. Add mixture to wine, stir gently and microwave 4 – 6 minutes or until cheese melts, stirring every minute. Stir in brandy and serve with bread cubes. Keep fondue warm over a spirit burner or reheat in the microwave oven as needed.
Serves 4

Chocolate fondue

Full Power
3½ minutes

45 mℓ (3 tablespoons) honey
125 mℓ (4 fl oz) single cream
100 g (3½ oz) plain chocolate, broken in
   pieces
100 g (3½ oz) milk chocolate, broken in pieces
few drops of vanilla extract
7 g (¼ oz) butter
15 – 30 mℓ (1 – 2 tablespoons) orange liqueur

Combine honey, cream and chocolate in a 1-litre (1¾-pint) casserole. Microwave on Full Power for 2½ – 3 minutes. Stir until completely smooth. Add vanilla, butter and liqueur, and mix well. Serve with cubes of fruit cake, strawberries, marshmallows, banana chunks and orange sections.
Serves 6

FRANKFURTERS

Originally from Germany, these lightly smoked sausages have become famous worldwide. Whether purchased loose or vacuum-packed, frankfurters are pre-cooked and are ideally suited to quick re-heating in the microwave. Add to soups and casseroles, use in dips, turn into mini kebabs or serve with sauerkraut.
See also Hot Dogs.

Barbecued frankfurters

Full Power
8 minutes

500 g (18 oz) frankfurters, sliced into 3-cm (1¼-inch) lengths
250 mℓ (8 fl oz) tomato sauce (as served with pasta)
125 g (4 oz) spicy chutney
45 mℓ (3 tablespoons) A1 sauce
45 g (1½ oz) soft brown sugar
10 mℓ (2 teaspoons) Worcestershire sauce
5 mℓ (1 teaspoon) dry mustard
2.5 mℓ (½ teaspoon) grated horseradish

Place all the ingredients except frankfurters, into a medium-sized bowl. Microwave on Full Power for 4 – 5 minutes. Stir at least twice during cooking time. Add frankfurters, cover and microwave for 4 – 6 minutes, until piping hot, stirring from time to time. Pour into a heated serving bowl and serve with plenty of cocktail sticks.
Serves about 15, as a cocktail snack

FREEZING

See also Defrosting, and for vegetables *see* Blanching.

Teaming the microwave with the deep-freeze means really quick and convenient cooking. It is easy to prepare extra portions of food to freeze for busy days or unexpected guests. Even individual meals, soups or portions can be frozen, then defrosted and reheated in only a few minutes in the microwave oven.

Select containers that are suitable for both the freezer and microwave, so that cooking, freezing, defrosting and reheating can be done in the same dish. Be sure to label food for the freezer clearly, and add microwave cooking instructions, such as 'heat on High (70%) for 5 minutes', so anyone wishing to eat the meal knows exactly how to prepare it. To freeze casseroles so that they do not occupy your favourite dish for several weeks, line the dish with plastic wrap or foil, add the food and freeze. Once frozen, remove food from the dish, wrap and label, and return to the freezer. Meanwhile, you can continue to use your dish for other meals. When you are ready to reheat the frozen food, take it out of the freezer, unwrap it and return it to the dish. There are numerous ovenproof disposable dishes available on the market which are ideal for freezing and reheating in the microwave. They are inexpensive and practical to use for informal meals.

Freezing guidelines

☐ Some foods do not freeze well: hard-boiled eggs become tough and rubbery, bananas go black in the freezer, and mayonnaise and custard may separate if frozen.
☐ When preparing dishes for the freezer, take care not to overcook them. Remember, they will continue to cook when you reheat them in the microwave oven.
☐ The flavour of many seasonings may change when foods are frozen. For example, cloves, garlic, pepper and sage become more pronounced, while salt and onions lose their flavour. You may need to correct the seasoning during reheating.
☐ Freeze foods like sausages, bacon and chops in usable portions so you take out only what you need at one time.
☐ Pizzas, tarts, flans, cakes and quiches can be cut into individual portions before freezing, and can be thawed and reheated quickly and easily.

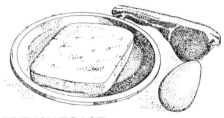

FRENCH TOAST

A delicious breakfast dish made from bread which has been dipped into an egg and milk mixture. Once fried the toast can be topped with a variety of sweet or savoury flavourings.

French toast

Full Power
6 minutes

2 eggs
45 mℓ (3 tablespoons) milk
pinch of salt
few drops of vanilla extract
90 g (3 oz) butter
6 slices of bread

Toppings
cinnamon and sugar
maple or golden syrup
jam and cream
bacon

Mix together eggs, milk, salt and vanilla. Preheat browning dish on Full Power for 5 minutes. Add one-third of the butter and microwave 30 seconds. Dip two bread slices in egg mixture and microwave in browning dish on Full Power for 30 – 40 seconds. Turn slices and microwave for 15 – 25 seconds. Serve with topping of your choice. Repeat process with remaining bread slices, adding more butter as needed.
Serves 6

FRIANDISES

Friandises are small pieces of fruit or nuts coated with a thin layer of crisp caramel sugar. Serve them with coffee after a formal dinner.

Friandises

300 mℓ (10 fl oz) sugar caramel*
fruits such as tangerine segments, grapes, strawberries and cherries
dates
selection of nuts

Remove pith from tangerine segments. Leave stems on grapes, strawberries and cherries. Wash and dry thoroughly. Make caramel, removing from microwave when light golden in colour. Have ready two oiled forks and a well oiled baking sheet. Dip fruit sections, one at a time, into caramel, remove and allow excess to drip off. Place on baking sheet. Continue until all the fruit has been used up. Should the caramel become too thick to work with, microwave for 1 minute on High (70%). Continue as before. When caramelized fruits are hard, lift off baking sheet, trim off excess caramel and serve in tiny paper cases.
Makes 50 friandises

FRIKKADELS

Frikkadels are meat balls or rissoles made from raw or cooked meat. If raw meat is used, it is minced and mixed with such ingredients as breadcrumbs, eggs and seasoning, then shaped and fried. When cooked meat is used, it is chopped and mixed with mashed potato, onion, egg and seasoning, then shaped and fried. Frikkadels cook quickly in the microwave and are moist and juicy, but they do not crisp as much on the outside as when fried conventionally. Frikkadels are often served with a piquant sauce.

Frikkadels in soured cream sauce

Full Power
15 minutes

500 g (18 oz) minced beef
250 g (9 oz) minced pork
30 g (1 oz) soft breadcrumbs
150 mℓ (5 fl oz) milk
2 eggs
30 mℓ (2 tablespoons) chopped onion
5 mℓ (1 teaspoon) salt
pinch of allspice
pinch of grated nutmeg
oil
250 mℓ (8 fl oz) water
30 mℓ (1 tablespoon) plain cake flour
250 mℓ (8 fl oz) soured cream
10 mℓ (2 teaspoons) lemon juice
10 mℓ (2 teaspoons) fresh chopped dill or 2.5 mℓ (½ teaspoon) dried dill

Mix together the meats, breadcrumbs, milk, eggs, onion, salt, allspice and nutmeg. Shape into balls about 1 cm (½ inch) in diameter.

Place frikkadels in a shallow casserole with 15 ml (1 tablespoon) oil and brush with a little oil. Microwave on Full Power for 6 – 8 minutes, rearranging twice. Remove meat and keep warm. Pour off any excess fat, then stir water into pan drippings. Microwave for 1 – 1½ minutes or until boiling. Stir flour into soured cream, mix a small amount of pan juices into soured cream and return mixture to the dish. Add lemon juice and dill and microwave for 2 – 3 minutes, stirring every minute until thickened. Return meat balls to the dish and microwave for 1 – 2 minutes to heat through. Serve with hot cooked noodles if desired. *Serves 6*

FRITTERS

Fritters are pieces of food cooked in batter and fried in deep fat. They cannot be microwaved successfully.

FRUIT

Fruit is so versatile, it can be used for the simplest of dishes, or as part of a spectacular presentation. If you wish to keep cooked fruit whole, poaching is the ideal method of cooking. In the microwave, fruit poaches in a fraction of the normal time and keeps its shape and colour. Either cook fruit in a small quantity of sugar syrup (see below) or sprinkle it with a little sugar. Place in a covered casserole or in a roasting bag and microwave for suggested time.

Guidelines for microwaving fruit
☐ Those fruits which are cooked whole, with skins on, should be pricked before microwaving.
☐ Slightly overripe fruits can be cooked without additional liquid. They are easily puréed and make delicious toppings for desserts.
☐ Stand cooked fruit for 5 minutes before serving.

Frozen fruit should be partly defrosted in the microwave so that it is still icy. Allow to stand at room temperature until completely thawed.

Sugar syrup

Full Power
7 minutes

300 ml (10 fl oz) water
125 g (4 oz) caster sugar

Place water and sugar in a large bowl, microwave on Full Power for 3 minutes, stir well to dissolve crystals. Brush the sides of the bowl with water. Microwave for 4 minutes, use as required.
Sufficient to poach 450 g (1 lb) fruit

Variations
☐ Add a little lemon juice and rind to syrup.
☐ Add a cinnamon stick to syrup.
☐ Add liqueur of your choice to cooked fruit.
☐ Cook sugar syrup to caramel stage, add extra water and liqueur, soak fresh fruit in this.

FRESH FRUIT COOKING CHART

FRUIT	QUANTITY	COOKING TIME Full Power	PREPARATION
Apricots	450 g (1 lb)	7 – 9 minutes	Cut in half and stone. Sprinkle with sugar to taste
Cape gooseberries	450 g (1 lb)	4 – 5 minutes	Prick with needle. Sprinkle with sugar to taste
Cooking apples, puréed	450 g (1 lb)	8 – 10 minutes	Peel, core and slice. Add sugar to taste
Cooking apples, baked whole	4	7 – 8 minutes	Core and stuff, if desired
Guavas	450 g (1 lb)	8 – 10 minutes	Peel and halve, poach in sugar syrup*
Peaches	4 medium	4 – 6 minutes	Peel, halve and stone. Cook halves or slices. Add sugar to taste
Pears	4 medium	7 – 9 minutes	Peel, halve and core. Sprinkle with a little lemon juice or cook in a syrup made of 60 g (2 oz) caster sugar, 75 ml (2½ fl oz) water, piece cinnamon stick
Plums and cherries	450 g (1 lb)	4 – 5 minutes	Cut plums in half. Remove stones. Remove cherry stalks. Add a strip of lemon rind and sugar to taste
Quinces	450 g (1 lb)	6 – 8 minutes	Peel, core and slice thickly. Cook in sugar syrup*
Rhubarb	450 g (1 lb)	8 – 10 minutes	Wash and cut into 3-cm (1¼-inch) lengths. Add 100 g (3½ oz) caster sugar and a strip of lemon rind
Soft Fruits			
Loganberries	450 g (1 lb)	4 – 5 minutes	Add sugar to taste
Mulberries	450 g (1 lb)	4 – 5 minutes	Remove stems and add sugar to taste
Strawberries	450 g (1 lb)	4 – 5 minutes	Hull and add sugar to taste

Note: Most fruits can be poached in a sugar syrup*

FRUIT CAKE

Rich, dark fruit cakes, a wonderful combination of dried fruit and nuts, are usually made for Christmas or special celebrations. They take a little time to mature, but will last for months and months. Light fruit cakes can be made at the last minute and are ideal to serve at any time. Bake them in round, square or tube dishes.
See also Christmas Cake.

Light fruit cake

High (70%)
9 minutes

100 g (3½ oz) glacé cherries, quartered
350 g (12 oz) mixed dried fruit
12 dried apricots, roughly chopped
60 g (2 oz) almonds, chopped
250 g (9 oz) margarine
250 g (9 oz) caster sugar
4 eggs
grated rind and juice of 1 lemon
2.5 ml (½ teaspoon) bicarbonate of soda
150 ml (5 fl oz) yoghurt
350 g (12 oz) self-raising flour
pinch of salt
1 quantity lemon icing*

Combine the fruits and nuts in a bowl, add 45 g (1½ oz) of the flour and toss so as to coat fruit with a little flour. Cream margarine well, add caster sugar, beat until light and fluffy. Add eggs one at a time, beating well after each addition. Combine lemon juice and rind, bicarbonate of soda and yoghurt. Sift flour and salt. Add about one-third of the dry ingredients to creamed mixture, beat well, than add one-third of the yoghurt mixture, beat well. Repeat twice until all the ingredients have been combined. Stir in the fruit. Pour into a greased 20-cm (8-inch) deep round pan or a 25-cm (10-inch) ring pan. Microwave on High (70%) for 9 – 11 minutes. Stand in pan for 15 minutes before turning out on to a cake rack. When cool drizzle with lemon icing.
Makes 1 x 20-cm (8-inch) cake

FRUIT SALAD

It is not necessary to have a recipe for fruit salad. Almost any combination of fresh fruits can begin or end a meal and a light splash of sugar syrup, liqueur or fruit juice gives the fruit added flavour. Use the microwave to melt sugar with liqueur or fruit juice and pour over fruits.

Try these syrup combinations
☐ Microwave a little brown sugar with some red wine on Medium (50%) to just melt sugar. Cool the mixture, then pour over sliced strawberries and peeled sliced kiwi fruits. Serve with a glass of the same wine.

☐ Microwave 250 ml (8 fl oz) orange juice, 45 ml (3 tablespoons) lemon juice, 45 g (1½ oz) caster sugar and 15 ml (1 tablespoon) chopped fresh mint on Medium (50%) for 2 minutes, then cool. Strain and pour over three kinds of melon balls. Garnish with fresh mint.

☐ Microwave 250 ml (8 fl oz) orange juice, 45 ml (3 tablespoons) light rum, 10 ml (2 teaspoons) grated orange rind on Medium (50%) for 2 minutes. Let cool, then pour over a combination of seedless green grapes, sweet melon balls and fresh or frozen, thawed blueberries.

☐ Microwave 30 ml (2 tablespoons) lime juice, 125 ml (4 fl oz) orange juice, 30 ml (2 tablespoons) honey and 5 ml (1 teaspoon) fresh mint leaves on Medium (50%) for 2 minutes. Cool and strain, then toss with chilled grapefruit and orange sections.

Fruits in port wine

Medium (50%)
3 minutes

350 g (12 oz) strawberries, hulled
500 g (18 oz) seedless green grapes
375 mℓ (12 fl oz) ruby port
60 g (2 oz) caster sugar
2 x 2.5-cm (1-inch) cinnamon sticks
4 whole cloves

Combine strawberries and grapes in a large serving bowl. Combine port, sugar, cinnamon sticks and cloves in a large jug and microwave on Medium (50%) for 3 minutes. Cool, strain and pour over the fruits. Cover and refrigerate for several hours, stirring gently occasionally.
Serves 6

FUDGE

Fudge is a creamy sweet made with sugar and condensed milk or cream to which various flavourings such as vanilla, al-

monds, chocolate and nuts or cherries are added. The microwave makes short work of fudge-making and the results are delicious. Take care to use a large bowl, as the ingredients become very hot and increase in volume.

Amazing fudge

High (70%)
3 minutes

200 g (7 oz) processed cheese slices
175 g (6 oz) butter
800 g (1 lb 14 oz) icing sugar
75 g (2½ oz) cocoa powder
few drops of vanilla extract
100 g (3½ oz) nuts or raisins, or 100 g (3½ oz) marshmallows, roughly chopped

Melt cheese and butter together in microwave on High (70%) for 2½ – 3 minutes, stirring every minute. Turn into a large mixing bowl. Sift icing sugar and cocoa and mix into the cheese mixture, along with the vanilla. Beat until smooth. Fold in chopped nuts, raisins or marshmallows. Spread into a lined 22.5 x 32.5-cm (9 x 13-inch) shallow tin. Chill well. Cut into squares and serve. For best results keep this fudge refrigerated.
Makes about 70 squares

Quick chocolate fudge

Full Power
2 minutes

500 g (18 oz) icing sugar
60 g (2 oz) cocoa powder
125 g (4 oz) butter
60 mℓ (4 tablespoons) single cream
few drops of vanilla extract
100 g (3½ oz) nuts, chopped

Combine sifted icing sugar and cocoa in a large deep bowl. Add butter, cut into chunks, and stir in cream and vanilla. Cover with waxed paper and microwave on Full Power for 2 minutes. Stir hot mixture well to incorporate melted butter, then beat well until mixture loses some of its gloss. Stir in half the nuts and turn into a greased 20-cm (8-inch) shallow square tin. Sprinkle remaining nuts over and lightly press into the fudge. Chill until firm, then cut into squares to serve.
Makes about 64 squares, depending on size

Creamy fudge

High (70%)
14 minutes

400 g (14 oz) canned condensed milk
25 g (4 oz) margarine
500 g (18 oz) icing sugar
few drops of vanilla extract

Combine all the ingredients in a large bowl. Microwave on High (70%) for 2 minutes, stir. Microwave for 12 – 14 minutes, stirring frequently. The fudge should be light golden in colour. Beat with a wooden spoon for 1 minute. Pour into a greased 20-cm (8-inch) shallow square tin. Cool until just setting, then mark into squares. Cool completely then cut into squares. Store in an air-tight container.
Makes about 50 squares

GALANTINE

A galantine is a dish of chicken or meat which is boned and stuffed, and restored as far as possible to its original shape. It is then rolled or tied in cheesecloth and simmered in stock until tender. If it is to be served cold, the galantine is chilled before being sliced thinly. Cooking a galantine in a microwave really saves time, as it takes only one-quarter to one-third the time the dish would take if cooked conventionally. Soaked clay pots are ideal for microwaving galantines but remember to extend the cooking time by a few minutes.

Galantine of lamb

Full Power
52 minutes

1 x 2 kg (4¼ lb) leg of lamb, boned
375 mℓ (12 fl oz) dry white wine
10 mℓ (2 teaspoons) chopped fresh mint leaves
10 mℓ (2 teaspoons) crushed fresh rosemary
peppercorns, bruised
3 garlic cloves, bruised
5 mℓ (1 teaspoon) salt

Stuffing
500 g (18 oz) boned, skinned chicken breasts
125 g (4 oz) cooked ham, diced
4 bacon rashers, chopped
30 g (1 oz) pecan nuts
10 mℓ (2 teaspoons) grated lemon rind
1 garlic clove, finely chopped
5 mℓ (1 teaspoon) chopped fresh mint leaves
5 mℓ (1 teaspoon) chopped fresh rosemary
15 g (½ oz) butter
250 g (9 oz) chicken livers
125 mℓ (9 oz) white wine
30 mℓ (2 tablespoons) whisky
pepper

Pat lamb dry and place in a large glass container. Pour wine over, sprinkle with mint, rosemary and peppercorns. Marinate overnight in the refrigerator, turning several times. Drain well and reserve marinade.

For the stuffing, cut 1 chicken breast in thin strips and set aside. Chop remaining chicken breasts and place in a food processor. Add ham, bacon, nuts, lemon rind, garlic, mint and rosemary, process until well blended. Microwave butter in a casserole on Full Power for 30 seconds to melt. Prick chicken livers, add to casserole, cover and microwave for 3 – 4 minutes, or until just cooked. Centres should still be pink. Remove livers with a slotted spoon, add livers to chicken mixture and blend well. Add wine to liquid remaining in the casserole and microwave for about 3 minutes, uncovered, or until reduced by half. Stir into chicken mixture along with the whisky. Season with pepper to taste. Layer stuffing in pocket of lamb alternately with strips of chicken breast. Sew up neatly.

Roll lamb in a double thickness of cheesecloth and shape neatly. Tie ends securely. Place lamb in a large casserole and pour over reserved marinade. Add just enough water to cover the meat. Add bruised garlic and salt. Cover and microwave on Full Power for 8 – 11 minutes per 500 g (18 oz), depending on how well done you like lamb. To serve hot, remove lamb from liquid and stand for 20 minutes before carving. To serve cold, remove lamb from liquid, cool, then chill well. Remove cheesecloth and slice thinly. Place on a platter and garnish as desired.
Serves 10 – 12

Galantine of chicken

Full Power, High (70%)
30 minutes

1 chicken
salt and pepper
30 mℓ (2 tablespoons) brandy
oil
1.5 litres (2¾ pints) good chicken stock

Stuffing
300 g (11 oz) sausage meat, skins removed
100 g (3½ oz) minced veal
salt and pepper
60 mℓ (4 tablespoons) chopped parsley
5 mℓ (1 teaspoon) dried tarragon
15 mℓ (1 tablespoon) finely grated orange rind
30 mℓ (2 tablespoons) orange juice
45 mℓ (3 tablespoons) brandy
30 g (1 oz) soft breadcrumbs
1 egg, slightly beaten
45 g (1½ oz) whole walnuts

To bone chicken, start with the breast side down. Make a slit in the skin along backbone from neck to tail. Starting at the tail, work meat away from the bone. Cut tips off drumsticks and remove wing tips at second joint. With a sharp knife, work flesh away from thigh bone and continue over drumstick. Be sure to cut sinews but be careful not to puncture the skin. Work down toward the breast, stopping when you reach the top of the breastbone. Repeat process on other side of the chicken. When the breastbone is reached, gently pull the carcass away from the flesh. Sprinkle flesh with salt and pepper and brandy. Set aside while preparing the stuffing.

To make the stuffing, mix all ingredients, except walnuts. Season with salt and pepper. Place half the stuffing down the centre of the boned chicken. Place whole walnuts on stuffing, then cover with remaining stuffing. Wrap flesh and skin around stuffing, and sew together neatly. Shape into a neat oblong. Brush skin with a little oil and wrap tightly in clean cheesecloth. Tie ends securely. Place in

a large casserole and cover with chicken stock. Cover and microwave on Full Power for 10 minutes. Reduce power to High (70%) and microwave for 18 – 20 minutes. Remove chicken roll from stock and cool, then chill. To serve, remove cloth and slice thinly. Arrange slices on a platter and garnish as desired.
Makes about 20 slices

GARLIC

Although it is thought to originate in Eastern Europe, this pungent herb is now cultivated worldwide. The strong taste of garlic is not enjoyed by everyone, but used in moderation garlic adds a wonderful flavour and provides dishes with a certain zest. Garlic cooks perfectly in the microwave, but as with conventional cooking, be sure to combine it with other ingredients as on its own it may scorch.

Garlic bread

High (70%)
2 minutes

1 long stick of French bread
1 quantity garlic and parsley butter*
60 g (2 oz) Cheddar cheese, grated

Cut French bread in half. Slice thickly at an angle, but do not cut completely through the slices. Spread bread thickly with garlic and herb butter. To reshape, push slices together firmly. Spread a little butter along the top of the bread. Sprinkle with cheese. Place each piece of the bread in a roasting bag and tie ends with string. Microwave on High (70%) for 2 minutes. Serve immediately.
Makes 2 x 40-cm (16-inch) loaves

Garlic mushroom starter

Full Power
8 minutes

12 – 14 large mushrooms, wiped clean
75 g (2½ oz) butter
2 garlic cloves, crushed
15 mℓ (1 tablespoon) lemon juice
generous pinch of dried tarragon
pinch of cayenne pepper
salt and black pepper
2.5 mℓ (½ teaspoon) cornflour
45 mℓ (3 tablespoons) white wine
15 mℓ (1 tablespoon) finely chopped chives

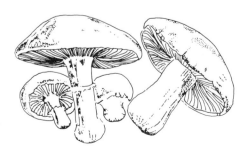

Place mushrooms in a greased shallow casserole. Overlap mushrooms if necessary as they shrink a great deal when cooked. Place butter in a small bowl, microwave on Full Power for 2 minutes. Add remaining ingredients, except chives. Brush each mushroom with butter mixture. Pour leftover butter into casserole dish. Cover with vented plastic wrap. Microwave 5 – 6 minutes. Do not overcook, as mushrooms continue to cook for some time after they have been removed from microwave. Sprinkle with chives.
Serves 6

GEFILTE FISH

Gefilte fish is a traditional Jewish dish made in advance and served during Passover.

Gefilte fish

Full Power, High (70%)
22 minutes

750 g (1¾ lb) hake
2 carrots
1 medium-sized onion
1 celery stick
30 mℓ (2 tablespoons) matzo meal
salt and black pepper
15 mℓ (1 tablespoon) oil
3 eggs
500 mℓ (16 fl oz) boiling water
5 mℓ (1 teaspoon) yellow food colouring
15 mℓ (1 tablespoon) powdered gelatine

To garnish
1 carrot, sliced
5 mℓ (1 teaspoon) water
parsley sprigs

Mince or process fish, carrots, onion and celery. Add matzo meal, seasonings, oil and egg, mix well. Roll fish mixture into 12 large balls. Arrange in a single layer in a large casserole. Add water, food colouring and gelatine, cover. Microwave on High (70%) for 20 minutes. Uncover and allow to cool. Refrigerate until well chilled. Place sliced carrot in a small bowl, add water. Microwave on Full Power for 2 minutes, cool. To serve, arrange fish balls on a flat serving platter with the jellied liquid. Garnish each fish ball with slices of carrot and parsley.
Makes 12

Note: Traditionally gefilte fish has fish bones and heads cooked in the liquid. If made this way, omit the gelatine.

GELATINE

Gelatine is an odourless and tasteless extract of animal protein used to set many sweet and savoury dishes, such as cold fruit soufflés, fish or vegetable mousses, jellies, pie fillings, ice creams and other moulded dishes. It can be used with almost any food with the exception of raw pineapple and pawpaw. These foods contain an enzyme that prevents the gelatine from setting, but

if pineapple or pawpaw is cooked or canned, the enzyme is destroyed and the fruit can be used successfully in gelatine mixtures.

As a general rule, use 15 mℓ (1 tablespoon) powdered gelatine to set 500 mℓ (16 fl oz) of liquid. If the jelly is to be unmoulded, it is a good idea to use about 2.5 mℓ (½ – 1 teaspoon) more gelatine to make the mould firmer and easier to handle.

Dissolving gelatine in any liquid is easily done with the help of the microwave. Fewer utensils are used and time is reduced when the microwave is used for this step in cooking. Simply measure the required liquid in a microwave jug or bowl, sprinkle gelatine over and stand for a few minutes until softened. Microwave, uncovered, on Medium (50%) until dissolved. The timing will depend on the amount of liquid and gelatine used, but 45 seconds to 1 minute is sufficient for 45 – 90 mℓ (3 – 6 tablespoons) or slightly longer for larger amounts. Stir well to make sure all the gelatine has dissolved and the liquid is clear, then use as directed in the recipe. If gelatine mixtures start setting and become too solid to mould or use, a few seconds on Medium (50%) will soften them. Most gelatine mixtures should not be boiled as this will weaken the setting power. Gelatine mixtures with a high fat content can be frozen.

Irish coffee parfait

Medium (50%)
1 minute

100 g (3½ oz) caster sugar
815 mℓ (26 fl oz) hot strong coffee
30 mℓ (2 tablespoons) gelatine
75 mℓ (2½ fl oz) Irish whiskey
250 mℓ (8 fl oz) cream
30 g (1 oz) caster sugar
45 g (1½ oz) plain chocolate, grated (optional)

Stir sugar into coffee and let dissolve. Sprinkle gelatine over Irish whiskey and stand for 5 minutes. Microwave on Medium (50%) for about 45 seconds, or until dissolved. Stir into the coffee and cool mixture to the consistency of unbeaten egg white. Pour into eight parfait or dessert glasses and chill until firm, about 2 hours. Beat cream with sugar until stiff and spoon on top of coffee mixture. Sprinkle with grated chocolate, if desired.
Serves 8

Tangy tomato aspic

Full Power, High (70%), Medium (50%)
20 minutes

A delicious summer salad for a cold buffet

1.5 litres (2¾ pints) tomato juice
1 large onion, coarsely chopped
3 celery sticks, coarsely chopped
5 mℓ (1 teaspoon) dried basil
60 mℓ (4 tablespoons) Worcestershire sauce
pinch of chilli powder
garlic salt
45 mℓ (3 tablespoons) gelatine, powdered
150 mℓ (5 fl oz) dry white wine
30 mℓ (2 tablespoons) dry sherry
225 g (8 oz) canned water chestnuts, drained
   and sliced
30 g (1 oz) finely chopped spring onion
60 mℓ (4 tablespoons) oil
45 mℓ (3 tablespoons) finely chopped spring
   onion
30 mℓ (2 tablespoons) red wine vinegar
5 mℓ (1 teaspoon) dried basil
15 mℓ (1 tablespoon) Dijon mustard
salt and pepper

Garnish
sliced tomatoes

Combine tomato juice, onion, celery, basil, Worcestershire sauce, chilli powder and garlic salt to taste in a large casserole. Microwave on Full Power for about 6 – 8 minutes, or until mixture comes to a boil. Reduce power to High (70%), cover and microwave for 10 minutes or until vegetables are soft. Purée tomato mixture in batches and strain into a clean bowl. Sprinkle gelatine over wine and sherry in a small bowl and stand for 10 minutes. Microwave on Medium (50%) for 1½ – 2 minutes, or until completely dissolved. Stir gelatine into tomato mixture, mixing well. Pour half the mixture into a 2-litre (3½-pint) mould and chill until nearly set.

Meanwhile, mix water chestnuts, spring onion and lemon juice. Toss lightly, then drain. Add the mixture to the mould and spoon in remaining tomato mixture. Chill until firm, 3 – 4 hours. Combine oil, spring onion, vinegar, basil, mustard, salt and pepper in a blender and blend well.

To serve, unmould tomato mixture on to a platter. Surround with sliced tomatoes and spoon oil and vinegar mixture over.
Serves 8

GHEE
This is the Indian name given to clarified butter or margarine. It is used extensively in Indian poultry, beef and rice dishes.
See Butter.

GIBLETS
Giblets comprise the neck, ends of wings, liver, heart and gizzard of chickens or other birds and are used in making stock or as a base for delicious soups, sauces and gravies. The microwave makes short work of simmering the giblets to make a rich stock.

Giblets are usually packed inside the body cavity of poultry and should be removed as soon as possible when thawing the bird in the microwave. Always wash and trim giblets before cooking.

Rich giblet stock

Medium (50%)
22 minutes

giblets, including neck (use of liver optional)
1 celery stick, sliced
1 carrot, sliced
1 small onion, sliced
3 parsley sprigs
375 mℓ (12 fl oz) water
salt
2 peppercorns
1 whole clove
1 bay leaf

Remove skin from neck if necessary and slash giblets on all sides with a sharp knife to prevent them from bursting. Set liver aside. Place giblets in a 1-litre (1¾-pint) casserole and add all remaining ingredients. Microwave, covered, on Medium (50%) for 10 minutes. Stir, cover again and microwave for 10 – 12 minutes until giblets are tender. Add liver, if used, during last 5 minutes of cooking time. Chill stock, then remove giblets and neck. Coarsely chop giblets and strain stock. Giblets can be added to the stock or to the dish made with stock.
Makes about 375 mℓ (12 fl oz)

Giblet gravy

Full Power
3½ minutes

30 g (1 oz) pan dripping from chicken or turkey
30 mℓ (1 tablespoon) plain flour
250 mℓ (8 fl oz) giblet stock*
chopped cooked giblets (optional)
salt and pepper

Place dripping in a 1-litre (1¾-pint) jug. Stir in flour, microwave on Full Power for 30 seconds. Stir in stock and microwave for 2 – 3 minutes until thickened, stirring every minute. Stir in

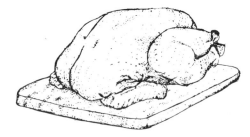

chopped giblets and sprinkle with salt and pepper.
Makes about 250 mℓ (8 fl oz)

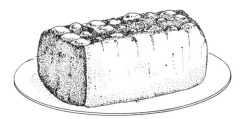

GINGERBREAD
As early as the 14th century, gingerbread was a favoured delicacy. It was a well spiced, hard cake containing honey as a sweetener and was often extravagantly decorated with gold leaf, studded with cloves and presented as a gift in a similar way a box of chocolates would be given today. The modern version of gingerbread can be microwaved to delicious perfection. As with other baked goods and cakes, the best results are often obtained by using a ring dish, rather than the more traditional loaf dish.

Upside-down gingerbread

Full Power, High (70%)
14 minutes

Topping
60 g (2 oz) butter or margarine
100 g (3½ oz) soft brown sugar
9 maraschino cherries
400 g (14 oz) canned apricot halves, drained

Cake
100 g (3½ oz) butter or margarine
100 g (3½ oz) soft brown sugar
60 mℓ (4 tablespoons) honey
2 eggs, beaten
225 g (8 oz) plain flour
15 mℓ (1 tablespoon) ground ginger
5 mℓ (1 teaspoon) bicarbonate of soda
30 g (1 oz) mixed dried fruit or 30 g (1 oz)
   carrot, finely grated

For the topping, place butter in a 20-cm (8-inch) square baking dish and microwave on Full Power for 1 minute. Sprinkle with brown sugar. Arrange cherries in three rows, then cover with apricot halves, cut side down. Place butter, sugar and honey in a bowl and microwave for 3 minutes. Cool slightly, then beat in the eggs. Sift dry ingredients together and fold into the egg mixture with dried fruit or grated carrot. Carefully spoon mixture over apricots. Smooth top and shield corners with aluminium foil. Microwave on High (70%) for 9 – 10 minutes. The gingerbread should begin to pull away from the sides of the dish and feel almost dry to the touch.

Stand for 5 minutes, then invert on to a serving dish. Leave the baking dish over the cake for another 5 minutes. Serve with cream or custard.
Serves 9

GLAZE

Food is usually glazed to improve the appearance and make it look more appetizing. The flavour of the glaze should complement that of the food. Cold savoury dishes are often glazed with Aspic Jelly (page 16) while sweet dishes may be glazed with Lemon Jelly (page 120) or melted jams or jellies such as smooth apricot jam or red currant jelly. Glazes are made in a few seconds in the microwave, and they do not 'catch' whilst being heated.

Fruit glaze

Full Power, Medium (50%)
4 minutes

30 mℓ (2 tablespoons) water
30 mℓ (2 tablespoons) jelly crystals, strawberry or raspberry
100 g (3½ oz) red currant jelly

Place water in a bowl, microwave on Full Power for 30 seconds, add jelly powder and stir to dissolve. Add red currant jelly, microwave on Medium (50%) for 3 – 4 minutes until the red currant jelly has melted. Cool slightly and use for brushing over strawberries, apricots or peaches.
Makes about 185 mℓ (6 fl oz)

Honey glaze

Full Power
1½ minutes

60 mℓ (4 tablespoons) honey
30 mℓ (2 tablespoons) soy sauce
30 mℓ (2 tablespoons) orange juice
2.5 mℓ (½ teaspoon) dry mustard

Place all ingredients in a small bowl. Mix well and microwave on Full Power for 1 – 1½ minutes. Stir well, and use with cooked carrots or baby onions.
Makes about 125 mℓ (4 fl oz)

Whisky glaze

Full Power
1½ minutes

90 g (3 oz) red currant jelly
15 g (½ oz) butter
generous pinch of dry mustard
2.5 mℓ (½ teaspoon) prepared mustard
30 mℓ (2 tablespoons) whisky

Place jelly in a jug and microwave on Full Power for 1 – 1½ minutes. Add remaining ingredients and mix well. Use for cooked carrots or baby onions.
Makes about 90 mℓ (3 fl oz)

Savoury glaze

Full Power
1 – 1½ minutes

125 mℓ (4 fl oz) tomato sauce (as served with pasta)
30 g (1 oz) soft brown sugar
5 mℓ (1 teaspoon) prepared mustard
pinch of chilli powder

Combine ingredients in a small bowl and microwave on Full Power for 1 – 1½ minutes. Use with green beans or other vegetables.
Makes about 125 mℓ (4 fl oz)

GLITTER

Edible glitter can be made in a variety of colours to give a sparkling finish to cakes and cookies. Liquid glitter can also be painted on to icing decorations, holly leaves, berries and pine cones for added sheen at Christmas time. Gum arabic, an essential ingredient, is available from chemists and specialist cake decorating suppliers.

Edible glitter

Medium (50%)
2 minutes

125 mℓ (4 fl oz) water
60 mℓ (4 tablespoons) gum arabic
food colouring

Combine water and gum arabic in a bowl, microwave on Medium (50%) for 1½ – 2 minutes. Strain through a fine sieve, then colour gum mixture. Paint a thick layer of mixture on an ungreased metal baking sheet. Stand in a sunny place, out of the wind. As the glitter dries, it flakes off the tray. Turn dried glitter on to a piece of brown paper, fold paper over and crush with a rolling pin. Store in an air-tight container. This mixture may also be kept in a liquid form in the refrigerator for up to two years.
Makes about 100 g (3½ oz)

GOOSEBERRIES, CAPE AND GREEN

Sometimes known as golden berries, Cape gooseberries are smooth and round with a pleasant, tangy taste. They are extremely versatile. Use them for making jam or as part of a sauce to serve with game. The berries can also be stewed and are good as a pie or flan filling. They are available fresh for only two to three months of the year, but the canned variety makes an excellent substitute. When microwaving either fresh or green gooseberries, you should prick them with a needle to prevent them bursting.
See also Jam and Fruit.

Gooseberry and cream tart

Full Power
4 minutes
Bake 200 °C / 400 °F / gas 6
8 minutes

1 x 22.5-cm (9-inch) biscuit or pie crust*

Filling
400 g (14 oz) canned gooseberries
7.5 mℓ (1½ teaspoons) custard powder
7.5 mℓ (1½ teaspoons) cornflour
15 mℓ (1 tablespoon) water
1 egg yolk

Topping
2 egg yolks
100 mℓ (3½ fl oz) single cream
15 mℓ (1 tablespoon) chopped almonds

Drain juice from gooseberries into a large jug, microwave on Full Power for 2 – 3 minutes until boiling. Combine custard powder and cornflour with water, stir well. Pour a little of the boiling liquid on to the mixture. Return the cornflour mixture to the boiling liquid, stir well. Microwave for 45 seconds to thicken. Stir in egg yolk and mix very well. Add fruit and cool slightly before pouring into prepared crust.
  To make the topping, beat yolks well. Microwave cream for 1 minute, pour on to yolks and beat to combine. Pour over fruit and sprinkle with almonds. Place in a conventional oven at 200 °C / 400 °F /gas 6 for 8 – 10 minutes until golden in colour. Serve warm.
Makes 1 x 22.5-cm (9-inch) pie

GOULASH *See* Beef

GRAPEFRUIT

The grapefruit is a large, slightly bitter tasting fruit of the citrus family. It may be round or slightly oval, and the flesh ranges from pale yellow to pink or even red. Fresh or canned grapefruit can be used in salads, fruit cups, preserves and in most of the ways that oranges are used. When eaten for breakfast, grapefruit are usually cut in half, the sections loosened and sprinkled with sugar, or they may be sprinkled with sugar and sherry or rum, microwaved until hot and served as a starter.

See also Marmalade

Spiced grapefruit and orange cups

Full Power
1½ minutes

2 grapefruit, peeled and segmented
2 oranges, peeled and segmented
30 ml (2 tablespoons) honey
15 ml (1 tablespoon) brown sugar
generous pinch of cinnamon
pinch of allspice
pinch of nutmeg
15 – 30 ml (1 – 2 tablespoons) medium sherry
  (optional)
brown sugar

To decorate
mint leaves

Place fruit segments in a bowl. Combine honey, brown sugar, spices and sherry if used. Gently mix into fruit and microwave on Full Power for 1½ minutes. Spoon into four individual serving dishes and sprinkle with sugar. Decorate with mint leaves. Serve hot or cold.
Serves 4

Baked grapefruit

Full Power
3 minutes

1 large grapefruit
30 ml (1 tablespoon) fruit juice, such as apple
  or orange
30 ml (1 oz) soft brown sugar
pinch of cinnamon

Cut grapefruit in half, remove pips and cut around sections to loosen. Place halves in

individual bowls and spoon juice over. Mix sugar and cinnamon and sprinkle on top. Microwave on Full Power for 2 – 3 minutes. Serve immediately.
Serves 2

GRAPES

The fruit of the vine has been popular for centuries, both for eating and drinking. Dessert or table grapes are delicious served just as they are; however, grapes may also be added to delicate meat, fish and poultry dishes. They do not need cooking, only heating through.

Cod Véronique

Full Power, High (70%)
19 minutes

1 kg (2¼ lb) cod or any other firm white fish
125 ml (4 fl oz) cider or semi-sweet white wine
75 ml (2½ fl oz) water
salt and black pepper
10 ml (2 teaspoons) lemon juice
30 g (1 oz) butter
6 spring onions, chopped

Cream sauce
30 g (1 oz) butter
30 ml (1 tablespoon) plain flour
125 ml (4 fl oz) single cream
15 g (½ oz) extra butter
150 g (5 oz) green grapes, skinned, halved and
  pips removed

To garnish
grapes
parsley sprigs

Cut fish into serving portions, arrange in a shallow casserole. Add cider, water, seasonings and lemon juice. Place butter in a bowl, microwave on Full Power for 1 minute. Add spring onion, stir to coat with butter and microwave for 2 minutes. Add to fish. Cover with vented plastic wrap, microwave for 6 – 8 minutes, depending on the thickness of the portions. The fish should flake easily. Remove fish and keep warm. Return liquid to the microwave for 4 – 5 minutes until reduced to about 150 ml (5 fl oz), then strain.
  For the sauce, place butter in a large bowl, microwave for 1 minute. Whisk in flour, then cream and reduced liquid. Microwave on High (70%) for 3 – 4 minutes, until thickened. Whisk every 30 seconds. Whisk in extra butter and adjust seasoning. Add grapes, microwave for a further 2 minutes. Pour sauce over fish, garnish with grapes and parsley sprigs.
Serves 4 – 6

GRAVY

Gravy-making is so easy with the help of the microwave. Just measure pan dripping or juices from roast meat or poultry into a jug. Add flour and stock, wine or water, or a combination of liquids and microwave, stirring occasionally, until thick. Gravy should be well-seasoned.

Gravy

Full Power
5 minutes

30 ml (2 tablespoons) pan juices
25 ml (5 teaspoons) plain flour
300 ml (½ pint) well-flavoured stock
salt and pepper

Place pan juices in a glass bowl or large jug and stir in flour. Microwave on Full Power for 1 – 2 minutes, then gradually add liquid. Microwave for 2 – 3 minutes, stirring every minute, until thick and smooth. Season to taste. Finish off with a little cream or soured cream if desired.
Makes about 300 ml (10 fl oz)

GREEN PEPPER *See* Peppers

GRILLING

Although it is not possible to grill in the microwave, foods such as meat, poultry or fish can be successfully browned and cooked in a browning dish.
See Browning Dish

GUAVA

Guavas are a tropical fruit with a yellow or pink flesh. They can be eaten raw, stewed, or turned into jam, jelly or fruit purée. They overripen very quickly and should be eaten or cooked as soon as possible after being purchased.
See also Fruit, Jams and Jellies

Spiced guavas

Full Power
18 minutes

1 kg (2¼ lb) firm guavas
500 g (18 oz) caster sugar
250 ml (8 fl oz) white vinegar
2.5 ml (½ teaspoon) whole cloves
1 cinnamon stick
5 ml (1 teaspoon) mustard seed
generous pinch of salt

Peel guavas, quarter and remove the seeds, set aside. In a large bowl, combine sugar, vinegar and spices. Microwave on Full Power for 8 minutes, stirring at least twice during cooking time. Add guavas, microwave for 10 minutes, stirring from time to time. Pack into warm sterilized jars and seal. These guavas are delicious served with roast pork, ham or venison.
Makes about 750 g (1¾ lb)

H

HADDOCK

Smoked haddock has a fairly strong flavour and is often combined with other fish. Poached or steamed, it plays an important role in an invalid's diet. The fillets microwave perfectly in minutes.

Poached haddock

Full Power
7 minutes

500 g (18 oz) haddock (fresh or smoked)
150 mℓ (5 fl oz) milk or milk and water
   combined
bay leaf (optional)
black peppercorns
onion, sliced (optional)
15 g (½ oz) butter

Arrange haddock in a shallow casserole, pour milk over and add bay leaf, a few peppercorns and onion. Dot with butter and cover with vented plastic wrap. Microwave on Full Power for 7 – 8 minutes. Remove from liquid and use as required. Serves 4

Note: Sometimes haddock is a little salty. To avoid this, pour boiling water over fish, stand 30 seconds. Repeat once, continue as above.

Haddock mousse

Full Power, Medium (50%)
4 minutes

500 g (18 oz) poached haddock* (fresh or
   smoked)
250 mℓ (8 fl oz) single cream
30 g (1 oz) butter
30 mℓ (1 tablespoon) plain flour
250 mℓ (8 fl oz) milk
5 mℓ (1 teaspoon) dry mustard
black pepper
15 mℓ (1 tablespoon) chopped dill
2 eggs, separated
15 mℓ (1 tablespoon) lemon juice
45 mℓ (4 tablespoons) water
15 mℓ (1 tablespoon) gelatine

To garnish
15 mℓ (1 tablespoon) capers
cucumber slices

Skin and bone fish. Place in a food processor with cream, process until smooth. Place butter in a 1-litre (1¾-pint) jug, microwave on Full Power for 1 minute, add flour and stir. Add milk, stir well. Microwave for 2 minutes, stirring every 30 seconds during cooking time. Add mustard, black pepper, dill, egg yolks and lemon juice. Stir well, then cool slightly. Combine fish mixture and sauce. Combine water and gelatine, stand 2 minutes. Microwave on Medium (50%) for 1 minute to dissolve. Stir gelatine into fish mixture. Beat egg whites to a soft peak consistency, fold into fish mixture. Pour into soufflé dish or glass dish. Place in the refrigerator for 3 – 4 hours to set. Decorate with slices of cucumber and capers.
Serves 6

HAKE See Fish, also Orange hake with capers (page 160)

HAM AND GAMMON

Ham is the cured meat of the hind leg of the pig. The curing process has been known for over 2 000 years, and the best hams today are not very different from the ancient ones. Curing may be done with many mixtures, although all are based on salt. Other ingredients, including sugar, molasses, vinegar, herbs and spices may be added to improve the texture and flavour. Hams may also be smoked with any number of woods and herbs such as hickory, apple, pine, bay leaf, sage or juniper berries. These combinations give a variety of flavours.

  Ham and gammon are very versatile as they can be cooked whole and glazed, served sliced, hot or cold. They can also be minced for a variety of dishes or included in any number of casseroles. Most hams are now precooked and are microwaved quickly and easily. The meat will be juicy and tender if care is taken not to overcook.

To microwave cooked ham
(Including canned hams)
Medium (50%)
10 – 13 minutes per 500 g (18 oz)
Place the ham in a roasting dish. Precooked hams should be placed with the fat side up and shielded on the thin edge with a strip of foil. Cover tightly with vented plastic wrap, and microwave on Medium (50%) for minimum time. Test internal temperature by inserting a meat thermometer and allow 2 minutes for the temperature to register. If the internal temperature has not reached 46°C (115°F), remove thermometer and return ham to the microwave for a few more minutes. Let ham stand for 5 – 10 minutes after cooking.

To microwave raw ham or gammon
Medium (50%)
14 – 16 minutes per 500 g (18 oz)
Shield top cut edge with a thin strip of foil. Place the ham or gammon in a roasting dish and cover tightly with vented plastic wrap, or place ham in a cooking bag and tie ends. Make at least two holes in the bag to allow steam to escape. Microwave on Medium (50%) for the minimum time, then check internal temperature by inserting a meat thermometer and allow 2 minutes for temperature to register. If the internal temperature has not reached 71°C (160°F), remove thermometer and return ham or gammon to the microwave for a few more minutes. Let ham or gammon stand for 5 – 10 minutes after cooking.

Glazes for ham and gammon
It is often a good idea to leave glazing ham or gammon to the last 3 – 5 minutes of cooking time only, as adding a sugary glaze any sooner may result in an overcooked outer layer of meat.

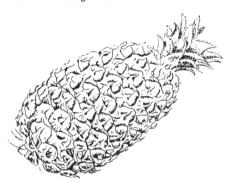

Pineapple mustard glaze

Full Power
4 minutes

400 g (14 oz) canned pineapple slices
100 g (3½ oz) soft brown sugar
30 mℓ (2 tablespoons) pineapple syrup from
   the can
30 mℓ (2 tablespoons) prepared mustard

Arrange pineapple slices over the ham or
gammon and secure with wooden cocktail
sticks. Combine brown sugar, pineapple syrup
and mustard and pour over the finished ham or
gammon. Microwave on Full Power for 3 – 4
minutes.

Honey and soy glaze

60 mℓ (4 tablespoons) honey
60 mℓ (4 tablespoons) soy sauce
5 mℓ (1 teaspoon) dry mustard

Combine all ingredients and brush over the
microwaved ham or gammon. Stand for a few
minutes to set.

Ham and noodle bake

Full Power
9 minutes

350 g (12 oz) cooked ham or gammon cut into
   bite-sized pieces
400 g (14 oz) canned cream of celery soup
185 mℓ (16 fl oz) water
225 g (8 oz) canned water chestnuts, drained
   and sliced
200 g (7 oz) noodles, cooked
3 celery sticks, sliced
175 g (6 oz) frozen peas
½ small onion, chopped
125 g (4 oz) mushrooms, sliced
60 g (2 oz) flaked almonds
30 mℓ (1 tablespoon) chopped parsley
1 chicken stock cube
salt and pepper
45 g (1½ oz) potato crisps, crushed

Combine all ingredients except potato crisps in
a casserole dish. Cover with vented plastic
wrap and microwave on Full Power for 8 – 10
minutes, or until heated through. Sprinkle crisps
on top and microwave for 1 minute more. Stand
for 5 minutes before serving.
Serves 6

Ham and potato casserole

Full Power
12 minutes

15 g (½ oz) butter
60 g (2 oz) savoury biscuit crumbs
30 g (1 oz) butter
2 celery sticks, chopped
½ small onion, chopped
30 g (1 oz) red pepper, chopped
300 g (11 oz) frozen peas
3 cooked potatoes, diced
10 mℓ (2 teaspoons) prepared mustard
375 mℓ (12 fl oz) white sauce*
salt and pepper

To garnish
parsley

Microwave butter for 30 seconds on Full Power
and stir in biscuit crumbs. Set aside. Place
butter in a casserole and microwave for 30 – 45
seconds to melt. Stir in celery, onion and red
pepper. Cover and microwave for 3 minutes,
stirring once. Add frozen peas, potatoes,
mustard and white sauce and season to taste
with salt and pepper. Mix gently, then
microwave, covered, for 7 – 8 minutes, or until
heated through. Sprinkle with buttered crumbs
and garnish with parsley.
Serves 4 – 6

HAMBURGERS

Minced beef patties or hamburgers are a
popular food and microwave very well. A
browning dish will give the hamburger patties a better appearance, but they are just
as delicious cooked on a glass or ceramic
dish. For low calorie hamburgers, place
patties on a bacon or roasting rack so that
the fat can drain away during microwaving.
An even more attractive appearance will
be obtained by brushing the patties with
any one of several browning agents suggested for meats (see page 39).

HAMBURGER COOKING CHART

NUMBER OF PATTIES	PREHEAT BROWNING DISH	COOKING TIME (Full Power)
1	4 minutes	2 – 3 minutes
2	6 minutes	3 – 4 minutes
3	6 minutes	4 – 5 minutes
4	7 minutes	5 – 6 minutes

The exact time depends on the desired
degree of cooking. To cook hamburgers in
a glass dish, increase the cooking time by
about 20 seconds per patty.

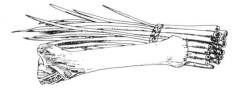

Cheese and wine burgers

Full Power
14 minutes

500 g (18 oz) minced beef
45 mℓ (3 tablespoons) tomato sauce (as served
   with pasta)
60 mℓ (4 tablespoons) dry red wine
90 g (3 oz) Cheddar cheese, grated
salt and pepper
30 mℓ (2 tablespoons) chopped onion
4 slices of cheese
4 hamburger buns, lightly toasted

Combine beef, tomato sauce, wine, cheese,
salt and pepper and chopped onion. Mix well
and shape into four patties. Preheat browning
dish on Full Power for 6 – 7 minutes. Place
patties in dish, cover and microwave for
2 minutes. Turn patties, cover and microwave
for 2 – 3 minutes more, depending on desired
degree of cooking. Top each patty with a slice
of cheese and microwave 30 – 60 seconds to
melt. Serve on toasted buns.
Serves 4

HARD SAUCE

Also known as brandy or rum butter, this
sauce is a traditional accompaniment to
Christmas pudding. It is also good served
with mince pies and hot winter puddings.

Hard sauce

Defrost (30%)
1 minute

100 g (3½ oz) butter
200 g (7 oz) caster sugar
1 egg yolk
30 – 45 mℓ (2 – 3 tablespoons) brandy or rum
15 mℓ (1 tablespoon) lemon juice
100 mℓ (3½ fl oz) whipping cream

Place butter in a medium-sized bowl.
Microwave on Defrost (30%) for 1 – 2 minutes to
soften. Cream butter and sugar until pale in
colour. Add egg yolk, brandy or rum to taste
and lemon juice, beat again. Now carefully beat
in cream, do not overbeat. Pile into a glass
serving bowl and refrigerate until required.
Makes about 300 mℓ (10 fl oz)

HAZELNUTS

A small, shiny round nut, known in some
countries as a filbert. Hazelnuts are especially popular in Austria, where they are
used extensively in cakes and tortes. The
nuts are often finely ground and used as a
flour substitute when baking. They are also
used whole or chopped in stuffings and
meat dishes.
   Hazelnut kernels are covered with a thin
dark skin which is inclined to give a bitter
taste to the nuts. Warm the kernels for a
few seconds in the microwave to remove
this skin.

To skin hazelnuts, place 100 g (3½ oz) hazelnuts on a paper plate, microwave on Full Power for 2 – 3 minutes until hot. Rub nuts between the palms of your hands to loosen as much of the skin as possible.
To toast hazelnuts *see* Almonds.

HERBS

Herbs, fresh and dried, add flavour and interest to most savoury dishes. When microwaving foods, fresh herbs can be added generously, but dried herbs should be used in smaller amounts. To substitute dried herbs for fresh, use 5 ml (1 teaspoon) dried for every 15 ml (1 tablespoon) fresh given in the recipe. Crumble the dried herbs before using to release the essential oils that flavour the food. Dried herbs will not last forever; when they have lost aroma, they have also lost flavour.

Fresh herbs can be quickly dried in the microwave oven and should be stored in an air-tight container, away from heat and strong light.

To dry herbs
Make sure the fresh sprigs are clean and dry. Leafy herbs should have heavy stems removed. Place 60 g (2 oz) fresh herbs between layers of kitchen paper on a paper plate. Microwave on Full Power for 4 – 6 minutes until dry and brittle, rearranging the herbs halfway through the cooking time. Cool between the layers of paper towel, then coarsely crush the leaves and store in an air-tight container.

Pickled herbs

Full Power
4 minutes

Pickled herbs are good to use anywhere herbs are required, or to toss in salads, mix with dressings or to use as garnishes.

fresh tarragon, basil, dill or oregano sprigs
white wine vinegar

Wash herbs and pat dry. Pack sprigs into small, hot, sterilized jars. Microwave vinegar, 500 mℓ (16 fl oz) at a time, on Full Power for 4 – 5 minutes, or until boiling. Slowly pour vinegar over herbs, filling the bottles. Seal and use as desired.

HOLLANDAISE SAUCE *See* Sauces

HONEY

The flavour of honey varies a great deal, depending on the type of flowers on which the bees feed. The colour, too, may vary from white or cream to a very dark brown. Honey granulates very easily, so microwave for a few seconds to return it to a smooth, runny consistency.

To clarify honey, remove the lid and microwave the jar on Full Power for 1 – 2 minutes. Stir well and use as desired.

Uses for honey
☐ Honey makes a good base for an upside-down cake.
☐ Drizzle a little warmed honey over hot winter puddings before serving.
☐ Use a little honey to moisten brown sugar and nuts before using as a topping.
☐ Brush a little warmed honey over cup cakes before sprinkling with a topping.

HONEYCOMB

A waxy structure made of many regularly shaped hexagonal cells in which honey is stored. The name also refers to something resembling this structure, hence honeycomb pudding and honeycomb toffee.

Honeycomb toffee

Full Power
13 minutes

400 g (14 oz) caster sugar
220 mℓ (7 fl oz) water
10 mℓ (2 teaspoons) vinegar
2.5 mℓ (½ teaspoon) bicarbonate of soda

Place sugar, water and vinegar in a large bowl. Microwave on Full Power for 3 minutes. Stir to dissolve sugar crystals and brush sides of the bowl with water. Microwave for 10 – 12 minutes, until very pale golden in colour (soft crack stage). Remove from microwave, and stir in bicarbonate of soda. Pour into a greased 17.5-cm (7-inch) pan. Mark into squares before completely set.
Makes about 30 squares

Honeycomb pudding

Full Power, Defrost (30%), Medium (50%)
6 minutes

A light custard-based dessert, which separates into three layers as it sets.

300 mℓ (½ pint) milk
2 eggs, separated
30 g (1 oz) caster sugar
few drops of vanilla extract
12.5 mℓ (2½ teaspoons) powdered gelatine
20 mℓ (4 teaspoons) water

Place milk in a jug, microwave on Full Power for 2 minutes. Beat yolks and sugar, pour on hot milk and beat to combine. Microwave on Defrost (30%) for 3 – 4 minutes, stirring every 30 seconds. Add vanilla, stir and set aside. Combine water and gelatine in a small jug, stand for 2 minutes. Microwave on Medium (50%) for 1 minute, stir and add to custard mixture. Cool until mixture thickens. Beat egg whites until soft peak consistency, fold into custard mixture. Pour into a rinsed mould and allow to set. Turn out and serve.
Serves 4

HOT DOG

A hot frankfurter eaten in a long, buttered bread roll with mustard, tomato sauce, relish or other garnishes. You can either heat the frankfurter separately in the microwave or heat the roll and sausage together. Both methods are given here.

To heat frankfurters
Place 4 frankfurters on a piece of kitchen paper on a plate. Prick each with a skewer to prevent it from bursting and microwave frankfurters on Full Power for about 2 minutes. Exact timing will depend on the starting temperature of the frankfurters. Use as desired.

Hot dogs

Full Power

Place each frankfurter in a buttered roll. Add mustard, tomato sauce or relish. Wrap each in a sheet of kitchen paper. Microwave on Full Power for the following times:

1 hot dog	45 – 60 seconds
2 hot dogs	1 – 1½ minutes
4 hot dogs	2 minutes
5 hot dogs	3 – 3½ minutes

I

ICE CREAM

Ice cream has been one of the world's most popular desserts since the 17th century and the variations are endless. It may be made from a custard, milk, cream, evaporated or condensed milk, or a sugar syrup base. Use your microwave oven to heat the liquid, make the custard or to boil the sugar syrup. *See also* Sorbet.

Hint: To soften ice cream which has frozen solid, place in the microwave oven and set Defrost (30%) for 1½ minutes.

Chocolate parfait ice cream

Full Power
3 minutes

150 g (5 oz) caster sugar
45 g (1½ oz) cocoa powder
10 mℓ (2 teaspoons) instant coffee powder
75 mℓ (2½ fl oz) water
4 egg yolks
250 mℓ (8 fl oz) whipping cream, lightly beaten
30 mℓ (2 tablespoons) rum
2 egg whites

Combine sugar, cocoa, coffee and water in a jug. Microwave on Full Power for 3 minutes, stirring every minute. Beat yolks until thick, add chocolate mixture and beat very well. Fold in the cream and rum. Beat egg whites until peaking consistency, fold into ice cream. Freeze for at least 6 hours.
Serves 6

Caramel ice cream

400 g (14 oz) canned condensed milk, caramelized*
4 eggs, separated
few drops of vanilla extract
500 mℓ (16 fl oz) whipping cream, lightly beaten

To decorate
whipped cream
nuts

Line the base of a 32.5 x 10-cm (13 x 4-inch) loaf pan with foil. Beat condensed milk, egg yolks and vanilla very well. Fold cream into mixture. Beat whites until stiff, but not dry, and fold into caramel mixture. Pour into prepared loaf pan and freeze overnight. Run a spatula around the edges of the pan. Turn ice cream out on to a plate. Decorate immediately with rosettes of cream and a few nuts. Return ice cream to freezer until ready to serve.
Serves 12

Chocolate biscuit ice cream

High (70%)
6 minutes

2 eggs, beaten
250 ml (8 fl oz) milk
125 g (4 oz) caster sugar
375 mℓ (12 fl oz) single cream
few drops of vanilla extract
1 egg white
10 chocolate biscuits
60 g (2 oz) toasted almonds, chopped

Combine beaten eggs, milk and sugar in a deep bowl. Microwave on High (70%) for 5 – 6 minutes, stirring every minute, until the mixture coats the back of a spoon. Place a piece of waxed paper on the surface of the custard and chill. Stir the cream and vanilla into the chilled custard. Pour into a freezer container and freeze until partially frozen. Break up the mixture and transfer to a large, chilled mixing bowl. Beat with an electric mixer until smooth, but do not let the ice cream melt completely. Return to the container and refreeze until partially frozen.

Beat the egg white to soft peaks. Use a food processor to crush the biscuits. Break up ice cream, transfer to a chilled mixing bowl and beat until smooth. Fold in egg white, biscuit crumbs and almonds, return to the freezer container and freeze until solid. This ice cream should be served within 3 – 4 days of preparation.
Serves 6 – 8

1. Creamy Rhubarb Sorbet (page 200); **2.** Plum Ice Cream (page 171); **3.** Chocolate Biscuit Ice Cream (page 110); **4.** Campari Sorbet (page 200); **5.** Apple Sorbet (page 201); **6.** Apricot Ice Cream (page 112)

Apricot ice cream

High (70%)
16 minutes

100 g (3½ oz) dried apricots
water
3 egg yolks, beaten
60 mℓ (4 tablespoons) water
30 mℓ (1 tablespoon) brandy
3 egg whites
100 g (3½ oz) caster sugar
250 mℓ (8 fl oz) cream
45 g (1½ oz) pecan nuts, chopped

Place apricots in a bowl and cover fruit with water. Cover the bowl and microwave on High (70%) for 10 – 12 minutes. Drain apricots and place in the container of an electric blender. Blend until smooth. Combine purée with egg yolks and water. Microwave for 3 – 4 minutes, stirring after every minute until mixture thickens. Add the brandy, then cool the mixture.
   Beat egg whites to soft peaks, then gradually add sugar and beat until stiff. Fold into the cooled apricot mixture. Whip cream to soft peaks and fold into the apricot mixture along with the pecans. Turn into a 32.5 x 22.5-cm (13 x 9-inch) pan, cover and freeze until firm.
Serves 6 – 8

Tangy apricot ice cream

Full Power
17 minutes

500 g (18 oz) fresh apricots, halved and stoned
45 mℓ (3 tablespoons) water
45 g (1½ oz) dried apricots
90 g (3 oz) caster sugar
100 mℓ (3½ fl oz) water
45 mℓ (3 tablespoons) apricot brandy
400 mℓ (13 fl oz) whipping cream,
   lightly whipped

Place fresh apricots in a shallow casserole, add water. Cover with vented plastic wrap and microwave on Full Power for 9 minutes. Cool and purée. Cover dried apricots with water, stand 20 minutes. Drain off any excess water, cover with vented plastic wrap and microwave for 5 minutes. Purée roughly. Combine sugar and water. Microwave for 3 minutes, stirring once during the cooking time. Combine both purées, sugar syrup and apricot brandy. Allow to cool. Fold into cream, pour into a container and freeze. Stir mixture two or three times during freezing.
Makes about 1.25 litres (2¼ pints)

ICE CREAM SAUCES
Try these delicious tasting sauces with your favourite ice cream. Some are poured hot over ice cream, while others are served chilled.

Amaretto orange ice cream sauce

Full Power
4 minutes

30 g (1 oz) cornflour
100 g (3½ oz) caster sugar
90 g (3 oz) frozen orange juice concentrate
125 mℓ (4 fl oz) Amaretto liqueur
250 mℓ (8 fl oz) water

Combine cornflour and sugar in a deep bowl. Thaw orange juice, stir into the cornflour mixture with the Amaretto and water. Microwave on Full Power for 3 – 4 minutes, or until sauce thickens and becomes clear, stirring every minute. Cool in a covered container and chill. Serve over vanilla or chocolate ice cream.
Serves 6

Pecan caramel ice cream sauce

Full Power
4 minutes

20 g (¾ oz) soft brown sugar
15 g (½ oz) cornflour
pinch of salt
125 mℓ (4 fl oz) water
185 mℓ (6 fl oz) single cream
60 mℓ (4 tablespoons) golden syrup
60 g (2 oz) pecan nuts, coarsely chopped
30 g (1 oz) butter
15 mℓ (1 tablespoon) rum or coffee liqueur

Combine brown sugar, cornflour and salt in a deep bowl. Stir in water and mix in cream and syrup. Microwave on Full Power for about 4 minutes, stirring every minute. The mixture should be thickened, and may appear curdled. Add pecans, butter and rum and beat well. Serve warm or chilled.
Makes about 500 mℓ (16 fl oz)

Chocolate sauce

Full Power
2 minutes

60 g (2 oz) cocoa powder
125 g (4 oz) caster sugar
250 mℓ (8 fl oz) water
45 mℓ (3 tablespoons) golden syrup
few drops of vanilla extract

Sift cocoa into a bowl, add sugar and gradually add water, mixing all the time. Add remaining ingredients, stir well. Microwave on Full Power for 2 – 3 minutes, until boiling. Stir every 30 seconds. Serve hot over ice cream.
Makes about 350 mℓ (11 fl oz)

Rum and raisin sauce

Full Power
13 minutes

500 g (18 oz) soft brown sugar
650 mℓ (21 fl oz) water
30 g (1 oz) instant coffee powder
375 mℓ (12 fl oz) dark rum
125 mℓ (4 fl oz) red Cinzano
1.5 kg (3 lb) seedless raisins
few drops of vanilla extract

Sauce
5 mℓ (1 teaspoon) cornflour
10 mℓ (2 teaspoons) water

Combine sugar and water in a large bowl. Microwave on Full Power for 10 minutes, stirring from time to time. Add instant coffee and allow to cool. Add remaining ingredients and stand, covered, in a cool place for at least 2 weeks. This mixture will last for a few months if stored in a cool place.
   To serve as a hot sauce, measure 250 mℓ (8 fl oz) of the mixture into a jug or small casserole dish. Microwave on Full Power for 2 minutes. Combine cornflour and water, add a little of the hot mixture to the cold, then add cornflour mixture to the boiling liquid, stir well. Microwave for 1 minute more, stir well and serve hot over ice cream.
Makes about 2 litres (3½ pints)

Butterscotch sauce

Full Power, High (70%)
6 minutes

150 g (5 oz) golden syrup
125 g (4 oz) caster sugar
125 mℓ (4 fl oz) single cream
30 g (1 oz) butter
few drops of vanilla extract

Combine all ingredients in a large jug. Microwave on Full Power for 2 minutes, stir well. Microwave on High (70%) for 4 – 5 minutes more. Stir well and pour over ice cream.
Makes 400 mℓ (13 fl oz)

ICING
A coating of fine sugar mixed to a paste with other ingredients, used to decorate or fill cakes, biscuits and some pastries. Icings add flavour to cakes and also help to keep them moist. The preparation time of many icings can be shortened by melting chocolate, boiling a sugar syrup, or making a custard base in the microwave oven.

Fluffy white icing

Full Power
7 minutes

200 g (7 oz) icing sugar
75 mℓ (2½ fl oz) water
pinch of cream of tartar
pinch of salt
2 egg whites
few drops of vanilla extract

Combine sugar, water, cream of tartar and salt in a deep bowl. Microwave on Full Power for 3 minutes. Scrape down sides of the bowl with a spatula and microwave for a further 3 – 4 minutes, stirring every minute until mixture is boiling and sugar has dissolved. Very slowly pour sugar syrup into unbeaten egg whites in a mixing bowl. Beat constantly with an electric mixer for about 7 minutes, or until stiff peaks form. Add the vanilla and beat to mix.
Ices tops and sides of 2 x 20 – 22.5-cm (8 – 9-inch) layers, or 1 x 25-cm (10-inch) ring cake

Chocolate icing

Medium (50%)
2 minutes

60 g (2 oz) plain chocolate
45 g (1½ oz) butter
200 g (7 oz) icing sugar, sifted
pinch of salt
1 small egg
185 mℓ (6 fl oz) single cream
few drops of vanilla extract

Place chocolate and butter in a jug and microwave on Medium (50%) for 1 – 2 minutes, or until melted. Place in a large bowl and beat in icing sugar, salt and egg. Beat until smooth. Chill mixture well, then beat in cream and vanilla and continue to beat for 3 – 4 minutes or until thick. Chill until used.
Makes enough for 2 x 22.5-cm (9-inch) layers

Chocolate fudge icing

High (70%)
2 minutes

125 g (4 oz) icing sugar
few drops of vanilla extract
15 g (½ oz) cocoa powder
15 g (½ oz) margarine
30 mℓ (2 tablespoons) milk

Place all ingredients in a 1-litre (1¾-pint) jug, stir. Microwave on High (70%) for 2 minutes, stir very well. Pour over cake.
Ices 1 x 20-cm (8-inch) cake

Coconut icing

High (70%)
5 minutes

1 egg
150 mℓ (5 fl oz) evaporated milk
150 g (5 oz) caster sugar
60 g (2 oz) butter
pinch of salt
100 g (3½ oz) desiccated coconut
60 g (2 oz) nuts, such as pecans or hazelnuts, chopped

Combine egg, milk, sugar, butter and salt. Microwave on High (70%) for 4 – 5 minutes, or until thickened and bubbly. Add coconut and nuts. Cool and use.
Ices top and sides of 2 x 20 – 22.5 cm (8 – 9-inch) layers, or 1 x 25-cm (10-inch) ring cake

Cream cheese icing

Defrost (30%)
1 minute

60 g (2 oz) butter
125 g (4 oz) cream cheese
250 g (9 oz) icing sugar
few drops of vanilla extract

Soften butter in microwave on Defrost (30%) for 1 – 2 minutes if necessary. Using an electric mixer, beat butter and cream cheese together. Slowly add sifted icing sugar, then vanilla, beating well after each addition. Use as required.
Iced 1 x 22.5 – 25-cm (9 – 10 inch) ring cake

Note: If a thicker icing is required, substitute caster sugar for icing sugar.

Creamy icing

Full Power
3 minutes

300 mℓ (½ pint) milk
45 g (1½ oz) cornflour
175 g (6 oz) butter or margarine
175 g (6 oz) caster sugar
few drops of vanilla extract

Microwave 280 mℓ (9 fl oz) milk on Full Power for 2 minutes. Combine remaining milk with cornflour, pour on boiling milk and stir well. Microwave for 1 minute until very thick, beat well. Cool until just warm. Meanwhile cream butter and sugar well, add vanilla. Beat in cornflour mixture about a quarter at a time, beat very well. Use for filling and icing sponge-type cakes.
Sufficient to fill and ice 1 x 20-cm (8-inch) cake

Lemon icing

Full Power
30 seconds

200 g (7 oz) icing sugar, sifted
30 mℓ (2 tablespoons) lemon juice
15 g (½ oz) butter
water

Garnish
little lemon rind

Place icing sugar in a bowl, add lemon juice. Microwave butter for 30 seconds on Full Power, cool slightly and add to icing sugar. Beat until smooth, adding a little water if necessary to form a coating consistency.
Sufficient to drizzle over 1 x 22.5 – 25-cm (9 – 10-inch) ring cake

Variation
Orange Icing: Substitute orange juice for the lemon juice. Decorate with orange rind.

IRISH COFFEE *See* Coffee

Overleaf left: Vegetable crudités with Broccoli Dip (page 84) and Aubergine Caviar (page 84)
Overleaf right: Leek Pie and Leeks à la Grecque (page 131)

J

JAMBALAYA

A Creole dish, similar to risotto, made with rice, pork or ham, chicken or shellfish and a mixture of onion, garlic and vegetables. The ingredients are heated until all the liquid is absorbed. This microwave recipe is quick and easy.

Shrimp jambalaya

Full Power
15 minutes

250 g (9 oz) cooked ham or gammon, cubed
½ green pepper, chopped
1 small onion, chopped
1 garlic clove, finely chopped
30 g (1 oz) butter
400 g (14 oz) canned condensed tomato soup
75 mℓ (2½ fl oz) water
125 g (4 oz) cooked shrimps
2.5 mℓ (½ teaspoon) dried basil
2.5 mℓ (½ teaspoon) dried oregano
salt and pepper
200 g (7 oz) rice, cooked

Combine ham, green pepper, onion, garlic and butter in a casserole. Microwave on Full Power 5 – 6 minutes or until vegetables are tender. Mix in soup, water, shrimps, basil, oregano, salt and pepper and microwave for 3 minutes. Add rice, stir and microwave for 5 – 6 minutes or until heated through.
Serves 4 – 6

JAMS AND JELLIES

Jams and jellies microwave perfectly in minutes while the kitchen remains cool and steam-free. Rapid cooking ensures the fruit retains its shape and the preserve is bright and clear in colour and rich in flavour. Jams and jellies made in the microwave require very little stirring and seldom need any skimming. Microwave energy is particularly attracted to sugar molecules, so there is a possibility of the preserve boiling over. Always choose very large, deep ovenproof bowls to allow the mixture to boil rapidly. Remember the bowl may become very hot, so use oven gloves when handling it. For best results, use fresh but slightly under-ripe fruits. Those high in pectin, such as citrus fruits and apples, preserve especially well.

Hint: To soften jams and jellies to a spreading consistency, microwave on Full Power for 3 seconds per 250 g (9 oz).

When preserving fruits
□ Select good quality, barely ripe fruit. Soft or bruised fruit will result in an inferior product. Wash, wipe and peel the selected fruit according to the type.
□ Wash jars well. Sterilize according to instructions (right).
□ Using a brush dipped in water, remove any sugar crystals which may have adhered to the sides of the bowl.
□ To test whether jam or marmalade is ready:
● Stand a sugar thermometer in the preserve but do not leave the thermometer in the microwave when it is switched on, unless it is specifically designed for microwave use. For a good set when making jam, the temperature should reach 105°C (220°F).
● Spoon a little jam on to a saucer and when it is cool push the surface gently with your finger. If the jam wrinkles, it is set.
● When you think the jam is ready, stir well with a wooden spoon. Lift a spoon-

ful of jam out of the bowl, cool slightly then allow the jam to drop off the spoon. It should drop off in 'flakes'.
□ Allow the jam to cool only slightly before pouring it into hot, sterile jars. Fill them right to the top and when the jam is cool, top up the jars once more and cover with brandy papers or waxed papers. To make brandy papers, cut circles of grease-proof or parchment paper the size of the top of the jars. Dip into brandy and place on cooled jam. To make waxed papers, dip the circles of paper into melted candle wax. Allow to set before placing on top of jam.
□ To prevent air bubbles from forming, do not allow the jam to cool for too long before pouring it into jars. If the jam is poured into jars while still too hot, the fruit may rise in the jars.

To sterilize jars for preserving

Pour a little water into the jars. Place no more than three jars in the microwave oven. Microwave on Full Power for up to 5 minutes, depending on the size of the jars and on the thickness of the glass. Pour out the water and stand the jars upside down to drain. Plastic lids, each containing a little water, may be sterilized in the microwave but do not sterilize metal lids this way.

Fig jam

Full Power
26 minutes

500 g (18 oz) coarsely chopped figs
5 mℓ (1 teaspoon) grated lemon rind
5 mℓ (1 teaspoon) grated orange rind
30 mℓ (2 tablespoons) lemon juice
5 mℓ (1 teaspoon) grated fresh ginger
400 g (14 oz) preserving sugar
30 mℓ (2 tablespoons) brandy

Combine fruit and spices in a large bowl. Microwave on Full Power for 8 minutes. Add sugar, stir well. Microwave for 18 – 22 minutes. The jam should now be at setting point. Allow to

cool slightly, stir in brandy, then pour into warm, dry, sterilized jars. Top up jars with extra jam when cold. Cover top of jam with a disc of brandy paper or waxed paper. Seal, label and store.
Makes about 450 g (1 lb)

Apricot jam

Full Power
35 minutes

1 kg (2¼ lb) semi-ripe apricots
1 kg (2¼ lb) preserving sugar
juice of 1 lemon

Wash fruit well. Cut in half and remove stones. Combine apricots, sugar and a few stones in a large bowl. Allow to stand overnight. Add lemon juice and stir well. Cover with vented plastic wrap and microwave on Full Power for 10 minutes, stirring every 2 minutes. Uncover and brush sides of the bowl with water to remove sugar crystals. Microwave for 25 minutes, stirring every 5 minutes. The jam should be at setting point. Remove from microwave. Allow jam to cool at least 30 minutes to prevent fruit from rising in the jar when it has cooled. Pour warm jam into warm, dry, sterilized jars. When cool, top up with a little more jam. Cover top of jam with a disc of brandy paper or waxed paper. Cover, label and store.
Makes about 1.5 kg (3 lb)

Variations
Peach Jam: Slice fruit. Use 800 g (1 lb 14 oz) preserving sugar to 1 kg (2¼ lb) fruit. Proceed as for apricot jam.
Pear and Red Wine Jam: Peel, core and slice fruit. Proceed as for apricot jam. Add 100 mℓ (3½ fl oz) red wine to uncooked mixture.
Plum Jam: Make as for apricot jam.

Strawberry jam

Full Power
25 minutes

500 g (18 oz) strawberries
30 mℓ (2 tablespoons) lemon juice
350 g (12 oz) preserving sugar

Wash strawberries, drain well. Combine fruit and lemon juice in a large bowl, microwave on Full Power for 7 minutes. Add sugar and mix well. Microwave for 18 – 22 minutes, until setting point is reached. Cool slightly before pouring into warm, dry, sterilized jars.
Makes about 450 g (1 lb)

Variations
Strawberry and Rhubarb Jam: Use 250 g (9 oz) strawberries, 250 g (9 oz) rhubarb, finely cut up, 1 kg (2¼ lb) preserving sugar. Proceed as for strawberry jam.
Cape Gooseberry Jam: Proceed as for strawberry jam.
Loganberry Jam: Proceed as for strawberry jam.
Mulberry Jam: Proceed as for strawberry jam.

Crab-apple jelly

Full Power
42 minutes

500 g (18 oz) crab-apples
500 mℓ (16 fl oz) water
grated rind of 1 lemon
2.5 cm (1-inch) piece of cinnamon stick
preserving sugar

Wash crab-apples and quarter. Place in a 5-litre (9-pint) bowl, add water, lemon rind and cinnamon stick, cover with vented plastic wrap. Microwave on Full Power for 15 minutes. Pour pulp and liquid into a jelly bag and allow to drain for about 1 hour. Do not force liquid through the bag. Measure liquid and place in the bowl. Add 350 g (12 oz) preserving sugar to every 500 mℓ (16 fl oz) juice. Microwave for 6 minutes, stirring every 2 minutes. Now microwave for 20 – 25 minutes until setting point is reached. Skim the surface if necessary. Allow jelly to cool, pour into warm, dry, sterilized jars. Cover, label and store.
Makes about 675 g (1½ lb)

Variations:
Apple Jelly: Use 1 kg (2¼ lb) cooking apples, 1 litre (1¾ pints) water, 3 whole cloves. Cut fruit into pieces. Proceed as for crab-apple jelly.
Guava Jelly: Use 1 kg (2¼ lb) guavas, 500 mℓ (16 fl oz) water, grated rind and juice of 1 lemon. Proceed as for crab-apple jelly.
Mulberry Jelly: Use 400 g (14 oz) mulberries, 1 large cooking apple, 250 mℓ (7 fl oz) water, 30 mℓ (2 tablespoons) brandy. Proceed as for crab-apple jelly. Add brandy before pouring into jars.

Grape jelly

Full Power
59 minutes

2 kg (4¼ lb) grapes
250 mℓ (8 fl oz) water
preserving sugar
strip of lemon rind

Wash grapes and remove stems, place in a large bowl. Microwave grapes on Full Power for 10 minutes. Using a potato masher, crush grapes to release juice, add water, microwave for 15 minutes. Tie a jelly bag or cloth on a stand, pour boiling water through bag to sterilize. Place a clean bowl under bag, pour in boiling grapes and allow to drip through. Do not stir or the juice will become cloudy.

Measure juice, it should be approximately 815 mℓ (26 fl oz), and pour into a large bowl. Measure an equal quantity of sugar, add to juice with lemon rind. Microwave for 10 minutes, stirring every 2 minutes to dissolve the sugar. Now microwave for 24 – 28 minutes, stirring every 5 minutes until setting point is reached. Skim top if necessary before stirring. Allow boiled jelly to stand 5 minutes, remove lemon rind. Skim and pour slowly into warm, sterilized jars. When cool, top up jars with more jelly. Cover with circles of parchment paper dipped in brandy, seal, label and store.
Makes about 900 g (2 lb)

Mint jelly

Full Power, Medium (50%)
4 minutes

250 mℓ (8 fl oz) clear apple juice
15 g (½ oz) sugar
45 mℓ (3 tablespoons) shredded fresh mint leaves
15 mℓ (1 tablespoon) wine vinegar
30 mℓ (2 tablespoons) water
10 mℓ (2 teaspoons) powdered gelatine

Pour apple juice into a jug, microwave on Full Power for 3 minutes, add sugar and stir to dissolve. Pour over mint and stand for 20 minutes. Strain and add wine vinegar. Combine water and gelatine, stand for a few minutes. Microwave on Medium (50%) for 45 seconds, stir well, then add to apple liquid. Pour into warm sterilized jars, cool, seal and label. To serve, chop jelly and use as an accompaniment to lamb, mutton, pork or venison.
Makes about 350 g (12 oz)

Variations
In place of apple juice and mint leaves, use any of the following:
☐ Apricot juice and a small cinnamon stick
☐ Orange juice and oregano
☐ Apple juice, lemon juice and thyme
☐ Loganberry juice and cloves

Overleaf left: Spinach and Salmon Pasta (page 164)
Overleaf right: Noisettes of Lamb with Blue Cheese (page 131) served with mashed potatoes and tomatoes

Lemon jelly

Full Power
10 minutes

500 mℓ (16 fl oz) water
100 mℓ (3½ fl oz) lemon juice
pared rind of 1 lemon
5 mℓ (1 teaspoon) oil of lemon
75 g (2½ oz) caster sugar
small piece of cinnamon stick
75 mℓ (2½ fl oz) dry sherry
1 clove
2 egg whites
shells of 2 eggs
40 mℓ (8 teaspoons) powdered gelatine

Mix all the ingredients in a large bowl.
Microwave on Full Power for 5 minutes,
whisking with a balloon whisk every minute.
Whisk briskly until a good 'head' of foam has
formed. Continue to microwave for a further
5 minutes, opening the door every 30 – 40
seconds as the mixture boils up. Do not allow
the liquid to boil up through the 'head'. Allow to
settle for 5 minutes. Tie a jelly bag or suitable
cloth on to a stand, and pour boiling water
through the cloth to scald it. Strain jelly through
the warmed cloth. The mixture should be clear.
Re-strain if necessary. Use for lining sweet
moulds, or chill, then chop and use to garnish
cold moulded desserts.
Makes about 575 g (1¼ lb)

Variations
Champagne Jelly: Substitute champagne or
sparkling wine for lemon juice and dry sherry.
Proceed as for lemon jelly.
Port Jelly: Substitute port for lemon juice and
dry sherry. Add a few drops of wine red food
colouring and 30 mℓ (2 tablespoons) red
currant or crab-apple jelly. Proceed as for
lemon jelly.

JAMS, DIABETIC
Making diabetic jams with fructose is as
simple as making jams with sugar, and because fructose has three times the sweetening power of sugar, you will use less in proportion to fruit. Usually only one person in
the family will be eating jam made with
fructose and for this reason small quantities will be required. Using your microwave, a jar or two of jam is easily made
whenever you have a small excess of fruit.
Jams made with fructose are inclined to
harden after a time. If this happens, turn
the jam into an ovenproof bowl and microwave for 6 – 7 minutes until well boiled.
Pour into sterilized jars and use as soon as
possible. Provided the jam is used in small
quantities, the following recipe is suitable
for diabetics and slimmers.

Diabetic peach jam

Full Power
25 minutes

600 g (1 lb 5 oz) peaches, peeled and stoned
200 g (7 oz) fructose
150 mℓ (5 fl oz) water
45 mℓ (3 tablespoons) lemon juice
2.5 mℓ (½ teaspoon) powdered gelatine

Mince or finely chop peaches in a food
processor. Turn into a large bowl, add fructose,
130 mℓ water and lemon juice. Microwave on
Full Power for 25 minutes, stirring every
5 minutes. Combine remaining water and
gelatine in a small bowl, stand for a few
minutes, stir into hot jam. Allow jam to cool
slightly before pouring into a sterilized jar. Store
in the refrigerator.
Makes about 450 g (1 lb)

Note: 5 mℓ (1 teaspoon) of this jam contains
2 grams of carbohydrate and 35 kilojoules.

JUNKET
A traditional English milk pudding, made
from milk, sugar and flavouring coagulated
with rennet. Rennet is made with the enzyme rennin, which is extracted from the
lining of a cow's stomach. Flavoured jun-
ket mixes are also available.

Old fashioned junket

Full Power
2 minutes

500 mℓ (16 fl oz) milk
15 g (½ oz) caster sugar
few drops of vanilla extract
5 mℓ (1 teaspoon) rennet
grated nutmeg (optional)

Microwave milk on Full Power for 2 minutes. Stir
in sugar, vanilla and rennet. Pour into a serving
dish. Sprinkle with a little nutmeg. Allow to
stand at room temperature until set.
Serves 4

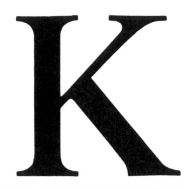

KEBABS

The kebab, as it is now known, comes from the Turkish 'shish kebab' – 'shish' meaning skewer and 'kebab' meaning grilled. Kebabs consist of cubes of meat (such as lamb, pork or beef), poultry or fish threaded on to skewers alternately with pieces of fruit or vegetables, or they may consist of any of these ingredients on their own. The ingredients are usually marinated or seasoned before being assembled and the kebabs are brushed with marinade or sauce while cooking. This generous use of seasonings and marinades gives kebabs their characteristic spicy flavour. Serve with rice and salad for a complete meal.

Note: When microwaving kebabs, be sure to use wooden skewers.

Mixed vegetable kebabs

Full Power
12 minutes

1 green pepper, cut in cubes
1 onion, cut in wedges
60 mℓ (4 tablespoons) water
250 mℓ (8 fl oz) Italian dressing
60 mℓ (4 tablespoons) white wine
10 mℓ (2 teaspoons) Worcestershire sauce
5 mℓ (1 teaspoon) soy sauce
2.5 mℓ (½ teaspoon) mixed herbs
8 mushrooms
2 courgettes, cut in chunks
8 cherry tomatoes

Place green pepper cubes and onion wedges in a bowl. Add water, cover and microwave on Full Power for 4 minutes. Drain, reserving liquid. Add Italian dressing, wine, Worcestershire sauce, soy sauce, and herbs to the reserved liquid and mix well. Microwave for 3 minutes. Add all vegetables, except tomatoes, cover and marinate for about 45 minutes. Drain vegetables and reserve liquid. Thread vegetables on to wooden skewers, adding tomatoes. Place in a baking dish and spoon some of the reserved liquid over. Cover with vented plastic wrap and microwave for 5 minutes, brushing with marinade once. Stand for 2 minutes before serving.
Serves 4

Marinated chicken kebabs with peanut sauce

Full Power, Medium (50%)
14 minutes

1 kg (2¼ lb) whole, boneless chicken breasts
60 mℓ (4 tablespoons) soy sauce
15 mℓ (1 tablespoon) Worcestershire sauce
20 mℓ (4 teaspoons) oil
25 mℓ (1 tablespoon) lemon juice
5 mℓ (1 teaspoon) sugar
5 mℓ (1 teaspoon) freshly grated ginger
1 garlic clove, finely chopped
1 pineapple, peeled and cut into 2.5-cm (1-inch) cubes

Peanut sauce
30 mℓ (2 tablespoons) finely chopped spring onion
10 mℓ (2 teaspoons) oil
75 g (2½ oz) peanut butter
60 mℓ (4 tablespoons) water
15 mℓ (1 tablespoon) lemon juice
5 mℓ (1 teaspoon) Worcestershire sauce

Remove skin from chicken breasts and cut into 2.5-cm (1-inch) pieces. Combine soy sauce, Worcestershire sauce, oil, lemon juice, sugar, ginger and garlic. Add to chicken pieces and toss to coat. Marinate in the refrigerator for 30 minutes to 1 hour.

To make the sauce, place onion and oil in a deep bowl. Microwave on Full Power for 1 minute. Add remaining ingredients and mix well. Microwave on Medium (50%) for about 1 minute. Mix well and set aside.

Remove chicken from marinade, reserving liquid. Thread wooden skewers with chicken and pineapple pieces. Brush with reserved marinade. Arrange half the skewers on a flat platter, cover with waxed paper and microwave on Full Power for about 6 minutes, or until chicken is cooked. Rearrange kebabs halfway through the cooking time. Repeat with the remaining kebabs. Serve with peanut sauce.
Serves 6

Pork kebabs

High (70%)
9 minutes

400 g (14 oz) canned pineapple rings, drained
6 bacon rashers, rinds removed
300 g (11 oz) pork fillet, cut into large cubes
12 small cherry tomatoes
12 button mushrooms, wiped

Marinade
30 mℓ (2 tablespoons) oil
45 mℓ (1½ fl oz) white wine
2.5 mℓ (½ teaspoon) curry paste
pinch of paprika
salt and black pepper

Cut each pineapple ring into three, wrap a small piece of bacon around each portion. Thread bacon and pineapple on to skewers alternately with cubes of meat, cherry tomatoes and mushrooms. Combine all the ingredients for the marinade, pour over kebabs and stand 3 – 4 hours, turning from time to time. Remove kebabs from marinade, arrange on a flat container and cover loosely with waxed paper. Microwave on High (70%) for 7 – 9 minutes. Pour remaining marinade into a small jug, microwave for 2 minutes. Pour over cooked kebabs and serve with rice.
Makes 6

Overleaf left: Galantine of Lamb (page 102) for a special buffet
Overleaf right: from top to bottom, Tangy Tomato Aspic (page 104) and Parma Ham Mousse (page 153)

KEDGEREE

This old-fashioned breakfast dish uses left-over cooked rice. Kedgeree may be made easily in the microwave oven, and the rice reheats with excellent results.

Haddock kedgeree

Full Power, High (70%), Medium (50%)
19 minutes

500 g (18 oz) haddock (fresh or smoked)
75 mℓ (2½ fl oz) milk and 75 mℓ (2½ fl oz)
    water, combined
1 bay leaf
1 onion slice
black peppercorns
60 g (2 oz) butter
600 g (1 lb 5 oz) cooked rice
5 – 10 mℓ (1 – 2 teaspoons) curry paste
30 mℓ (2 tablespoons) chopped parsley
salt and black pepper
125 mℓ (4 fl oz) single cream
4 hard-boiled eggs, sieved
parsley sprigs

Place haddock in a shallow casserole, add milk, water, bay leaf, onion and peppercorns. Cover, microwave on Full Power for 7 – 8 minutes. Transfer fish from liquid, remove skin and bones, and flake with two forks. Place butter in a large bowl, microwave for 1 minute. Add fish, rice, curry paste, parsley, seasonings, cream and half the eggs. Mix lightly to combine, microwave on High (70%) for 4 minutes, stir well. Pack into a well-greased bowl or loaf dish and cover with vented plastic wrap. Microwave on Medium (50%) for 7 minutes. Turn kedgeree out on to a heated serving dish, garnish with remaining sieved egg and parsley sprigs.
Serves 6 – 8

KIDNEYS

Kidneys cook almost instantly in the microwave oven. Cover with waxed paper to prevent splattering.

Sautéed kidneys

Full Power
7 minutes

6 lambs' or calves' kidneys
salt and black pepper
15 g (½ oz) butter

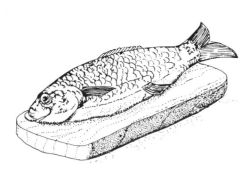

Remove and discard the skin from the kidneys. Cut in half, remove the cores and season. Microwave browning dish on Full Power for 5 minutes. Add butter, microwave 30 seconds. Arrange kidneys, cut side downwards, on browning dish and microwave for 30 seconds. Turn kidneys over, microwave 1 minute more. Serve immediately.
Serves 4 – 6 at breakfast

Devilled kidneys

Full Power
8 minutes

8 lambs' or calves' kidneys
15 mℓ (1 tablespoon) plain flour
salt and black pepper
45 mℓ (1½ oz) butter
2 bacon rashers, chopped
100 g (3½ oz) button mushrooms, sliced
75 mℓ (2½ fl oz) white wine
15 mℓ (1 tablespoon) tomato paste
10 mℓ (2 teaspoons) mustard
5 mℓ (1 teaspoon) Worcestershire sauce
15 mℓ (1 tablespoon) chutney
2.5 mℓ (½ teaspoon) vegetable extract
few drops of Tabasco

To serve
15 mℓ (1 tablespoon) chopped parsley
4 slices of toast

Remove and discard the skins and cores from the kidneys, slice each kidney into four. Toss in flour and seasonings. Microwave butter in a shallow casserole on Full Power for 1 minute. Add bacon and microwave for 1 minute. Now add kidneys, toss to coat with butter, then microwave for 1 minute. Add all the remaining ingredients, stirring well. Cover, microwave for 5 – 7 minutes, stirring at least once during the cooking time. Sprinkle with parsley and serve with hot toast.
Serves 4

KIPPERS

Herrings which have been cleaned, split open, soaked in brine and smoked, are called kippers. A typical breakfast dish, kippers may be defrosted or cooked in the microwave in a couple of minutes. Take care not to microwave too long, as kippers need very little cooking. Remember, if using 'boil-in-the-bag' kippers, pierce the bag before defrosting and microwaving.

To defrost kippers

Place 250 g (9 oz) kippers on a plate. Microwave on Defrost (30%) for 3 – 4 minutes, turning once during defrosting time. Stand 5 minutes before cooking.

To microwave kippers

Place 250 g (9 oz) kippers in a shallow dish, overlap tails to ensure even cooking. Dot with a little butter and cover with vented plastic wrap. Microwave on Full Power for 3 – 5 minutes, depending on the thickness or size of the kippers.

Kipper pâté

Full Power
1 minute

250 g (9 oz) kippers, cooked*
75 g (2½ oz) butter
75 g (2½ oz) cream cheese
75 mℓ (2½ fl oz) single cream
10 mℓ (2 teaspoons) lemon juice
generous pinch of dried thyme
black pepper
parsley sprigs
lemon twists

Remove skin and bones from kippers, and place in a food processor bowl. Microwave butter on Full Power for 1 minute. Add butter and cream cheese to kippers, process until smooth. Add remaining ingredients, process to combine. Spoon pâté into a serving bowl and decorate with parsley and lemon. Serve with hot toast.
Serves 4

KOHLRABI

This swollen-stemmed vegetable is not yet particularly well known but it is sold in an increasing number of large supermarkets. Choose small, young kohlrabi as mature ones tend to become fibrous once microwaved.

To microwave kohlrabi

Trim off root ends and leaf stems of 500 g (18 oz) kohlrabi. Peel thickly and slice into 5-mm (¼-inch) thick slices. Place in a shallow casserole, add 60 ml (4 tablespoons) water and a pinch of salt. Cover, microwave on Full Power for 4 – 8 minutes, stirring once during cooking time. Stand 2 minutes before draining.

Serving suggestions

☐ Toss in melted butter, top with chopped parsley or chives.
☐ Coat with white sauce and top with parsley.
☐ Purée and add a dash of nutmeg.
☐ Serve with soured cream.

KUMQUAT

A member of the citrus family with small fruits similar to tiny oranges. Though bitter when eaten fresh, the fruits make an interesting preserve.

Kumquat preserve

Full Power
44 minutes

750 g (1¾ lb) kumquats
800 mℓ (26 fl oz) boiling water
20 mℓ (4 teaspoons) bicarbonate of soda
400 g (14 oz) preserving sugar
150 mℓ (5 fl oz) water
30 mℓ (2 tablespoons) lemon juice

Wash kumquats and place in a large bowl. Pour boiling water over the fruit and add bicarbonate of soda. Cover with vented plastic wrap, microwave on Full Power for 5 minutes. Allow to cool. Drain off water and rinse well in cold water. Using a small, sharp, pointed knife, make incisions right through the sides of fruit. Place fruit once again in a large bowl, cover with boiling water and plastic wrap. Microwave on Full Power for 10 minutes. Allow to cool slightly, then squeeze out the pips.

Place sugar and water in a large bowl. Microwave, uncovered, on Full Power for 10 minutes, stirring every few minutes. Strain syrup through a sieve lined with cotton wool. Return to bowl, then microwave for 3 – 4 minutes until syrup is boiling once more. Add kumquats and lemon juice. Microwave, uncovered, on Full Power for 15 minutes. The syrup should be thickened, and the fruit shoud be translucent. Pour into sterilized bottles. Cover loosely and allow to cool. Once cool, top up with syrup. Cover tightly, label and store.
Makes about 900 g (2 lb)

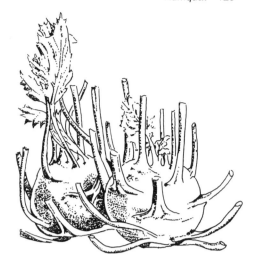

Overleaf:
Jams and jellies (page 116): clockwise, Strawberry Jam, Apricot Jam, Mint Jelly, Crab-apple Jelly (page 117), Peach Jam (page 120)
Centre: Fig Jam (page 116)

L

LAMB

The colour of good lamb may vary from pale pink to dark red and the flesh should be covered with a thin, even fatty layer. Do not cut off the rollermark, as the flesh will be exposed, causing the meat to become dry and tasteless during microwaving. All cuts of lamb are tender and suitable for cooking in the microwave. However, the cuts are not always a uniform shape, so knuckle ends and rib bones may need shielding wih small strips of foil and chops should be arranged so that the thickest parts are towards the outside.

Braised lamb with wine sauce

Full Power, Medium (50%)
2 hours 15 minutes

1.5 kg (3 lb) boned lamb shoulder, cut in
    2.5-cm (1-inch) cubes
60 g (2 oz) plain flour
salt and pepper
150 mℓ (5 fl oz) oil
30 g (1 oz) butter
2 large onions, chopped
1 large carrot, coarsely chopped
1 green pepper, cut in cubes
2 garlic cloves, finely chopped
20 mℓ (4 teaspoons) paprika
generous pinch of cayenne
2.5 mℓ (½ teaspoon) dried rosemary
2.5 mℓ (½ teaspoon) dried marjoram
2.5 mℓ (½ teaspoon) ground cumin
1 large bay leaf
350 mℓ (11 fl oz) beef stock
325 mℓ (10 fl oz) dry red wine
100 g (3½ oz) cooked gammon, diced
20 mℓ (4 teaspoons) cornflour
30 mℓ (2 tablespoons) dry red wine

Dredge the cubes of lamb with flour, salt and pepper. Preheat a browning dish according to the manufacturer's instructions, approximately 6 minutes. Add one-third of the oil and brown one-third of the meat by microwaving on Full Power for 2 minutes, turning meat and microwaving 2 – 3 minutes more, stirring once. Wipe the browning dish clean, reheat and repeat process twice more until all meat has been browned.

Microwave butter on Full Power for 30 seconds, add onions, carrot, green pepper and garlic. Toss to coat, then microwave for 5 – 7 minutes or until vegetables are tender, stirring once. Place lamb in a large casserole along with any juices. Stir in paprika, cayenne, rosemary, marjoram, cumin, bay leaf and vegetables. Cover and microwave for 5 minutes to blend flavours. Add stock, wine and gammon. Cover and microwave on Medium (50%) for 1¼ – 1½ hours, or until lamb is tender. Mix cornflour with dry red wine and stir into the lamb mixture, mixing well. Cover and microwave for a further 10 – 15 minutes to thicken, stirring several times. Serve with hot buttered rice.
Serves 6

Lamb stew with dumplings

Full Power
55 minutes

1 kg (2¼ lb) lean stewing lamb
30 mℓ (2 tablespoons) oil
5 mℓ (1 teaspoon) soft brown sugar
15 mℓ (1 tablespoon) plain flour
400 mℓ (13 fl oz) beef stock
100 mℓ (3½ fl oz) red wine
salt and pepper
2.5 mℓ (½ teaspoon) mixed herbs
30 mℓ (2 tablespoons) tomato paste
1 onion, sliced
2 carrots, thinly sliced
1 potato, diced

Dumplings
90 g (3 oz) self-raising flour
45 g (1½ oz) butter or margarine
salt and pepper
15 mℓ (1 tablespoon) chopped chives or spring
    onion
water

Cut meat into 2.5-cm (1-inch) cubes. Place oil in a shallow casserole and microwave on Full Power for 60 seconds. Add meat, cover with vented plastic wrap and microwave for 12 – 14 minutes, stirring occasionally. Remove meat and keep warm. Reserve 30 mℓ (2 tablespoons) of the fat and stir in sugar and flour. Microwave for 30 seconds, then stir in stock, wine, salt and pepper, herbs and tomato purée. Microwave 2 – 3 minutes, stirring once. Add onion, carrots, potato and meat. Cover and microwave for 18 – 20 minutes, or until lamb is tender, stirring at least twice.

To make dumplings, rub flour and butter together until mixture resembles fine crumbs. Mix in salt, pepper and chives. Add enough water to form a soft, but not sticky, dough. Carefully spoon dough in twelve portions into the casserole. Cover and microwave for 7 minutes.
Serves 6

Overleaf left: A Swiss Cheese Fondue (page 98) with an interesting variety of foods for dipping
Overleaf right: Ratatouille (page 185)

Chutney chops

High (70%)
23 minutes

4 lamb loin chops, about 2.5-cm (1-inch) thick
300 g (11 oz) canned mandarin segments
60 g (2 oz) caster sugar
150 g (5 oz) fruit chutney
30 mℓ (2 tablespoons) lemon juice
generous pinch of dried mint
salt and pepper
10 mℓ (2 teaspoons) cornflour

To garnish
mint sprigs

In a casserole, arrange chops so that the thickest parts are towards the outside. Cover with waxed paper and microwave on High (70%) for 10 minutes. Drain fat and turn chops over. Drain mandarin segments, saving the syrup. Arrange segments on top of the chops. Combine 75 mℓ (2½ fl oz) mandarin syrup, sugar, chutney, lemon juice and mint and spoon over the chops. Season to taste with salt and pepper. Cover with waxed paper and microwave for 10 minutes or until chops are tender. Remove chops to serving platter and keep warm. Mix cornflour with 30 mℓ (2 tablespoons) mandarin syrup, stir into the chutney mixture and microwave for 2 – 3 minutes, stirring at least once. Serve chops with the sauce spooned over and garnish with mint.
Serves 4

Crown roast of lamb

Full Power
28 minutes

2 racks of lamb, of 6 chops each

Stuffing
1 onion, chopped
60 g (2 oz) butter
1 garlic clove, crushed
125 g (4 oz) soft breadcrumbs
2.5 mℓ (½ teaspoon) dried rosemary
salt and pepper
2.5 mℓ (½ teaspoon) grated lemon rind
5 mℓ (1 teaspoon) grated orange rind
30 mℓ (2 tablespoons) orange juice or orange
   liqueur
45 g (1½ oz) sultanas
1 egg, beaten

Basting sauce
45 mℓ (3 tablespoons) apricot jam
15 mℓ (1 tablespoon) orange juice or orange
   liqueur

Ask the butcher to form the crown roast or bend each rack into a semi-circle with the fat side inwards. Cut between chop bones, but do not cut all the way through. Sew ends of racks together to form a circle.
   To make the stuffing, place onion, butter and garlic in a bowl and microwave on Full Power for 3 minutes. Stir in breadcrumbs, rosemary,

LAMB CHART

LAMB CUT	DEFROST TIME Per 500 g (18 oz) On Defrost (30%)	COOKING TIME Per 500 g (18 oz) On Full Power	METHOD
Leg	8 – 10 minutes, stand 30 minutes	8 – 11 minutes, stand 15 minutes	Shield bone-end during defrosting and halfway through cooking
Shoulder or loin	7 – 8 minutes, stand 30 minutes	8 – 11 minutes, stand 15 minutes	Shield thin portion during defrosting and three quarters of the way through cooking.
Chops	3 – 5 minutes, stand 5 – 10 minutes	8 – 10 minutes, stand 1 minute	Separate chops during defrosting. Microwave in browning dish, turn after 2½ minutes

salt and pepper to taste, lemon and orange rind, orange juice, sultanas and beaten egg.
   To make the basting sauce, mix apricot jam with orange juice and microwave for 45 seconds.
   Stuff centre of crown with the stuffing and place on a microwave roasting rack. Cover the stuffing, but not the roast, with waxed paper and microwave for 15 minutes, brushing roast with basting sauce after 10 minutes. Remove waxed paper, brush again with basting sauce and microwave another 10 minutes. Remove from the oven, cover with aluminium foil and stand in a warm place for 20 – 25 minutes. Garnish bone ends with paper frills or green stuffed olives if desired.
Serves 6

Lamb with plum sauce

Full Power, High (70%)
49 minutes

1.5 kg (3 lb) leg of lamb, boned
salt and black pepper
5 mℓ (1 teaspoon) powdered gelatine
gravy browning
paprika
15 g (½ oz) butter

Stuffing
45 mℓ (3 tablespoons) oil
1 onion, chopped
1 garlic clove, crushed
100 g (3½ oz) chicken livers
125 g (4 oz) cooked rice*
5 mℓ (1 teaspoon) chopped rosemary
2.5 mℓ (½ teaspoon) turmeric
generous pinch of coriander
75 g (2½ oz) raisins
1 egg

Plum sauce
100 g (3½ oz) plum jam
10 mℓ (2 teaspoons) lemon juice
5 mℓ (1 teaspoon) Dijon mustard
45 mℓ (3 tablespoons) water
30 mℓ (2 tablespoons) red wine
5 – 10 mℓ (1 – 2 teaspoons) gravy granules
15 mℓ (1 tablespoon) water

First make the stuffing. Place oil in a large bowl, microwave on Full Power for 1 minute. Add onion and garlic, microwave 2 minutes. Prick the membranes of the chicken livers, chop chicken livers roughly, add to bowl and stir to coat with oil. Cover and microwave for 2 minutes. Add remaining ingredients, season well.
   Lay meat flat, season and sprinkle with gelatine. Add stuffing, roll up and sew with thick thread. Brush outside of meat with gravy browning, season with salt, pepper and paprika, spread butter on top. Place in a roasting bag, tie loosely with string. Stand meat on a meat rack or on a plate with an inverted saucer underneath. Microwave on High (70%) for 12 – 13 minutes per 500 g (18 oz). Stand for 10 minutes before serving.
   To make the sauce, place all ingredients except gravy powder and 15 mℓ water into a jug, microwave on Full Power for 3 minutes, stir well. Add some of the liquid from the cooking bag, stir. Combine gravy granules and water, add to the sauce. Microwave for 3 minutes, stir well and serve.
Serves 4 – 6

Lamb curry

Full Power, High (70%), Medium (50%)
66 minutes

750 g (1¾ lb) stewing lamb, cubed
30 g (1 oz) plain flour
salt and black pepper
60 mℓ (4 tablespoons) oil
2 onions, chopped
1 green pepper, chopped
2 garlic cloves, crushed
1 small piece of fresh ginger, chopped
15 mℓ (1 tablespoon) curry powder or blended
   curry spices
400 g (14 oz) canned tomatoes, coarsely
   chopped
15 mℓ (1 tablespoon) tomato paste
25 mℓ (5 teaspoons) fresh coriander, chopped
   (optional)
15 mℓ (1 tablespoon) fruit chutney
10 mℓ (2 teaspoons) biryani spices
beef stock, if necessary

Toss lamb in flour, salt and pepper. Microwave browning dish on Full Power for 5 – 6 minutes. Add half the oil, microwave for 2 minutes. Add lamb and stir to coat with oil. Microwave for 3 – 4 minutes, stirring twice during cooking time. Pour remaining oil into a 2.5 – 3-litre (4¼ – 5-pint) casserole, microwave for 2 minutes. Add onions, green pepper, garlic, ginger and curry powder. Stir to combine, microwave for 4 minutes, stirring once during cooking time. Add browned meat, tomatoes and liquid, tomato paste, coriander and chutney. Tie biryani spices in a small piece of muslin, add to curry, stir to combine ingredients. Cover, microwave for 5 minutes. Reduce power to High (70%) and microwave for 15 minutes. Stir, reduce power to Medium (50%) and microwave uncovered for 30 minutes, stirring once or twice. Add a little stock if necessary. Remove spices, stand for 10 – 15 minutes. Serve with rice and a selection of sambals.
Serves 4 – 6

Suggested sambals: poppadums, roti, onion and tomato, sliced banana, cucumber with mint and yoghurt, chopped green pepper, sliced pineapple, lime pickle, chutney, Bombay duck.

Noisettes of lamb with blue cheese

Full Power
19 minutes

8 noisettes of lamb
8 streaky bacon rashers, rinds removed
salt and black pepper
30 mℓ (2 tablespoons) red wine
1 onion, sliced
1 celery stick, sliced
100 g (3½ oz) mushrooms, sliced
15 mℓ (1 tablespoon) plain flour
125 mℓ (4 fl oz) chicken stock
60 mℓ (4 tablespoons) tomato purée
generous pinch of dried rosemary
30 g (1 oz) blue cheese, crumbled

Cut bacon into lengths that will fit around noisettes, wrap around and secure with string. Season lightly with salt and pepper. Arrange noisettes in a shallow casserole, cover with kitchen paper and microwave on Full Power for 7 – 8 minutes. Turn meat over and rearrange halfway through cooking time. Remove meat and set aside. Add red wine and vegetables to casserole, stir well. Microwave for 4 minutes, stirring once during cooking time. Stir in flour, chicken stock, tomato purée and rosemary. Microwave for 5 minutes, stirring once. Add chops, spoon a little sauce over each chop, sprinkle with blue cheese. Cover, microwave for 3 minutes and serve immediately.
Serves 4

Spicy skewered lamb

Full Power, Medium (50%)
24 minutes

45 mℓ (1½ oz) butter or margarine
1 large onion, finely chopped
15 mℓ (1 tablespoon) curry powder
5 mℓ (1 teaspoon) ground coriander
2.5 mℓ (½ teaspoon) ground turmeric
125 mℓ (4 fl oz) lemon juice
125 mℓ (4 fl oz) water
30 mℓ (2 tablespoons) apricot jam
15 mℓ (1 tablespoon) soft brown sugar
150 g (5 oz) dried apricots
1.5 kg (3 lb) fatty leg of lamb or mutton
salt and pepper
4 bay leaves
1 garlic clove, finely chopped
5 mℓ (1 teaspoon) freshly chopped hot chillies
15 mℓ (1 tablespoon) plain flour
30 mℓ (2 tablespoons) cold water

Microwave butter in a large casserole on Full Power for 30 – 45 seconds to melt. Stir in onion and microwave 2 – 3 minutes or until just soft. Add curry powder, coriander and turmeric and microwave for 1 minute. Stir in lemon juice and water, apricot jam and brown sugar. Microwave 2 – 3 minutes, or until mixture comes to the boil. Reduce power to Medium (50%) and simmer, loosely covered, for 6 minutes. Add apricots and cool mixture to room temperature.
  Meanwhile, cut mutton into 2.5 – 3 cm (1 – 1¼-inch) cubes. Sprinkle with salt and pepper, then add to cooled marinade along with bay leaves, garlic and chillies. Marinate, refrigerated, for at least 12 hours, stirring occasionally. Thread meat alternately with apricots on wooden skewers and microwave, a few at a time, on Medium (50%) for 5 – 6 minutes. Then place over glowing coals and barbecue until cooked.
  To make a sauce, mix flour with cold water, add to the marinade and microwave on Full Power for 3 – 4 minutes or until sauce thickens, stirring every minute.
Serves 6 – 8

LANGOUSTINE *See* Crayfish

LEEK
This member of the onion family is frequently neglected. When topped and tailed, its even shape makes it ideal for microwave cooking. This versatile vegetable may be served hot or cold, in a casserole or as a soup. *See also* Vichyssoise.

To microwave leeks
Trim the roots and leaves off 8 medium-sized leeks. Arrange in a shallow casserole, and add 60 ml (4 tablespoons) water. Cover and microwave on Full Power for 11 – 15 minutes. Drain.

Serving suggestions
☐ Toss in melted butter, sprinkle with parsley.
☐ Coat with a béchamel or cheese sauce.

☐ Toss in melted butter, sprinkle with cooked crumbled bacon.

Leek pie

Full Power, Medium (50%)
18 minutes

1 x 22.5-cm (9-inch) savoury biscuit crust*
30 g (1 oz) butter
6 leeks, thinly sliced
15 mℓ (1 tablespoon) plain flour
150 mℓ (5 fl oz) chicken stock
black pepper
2 eggs
1 egg yolk
150 mℓ (5 fl oz) single cream
100 g (3½ oz) Cheddar cheese, grated
15 mℓ (1 tablespoon) chopped parsley

For the filling, microwave butter on Full Power in a large bowl for 1 minute, add leeks, stir to coat with butter. Microwave for 4 minutes, stirring at least once during cooking time. Stir in flour, then chicken stock and pepper. Microwave for 2 minutes, stir well. Beat eggs, egg yolk and cream, stir into leek mixture, season, and add half the cheese. Pour into prepared pie crust. Microwave on Medium (50%) for 11 – 13 minutes. Add remaining cheese 3 minutes before the end of the cooking time. Stand for 5 minutes before serving. Garnish with chopped parsley.
Serves 6

Leeks à la Grecque

Full Power
5 minutes

8 cooked leeks*

Dressing
1 tomato, skinned, seeded and chopped
150 g (5 oz) button mushrooms, sliced
45 mℓ (3 tablespoons) oil
1 garlic clove, crushed
2.5 mℓ (½ teaspoon) dried tarragon
salt and black pepper
1 bay leaf
15 mℓ (1 tablespoon) lemon juice

To serve
15 mℓ (1 tablespoon) chopped parsley
slices of brown bread and butter

Place all the ingredients for the dressing into a large bowl. Cover with vented plastic wrap. Microwave on Full Power for 5 minutes, stir well and allow to cool slightly. Remove bay leaf and pour over the leeks. Chill well before serving. Sprinkle with parsley and serve with fresh brown bread.
Serves 4

Overleaf left: Cheese and Wine Burgers cooked in a browning dish (page 108)
Overleaf right: Marinated Chicken Kebabs with Peanut Sauce (page 121)

LEMON

Both the juice and the rind of the lemon are used in all types of cookery. To obtain the maximum amount of juice, lightly prick the skin of a whole lemon with a skewer. Microwave on Full Power for 10 – 15 seconds, then cut in half and squeeze.

Lemon chicken breasts

Full Power, High (70%)
30 minutes

6 chicken breasts, boned

Marinade
1 onion, sliced
45 mℓ (3 tablespoons) lemon juice
salt and black pepper
10 mℓ (2 teaspoons) dry mustard

Sauce
30 g (1 oz) butter
1 leek, sliced
1 garlic clove, crushed
1 carrot, sliced
1 celery stick, chopped
1 bacon rasher, rind removed and chopped
200 mℓ (6½ fl oz) sparkling white wine
400 mℓ (13 fl oz) chicken stock
10 mℓ (2 teaspoons) dry mustard
2.5 mℓ (½ teaspoon) Dijon mustard
5 mℓ (1 teaspoon) sugar
30 mℓ (2 tablespoons) lemon juice
15 g (½ oz) cornflour

To garnish
1 leek, cut in julienne
1 carrot, cut in julienne
30 g (1 oz) butter

First make the garnish. Place vegetable julienne in a bowl with water and a few ice cubes. Refrigerate for at least 2 hours. Place chicken in a shallow glass dish, combine marinade ingredients and pour over chicken. Cover, marinate for 2 hours, turning chicken from time to time.

To make the sauce, microwave butter in a shallow casserole on Full Power for 1 minute. Add leek, garlic, carrot, celery and bacon, toss to coat with butter. Microwave for 4 minutes, add remaining ingredients, except the lemon juice and cornflour, and stir well. Microwave for 10 minutes. Strain sauce, return liquid to casserole and discard vegetables. Combine lemon juice and cornflour, stir in a little of the hot liquid, then add cornflour mixture to remaining hot liquid. Microwave for 2 minutes.

Remove chicken breasts from marinade and pat dry. Arrange in the sauce, spooning a little liquid over each portion. Cover and microwave on High (70%) for 10 – 12 minutes, turning chicken over halfway through cooking time. Remove from microwave and keep warm.

Drain vegetable julienne from iced water, place in a bowl, cover with vented plastic wrap. Microwave on Full Power for 2 – 3 minutes, add butter and microwave for 30 seconds. Toss vegetables to coat with butter. Arrange vegetable julienne on top of chicken and serve.
Serves 4

Lemon curd

Full Power, High (70%), Medium (50%)
7 minutes

125 g (4 oz) butter
4 eggs
200 g (7 oz) caster sugar
125 mℓ (4 fl oz) lemon juice
finely grated rind of 2 lemons
5 mℓ (1 teaspoon) cornflour

Place butter in a large bowl and microwave on Full Power for 2 minutes. Beat eggs and sugar until light and fluffy. Add remaining ingredients and beat to combine. Pour in melted butter, mix well. Microwave for 2 minutes, stir well. Now microwave on High (70%) for 2 minutes more, stirring at the end of each minute. Reduce power setting to Medium (50%) and microwave for 1 – 2 minutes more. Beat well. The mixture should be thick enough to coat the back of a wooden spoon. Cool slightly. Pour into two medium-sized jars, top with waxed or brandy papers. Cover when cold. Label and store in the refrigerator.
Makes about 900 g (2 lb)

Spicy lemon sauce

Full Power
5 minutes

generous pinch of cinnamon
pinch of cloves
pinch of nutmeg
100 g (3½ oz) caster sugar
15 mℓ (1 tablespoon) cornflour
juice of 2 lemons
300 mℓ (10 fl oz) water
few drops of vanilla extract

Combine cinnamon, cloves, nutmeg, sugar and cornflour. Combine lemon juice, water and vanilla and stir into the spice mixture. Microwave on Full Power for about 5 minutes, stirring every minute until sugar has dissolved and mixture has thickened. Serve warm over bread pudding, steamed pudding or Madeira cake.
Makes enough for 6 servings

Lemon filling

Full Power, Medium (50%)
4 minutes

When lemons are plentiful, use this to fill cream puffs or pastries

250 g (9 oz) caster sugar
30 g (1 oz) cornflour
salt
375 mℓ (12 fl oz) water
3 egg yolks
7 mℓ (2½ fl oz) lemon juice
60 g (2 oz) butter

In a large jug, combine sugar, cornflour and salt, add water and stir well. Microwave on Full Power for 2 – 3 minutes, until boiling, stirring every 30 seconds during cooking time. Beat yolks lightly, stir in a little of the boiling liquid, return to hot mixture. Microwave on Medium (50%) for 2 minutes, beat well. Stir in lemon juice and butter, cool, then refrigerate until chilled.
Makes about 600 mℓ (19 fl oz)

LENTILS

Lentils are a good source of protein and one of our most nourishing foods, more easily digested than either dried beans or peas and used extensively in vegetarian and Indian cookery.

There are many varieties of lentils, the most popular being red, brown and black. Whole brown or black lentils should be soaked in plenty of cold water for at least 6 hours before being cooked. Red lentils have had the dark seed removed and resemble small, reddish-yellow split peas. They do not need to be soaked before cooking, and are popularly used in lentil soup.

To microwave whole lentils
Soak 250 g (9 oz) lentils for 6 hours, drain. Place in a casserole, cover with about 600 ml (19 fl oz) water, add generous pinch of salt and a chicken stock cube. Cover and microwave on High (70%) for 25 minutes, stirring at least twice.

Serving suggestions
☐ To serve cooked lentils, add 100 ml (3½ fl oz) French dressing, 5 ml (1 teaspoon) turmeric, 5 ml (1 teaspoon) curry paste, 1 chopped onion, 1 crushed garlic clove and 45 ml (3 tablespoons) lemon juice. Stand overnight before serving.

Dhall

Full Power, High (70%)
30 minutes

60 mℓ (4 tablespoons) oil
2 large onions, chopped
2 garlic cloves, crushed
5 mℓ (1 teaspoon) chopped fresh ginger
1 – 2 green chillies, chopped
5 mℓ (1 teaspoon) turmeric
250 g (9 oz) whole lentils, soaked
595 mℓ (19 fl oz) coconut cream*
salt and black pepper
½ chicken stock cube

Pour oil into a large casserole, microwave for 3 minutes on Full Power. Add onion, garlic, ginger, chillies and turmeric, stir well. Microwave for 5 minutes. Add remaining ingredients and stir well. Cover and microwave on High (70%) for 25 – 28 minutes, stirring at least twice during the cooking time. Serve as a side dish with curry or any spicy dish.
Serves 8

LIMA BEANS *See* Beans

LIQUEUR

Liqueurs are often made by infusing flavourings, such as fruit, herbs and spices, in alcohol. Originally, liqueurs were considered medicinal and, even today, they may be looked on as digestives to be served at the end of a meal. In the kitchen, they are useful for flavouring desserts, sweet sauces, puddings and beverages. To simplify the making of liqueurs at home, use the microwave to make the sugar syrups and infuse flavours.

Spiced orange liqueur

High (70%)
3 minutes

2 oranges
250 mℓ (8 fl oz) brandy
300 g (11 oz) caster sugar
5 mℓ (1 teaspoon) coriander seeds
2.5-cm (1-inch) piece of cinnamon stick
2 cloves

Using a zester, remove peel from oranges in thin strips. Squeeze oranges, juice should measure 250 mℓ (8 fl oz). In a jug, combine brandy, sugar and spices. Microwave on High (70%) for 3 minutes, stir well. Add orange juice and rind. Cover and stand for 2 days, stirring occasionally. Strain through a filter coffee paper. Pour into a clean, dry bottle, seal and store for 3 weeks before drinking.
Makes about 700 mℓ (22 fl oz)

Loganberry liqueur

Full Power
3 minutes

250 g (9 oz) fresh loganberries
200 g (7 oz) caster sugar
750 mℓ (1¼ pints) gin

Wash loganberries and drain. Place sugar and 125 mℓ (4 fl oz) of the gin in a measuring jug and microwave on Full Power for 2 minutes. Stir and microwave for 1 minute. Pour sugar mixture over berries and stir gently. Cool to room temperature, then place mixture in a large jar with a tight-fitting lid. Add remaining gin. Seal and keep in a cool place. Turn jar every few days for about three weeks. The liqueur is better if left for about two months before serving.
Makes about 750 mℓ (1¼ pints)

Coffee liqueur

Full Power
5 minutes

250 mℓ (8 fl oz) water
400 g (14 oz) caster sugar
15 mℓ (1 tablespoon) instant coffee powder
400 mℓ (13 fl oz) cane spirit or vodka
125 mℓ (4 fl oz) brandy
few drops of vanilla extract

Combine water and sugar and microwave on Full Power for 2 minutes. Stir and microwave about 3 minutes more, stirring twice, until sugar has dissolved. Stir in instant coffee and cool the mixture. Stir in cane spirit or vodka, brandy and vanilla. Bottle and mature for about two months before serving.
Makes about 850 mℓ (27 fl oz)

Chocolate liqueur

Full Power
5 minutes

1 egg
250 g (9 oz) caster sugar
500 mℓ (16 fl oz) vodka
250 mℓ (8 fl oz) water
45 g (1½ oz) cocoa powder
2.5-cm (1-inch) piece of cinnamon stick
20 mℓ (4 teaspoons) grated orange peel
few drops of vanilla extract

Combine the egg with 45 g (1½ oz) of the sugar and beat well. Slowly beat in the vodka, mixing well. Combine remaining sugar, water, cocoa, cinnamon stick, orange peel and vanilla. Microwave on Full Power for 2 minutes, then stir well. Microwave for about 3 minutes longer, stirring twice, until sugar has dissolved completely. Cool the mixture, strain to remove cinnamon stick and orange peel, then beat slowly into the vodka mixture. Bottle and mature for at least 6 weeks before serving.
Makes about 750 mℓ (1¼ pints)

Liqueur cream sauce

High (70%)
4 minutes

Serve with cake or warm over ice cream

90 g (3 oz) butter
200 g (7 oz) icing sugar
45 mℓ (3 tablespoons) liqueur such as Crème de Cacao, Tia Maria or brandy
2 egg yolks
125 mℓ (4 fl oz) single cream

Microwave butter on High (70%) for 45 seconds. Gradually beat in icing sugar, then slowly stir in liqueur. Add egg yolks, one at a time, beating well after each addition and finally stir in the cream. Microwave for about 3 minutes, stirring every minute until the mixture is slightly thickened. Serve warm or cool.
Makes about 375 mℓ (12 fl oz)

LIVER

Microwaving liver takes only a few minutes, and the results are delicious. Liver should not be overcooked as it may toughen, so follow instructions carefully.

To defrost liver, place 250 (9 oz) liver on a shallow dish. Cover with waxed paper and microwave on Defrost (30%) for 4 minutes. Stand 10 minutes before using.

Fried liver

Full Power
7 minutes

250 g (9 oz) liver, thinly sliced
30 g (1 oz) plain flour
salt and pepper
15 mℓ (1 tablespoon) oil
15 g (½ oz) butter

Lightly dredge liver with mixture of flour, salt and pepper. Preheat a browning dish according to manufacturer's instructions, about 6 minutes on Full Power. Add oil and butter and stir to mix. Add liver and microwave 1 – 1½ minutes on each side, depending on desired doneness and thickness of slices.
Serves 3 – 4

Braised liver and onions

Full Power, Medium (50%)
16 minutes

30 g (1 oz) butter
1 large onion, sliced
30 mℓ (1 tablespoon) plain flour
salt and pepper
200 g (7 oz) calf's or lamb's liver, trimmed and thinly sliced
15 g (½ oz) butter
15 mℓ (1 tablespoon) oil
125 mℓ (4 fl oz) chicken stock
2.5 mℓ (½ teaspoon) dried thyme
2 bacon rashers, rinds removed, cooked and chopped

Microwave butter on Full Power for 45 seconds. Add onion, toss to mix and microwave for 3 minutes. Remove and set aside. Combine flour with salt and pepper and lightly dredge liver slices. Preheat a browning dish according to manufacturer's instructions, about 6 minutes. Add butter and oil and stir to heat. Add liver to browning dish and microwave 1 minute on each side. Remove from oven, add stock, thyme and bacon. Cover and microwave on Medium (50%) for 6 – 8 minutes until liver is tender. Check seasoning and thicken the sauce with a little cornflour or flour if desired.
Serves 3

Overleaf left: A selection of Friandises (page 99)
Overleaf right: Fresh Fruit Savarin (page 197)

Liver flambéed with bourbon

Full Power
10 minutes

125 g (4 oz) calf's liver, trimmed and thinly
　sliced
30 mℓ (1 tablespoon) plain flour
salt and pepper
15 g (½ oz) butter
15 mℓ (1 tablespoon) oil
10 mℓ (2 teaspoons) chopped fresh sage
　leaves or 2.5 mℓ (½ teaspoon) dried sage
15 mℓ (1 tablespoon) raspberry vinegar
30 mℓ (2 tablespoons) bourbon

Dredge liver slices with a mixture of flour, salt
and pepper. Microwave butter and oil for 30
seconds on Full Power. Stir in sage leaves and
set aside. Preheat a browning dish according
to manufacturer's instructions, about 6 minutes.
Add oil mixture, then liver slices. Microwave
1 – 1½ minutes on each side. Remove dish
from the oven. Sprinkle with vinegar and pour
the bourbon over. Flambé, and serve
immediately when the flame dies, spooning
some of the sauce over each serving.
Serves 2 – 3

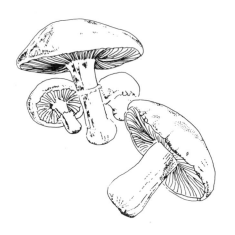

LOGANBERRY
This berry is a cross between a raspberry
and a blackberry. Though the fruit resembles the raspberry in character, it is larger
and darker in colour. Loganberries are
highly perishable and are more usually
found canned or bottled than fresh.
See also Jam and Liqueur.

Loganberry mousse

Medium (50%)
1 minute

3 eggs, separated
90 g (3 oz) caster sugar
400 g (14 oz) canned loganberries
20 mℓ (4 teaspoons) powdered gelatine
45 mℓ (3 tablespoons) water
30 mℓ (2 tablespoons) Kirsch
15 mℓ (1 tablespoon) lemon juice
125 mℓ (4 fl oz) whipping cream

Beat egg yolks and sugar together until thick
and light in colour. Drain berries, reserving
liquid. Purée berries and strain. Make up to
250 mℓ (8 fl oz) with some of the liquid if
necessary. Mix purée into egg yolk mixture.
Sprinkle gelatine over water and stand for
5 minutes. Microwave on Medium (50%) for
45 – 60 seconds, until completely dissolved.
Add to fruit mixture along with the Kirsch and
lemon juice. Chill until just beginning to thicken.
Beat egg whites until stiff and whip cream to
soft peaks. Fold both into the fruit mixture. Turn
into a serving bowl and chill until firm. Decorate
with whipped cream if desired. *Serves 6*

MACADAMIA NUTS

Macadamias are members of the Protea family and native to Australia. The firm, round nuts have become one of Hawaii's major crops and are now very popular worldwide. Macadamia nuts are prized for their rich, delicate flavour. The hard outer husk is almost impossible to remove which is why they are sold preshelled. Lightly toasted, usually in coconut oil, and lightly salted, these tasty nuts are used in baking, sprinkled on chicken salads and fruit desserts, and are delicious when teamed up with chocolate.

Macadamia and banana cream pie

Full Power
3 minutes

Crust
100 g (3½ oz) Marie biscuit crumbs
100 g (3½ oz) macadamia nuts, finely chopped
75 g (2½ oz) caster sugar
5 mℓ (1 teaspoon) cinnamon
90 g (3 oz) butter
45 mℓ (3 tablespoons) single cream

Filling
2 bananas
10 mℓ (2 teaspoons) lemon juice
250 g (9 oz) low-fat soft cheese
30 mℓ (2 tablespoons) Coco Rico liqueur or Créme de Cacao
400 mℓ (13 fl oz) milk
1 packet vanilla instant pudding mix

For the crust, mix biscuit crumbs with chopped nuts, caster sugar and cinnamon. Microwave butter on Full Power for 45 seconds, then mix into crumb mixture. Add the cream. Press mixture into bottom and sides of a 22.5-cm (9-inch) pie dish. Microwave for 2 minutes, then cool.
    For the filling, slice bananas and sprinkle with lemon juice. Mix soft cheese with liqueur and 125 mℓ (4 fl oz) of the milk. Mix pudding mix with remaining milk, beating for 1 minute.

Combine soft cheese and pudding mixtures and mix well. Arrange banana slices on the cooled crust and pour filling over. Chill until set. Decorate with whipped cream, slices of banana and macadamia nuts if desired.
Serves 6 – 8

Macadamia chocolate bark

Medium (50%)
5 minutes

350 g (12 oz) plain chocolate, broken into pieces
125 g (4 oz) macadamia nuts, coarsely chopped

Place chocolate in a large casserole. Cover and microwave on Medium (50%) for 5 minutes. Stir well, then mix in nuts. Turn mixture out on a piece of waxed paper on a baking sheet and spread in a thin layer. Place in a cool spot until firm, then break into pieces.
Makes about 475 g (17 oz)

MARINADES

Marinades improve the flavour of fish or poultry and may also be used to tenderize and impregnate with juice and oil meats such as venison, which would otherwise be dry. Some meats should be marinated for several hours or overnight to tenderize, while others may need only an hour or so in the marinade liquid for added flavour. To avoid having to clean dishes and to make turning the meat easier, place meat and marinade in a large roasting bag. Simply rearrange the bag from time to time to ensure all parts are well marinated.
    Marinades also make excellent basting sauces, preventing meat, poultry or fish from drying out during cooking. They are easily cooked in the microwave and can be heated and thickened and served as a sauce.

Basic marinade

High (70%)
5 minutes

250 mℓ (8 fl oz) water
250 mℓ (8 fl oz) red wine
1 garlic clove, crushed
1 large onion, finely chopped
2 carrots, sliced
5 mℓ (1 teaspoon) dried rosemary
2 bay leaves
black pepper
6 allspice berries

Combine all the ingredients in a jug. Microwave on High (70%) for 5 minutes. Stand for 24 hours before using marinade. Use for steaks, chops or chicken. *Makes 500 mℓ (16 fl oz)*

Red wine marinade

High (70%)
2 minutes

250 mℓ (8 fl oz) dry red wine
250 mℓ (8 fl oz) oil
30 mℓ (2 tablespoons) vinegar
4 spring onions, chopped
10 mℓ (2 teaspoons) grated lemon rind
1 garlic clove, finely chopped
10 mℓ (2 teaspoons) salt
20 mℓ (4 teaspoons) sugar
5 mℓ (1 teaspoon) pepper
2.5 mℓ (½ teaspoon) dry mustard
2.5 mℓ (½ teaspoon) thyme
generous pinch of basil

Combine all ingredients and microwave on High (70%) for 2 minutes. Cool and use to marinate steak for several hours or overnight. Reserve marinade to brush on steak during cooking. *Makes about 500 mℓ (16 fl oz)*

Overleaf left: Eggs Florentine (page 89)
Overleaf right: Snail-stuffed Mushrooms (page 200), Spinach-stuffed Mushrooms (page 156) and Garlic Mushrooms (page 156)

Apricot marinade

Full Power
13 minutes

60 g (2 oz) dried apricots
200 mℓ (6½ fl oz) water
30 g (1 oz) butter
2 large onions, chopped
1 garlic clove, chopped
about 15 mℓ (1 tablespoon) curry powder
15 mℓ (1 tablespoon) sugar
2.5 mℓ (½ teaspoon) salt
45 mℓ (3 tablespoons) vinegar
cayenne
6 lemon leaves (optional)

Place apricots and water in a jug and
microwave on Full Power for 3 minutes, then
cool. Drain apricots and purée in a blender or
food processor. Microwave butter for 30
seconds, add onion and garlic and toss to coat.
Microwave for 3 minutes, stirring once. Mix in
curry powder and microwave 1 minute more.
Add apricot purée and remaining ingredients.
Microwave for 5 minutes, stirring once, then
cool. Use to marinate ribs, lamb or chops.
Makes about 250 mℓ (8 fl oz)

MARMALADE
Many people consider breakfast incom-
plete without a pot of golden, fruity marmalade. Marmalades microwave quickly
and do not make the kitchen hot and
sticky. To ensure you have a good selection
of marmalades year round, make small
batches whenever citrus fruit is plentiful.

Orange ginger marmalade

Full Power
40 minutes

3 oranges
1 litre (1¾ pints) water
500 g (18 oz) green apples
1.5 kg (3 lb) sugar
small piece of fresh ginger, grated
25 mℓ (5 teaspoons) chopped preserved
   ginger
generous pinch of ground ginger

Wash oranges well. Squeeze the juice. Remove
membranes and pips, then mince or chop peel
finely. In a large bowl, combine orange juice,
minced peel and water. Tie membranes and
pips in a piece of muslin and add to bowl.
Cover bowl with vented plastic wrap and
microwave on Full Power for 20 minutes.
Remove the muslin bag. Peel, core and dice
apples finely. Add all the remaining ingredients
to the bowl. Microwave, uncovered, on Full
Power for 15 – 20 minutes, stirring every 5
minutes. Check for setting point, allowing extra
time if necessary. Pour into warm, sterilized
jars. Cover loosely when cold, top up jars and
cover tightly. Label and store.
Makes about 1.5 kg (3 lb)

Grapefruit jelly marmalade

Full Power
1 hour 45 minutes

1 kg (2¼ lb) grapefruit
1 lemon
2 litres (3½ pints) water
1.25 kg (2¾ lb) preserving sugar

Using a zester remove the zest from the
grapefruit, or peel very thinly and cut rind into
fine shreds. Cover zest with boiling water, stand
10 minutes, then drain. Peel grapefruit and
lemon. Chop pulp, place in a large bowl and
add 1 litre (3¾ pints) water. Cover with vented
plastic wrap. Microwave on Full Power for 20
minutes. Strain pulp through a jelly cloth and
reserve liquid. Cover zest with 500 mℓ (16 fl oz)
water, microwave for 10 minutes. Drain and
add this liquid to the pulp. Return pulp to bowl,
add 500 mℓ (16 fl oz) water and cover.
Microwave on Full Power for 15 minutes. Strain
pulp again through jelly cloth. Reserve liquid
and discard pulp.
   In a large bowl, combine reserved liquid and
sugar. Microwave, uncovered, for 20 minutes,
stirring every 5 minutes. Add zest and
microwave for 30 – 35 minutes more, skim if
necessary and stir every 5 minutes. To prevent
marmalade from rising in the jar, allow to cool
slightly before pouring into warm, sterilized jars.
Cool completely, top up with more marmalade,
then cover tightly, label and store.
Makes about 1.5 kg (3 lb)

Variation
Add 45 mℓ (3 tablespoons) Grand Marnier to
slightly cooled marmalade.

Four-fruit marmalade

Full Power
55 minutes

2 oranges
2 grapefruit
2 lemons
2 tangerines or satsumas
850 mℓ (27 fl oz) boiling water
2 kg (4¼ lb) preserving sugar
15 mℓ (1 tablespoon) molasses or dark treacle
60 mℓ (4 tablespoons) whisky

Wash and dry fruit. Squeeze juice and set
aside. Remove pips and pith, and tie in a piece
of muslin. Slice peel according to taste – thin,
medium or coarse. Place juice, sliced peel and
muslin bag in a large mixing bowl. Add half the
boiling water, stand for 1 hour, then add
remaining boiling water. Cover with vented
plastic wrap and microwave on Full Power for
about 25 minutes. Uncover, remove muslin bag
and stir in sugar and molasses. Microwave,
uncovered, for 25 – 30 minutes until setting
point is reached, stirring every 5 minutes. If any
scum forms on top, scoop it off. Allow
marmalade to cool. Stir in the whisky, then pour
into sterilized jars. Cover, label and store.
Makes about 1.5 kg (3 lb)

MARSHMALLOW
A soft, spongy confection which is enjoyed
by many people in all age groups. The
sugar syrup boils quickly in the microwave
oven. When the soft ball stage is reached,
the gelatine is added and the mixture is
whipped with beaten egg whites until light
and fluffy.

Marshmallows

Full Power
16 minutes

400 g (14 oz) caster sugar
15 mℓ (1 tablespoon) golden syrup
350 mℓ (11 fl oz) water
35 mℓ (7 teaspoons) powdered gelatine
2 egg whites
few drops of vanilla extract
45 mℓ (3 tablespoons) cornflour
45 mℓ (3 tablespoons) icing sugar, sifted

Combine sugar, golden syrup and 250 mℓ (8
fl oz) water in a large bowl, microwave on Full
Power for 4 minutes, stir well. Microwave for
about 12 minutes more, until mixture reaches
soft ball stage. Meanwhile soak gelatine in
remaining water for 2 minutes. Add to boiling
syrup and stir to dissolve. Beat egg whites until
stiff, then gradually pour in boiling syrup.
Continue beating until mixture holds its shape,
add vanilla. Pour into a well-buttered 25 x 20-
cm (10 x 8-inch) pan. Leave to set in the
refrigerator. Cut into squares with a hot knife.
Combine cornflour with icing sugar and roll
each square in this mixture. Alternatively roll in
toasted coconut.
Makes about 50 squares

Grasshopper filling

Medium (50%)
3 minutes

12 marshmallows, roughly chopped
30 mℓ (2 tablespoons) Crème de Cacao
30 mℓ (2 tablespoons) Crème de Menthe
few drops of green colouring
250 mℓ (8 fl oz) whipping cream

Place marshmallows, liqueurs and colouring in
a bowl. Microwave on medium (50%) for 3 – 4
minutes, stirring at least once. Stir until smooth.
Allow to cool to room temperature. Beat cream
until beginning to thicken, fold in cooled
marshmallow mixture. Use to fill choux puffs,
meringues or a biscuit crust.
Makes about 500 mℓ (16 fl oz)

Baked Glazed Gammon (page 107)

Easy marshmallow cake

Medium (50%)
4 minutes

Very rich and very good.

225 g (8 oz) digestive biscuits, coarsely
  crushed
175 g (6 oz) candied mixed peel, chopped
175 g (6 oz) glacé cherries, chopped
100 g (3½ oz) seedless raisins
100 g (3½ oz) hazel or pecan nuts, coarsely
  chopped
5 mℓ (1 teaspoon) mixed spice
90 g (3 oz) marshmallows, chopped if large
45 mℓ (3 tablespoons) sweet sherry
45 mℓ (3 tablespoons) golden syrup
100 g (3½ oz) milk chocolate or plain
  chocolate, coarsely grated

Line a loaf dish with greased waxed paper and
set aside. In a large mixing bowl, combine
crumbled biscuits, mixed peel, cherries,
raisins, nuts and mixed spice. Place
marshmallows, sherry, syrup and chocolate in a
bowl. Microwave on Medium (50%) for 3 to 4
minutes, stirring every minute, until
marshmallows and chocolate are melted. Add
to biscuit mixture and blend well. Turn into the
loaf dish and spread evenly. Press mixture into
the dish and cover with foil or waxed paper.
Chill until firm, then unmould and slice to serve.
Store, well wrapped, in a cool place.
Makes 1 loaf cake

MARZIPAN

Marzipan is a sweet paste made from
ground almonds and a well-boiled sugar
syrup. Traditionally it is used to cover fruit
cakes, but it can also be moulded into interesting fruit and vegetable shapes. Boil
the sugar and water to the correct temperature in the microwave.

To cover fruit cake with marzipan

Before covering a fruit cake with marzipan, it is usually brushed with a little hot
apricot jam, but this sometimes oozes
through the marzipan if the weather is particularly hot. Use this method to simplify
the process:
Place about 125 g (4 oz) almond paste in a
bowl, add 30 ml (2 tablespoons) water.
Microwave on Medium (50%) for 1 – 2
minutes, until bubbling. Brush sparingly
on to fruit cake. Cover with rolled-out
marzipan. To soften marzipan, microwave
for a few seconds.

MAYONNAISE

A well-flavoured, smooth mixture of eggs,
oil, lemon juice or vinegar and seasonings.
Cooked mayonnaise is a joy to make in the
microwave, as it does not require constant
beating.

Boiled mayonnaise

Full Power
2 minutes

15 g (½ oz) caster sugar
10 mℓ (2 teaspoons) plain flour
salt and white pepper
10 mℓ (2 teaspoons) prepared mustard
60 mℓ (4 tablespoons) water
75 mℓ (2½ fl oz) white vinegar
1 egg
15 g (½ oz) butter
single cream or milk

Combine the dry ingredients, mustard and
water in a jug. Mix until smooth, then add
vinegar. Microwave on Full Power for 2 minutes,
stirring after 1 minute. Beat well with a small
whisk. The mixture must be boiling. Whisk egg
lightly, add vinegar mixture and butter, beat
well. Cover with greaseproof paper and allow to
cool. Thin with milk or cream before using.
Store in the refrigerator.
Makes about 150 mℓ (5 fl oz)

Variations

Curry Mayonnaise
Add the following to the mayonnaise:
2.5 mℓ (½ teaspoon) curry paste
garlic salt
5 mℓ (1 teaspoon) honey
pinch of ground ginger

Green Goddess Mayonnaise
Add the following to the mayonnaise:
1 garlic clove, crushed
2 anchovy fillets, chopped
45 mℓ (3 tablespoons) chopped spring onions,
  tops included
45 mℓ (3 tablespoons) chopped parsley
10 mℓ (2 teaspoons) lemon juice
100 mℓ (3½ fl oz) soured cream

Spiced mayonnaise

Full Power
2 minutes

1 garlic clove, crushed
5 mℓ (1 teaspoon) chopped fresh ginger
30 mℓ (2 tablespoons) red wine vinegar
15 mℓ (1 tablespoon) soft brown sugar
5 mℓ (1 teaspoon) biriani seeds
45 mℓ (3 tablespoons) soy sauce
2 eggs
10 mℓ (2 teaspoons) dry mustard
250 mℓ (8 fl oz) oil
few drops of chilli sauce
salt and black pepper

Combine garlic, ginger, vinegar, sugar, seeds
and soy sauce in a jug. Microwave on Full

Power for 2 minutes, stir well. Cool and strain.
Place eggs and mustard in the work bowl of a
food processor, process well, and add boiled
liquid. Slowly add oil. Season with chilli sauce,
salt and papper. Serve as a dip with crudités or
as a dressing for potato salad.
Makes about 375 mℓ (12 fl oz)

MEAT

See also individual names.
Microwaved meat such as pork and lamb
becomes tender and juicy in a third to half
the time it takes to cook it conventionally.
Most meat can be cooked on Full Power,
but a lower power setting will cook
tougher, more economical cuts until they
are tender and full of flavour. Larger joints
brown naturally during the cooking process, but small cuts cook too quickly to do
so. The addition of a browning agent (see
page 39) or basting with a marinade or
glaze improves both the appearance and
taste of these meats.

Reduced power levels

When microwaving large pieces of meat, or
less tender cuts, the power should be reduced so that the cooking period is longer.
Meat should be microwaved on High
(70%) for half the cooking time, then the
power reduced to Medium (50%) to complete the cooking process.
Example: 1.5 kg (3 lb) rolled beef – rare
Full Power method: Microwave for 24 – 30
minutes on Full Power. Stand for 10 minutes.
Alternative method: Microwave for 15 – 18
minutes on high (70%). Microwave on Medium (50%) for about 20 – 22 minutes.
Stand for 10 minutes.

Hints for microwaving meat

☐ Cover all meat before placing it in the
microwave. Joints of meat should be
placed in a roasting bag, a microwave
roasting dish or a shallow dish before cooking. When using a browning dish, meat
should be covered with kitchen paper to
prevent spattering.
☐ Defrost the meat completely for best results and even cooking.
☐ Joints of meat cook more evenly if they
are symmetrical – that is, boned or rolled.
☐ Thin parts or bone-ends should be
shielded with small strips of aluminium foil
during the first half of the cooking time to
prevent overcooking.
☐ When preparing casseroles or stews, cut
the ingredients to uniform size to promote
even cooking.
☐ Prevent spattering when cooking sausages, bacon or other fatty meats by covering with waxed paper or kitchen paper.
☐ To improve the natural browning of
meat, microwave in a covered glass casserole or in a pierced roasting bag fastened
with an elastic band or string.
☐ Reduce liquid in recipes such as casseroles as there is little evaporation during
microwave cooking.

☐ Shape meat mixtures into individual loaves, ring shapes or flat round shapes rather than one large loaf so that the meat will cook quickly and evenly.

☐ Arrange such foods as meat balls in a circle to promote even cooking. Meat such as chops or steaks should have the narrow end towards the centre of the oven.

MEAT BALLS

Meat balls microwave very well and need no special browning agents as they turn brown after a short standing time at the end of microwave cooking.
See also Frikkadels.

To microwave meat balls

Place meat balls about 2.5 cm (1 inch) apart in a shallow microwave dish. Re-arrange them after half the cooking time. To cook a few at a time, arrange them around the edge of a glass pie dish or round casserole. If your microwave does not have a turntable, it is a good idea to rotate the dish half a turn after half the recommended cooking time. Exact timing for microwaving meat balls depends on the size and desired degree of cooking, but as a guide, 500 g (18 oz) minced meat made into 12 – 15 meat balls can be microwaved on Full Power for 9 – 12 minutes.

Basic meat balls

Full Power
9 – 12 minutes

500 g (18 oz) minced beef
1 egg
60 g (2 oz) soft breadcrumbs
5 mℓ (1 teaspoon) salt
pepper

Combine beef, egg, breadcrumbs, salt and pepper and mix well. Shape into 12 – 15 balls and arrange in a circle on a glass pie dish or round casserole. Cover loosely with waxed paper. Microwave on Full Power for 9 – 12 minutes.
Makes 12 – 15 meat balls

Variations
Add any one of the following combinations to give added flavour:
☐ 15 mℓ (1 tablespoon) Worcestershire sauce, 2.5 mℓ (½ teaspoon) dry mustard and ½ onion, finely chopped.
☐ 30 mℓ (2 tablespoons) barbecue sauce and 1 garlic clove, finely chopped.
☐ 30 mℓ (2 tablespoons) tomato sauce, 10 mℓ (2 teaspoons) prepared mustard, 5 mℓ (1 teaspoon) mixed herbs and ½ onion, finely chopped.
☐ 30 mℓ (2 tablespoons) red wine, 30 mℓ (2 tablespoons) tomato sauce and 5 mℓ (1 teaspoon) dried basil.
☐ 15 mℓ (1 tablespoon) chilli sauce or 2.5 mℓ (½ teaspoon) crushed chillies, 30 g (1 oz) finely chopped green pepper and ½ onion, chopped.

Chilli meat balls

Full Power, Low (15%)
40 minutes

15 mℓ (1 tablespoon) oil
1 onion, chopped
1 green pepper, chopped
500 g (18 oz) minced beef
2.5 mℓ (½ teaspoon) Tabasco
30 g (1 oz) soft white breadcrumbs
1 egg
generous pinch of mixed herbs
salt and black pepper
125 g (4 oz) uncooked rice
400 g (14 oz) canned tomatoes, chopped
350 mℓ (11 fl oz) boiling water
1 beef stock cube
10 mℓ (2 teaspoons) soy sauce

Pour the oil into a small casserole. Microwave on Full Power for 1 minute. Add onion and green pepper and toss in the oil. Microwave for 4 minutes. In a large bowl, combine onion, green pepper, beef, Tabasco, breadcrumbs, egg, mixed herbs and seasonings. Form into small meat balls. Roll meat balls in rice thickly and place in a deep casserole dish. Combine all the remaining ingredients and pour over the meat balls. Finally, add any remaining rice, cover and microwave for 15 minutes, then reduce power level to Low (15%) for 20 minutes. Serve hot.
Serves 6

MEAT LOAF

Microwaved meat loaf cooks in about one third the time it takes in a conventional oven, and the flavour and texture are excellent. The containers used for cooking meat loaves in the microwave should be round rather than square or rectangular, because corners absorb microwaves readily and the meat loaf will be overcooked by the time the centre is ready. Microwave energy is also attracted to toppings containing sugar, syrup or preserves. When such toppings are used on meat loaves before microwaving, they should be applied to the top only, as they may cause the sides to become overcooked.

If a temperature probe is used, it should be inserted so that the tip is in the centre of the meat loaf. Make sure the tip of the probe does not touch the sides or bottom of the dish, or a false reading will be given. An internal temperature reading of between 73 °C (163 °F) and 75 °C (167 °F) indicates the meat loaf is cooked. Stand meat loaf for at least 5 minutes after cooking.

Glazed meat loaf

Full Power
18 minutes

75 g (2½ oz) rolled oats
250 mℓ (8 fl oz) milk
salt and pepper
2.5 mℓ (½ teaspoon) sage
2 eggs
5 mℓ (1 teaspoon) Worcestershire sauce
1 large onion, chopped
30 g (1 oz) green pepper, finely chopped
30 mℓ (2 tablespoons) finely chopped parsley
750 g (1¾ lb) lean minced beef
75 mℓ (2½ fl oz) chilli or tomato sauce
30 g (1 oz) soft brown sugar
5 mℓ (1 teaspoon) Dijon mustard
pinch of ground nutmeg

Mix together the oats, milk, salt, pepper, sage, eggs, Worcestershire sauce and onion. Add green pepper, parsley and beef and mix well. Pat mixture evenly into a 22.5-cm (9-inch) round glass microwave dish. Stir together the chilli or tomato sauce, sugar, mustard and nutmeg and spread evenly over the top of the meat loaf. Microwave on Full Power for 18 – 20 minutes, or to desired degree of cooking. Stand for at least 5 minutes before serving. To serve, cut in wedges.
Serves 6

MERINGUES

Light, crispy meringues are enjoyed by all and although it is not possible to cook traditional meringues in the microwave, the following recipe works well and the meringues can be made almost instantly.

Microwave meringues

Full Power
6 minutes

1 unbeaten egg white
flavouring, such as vanilla extract, rum or almond essence
pinch of salt
250 g (9 oz) icing sugar, sifted

Combine all ingredients, mix well until mixture forms a ball. Roll into smaller balls, about the size of a walnut. Place in paper baking cups. Arrange seven at a time on a plate, leaving a space between each as they puff up. Microwave on Full Power for 1½ minutes. Remove from oven and cool. Repeat until all the mixture has been microwaved.
Makes about 30

Variation
For colourful meringues add a few drops of food colouring to the mixture. These are particularly popular at children's parties.

Overleaf left: Escalopes of Veal with Artichokes (page 223)
Overleaf right: Mexican Beef Pittas (page 170)

MICROWAVE COOKING

Microwave cooking is a very versatile and efficient way to prepare a wide variety of tasty foods in a fraction of the time it normally takes and without mess or fuss. There is nothing difficult about cooking food in the microwave oven once you have mastered the basic techniques. Like any other appliance, the microwave has certain limitations and, to avoid disappointment, it will help you to know which foods microwave well and which do not.

Foods that microwave well

Some foods cooked in the microwave have such excellent flavour and texture that you may never want to cook them any other way. Foods that need constant stirring, such as puddings, sauces, custards or sweets, need only occasional stirring in the microwave. Many foods can be measured, mixed and cooked in the same dish, so cleaning up is easy. The following are foods that microwave exceptionally well:

Eggs when scrambled and cooked in the microwave are light and fluffy and have greater volume. Poached eggs can be microwaved in individual dishes for easy serving and omelettes are a treat to make.

Bacon can be microwaved to just the desired crispness. It is quick and easy and there is no pan to clean.

Snacks and appetizers can be heated in seconds, often on serving plates. It is easy to serve a variety of these foods, and there is little washing up to do later.

Fish microwaves to perfection, retaining moisture and flavour. It can be steamed to just the right texture with little extra liquid.

Chicken portions remain tender and juicy and are ready to serve quickly. A variety of coatings can be used to make the chicken look appetizing and to increase its flavour. *See* Crumbed Portions.

Casseroles can be reheated and served in the same dish and the flavour and texture will be just as good as when first cooked.

Meat loaf can be taken from the freezer, defrosted and cooked in the microwave in just over half an hour.

Leftovers can be reheated with no loss of texture or flavour. They stay moist and taste freshly cooked. Meat and rice can be reheated without overcooking.

Vegetables retain their bright colour and crisp, fresh texture when microwaved according to the chart on page 221.

Potatoes baked in the microwave for 4 – 5 minutes each, come out tender and moist.

Custards and puddings need only occasional stirring in the microwave. They cook smoothly and creamily and can be made and chilled in the same dish.

Hot fruit desserts require less liquid to cook, so fruits retain their natural juices and flavours.

Chocolate can be melted in a glass measuring cup with very little danger of scorching or overcooking. Washing up is easy too.

Upside-down cake takes just minutes to bake in the microwave, and can be prepared just before serving.

Coffee cake is another quickly and easily baked cake that has excellent flavour and texture.

Sweets that used to take constant stirring are simple to make in the microwave and the flavour is the same.

Preserves retain the colour and flavour of the fruit when made in the microwave, and there is no sticking or burning.

Foods that do not microwave well

There are some foods that should not be cooked in the microwave, either because the results are not good, or because conventional cooking is more efficient. For example, large food loads, such as a 10 kg (22 lb) turkey or a dozen potatoes, cook more efficiently in a conventional oven.

Eggs in shells should not be cooked in the microwave as they may burst. Do not attempt to heat hard-boiled eggs in shells.

Deep-frying should not be attempted in the microwave oven, as it is difficult to control the temperature of fat and food may burn.

Grilled toppings become bubbly, but will not crisp and brown in the microwave.

Pasta and rice need time to absorb moisture and become tender and, as they take almost as long to cook in the microwave, it may be better to cook these conventionally.

Pastry does not crisp or brown well. Puff pastry, which needs dry heat to crisp, rises in the microwave but falls when removed. Meats, such as sausages, wrapped in pastry do not brown. The pastry or dough coating becomes soggy because it absorbs moisture from the meat.

Batter recipes such as pancakes, crêpes and Yorkshire puddings need conventional cooking to form a crust and become crisp.

Conventional meringues should be cooked by conventional methods. However, for meringues cooked in a microwave, see recipe left.

Bottling requires a long period of high temperature and is better done conventionally.

How to check whether food is ready

One of the major differences between conventional recipes and microwave recipes is the cooking time. The appearance of some foods cooked in the microwave also differs from that of foods cooked conventionally, but many of the methods used for checking whether the food is done remain the same. Personal preference will affect some foods, so cooking times will have to be adjusted accordingly. It is important to learn when to remove the food from the microwave. Some foods must be removed while they look only partly cooked, as they will finish cooking during the standing time. Always undercook until you learn to judge accurately cooking times in your microwave, and become familiar with how food should look.

Cakes and sponge puddings are done when a wooden cocktail stick or skewer inserted in the centre comes out clean. Moist spots on the surface of the cake or pudding will dry during the standing time. Timing is very important with cakes and puddings, as overcooking will cause the outer edges to become hard and dry. Check whether cakes or puddings are done at the minimum suggested time.

Shortcrust pastries should be flaky, and the base should be dry and opaque. The pastry will not turn golden brown although a few brown spots may appear.

Custards and quiches should appear soft in the centre. A knife inserted halfway between the centre and the outer edge should come out clean. The centre will set during the standing time.

Reheated meals on plates are hot enough to serve when the base of the plate feels warm all over.

Vegetables should be fork-tender but not mushy because they continue to cook during the standing time.

A baked potato is heated through in 4 – 5 minutes, but if cut in half reveals an uncooked centre. The potato will finish cooking during standing time, and stay hot enough to serve for up to 30 minutes if wrapped in aluminium foil after cooking. This is a great help when planning menus.

Meat should be fork-tender when done. Less tender cuts should split at the fibres when tested with a fork. A temperature probe is one way of ensuring meat is done as desired, but remember that meat continues to cook during standing time. Only special microwave meat thermometers can be used in the microwave during cooking, but a conventional meat thermometer can be inserted to check the temperature after the joint has been removed from the microwave.

Whole chicken feels soft when pinched and the leg moves easily at the joint. The juices should run clear with no trace of pink. During standing time, cover the chicken with a tent of aluminium foil, shiny side in, to keep in the heat.

Fish flakes easily with a fork when it is cooked. The centre of a piece of fish may be slightly translucent, but will finish cooking during standing time. Fish becomes tough and dry if overcooked.

Shellfish turn pink and opaque when cooked. To avoid toughening, undercook slightly and let stand.

Microwave and conventional cooking

Many foods can be quickly and easily prepared by using a combination of microwave and conventional cooking. Use the microwave for its speed and conventional cooking for browning or baking. Remember to use a dish suitable for microwaving if you are cooking in both the conventional and the microwave oven.

☐ For toasted sandwiches, toast bread

conventionally, then place the sandwiches in the microwave to heat fillings and melt cheese.

☐ Brown meats conventionally, then finish cooking in the microwave but reduce the cooking time by a quarter to a half.

☐ Make pancakes or crêpes conventionally, but heat fillings and toppings in the microwave.

☐ Partially cook chicken portions or meat ribs in the microwave, and then finish cooking them over the barbeque, or under the grill.

☐ Bake double-crust pies conventionally, and reheat or defrost in the microwave.

☐ Prove yeast doughs in the microwave and bake conventionally for a crusty loaf.

☐ Bake a flan or quiche case conventionally, then add the filling and use the microwave to cook it quickly.

Convection microwave ovens

In some microwaves it is possible to cook by microwave energy or by convection, fan-forced hot air circulating around food, or to use a combination of microwave and convection cooking at the same time. These ovens give results that are similar to conventionally cooked dishes, but in a much shorter time. However, it is difficult to give general recipes for combination cooking because each model of convection/microwave oven is different and the instructions and timing vary from manufacturer to manufacturer.

MICROWAVE ENERGY

Microwaves work on the same principle as radio, television or light waves. They are simply a form of high-frequency electromagnetic energy that produces heat, depending on the substances with which they come into contact. Microwaves are not attracted to all substances; for example they cannot penetrate metal and so they are reflected by it. For this reason metal makes an ideal lining to microwave ovens as the waves bounce off the oven walls. Many other substances allow microwaves to pass straight through them without producing heat, for example, glass, pottery, china, paper, wood and some plastics. These make ideal containers as microwave energy passes through them directly into the food.

Microwaves are attracted by the moisture, sugar or fat content of foods and, depending on the size and density of the food, penetrate to a depth of 2 – 4 cm (1 – 1½ inch). The microwave energy causes molecules to vibrate at very high speeds – over two thousand million times a second – producing heat through friction. This heat spreads rapidly throughout the food from the point of penetration, thus cooking the food by conduction. However, smaller pieces of food are penetrated completely by the microwaves and therefore cook more quickly than larger, more solid foods. It should also be remembered that larger quantities will take longer to micro-

When the cake or sponge pudding is cooked, the surface may still appear moist, but a wooden cocktail stick inserted in the centre should come out clean.

Use a meat thermometer or a microwave meat probe to test the cooked roast in several places to ensure an internal temperature of at least 77 °C (171 °F) throughout the roast.

wave than smaller quantities because the microwave energy within the oven remains constant. Microwave ovens do not need preheating like conventional ovens, as microwaves react with the food instantly.

Although microwaves are similar to radio and television waves, they are of a much higher frequency. It is this high frequency which causes molecules in the food to vibrate at such high speeds that they produce heat. Microwaves should not be confused with X-rays, ultra-violet or gamma rays, all of which are ionizing and cause irreversible chemical and cellular changes with little or no temperature change. Microwave energy is a non-ionizing form of electromagnetic energy transmitted through space by microwaves, which are very short and travel in straight lines. Being non-ionizing, microwaves are not harmful, as they do not damage cells, nor do they accumulate in foodstuffs cooked in a microwave oven.

Microwaves have three important characteristics:

☐ They are reflected by metals.

☐ They are attracted by foodstuffs.

☐ They pass straight through glass, plastics and paper without affecting them.

MICROWAVE SAFETY

The microwave has no sharp edges or moving parts, and its form of heat generation helps prevent burns and scalding. As microwaves heat only the food, no energy is wasted heating the air inside, which remains cool, or the container. However, as the food is heated, the container may become hot by conduction, so care should always be exercised when taking food out of the microwave.

Special safety features are built into microwaves, making them one of the safest kitchen appliances. The see-through door incorporates a reflecting metal screen and the door frame is designed with special seals to keep microwaves safely within the oven. Cut-out devices ensure microwave energy is automatically switched off when the door is open.

☐ Do not attempt to operate the microwave with the door open. Do not tamper with the safety locking systems.

☐ Do not place any object between the door and the front of the microwave. Make sure that sealing surfaces are clean.

☐ Do not operate the microwave if it is damaged in any way. It is important that the door closes properly.

☐ Do not allow the microwave to be adjusted or repaired by anyone other than qualified microwave service personnel.

☐ Do not remove the outer casing or door at any time.

☐ Never line the oven with foil, paper or any other material.

☐ Do not lean heavily on the oven door.

☐ Do not use the oven for storing utensils.

☐ Do not operate the oven when it is empty, as this may damage the magnetron. A cup of water left in the oven when it is not in use will attract the microwave energy if the oven is accidentally turned on.

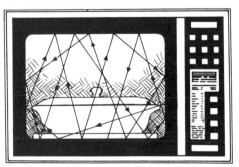

Microwaves are reflected by the metal lining of the oven and attracted by moisture in food.

Overleaf left: Baked Potatoes with Chive Topping, Tangy Topping and Bacon Cheese Topping (page 173)

Overleaf right: Pork Fillet with Spinach Stuffing (page 172) served with Peas and Onions (page 166) and sliced pears

MINCED MEAT

Minced meat is a basic ingredient for a wide variety of meat dishes, such as casseroles, hamburgers, meat balls and meat loaves (*see* individual entries).

Many recipes using crumbled minced beef call for the cooked minced beef to be drained before adding to other ingredients. An easy way to microwave and drain the minced beef is to put the meat in a microwave-proof colander. Place the colander in a casserole. Cover loosely and microwave as the recipe directs. While the minced beef cooks, the fat will drain away and the meat will be ready to use.

See Beef chart (page 29) for how to defrost minced beef.

Meat sauce

Full Power
24 minutes

This basic mince recipe freezes well and may be thawed in the microwave at a moment's notice. Add one or two extra ingredients and use for any number of dishes, including pasta dishes and as a base for a quick chilli con carne.

30 mℓ (2 tablespoons) oil
1 onion, chopped
1 celery stick, chopped
1 small green pepper, chopped
1 small garlic clove, crushed
750 g (1¾ lb) minced meat
pinch of mixed herbs
5 mℓ (1 teaspoon) Worcestershire sauce
1 bay leaf
salt and black pepper
400 g (14 oz) canned tomatoes, chopped
15 mℓ (1 tablespoon) tomato paste
45 – 60 mℓ (3 – 4 tablespoons) beef stock

Pour oil into a casserole, microwave on Full Power for 1 minute. Add onion, celery, green pepper and garlic, stir to coat with oil. Microwave for 3 minutes, stirring once. Add mince, breaking up meat with a fork and combining with vegetables. Microwave for 5 minutes, stirring every 2 minutes with a fork to break up the mince. Add remaining ingredients, stir well. Microwave for 15 minutes, stirring from time to time. Remove bay leaf and use as required.
Serves 4 – 6

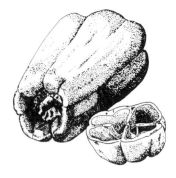

Variations
Stuffed French Loaf: Combine equal quantities of meat sauce and grated Cheddar cheese. Hollow out a small French loaf or a cottage-style loaf, fill with meat mixture. Replace 'lid' and place loaf in a roasting bag, tie end loosely. Microwave on High (70%) for 22 – 25 minutes, stand 5 minutes before serving.
Serves 6 – 8

Stuffed Green Peppers: Mix equal quantities of meat sauce and cooked rice, spoon into hollowed-out peppers. Top with grated cheese and dried breadcrumbs. For 4 stuffed peppers, microwave on High (70%) for 5 minutes.
Serves 4

MINT

A refreshing aromatic herb used in a variety of recipes: in mint sauce, mint jelly (*see* Jellies), iced teas, salads and with peas and new potatoes. Fresh mint can also be dried in the microwave (*see* Herbs) and sprinkled over cooked tomatoes or buttered vegetables.

Here is a delicious recipe which will complement lamb, veal or venison.

Mint sauce

Full Power
4 minutes

275 g (10 oz) apricot jam, sieved
100 g (3½ oz) caster sugar
250 mℓ (8 fl oz) white vinegar
45 – 60 g (1½ – 2 oz) mint, chopped

Combine jam, sugar and vinegar in a large bowl, microwave on Full Power for 4 – 5 minutes, stir very well to ensure that the sugar has dissolved. Stir in the mint, allow to cool, bottle and store. This will keep in the refrigerator for six months.
Makes about 600 mℓ (19 fl oz)

MIXED GRILL

A mixed grill is a platter of grilled bacon, kidneys, steak or chops, mushrooms and tomatoes usually topped with a fried egg. With the help of the microwave, a mixed grill is easily prepared at a moment's notice and served for breakfast, lunch or dinner. The preparation time is almost halved and very little mess is made.

Mixed grill

Full Power
24 minutes

4 – 6 bacon rashers, rinds removed
salt and black pepper
4 lamb's kidneys, cut in half
4 small rump steaks or 4 small lamb chops
4 large flat mushrooms
2 tomatoes, sliced thickly
30 g (1 oz) butter
4 eggs

To serve
potato chips

Arrange bacon rashers on a bacon rack and cover with waxed paper. Microwave on Full Power for about 5 minutes, depending on the size of rashers. Keep warm. Pour bacon fat into browning dish. Heat browning dish for 4 – 5 minutes. Season kidneys and steak or chops lightly. Arrange steak and kidneys on dish, placing kidneys on inside. Microwave for 4 minutes, turning after 2 minutes. Microwave an extra 1 – 2 minutes if steak is to be well done, or if cooking chops. Brush mushrooms with a little of the meat dripping, season lightly. Season tomatoes, then arrange mushrooms and tomatoes on a plate. Microwave for 3 – 4 minutes, keep warm. Heat butter in a shallow casserole for 2 minutes. Carefully break eggs into dish. Pierce each yolk twice with the point of a skewer. Cover dish and microwave on Full Power for 2 minutes. Stand for 1 minute. Microwave for about 1 minute more. The egg whites should be just set. Serve mixed grill with potato chips.
Serves 4

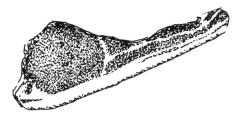

MOUSSAKA

This casserole dish has many variations, but usually consists of layers of sliced aubergine, alternating with layers of minced meat in a tasty tomato sauce. Sometimes the moussaka is covered with a layer of white sauce and cheese. In the recipe below, potatoes are cooked in the microwave, sliced thickly and layered with the more traditional ingredients.

Moussaka

Full Power, High (70%)
1 hour

2 aubergines, sliced
salt
oil
1 onion, chopped
2 garlic cloves, crushed
500 g (18 oz) minced beef
400 g (14 oz) canned peeled tomatoes
30 mℓ (2 tablespoons) tomato paste
generous pinch of oregano
2.5 mℓ (½ teaspoon) cinnamon
salt and black pepper
3 potatoes
60 g (2 oz) Cheddar cheese, grated
2 eggs
300 mℓ (10 fl oz) béchamel sauce*
15 mℓ (1 tablespoon) grated Parmesan cheese

Sprinkle aubergines with a little salt, set aside for 30 minutes. Drain and pat dry. Toss in a little oil. Arrange aubergine slices on the bottom of a large shallow dish, overlapping them slightly if necessary. Cover and microwave on Full Power for 6 minutes. They should not be completely cooked. Drain on kitchen paper. Pour a little oil into a casserole and microwave for 1 minute. Add onion and garlic and toss to mix. Microwave for 5 minutes, then add meat and microwave for 5 minutes more, stirring once. Add tomatoes, tomato paste, oregano, cinnamon and seasonings. Microwave for 12 minutes, stirring from time to time. Place washed potatoes on a plate. Microwave for 8 – 10 minutes, then peel and slice thickly.

Layer meat mixture, aubergine and potato in a large greased casserole. Add half the Cheddar cheese and the eggs to the sauce, mixing well. Pour sauce over top layer of potatoes. Sprinkle with remaining Cheddar cheese and Parmesan cheese. Microwave on High (70%) for 15 – 20 minutes. The mixture should be very hot and the tomatoes bubbling around the edges. Serve warm.
Serves 6

MOUSSE

Mousse is the French word for foam or froth. It is a rich, airy mixture made with beaten egg white or whipped cream or both, and can be either sweet or savoury. The microwave dissolves gelatine perfectly so the texture of the mousse is smooth and light.
For Loganberry Mousse see page 138.

Parma ham mousse

Medium (50%)
1 minute

250 mℓ (8 fl oz) single cream
90 mℓ (3 fl oz) Marsala
125 g (4 oz) Ricotta cheese
125 mℓ (4 fl oz) chicken stock
225 g (8 oz) Parma ham
15 mℓ (1 tablespoon) powdered gelatine
45 mℓ (3 tablespoons) water

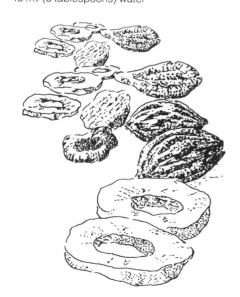

Place cream, Marsala, cheese and stock in the container of an electric blender. Reserve 3 – 4 slices of the ham, cut the remaining ham into pieces and add to the blender. Blend until smooth. Sprinkle gelatine over the water, stand for 5 minutes, then microwave on Medium (50%) for 45 – 60 seconds, or until dissolved. Add gelatine to ham mixture and blend to combine. Use reserved ham slices to line a lightly oiled loaf pan. Pour ham mixture into loaf pan and chill until set, 2 – 3 hours. To serve, turn out, slice and serve, garnished with slices of kiwi fruit or with halved fresh figs.
Serves 8 – 10

Note: This mixture has a strong flavour and needs no extra seasoning.

MUESLI

A nutritious mixture of oats, bran, wheat germ, seeds, dried fruits and nuts. Make a toasted muesli with honey and oil in the microwave. Store in an air-tight container and create new variations at breakfast time by adding stewed dried fruit, fresh fruit and yoghurt.

Muesli

Full Power, Medium (50%)
13 minutes

60 mℓ (4 tablespoons) honey
60 mℓ (4 tablespoons) oil
90 g (3 oz) rolled oats
90 g (3 oz) bran
45 g (1½ oz) sunflower seeds
15 g (½ oz) sesame seeds
30 g (1 oz) wheat germ
45 g (1½ oz) desiccated coconut
60 g (2 oz) raisins
60 g (2 oz) dried apple rings, chopped
60 g (2 oz) blanched almonds, chopped

Combine honey and oil in a large bowl. Microwave on Full Power for 1 minute, stir to combine. Add remaining ingredients, except raisins, dried apple rings and almonds. Stir very well. Spread mixture on to a microwave baking sheet. Microwave on Medium (50%) for 12 – 14 minutes, stirring every 2 minutes. Leave to cool, add raisins, apple rings and almonds. Store in an air-tight container.
Fills 1-litre (1¾-pint) container

Muesli and jam pudding

Full Power, High (70%)
12 minutes

100 g (3½ oz) apricot, gooseberry or
   loganberry jam
125 g (4 oz) margarine
25 g (4 oz) soft brown sugar
2 eggs
few drops of vanilla extract
75 g (2½ oz) plain flour
5 mℓ (1 teaspoon) baking powder
45 g (1½ oz) ground almonds
75 g (2½ oz) muesli
45 – 60 mℓ (3 – 4 tablespoons) milk

Topping
30 g (1 oz) soft brown sugar
30 g (1 oz) plain flour
45 g (1½ oz) muesli

Grease a 20-cm (8-inch) round pyrex dish, spread base with jam. Cream margarine and brown sugar until light. Add eggs one at a time, add vanilla and beat well. Sift flour and baking powder, beat into mixture. Mix in ground almonds and muesli, add milk and mix to a dropping consistency. Spoon into pyrex dish. Combine topping ingredients and sprinkle on top of mixture. Microwave on Full Power for 8 minutes. Reduce power to High (70%), microwave for 4 – 6 minutes. Stand for 10 minutes before serving. Serve with cream or custard.
Serves 8

MUFFINS, AMERICAN

American muffins are individually baked quick breads made with a batter that is poured into well-greased muffin pans. They are turned out as soon as they are done and are served piping hot. Make a batch of muffins for breakfast and spread with butter and jam or marmalade.

For best results when microwaving muffins, spoon batter into microwave muffin pans lined with paper cups and sprinkle with one of the delicious toppings given below. Do not microwave more than six muffins at a time.

Basic microwave American muffins

High (70%)

250 g (9 oz) plain flour
100 g (3½ oz) caster sugar
15 mℓ (1 tablespoon) baking powder
2.5 mℓ (½ teaspoon) salt
2 eggs, beaten
125 mℓ (4 fl oz) oil
125 mℓ (4 fl oz) milk

Sift together dry ingredients. Beat together eggs, oil and milk, and add to dry ingredients. Mix until just moistened. Half-fill paper muffin cups with batter and place in a microwave muffin pan. Microwave on High (70%) according to chart below. The muffins are done when a wooden cocktail stick inserted in the centre comes out clean.
Makes 10 – 12 muffins

Overleaf left: Mixed Grill (page 152) with steak, bacon, kidneys, mushrooms, egg and tomato
Overleaf right: Ploughman's Lunch with Pickled Onions, Mixed Vegetable Pickle, Cucumber Pickle and Pickled Red Cabbage (page 168)

NUMBER OF MUFFINS	TIME ON HIGH (70%)	METHOD
3	1½ – 2 minutes	Rotate the pan half a turn after half the cooking time.
4	2 – 3 minutes	
5	2½ – 3½ minutes	
6	3 – 5 minutes	

Variations
These muffins will take slightly longer to microwave than the times given for the basic recipe.

Cinnamon Apple Muffins: add 2.5 mℓ (½ teaspoon) cinnamon to dry ingredients and add 1 peeled, chopped apple with liquid. Top with cinnamon sugar topping.

Herby Cheese Muffins: Add 2.5 mℓ (½ teaspoon) mixed herbs, 5 mℓ (1 teaspoon) chopped parsley and pinch of dry mustard to dry ingredients. Stir in 45 g (1½ oz) grated cheese with liquid. Top with extra grated cheese.

Lemon Coconut Muffins: Add 5 mℓ (1 teaspoon) grated lemon rind and 30 g (1 oz) toasted coconut* to dry ingredients. Add 15 mℓ (1 tablespoon) lemon juice to liquid and top with more toasted coconut.

Orange Nut Muffins: Add 5 mℓ (1 teaspoon) grated orange rind and 45 g (1½ oz) chopped pecan nuts to dry ingredients. Replace 25 mℓ (5 teaspoons) of the milk with orange juice in the liquid. Top with streusel topping.

Muffin toppings
Streusel Topping: Combine 100 g (3½ oz) soft brown sugar, 30 mℓ (1 tablespoon) flour, 10 mℓ (2 teaspoons) cinnamon, 30 g (1 oz) butter and 45 g (1½ oz) chopped nuts.

Nut Crunch Topping: Combine 45 g (1½ oz) plain flour, 30 mℓ (1 tablespoon) soft brown sugar, 30 g (1 oz) butter, 30 g (1 oz) chopped nuts and 30 mℓ (1 tablespoon) cornflake crumbs.

Cinnamon Sugar Topping: Combine 5 g (½ oz) soft brown sugar with 2.5 – 5 mℓ (½ – 1 teaspoon) cinnamon.

30-day muffins

High (70%)
3 minutes

2 eggs
300g (11 oz) soft brown sugar
75 mℓ (2½ fl oz) oil
30 g (11 oz) plain flour
generous pinch of salt
7.5 mℓ (1½ teaspoons) bicarbonate of soda
175 g (6 oz) bran
500 mℓ (16 fl oz) milk
few drops of vanilla extract
125 g (4 oz) sultanas

Beat eggs and brown sugar well. Add oil and beat again. Sift flour, salt and bicarbonate of soda, add to mixture. Add remaining ingredients and mix well. Refrigerate until required in an air-tight container. When required, spoon about 20 mℓ (4 teaspoons) of the mixture into paper baking cups either on a plate or in a muffin pan. Microwave on High (70%) for 3 – 3½ minutes.
Makes about 50

Note: This mixture will last for up to thirty days in the refrigerator.

Variations:
Add the following ingredients to the mixture just before microwaving:
Banana Muffins: Add one or two mashed bananas and a little cinnamon.
Spicy Apple Muffins: Omit sultanas and add chopped fresh or canned pie apples and a little mixed spice.
Marmalade Muffins: Add a spoonful of marmalade.

MULBERRIES *See* Jam and Fruit

MUSHROOMS
This is the name given to a wide variety of edible fungi which have been used in cooking for centuries. All mushrooms microwave well and give delicious flavour to soups, casseroles and salads and are a favourite food on their own.
See also Duxelles.

To microwave mushrooms
Wipe 250 g (9 oz) mushrooms and slice if desired. Add 30 ml (2 tablespoons) water or stock. Cover and microwave on Full Power for 2 minutes. Stir, cover and microwave until tender, 1 – 3 minutes more. Leave to stand 1 minute, then drain and season as desired.

Garlic mushrooms

Full Power
3 minutes

30 g (1 oz) butter
1 small garlic clove, finely chopped
5 mℓ (1 teaspoon) cornflour
pinch of salt
pinch of oregano
300 g (11 oz) mushrooms, cleaned and sliced
chopped parsley

Microwave butter and garlic in a large casserole on Full Power for 30 seconds. Sprinkle cornflour, salt and oregano over mushrooms, tossing to mix and add to the casserole. Stir, then cover and microwave 1 minute. Stir, cover and microwave 1½ minutes longer. Sprinkle with chopped parsley.
Serves 4 as an accompaniment

Spinach-stuffed mushrooms

Full Power
6 minutes

10 large flat mushrooms
250 g (9 oz) cooked spinach*
1 egg
30 mℓ (2 tablespoons) thick white onion soup powder
90 g (3 oz) low-fat soft cheese
pinch of grated nutmeg
salt and pepper
15 g (½ oz) dry breadcrumbs
30 g (1 oz) Cheddar cheese, finely grated

Wipe mushrooms, remove stems and arrange on two microwave dishes. Drain and chop spinach and mix with remaining ingredients, reserving half Cheddar cheese. Place spoonfuls of the mixture on each mushroom and sprinkle with remaining cheese. Microwave each dish on Full Power for 2½ – 3 minutes. Smaller mushrooms will be cooked more quickly
Makes 10 mushrooms

Mushroom vegetable sauté

Full Power
8 minutes

3 – 4 carrots, cut in julienne
45 mℓ (3 tablespoons) water
45 g (1½ oz) butter
300 g (11 oz) button mushrooms, wiped clean and sliced
½ cucumber, cut in julienne
salt and black pepper
15 mℓ (1 tablespoon) chopped parsley or 5 mℓ (1 teaspoon) chopped dill

Place carrots and water in a bowl. Cover with vented plastic wrap, microwave on Full Power for 4 minutes. Stand for 5 minutes and drain. In a shallow casserole, microwave butter for 1 minute, add mushrooms, cucumber and carrots, toss to coat with butter. Cover, microwave for 3 – 4 minutes, stirring every minute. Season to taste. Sprinkle with parsley or dill before serving.
Serves 4 – 6

MUSSELS
Fresh mussels cook quickly and retain their flavour when cooked in the microwave. Canned mussels are already cooked and only need heating through.

Steamed fresh mussels

Full Power
8 minutes

1 kg (2¼ lb) fresh mussels
water
salt
black peppercorns
1 small garlic clove
1 lemon slice
60 mℓ (4 tablespoons) white wine (optional)

Soak mussels in plenty of cold water for about 1 hour. Scrub them very well, removing any foreign matter from the outside. Place in a large shallow casserole, add 300 mℓ (10 fl oz) water and the remaining ingredients. Cover, microwave on Full Power for 8 – 10 minutes, stirring at least once during cooking time. Discard any mussels which are tightly closed. Open remaining mussels, remove the 'beard' and rinse. Set aside. Strain remaining liquid

through a piece of muslin before using it as a sauce base.
Serves 4 – 6 as a starter

Mussel and leek starter

Full Power
24 minutes

1 – 1½ kg (2¼ – 3 lb) fresh mussels, steamed*
400 mℓ (4 fl oz) cooking liquid
10 saffron threads, crushed
375 mℓ (12 fl oz) sparkling dry white wine
500 mℓ (16 fl oz) cream
black pepper
75 g (2½ oz) butter
3 – 4 leeks, sliced thinly

Combine 200 mℓ (6½ fl oz) cooking liquid with saffron threads, stand for a few minutes, add wine. Microwave on Full Power for 4 minutes, add cream and pepper and microwave for about 10 minutes, until the liquid is reduced by half. Microwave butter for 2 minutes, add leeks, toss to coat with butter, microwave for 3 minutes, pour in remaining cooking liquid, microwave for 5 minutes. Add reduced sauce to leeks, stir to combine. To serve, spoon a generous layer of leeks on to six fish plates, top with a serving of mussels. Serve immediately. If necessary, reheat mussels for a few minutes before serving.
Serves 6 as a starter

MUTTON

Mutton is the meat of a mature sheep and although not nearly as tender as lamb, it is richer in flavour and is usually less expensive. Mutton can be used in any recipe for pot-roasted, casseroled or stewed lamb, but it takes longer to cook. *See also* Lamb.

NOODLES *See* Pasta

NOUGAT

Originating in France, this soft, chewy confection, wrapped in edible rice paper, is simple to make in the microwave. Two separate mixtures are made and then combined. Because the sugar syrup becomes very hot, large ovenproof bowls should be used.

Nutty nougat

Full Power
23 minutes

icing sugar
4 sheets of rice paper

Mixture 1
100 g (3½ oz) caster sugar
20 mℓ (4 teaspoons) water
60 mℓ (4 tablespoons) golden syrup
2 egg whites

Mixture 2
200 g (7 oz) caster sugar
200 g (7 oz) golden syrup
150 mℓ (5 fl oz) water
15 mℓ (1 tablespoon) powdered gelatine
15 g (½ oz) butter
few drops of vanilla extract
45 g (1½ oz) nuts, chopped
30 g (1 oz) glacé cherries or apricots, chopped

Grease a 12.5. cm (5-inch) square pan, and dust with a little icing sugar. Line base and sides with rice paper. Make the first mixture. In a large bowl, combine sugar, water and golden syrup. Microwave on Full Power for 2 minutes, stir well. Brush sides of the bowl with water to remove sugar crystals. Microwave for 5 – 6 minutes, until sugar reaches soft ball stage. Allow bubbles to subside. Beat whites until stiff, gradually pour in hot syrup and beat for 5 minutes. Stand mixture over a bowl of hot water.

For the second mixture combine sugar, golden syrup and 100 mℓ (3½ fl oz) of the water in a large bowl. Microwave for 4 minutes, stir well. Brush sides of the bowl with water to remove sugar crystals. Microwave for 12 – 14 minutes more until light crack stage is reached. Soak gelatine in remaining water, add to cooked syrup, stir to dissolve. Pour into first mixture and beat well, add butter and vanilla. Stir in nuts and fruit. Pour into prepared pan, cover with rice paper. Refrigerate until set. Cut into rectangular pieces with a hot, sharp knife.
Makes about 20 pieces

NUTS

Nuts react perfectly to microwave cooking and can be blanched or toasted. Heat unblanched almonds in a little water for a few minutes and the skins slide off easily. Warm hazelnuts for a few seconds in the microwave and rub the outer skin off with your fingers. Nuts are frequently used to add colour, texture and flavour to toppings for cakes and puddings cooked in the microwave oven.
See also individual names.

To toast nuts, place flaked or blanched nuts in a browning dish and microwave on Full Power for 4 – 5 minutes, stirring every minute.

To shell nuts, place 125 g (4 oz) unshelled nuts in a jug, cover with cold water. Microwave on Full Power for 2 – 3 minutes. Drain nuts and crack open shells immediately. If the kernels are slightly damp, place on a plate, microwave for 1 minute, then stand for 5 minutes before using.

A tangy Lemon Jelly (page 120) adds sparkle to any occasion

O

OATMEAL PORRIDGE *See* Porridge

OCTOPUS *See* Squid

OFFAL *See* individual names: Brains, Kidneys, Liver, Tongue and Sweetbreads

ORANGE

Oranges, one of the best known members of the citrus family, originally came from China and south-east Asia but are now grown in tropical and subtropical areas throughout the world. There are two main varieties: the bitter orange, such as Sevilles which are used for marmalade, and the sweet, such as Valencias and navels. Sweet oranges can also be used for marmalade but are usually used fresh for juice or in fruit salads or are combined with other ingredients such as meat, fish or poultry. Orange counteracts the richness of pork and duck.

To obtain all the juice from fresh oranges, prick the skin lightly and warm in the microwave for a few seconds before squeezing.

Spicy orange chicken

Full Power
35 minutes

1,5 kg (3 lb) chicken, cut into serving portions
7.5 mℓ (1½ teaspoons) salt
5 mℓ (1 teaspoon) paprika
pinch of pepper
2 onions, sliced
100 g (3½ oz) orange marmalade
60 mℓ (4 tablespoons) orange juice
20 mℓ (4 teaspoons) cornflour
30 mℓ (2 tablespoons) brown sugar
30 mℓ (2 tablespoons) lemon juice
generous pinch of ground ginger
pinch of nutmeg
pinch of cloves
1 orange, peeled and sliced

Arrange chicken portions in a baking dish with skin sides up and thickest parts towards the outside. Sprinkle with salt, paprika and pepper and arrange onion slices on top. Cover, microwave on Full Power for 15 minutes, and set aside. Combine marmalade, orange juice, cornflour, sugar, lemon juice, ginger, nutmeg and cloves. Add juices from the chicken and microwave for 2½ minutes. Stir, then microwave for 1½ – 2 minutes longer, or until sauce is thick and translucent. Add orange slices and spoon sauce over chicken. Cover loosely and microwave for 10 – 15 minutes, or until chicken is tender. Stand for 10 minutes before serving.
Serves 4 – 6

Orange hake with capers

Full Power
10 minutes

750 g (1¾ lb) hake steaks, skinned
20 mℓ (4 teaspoons) capers, chopped
grated rind and juice of 1 large orange
15 mℓ (1 tablespoon) chopped parsley
10 mℓ (2 teaspoons) finely chopped onion
60 g (2 oz) butter
salt and lemon pepper

To garnish
1 orange, sliced
parsley

Place fish steaks in a shallow casserole, arranging thin ends towards the centre. Sprinkle with capers, rind and juice of the orange, chopped parsley and onion. Dot butter over the fish, and season with salt and lemon pepper. Cover with vented plastic wrap and microwave on Full Power for 8 – 10 minutes, or until fish flakes easily. Stand for 5 minutes, then garnish with orange slices and parsley.
Serves 6

Orange and white chocolate mousse

Medium (50%)
6 minutes

450 g (1 lb) white chocolate, broken into squares
60 g (2 oz) butter
185 mℓ (6 fl oz) whipping cream
finely grated rind of 1 orange
30 mℓ (2 tablespoons) orange juice
30 mℓ (2 tablespoons) orange liqueur
2 eggs, separated
fresh strawberries

Place white chocolate in a large bowl. Microwave on Medium (50%) for 3 minutes. Stir, add butter, and microwave 2 – 3 minutes more or until completely melted. Stir well, then cool slightly. Beat the cream to soft peaks. Beat orange rind, orange juice and orange liqueur into the egg yolks and beat egg whites to stiff peaks. Stir orange liqueur mixture into the chocolate mixture, mixing well. Stir in cream, then fold in egg whites. Transfer to a serving dish or spoon into individual dishes and chill until firm. Serve with fresh strawberries sprinkled with sugar, if desired. *Serves 6*

Carrot and orange soup

Full Power
31 minutes

45 g (1½ oz) butter
2 onions, chopped
4 – 6 carrots, chopped
1 potato, cubed
700 mℓ (23 fl oz) chicken stock
250 mℓ (8 fl oz) fresh orange juice
salt and black pepper
5 mℓ (1 teaspoon) chopped fresh coriander or tarragon

To garnish
fresh coriander or tarragon sprigs
strip of orange zest
1 carrot

Microwave butter in a 2-litre (3½-pint) casserole on Full Power for 2 minutes. Add onion, stir and microwave for 4 minutes. Add carrots, potato and stock, cover and microwave for 20 minutes, or until carrot and potato are cooked. Purée until smooth in a blender, strain. Add orange juice, adjust seasoning and add coriander. Microwave for 5 minutes to reheat. Spoon into soup bowls, top with a sprig of coriander or tarragon and a strip of orange zest. Using a potato peeler, peel a few thin strips of carrot, form into a curl, and use as a garnish.
Serves 6 – 8

Note: This soup may also be served chilled with a swirl of cream.

OVEN CHIPS

Oven chips are designed to be baked in a conventional oven and need hot, dry air to develop their characteristic crisp texture. They become soggy when heated in the microwave oven.

OXTAIL

Meat that contains a high percentage of bone, such as oxtail, needs long, slow simmering to become tender and gelatinous in texture. Little time is saved and the oxtail tends to remain tough when it is cooked in the microwave, so for best results, cook it conventionally or use a slow cooker. Oxtail stews and casseroles are best prepared the day before serving, and can be reheated in the microwave.

OYSTER

These marine molluscs have been known to man since early times and are considered by some to be of great gastronomic merit. Different species of oyster vary considerably in flavour and texture and although the purists prefer their oysters raw, others like their oysters cooked.

Oysters for eating raw should be alive and fresh. To open oysters, a special knife with short, flat blade and a triangular point is normally used. The knife is inserted under the smooth lip of the shell and pushed between the upper and lower shells to prise them apart. The oyster is detached from the upper shell and served in the deeper bottom shell. Oysters when fresh should be plump and smell of the sea.

Oysters should be cooked very carefully in the microwave, as excess heat makes them tough and rubbery. They should just curl at the edges, and when used in casseroles or other dishes, should be added during the last few minutes, or be well covered with sauce or other ingredients during cooking.

Oysters are also available canned in brine or smoked.

Oyster and spinach soup

Full Power
10 minutes

300 g (11 oz) spinach
2 x 225 g (8 oz) cans of oysters in brine
125 mℓ (4 fl oz) chicken stock
125 mℓ (4 fl oz) milk
125 mℓ (4 fl oz) single cream
10 mℓ (2 teaspoons) Worcestershire sauce
5 – 10 mℓ (1 – 2 teaspoons) lemon juice
salt and black pepper
60 mℓ (4 tablespoons) soured cream
15 mℓ (1 tablespoon) finely chopped chives

Wash spinach well, drain and place in a large bowl with the water that clings to the leaves. Cover with vented plastic wrap, microwave on Full Power for 5 minutes, drain well. Blend spinach, liquid from oysters and half the oysters. Add chicken stock and blend until smooth. Pour soup into a large casserole, add milk, cream, Worcestershire sauce, lemon juice, seasonings and remaining oysters. Microwave for 5 – 7 minutes, until piping hot. Ladle into bowls, top with soured cream and chives.
Serves 6

Creamed oysters

Full Power
7 minutes

24 – 30 raw oysters
90 mℓ (3 fl oz) soured cream
Tabasco
10 mℓ (2 teaspoons) lemon juice
60 g (2 oz) grated Parmesan cheese
60 g (2 oz) savoury biscuit crumbs
pinch of dry mustard
15 mℓ (1 tablespoon) chopped parsley
salt and pepper
60 g (2 oz) butter

Divide oysters among six small ramekins. Combine soured cream, a few drops of Tabasco and lemon juice and spoon over oysters. Combine cheese, crumbs, mustard, parsley and salt and pepper. Microwave butter on Full Power for 30 – 45 seconds and stir into Parmesan mixture. Spoon over oysters. Arrange dishes in a circle on a large plate and microwave for 5 – 6 minutes or until mixture is heated through and cream is just bubbly.
Serves 6 as a starter

P

PAELLA

In Spain, a paella may vary from a simple peasant-style dish to an extremely elaborate affair. The ingredients, too, vary from region to region but usually include chicken, sausage, fish, shellfish and a selection of vegetables which are added to the basic rice and saffron mixture. The following is a quick paella, suitable for preparing in the microwave.

Quick paella

Full Power
25 minutes

few threads of saffron, crushed or a generous
   pinch of turmeric
425 mℓ (14 fl oz) boiling chicken stock
45 mℓ (3 tablespoons) oil, sunflower and olive
   combined
1 onion, chopped
1 – 2 garlic cloves, crushed
1 small green pepper, chopped
125 g (4 oz) rice
1 chicken stock cube
2 tomatoes, skinned and chopped
salt and black pepper
225 g (8 oz) canned clams
150 g (5 oz) monkfish
150 g (5 oz) haddock
45 mℓ (3 tablespoons) water
black peppercorns
lemon slice
175 g (6 oz) frozen peas
½ cooked chicken, cut in bite-sized pieces

To garnish
black olives
1 lemon, cut in wedges

Add saffron to stock, stand for a few minutes to infuse. In a large casserole, microwave oil on Full Power for 1 minute. Add onion, garlic and green pepper, toss vegetables to coat with oil. Microwave for 4 minutes, stirring once. Add rice, stock cube, stock, tomatoes, a little seasoning and juice from clams. Cover and microwave on Full Power for 12 minutes. Stand, covered, for at least 10 minutes until the rice has absorbed the stock.

Meanwhile, place monkfish and haddock in a shallow casserole. Add water, peppercorns, salt and lemon slice. Cover with vented plastic wrap, microwave for 3 minutes. Drain and cut into bite-sized pieces. Add fish, clams, peas, and chicken to rice, stir well. Cover, microwave for 5 minutes, stirring once. Garnish with a few olives and lemon wedges.
Serves 6 – 8

Variation
Add any of the following to the paella:
☐ canned artichoke hearts, sliced
☐ canned mussels
☐ crayfish or prawns
☐ crab sticks
☐ garlic sausage, cubed

PANCAKES *See* Crêpes

PARSLEY

Parsley is one of the best known and most widely used of all herbs. It can be used to garnish fish, eggs, meat and vegetables, or to flavour soups, sauces and stuffings. A parsley sprig is often included in a bouquet garni. The attractive, bright-green leaves are flat or curly, depending on the variety. Flat-leafed parsley has a stronger flavour than the more delicate curly-leafed variety. Parsley can be used fresh or dried, and can even be frozen with a little water in ice cube form for dropping into soups and stews.

Parsley rice

Full Power
15 minutes

200 g (7 oz) rice
500 mℓ (16 fl oz) boiling water
1 chicken stock cube
pinch of turmeric
45 mℓ (3 tablespoons) finely chopped onion
30 g (1 oz) butter
45 mℓ (3 tablespoons) chopped parsley
60 g (2 oz) Cheddar cheese, grated

Place rice in a casserole and add the water mixed with stock cube, turmeric and onion. Stir, cover with vented plastic wrap and microwave on Full Power for 15 minutes. Stand for 20 minutes, or until all liquid is absorbed. Stir in butter, chopped parsley and cheese before serving.
Serves 4 – 6

PARSNIP

A strongly flavoured white root vegetable, shaped like a carrot and cooked in much the same way. Young parsnips microwave extremely well, whereas older parsnips tend to have a tough, woody core and should be avoided.

To microwave parsnips
Peel and slice 500 g (18 oz) parsnips, place in a bowl. Add 75 ml (2½ fl oz) water and a little salt. Cover with vented plastic wrap, microwave on Full Power for 10 – 12 minutes. Stir once during cooking time. Drain off liquid and add black pepper to taste.

Serving suggestions
☐ Mash cooked parsnips, add 100 ml (3½ fl oz) single cream, sprinkle with chopped parsley.
☐ Mash cooked parsnips with 60 ml (2 oz) butter, sprinkle with paprika.
☐ Cut parsnips in julienne, cook with carrots and courgettes, toss in butter.

PASSIONFRUIT

The passionfruit granadilla originated in South America, but is now grown in many countries with warm climates. When picked, the fruit is about the size of a large egg and is greenish-brown with a smooth surface. As the fruit ripens further, the skin turns a darker colour and becomes wrinkled. Passionfruit pulp is very versatile. It is used to flavour ice cream, puddings, icings and cakes and can also be added to fresh fruit salad or turned into fruit cordials. Passionfruit pulp freezes well and small containers may be thawed in a minute or two in the microwave.

Passionfruit curd

Full Power, High (70%), Medium (50%)
7 minutes

125 g (4 oz) butter
3 eggs
125 g (4 oz) caster sugar
8 passionfruit (about 125 g (4 oz) pulp)
5 mℓ (1 teaspoon) grated lemon rind
juice of 3 lemons
5 mℓ (1 teaspoon) cornflour

Microwave butter on Full Power for 2 minutes. Meanwhile beat together eggs and caster sugar until light and fluffy. Add passionfruit pulp, lemon rind and most of the lemon juice. Mix remaining lemon juice and cornflour to a smooth paste and stir into egg mixture with melted butter. Microwave, uncovered, for 2 minutes. Stir well. Microwave on High (70%) for 2 minutes more, stirring at the end of each minute. Change setting to Medium (50%) and microwave for 1 minute. Stir very well. The mixture should be thick enough to coat the back of a wooden spoon. Cool slightly. Pour into two medium-sized jars and top with brandy papers or waxed papers. Cover when cold. Label and store in the refrigerator. Use in fruit flans, as a cake filling or in fruit tartlets.
Makes about 350 g (12 oz)

Passionfruit mould

Full Power, Medium (50%)
8 minutes

150 g (5 oz) passionfruit pulp (about 10 passionfruit)
75 g (2½ oz) caster sugar
150 mℓ (5 fl oz) milk
2 eggs, separated
100 mℓ (3½ fl oz) natural yoghurt
75 mℓ (2½ fl oz) water
20 mℓ (4 teaspoons) powdered gelatine
100 mℓ (3½ fl oz) whipping cream

To decorate
60 mℓ (4 tablespoons) whipping cream, whipped
2 – 3 cherries, quartered

Combine passionfruit pulp and sugar, microwave on Full Power for 3 minutes. Stir well,

set aside to cool. Pour milk into a jug, microwave for 2 minutes. Pour on to lightly beaten egg yolks and beat. Microwave on Medium (50%) for 2 minutes, stirring once during cooking time. Cool slightly. Combine custard, pulp and yoghurt. Pour water into a small jug, add gelatine and stir to combine. Stand for 2 minutes to soften. Microwave on Medium (50%) for 1 minute, stir and add to custard mixture. Stand over ice until the mixture begins to thicken, stirring from time to time. Beat the cream until thick, fold into the mixture. Now beat egg whites to peaking consistency and fold into the mixture. Rinse a 1-litre (1¾-pint) mould with cold water, pour in the thickening mixture. Refrigerate until set. To serve, dip mould into hot water for 3 seconds, loosen a small portion of the edge using your thumb, to introduce an air bubble down the side of the mould. Invert on to a plate, pipe with stars of whipped cream and decorate with cherries.
Serves 6

PASTA

Dried pasta needs to be reconstituted in plenty of boiling, salted water and the microwave does not speed up this process to any great extent. Some cooks say that the flavour of pasta is better when it is cooked in the microwave and the texture is firmer or 'al dente'. Others feel that because pasta takes almost the same amount of time to cook in the microwave as conventionally, it should be cooked conventionally, leaving the microwave free for making sauces or toppings.
See also Bolognese sauce.

To reheat pasta
Pasta reheats in the microwave with excellent results. Just place the pasta in a suitable container, cover and microwave on Full Power for 1 – 3 minutes, or longer, depending on quantities.

Tuna and noodles

Full Power
14 minutes

400 g (14 oz) canned tuna in brine, drained
400 g (14 oz) canned cream of celery soup
30 g (1 oz) butter
½ small green pepper, diced
2 celery sticks, thinly sliced
½ onion, chopped
2.5 mℓ (½ teaspoon) mild curry powder
125 mℓ (4 fl oz) milk
125 mℓ (4 fl oz) soured cream
salt and black pepper
250 g (9 oz) cooked noodles*
60 mℓ (4 tablespoons) toasted almonds*

Flake tuna and add to the soup in a large casserole. Microwave butter on Full Power for 30 seconds. Add green pepper, celery and onion. Stir, then microwave for 3 minutes. Stir in curry powder. Add vegetables to soup mixture and stir in milk and soured cream. Season to

taste and mix in cooked noodles. Microwave for 8 – 11 minutes or until heated through, then sprinkle with almonds.
Serves 6

Salmon and pasta bake

Full Power, Medium (50%)
23 minutes

45 mℓ (3 tablespoons) oil
2 onions, chopped
1 green pepper, chopped
200 g (7 oz) mushrooms, sliced
450 g (1 lb) canned salmon
400 g (14 oz) canned tomato purée
10 mℓ (2 teaspoons) Worcestershire sauce
30 mℓ (2 tablespoons) tomato sauce
5 mℓ (1 teaspoon) dry mustard
salt and black pepper
125 g (4 oz) Cheddar cheese, grated
250 g (9 oz) pasta shells, cooked*
15 g (½ oz) butter

Pour oil into a large bowl, microwave on Full Power for 2 minutes. Add onion and green pepper, toss to coat with oil and microwave for 4 minutes, stirring once during cooking time. Stir in mushrooms, fish, tomato purée, Worcestershire sauce, mustard and seasonings. Cover, microwave for 5 minutes. Stir in half the cheese and the pasta. Pour into a greased casserole, sprinkle with remaining cheese and dot with butter. Microwave on Medium (50%) for 12 – 15 minutes. For a crispy brown top, slide under the grill for a few minutes.
Serves 6

Spaghetti with spicy meat sauce

Full Power
15 minutes

500 g (18 oz) minced beef
1 small onion, chopped
1 garlic clove, finely chopped
400 g (14 oz) canned tomatoes, roughly chopped
185 mℓ (6 fl oz) tomato paste
60 mℓ (4 tablespoons) chilli sauce
125 g (4 oz) mushrooms, sliced
60 mℓ (4 tablespoons) chopped parsley
15 mℓ (1 tablespoon) soft brown sugar
2.5 mℓ (½ teaspoon) dried oregano
2.5 mℓ (½ teaspoon) dried basil
salt
350 g (12 oz) spaghetti, cooked*
grated Parmesan cheese

Crumble meat into a casserole. Add onion and garlic and microwave on Full Power for about 5 minutes or until meat is browned, stirring twice. Drain off excess fat, then stir in tomatoes and juice, tomato paste, chilli sauce, mushrooms, parsley, brown sugar, herbs and season to taste. Microwave, covered, for 10 minutes or until sauce is thickened. Serve over hot, cooked spaghetti. Sprinkle with Parmesan cheese.
Serves 6

Tagliatelle with prawns

Defrost (30%), Full Power, High (70%)
16 minutes

500 g (18 oz) peeled, deveined frozen prawns
300 g (11 oz) frozen peas
200 mℓ (6½ fl oz) cream
10 mℓ (2 teaspoons) chopped dill, or 300 mℓ
 (2 tablespoons) chopped sorrel
salt and black pepper
Tabasco
2 egg yolks
60 g (2 oz) Parmesan cheese, grated
300 g (11 oz) tagliatelle, cooked*
paprika

Place the bag of frozen prawns on a plate and pierce. Microwave on Defrost (30%) for 5 minutes. In a casserole, combine peas, cream, dill and seasonings. Microwave on Full Power for 2 minutes. Add prawns and some of the liquid, cover and microwave for 5 minutes. Mix yolks with a little of the hot liquid, then stir yolks into prawn mixture, add Parmesan cheese. Carefully combine pasta and prawns, place in a shallow casserole. Cover, microwave on High (70%) for about 4 minutes, until piping hot. Sprinkle with paprika.
Serves 4

Spinach and salmon pasta

Full Power, Medium (50%)
26 minutes

300 g (11 oz) spinach
5 fresh pink salmon steaks, about 1.5-cm
 (½-inch) thick
60 mℓ (4 tablespoons) water
15 mℓ (1 tablespoon) lemon juice
60 mℓ (4 tablespoons) white wine
salt and black pepper
bay leaf
15 g (½ oz) butter
15 mℓ (1 tablespoon) plain flour
75 mℓ (2½ fl oz) milk
2 egg yolks
250 mℓ (8 fl oz) single cream
75 g (2½ oz) Parmesan cheese, grated
300 g (11 oz) cooked pasta (tagliatelle or
 fettucini)
lemon twists

Wash spinach well, place in a bowl with the water that clings to the leaves. Cover with vented plastic wrap and microwave on Full Power for 5 minutes. Drain and chop coarsely. Set aside. Place salmon, water, lemon juice, wine, seasonings and bay leaf in a shallow casserole, cover. Microwave for 5 – 7 minutes, remove fish and cut into bite-sized pieces. The fish should not be completely cooked.

Microwave fish liquid for 3 minutes, strain. Microwave butter in a jug for 30 seconds, stir in flour, then add milk and reduced liquid, stir well. Microwave for 2 minutes, whisking every 30 seconds. Whisk in yolks and cream. In a large dish, combine spinach, salmon, sauce and half the Parmesan cheese. Add to pasta

and pour mixture into a shallow casserole. Sprinkle with remaining cheese, cover and microwave on Medium (50%) for 10 – 12 minutes. Garnish with lemon twists.
Serves 4 – 6

Tomato sauce for pasta

Full Power
13 minutes

30 mℓ (2 tablespoons) oil
1 onion, chopped
1 – 2 garlic cloves, crushed
4 – 5 tomatoes, skinned and chopped
30 mℓ (2 tablespoons) tomato paste
2.5 mℓ (½ teaspoon) caster sugar
salt and black pepper
10 mℓ (2 teaspoons) chopped marjoram or
 basil
1 bay leaf
15 mℓ (1 tablespoon) Italian olive oil

Place oil in a large casserole, microwave on Full Power for 1 minute. Add onion and garlic, toss to coat with oil, microwave for 4 minutes, stirring twice. Add tomato paste, sugar, seasonings, herbs and bay leaf, stir well. Cover, microwave for 8 – 10 minutes, stirring once. Remove bay leaf, stir in olive oil and serve with steaming hot pasta.
Serves 4

PASTRY

Shortcrust and suet pastries become tender and flaky when baked in the microwave, but do not brown. Brushing the pastry shell with a little egg yolk or vanilla extract mixed with water, or adding a few drops of yellow food colouring to the dough will improve the colour. Directions for microwaving shortcrust pastry are given in the recipe below.

Pastries such as puff pastry and choux pastry need hot dry air to give their characteristic finish and are not suitable for microwave cooking. Double crust pies are

also not successful as the bottom crust does not cook properly and tends to become soggy and unappetising.

Shortcrust pastry

Full Power
6 minutes

125 g (4 oz) plain flour
2.5 mℓ (½ teaspoon) salt
5 mℓ (1 teaspoon) sugar
60 g (2 oz) butter
1 egg yolk
45 mℓ (3 tablespoons) cold water

Combine flour, salt and sugar. Rub in butter until mixture resembles fine crumbs. Combine egg yolk and water and add enough to the dry ingredients to form a dough. Turn pastry on to a lightly floured surface and knead gently, then roll out and use as desired.

To microwave pastry shells line pie dish with pastry. Cut a long foil strip about 3-cm (1¼-inch) wide and line the edge of the pastry shell. Place a double layer of kitchen paper in the base of the pastry shell, pressing gently into the edges. Microwave on Full Power for 3½ – 4 minutes rotating dish after 2 minutes if necessary. Remove foil and kitchen paper and microwave for 1½ – 2 minutes. Use cooked pastry shells for pies and tarts with cold or uncooked fillings.
Makes a 20 – 22.5-cm (8 – 9-inch) single crust

Variations
Herb Pastry: Leave out sugar and add 5 mℓ (1 teaspoon) herbs, or herb of your choice.
Cheese Pastry: Omit sugar, add a pinch of dry mustard to the dry ingredients and stir in 60 mℓ (4 tablespoons) grated cheese after rubbing in the butter.
Sweet Pastry: Increase the sugar to 45 mℓ (3 tablespoons), add a few drops of vanilla extract, and proceed as for shortcrust pastry.
Nut Pastry: Add 60 mℓ (4 tablespoons) finely chopped nuts to dry ingredients.

PASTA MICROWAVING CHART

PASTA 250 g (9 oz)	COOKING TIME (On Full Power)	PREPARATION
Egg noodles and Tagliatelle	7 – 9 minutes, stand 5 minutes	Add 600 mℓ (19 fl oz) boiling water, 2.5 mℓ (½ teaspoon) salt, 10 mℓ (2 teaspoons) oil
Spaghetti	14 – 16 minutes, stand 5 minutes	Add 900 mℓ (29 fl oz) boiling water, 2.5 mℓ (½ teaspoon) salt, 10 mℓ (2 teaspoons) oil
Macaroni	10 – 12 minutes, stand 5 minutes	Add 600 mℓ (19 fl oz) boiling water, 2.5 mℓ (½ teaspoon) salt, 10 mℓ (2 teaspoons) oil
Lasagne	14 – 16 minutes, stand 5 minutes	Add 1 litre (1¾ pints) boiling water, 2.5 mℓ (½ teaspoon) salt, 10 mℓ (2 teaspoons) oil
Pasta shells	18 – 20 minutes, stand 5 minutes	Add 1 litre (1¾ pints) boiling water, 2.5 mℓ (½ teaspoon) salt, 10 mℓ (2 teaspoons) oil

PÂTÉ

The term pâté generally refers to a mixture of finely ground meats, liver, poultry or game, which is well-seasoned and flavoured. The mixture can be baked in a loaf dish or terrine, or it can be cooked and pressed into a serving dish or mould. The microwave cooks the ingredients for pâtés quickly and easily and makes a great saving on washing-up.
See also Terrine.

Smoked cod pâté

Full Power
11 minutes

250 g (9 oz) hake
1 small onion, sliced
1 bay leaf
peppercorns
100 ml (3½ fl oz) milk
100 ml (3½ fl oz) water
45 ml (3 tablespoons) white wine
125 g (4 oz) smoked cod
200 g (7 oz) butter
45 ml (3 tablespoons) lemon juice
5 ml (1 teaspoon) dried dill
45 ml (3 tablespoons) single cream
salt and pepper

Place hake, onion, bay leaf, peppercorns, milk, water and wine in a casserole. Cover and microwave on Full Power for 5 minutes. Drain fish, remove skin and bones from hake and cod and flake. Place butter, lemon juice and dill in a bowl. Microwave for 4 minutes, add flaked fish, cover and microwave for 2 minutes. Stir in cream. Purée mixture in a food processor or blender. Season with salt and pepper and turn into a serving dish or mould. Chill for at least 6 hours. If using a mould, turn out and garnish with lemon slices and herbs. To serve individually, place slices of pâté on lettuce and garnish as desired.
Serves 6

Chicken pâté

Full Power
12 minutes

750 g (1¾ lb) chicken breasts, skinned, boned and diced
250 g (9 oz) chicken livers, coarsely chopped
1 onion, chopped
2.5 ml (½ teaspoon) dried thyme
2.5 ml (½ teaspoon) dried sage
15 ml (1 tablespoon) freshly chopped parsley
1 garlic clove, finely chopped
1 bay leaf
15 ml (1 tablespoon) grated orange rind
30 ml (2 tablespoons) orange juice
30 ml (2 tablespoons) dry sherry
salt and pepper
60 g (2 oz) low-fat soft cheese

Place chicken breasts, liver, onion, herbs, garlic, bay leaf, orange rind and juice, sherry and salt and pepper in a casserole. Cover and

microwave on Full Power for 10 – 12 minutes, or until no pink remains in the chicken liver. Stir twice during cooking. Remove bay leaf and place ingredients in a food processor or blender. Process until smooth, then stir in cheese and correct seasoning. Spoon mixture into a serving dish and chill well.
Serves 6 – 8

Baked pork pâté

Full Power
18 minutes

500 g (18 oz) lean, boneless pork, diced
2 small onions, chopped
300 g (11 oz) pig's liver, coarsely chopped
3 garlic cloves, finely chopped
5 ml (1 teaspoon) dried or 15 ml
    (1 tablespoon) chopped fresh sage
5 ml (1 teaspoon) dried or 15 ml
    (1 tablespoon) chopped fresh oregano
2.5 ml (½ teaspoon) dried or 10 ml
    (2 teaspoons) chopped fresh thyme
2.5 ml (½ teaspoon) chopped fresh mint
2.5 ml (½ teaspoon) dried or 10 ml
    (2 teaspoons) chopped fresh rosemary
7.5 ml (1½ teaspoons) grated lemon rind
15 ml (1 tablespoon) lemon juice
1 beaten egg
45 ml (3 tablespoons) whisky
salt and black pepper
pinch of freshly grated nutmeg
250 g (9 oz) rashers streaky bacon, rinds removed

Place pork, onion, liver, garlic, herbs and lemon rind and juice in a large casserole. Cover and microwave on Full Power for 8 – 10 minutes or until no pink shows in the meat. Purée the mixture in a food processor or blender until smooth. Stir in egg and whisky, and season well with salt, pepper and nutmeg. Line a loaf dish with bacon rashers and spoon in meat mixture. Fold ends of bacon over mixture and cover with vented plastic wrap. Microwave for 8 minutes. Cover with foil, then place a heavy weight on top of the pâté. Cool, then chill overnight. To serve, turn out onto a platter and cut into slices. Garnish with herbs if desired.
Serves 8

PEACH

The peach has been cultivated in China for at least 1,500 years and has spread westwards through Asia, to Europe, Africa and America. There are more than 2,000 varieties, which are roughly divided into 'freestone' or 'clingstone' peaches. Because the season is short and the fresh fruits spoil easily, surplus peaches can be made into jam or chutney, or be preserved by canning or bottling.

To peel peaches, place a small amount of water in the bottom of a glass dish. Prick the peach skins and place peaches in the bowl. Cover and steam on High (70%) for about 2 minutes. Stand for 5 minutes, then peel.

To stew peaches, peel and halve four medium-sized peaches. Remove stones, sprinkle with 100 g (3½ oz) caster sugar, cover and microwave on Full Power for 4 – 5 minutes.

Spicy peaches

Full Power
6 minutes

4 large ripe peaches, peeled*
125 ml (4 fl oz) dry white wine or dry rosé
90 g (3 oz) caster sugar
2.5 ml (½ teaspoon) chopped preserved ginger
2 x 2.5 ml (1-inch) cinnamon sticks
4 whole cloves

Cut peaches in half and remove stones. Place peaches in a small, deep dish. Combine wine, sugar, ginger and spices in a jug and microwave on Full Power for 2 minutes. Pour over peaches. Cover with vented plastic wrap and microwave for 3 – 4 minutes. To serve, spoon fruit into individual bowls and add some of the liquid to each. Serve with cream or ice cream if desired.
Serves 4

Peach cobbler

High (70%)
11 minutes

400 g (14 oz) canned sliced peaches
few drops of almond essence
pinch of nutmeg
30 ml (2 tablespoons) brandy
5 ml (1 teaspoon) cornflour

Topping
125 g (4 oz) plain flour
15 ml (1 tablespoon) caster sugar
pinch of salt
5 ml (1 teaspoon) baking powder
60 ml (4 tablespoons) buttermilk
15 g (½ oz) butter, melted
30 ml (2 tablespoons) toasted almonds*

To make the topping, combine flour, sugar, salt and baking powder. Combine buttermilk and melted butter and mix into the dry ingredients to form a soft dough. Stir in almonds. Turn peaches and juice into a shallow casserole. Add almond essence, nutmeg and brandy. Stir in cornflour, mixing well. Microwave on High (70%) for 4 minutes, stirring twice. Drop spoonfuls of the dough in a circle on the hot peach mixture and microwave until top of dough is almost dry to the touch, about 5 – 7 minutes. Stand for 10 minutes before serving. Serve with cream or ice cream if desired.
Serves 6

PEARS

Fresh, juicy pears are at their best towards the end of summer, but modern cold storage makes it possible for pears to be available almost year round. Pears cook extremely well in the microwave, though the exact cooking time will vary a great deal depending on the variety and ripeness of the pears used. When poaching pears, always undercook slightly as they continue to cook while standing. Overcooked pears become pulpy and lose their shape.

Chocolate pear crisp

Full Power
10 minutes

75 g (2½ oz) plain flour
75 g (2½ oz) wholewheat flour
45 g (1½ oz) rolled oats
pinch of salt
60 g (2 oz) soft brown sugar
90 g (3 oz) margarine
30 g (1 oz) chocolate chips
800 g (1 lb 14 oz) canned pears

To serve
chocolate sauce* or custard*

Sift plain flour into a bowl, add wholewheat flour, oats, salt and brown sugar. Rub in margarine and add chocolate chips. Grease a 20-cm (8-inch) pie dish, arrange pears flat side downwards, add a little juice. Sprinkle topping over pears. Microwave on Full Power for 10 – 12 minutes. Stand for 5 minutes. Serve with chocolate sauce or custard.
Serves 6

Pears with sherry

Full Power
15 minutes

6 firm pears, peeled
6 whole cloves
100 mℓ (3½ fl oz) water
100 mℓ (3½ fl oz) orange juice
45 mℓ (3 tablespoons) lemon juice
30 mℓ (2 tablespoons) red currant jelly
30 mℓ (2 tablespoons) sweet sherry
pinch of ground cloves
pinch of cinnamon
15 mℓ (1 tablespoon) soft brown sugar
strip of orange rind
15 mℓ (1 tablespoon) cornflour
15 mℓ (1 tablespoon) water

To decorate
angelica, cut in leaves

Core pears from the base, leaving the stalk intact. Stick a clove into each pear next to the stalk. In a casserole, combine water, fruit juice, red currant jelly, sherry, spices, brown sugar and orange rind. Microwave on Full Power for 4 minutes, stir well. Add pears and cover. Microwave for 7 – 10 minutes until pears are just soft. The time will vary, depending on the

type and ripeness of the pears. Carefully remove pears, set aside and strain liquid. Combine cornflour and water, add to strained liquid, stir well. Microwave for 4 – 5 minutes, stirring every minute. Allow sauce to cool. Add pears, and spoon sauce over from time to time. Chill well. To serve, spoon sauce over pears, decorate with a leaf of angelica and serve with whipped cream.
Serves 6

PEAS

This popular vegetable microwaves extremely well in a matter of minutes. Add a little water to young, fresh peas before microwaving. Frozen peas, however, need only the addition of a pat of butter and a pinch of sugar to cook to perfection. Canned peas, emptied into a suitable container, will heat in 2 minutes.

To microwave frozen peas
Place 250 g (9 oz) frozen peas in a casserole, cover and microwave on Full Power for 6 – 7 minutes. Serve immediately.
To microwave fresh peas
Place 250 ml (9 oz) shelled peas and 30 ml (2 tablespoons) water in a bowl. Cover with vented plastic wrap and microwave on Full Power for 8 – 10 minutes, stirring once. Drain and serve.
Serves 4
Serving suggestions
☐ Add a pat of butter and a mint sprig.
☐ Purée peas with mint, butter and a little cream.
☐ Combine peas with carrots or mushrooms, toss in butter.

Peas and onions

Full Power
10 minutes

60 g (2 oz) butter
1 bunch of spring onions, chopped
1 small garlic clove, finely chopped
generous pinch of dry mustard
generous pinch of ground coriander
pinch of ground ginger
300 g (11 oz) frozen peas
salt and pepper

Microwave butter in a casserole on Full Power for 45 seconds. Add chopped onion, garlic, mustard, coriander and ginger and microwave, covered, for 3 minutes. Add peas, stir well, then microwave, covered, for 5 – 6 minutes. Season with salt and pepper.
Serves 4

Variation
Substitute 6 small pickling onions, halved, for spring onions and proceed as above.

Peas with lettuce and ham

Full Power
17 minutes

12 pickling onions
45 mℓ (3 tablespoons) water
2 butter head lettuces
400 g (14 oz) frozen petit pois
5 mℓ (1 teaspoon) sugar
1 mint sprig
15 g (1½ oz) butter
75 g (3 oz) ham, chopped
salt and black pepper
15 mℓ (1 tablespoon) chopped parsley

Place onions and water in a bowl, cover with vented plastic wrap. Microwave on Full Power for 7 – 8 minutes, stirring once. Drain and keep warm. Rinse lettuce well, do not dry. Cut each lettuce into four wedges, tie each wedge with string to hold the shape. Place lettuce, peas, sugar and mint into a casserole, cover. Microwave on Full Power for 8 – 9 minutes, stir carefully at least once. Carefully remove string from lettuce and remove mint. Microwave butter for 30 seconds, add ham, microwave for 1 minute. Stir ham and onions into peas, season lightly. Sprinkle with parsley.
Serves 8

PECAN NUTS

These nuts belong to the hickory family and are similar to walnuts except they are less bitter and have smooth, elongated shells. Pecans are used in cakes, desserts, pies and biscuits, and may be substituted in recipes requiring walnuts.

Pecan and brandy tart

High (70%)
15 minutes

250 g (9 oz) stoned dates, chopped
60 g (2 oz) sultanas
5 mℓ (1 teaspoon) bicarbonate of soda
250 mℓ (8 fl oz) boiling water
2 eggs
200 g (7 oz) caster sugar
60 g (2 oz) margarine
200 g (7 oz) plain flour
60 g (2 oz) pecan nuts, chopped

Sauce
175 g (6 oz) soft brown sugar
15 g (½ oz) margarine
250 mℓ (8 fl oz) boiling water
few drops of vanilla extract
125 mℓ (4 fl oz) brandy

Place dates, sultanas, bicarbonate of soda and boiling water in a bowl, set aside to cool. Beat eggs well, add half the sugar and beat well. Cream margarine and remaining sugar, combine both mixtures. Add date mixture and mix well. Sift flour, add to mixture about a third at a time, mixing well after each addition. Stir in nuts. Pour into a greased 22.5-cm (9-inch) pyrex dish or pie plate. Microwave on High (70%) for 13 – 15 minutes. Stand for 10 minutes.

To make the sauce, place all ingredients in a jug, microwave on High (70%) for 2 – 3 minutes, stirring at least once to dissolve the sugar. Carefully pour over the hot tart. Serve warm or cold with cream.
Makes 1 x 22.5-cm (9-inch) tart

Pecan pie

Full Power, Medium (50%)
20 minutes

1 x 22.5-cm (9-inch) shortcrust pastry shell, uncooked*
1 egg yolk
30 mℓ (2 tablespoons) golden syrup
60 g (2 oz) butter
3 eggs
1 extra egg white
350 g (12 oz) golden syrup
75 g (2½ oz) soft brown sugar
15 mℓ (1 tablespoon) plain flour
few drops of vanilla extract
15 mℓ (1 tablespoon) sherry
150 g (5 oz) pecan nuts

Brush the inside of the pastry shell with a mixture of egg yolk and syrup. Microwave on Full Power for 4 minutes. Microwave butter in a large bowl for 45 seconds. Add eggs and egg white to butter, mixing well. Mix in syrup, sugar, flour, vanilla extract and sherry. Add pecans and mix well. Pour into the pastry shell and microwave on Medium (50%) for 12 – 15 minutes. The top of the pie should be almost dry to the touch and nicely puffed. Cool, then cut into wedges to serve.
Serves 6 – 8

PEPPERS
Peppers are members of the large Capsicum family, which also includes the fiery chilli pepper. Sweet peppers are available in red, green or pale yellow varieties and have a strong, distinctive flavour when cooked. Red peppers are the ripened version of green peppers and have a sweeter flavour. Peppers can be eaten raw in salads, stuffed with rice, herbs or meat, or used in casseroles and stews.

To microwave peppers
Wash two peppers, remove stems, seeds and membranes. Cut into slices or rings. Place in a casserole, cover and microwave on Full Power for 2 minutes. Stir, cover and microwave for 2 – 3 minutes more, depending on desired doneness. Stand for 1 minute before serving. To serve, add butter, salt and pepper or combine with tomatoes and mushrooms or onions.

Pepper tomato bake

Full Power
10 minutes

2 green peppers, cut in chunks
1 onion, sliced
2.5 mℓ (½ teaspoon) oregano
salt and black pepper
30 mℓ (2 tablespoons) water
2 tomatoes, cut in wedges
60 g (2 oz) Cheddar cheese, grated

Place green pepper in a casserole. Separate onion slices into rings and arrange on top of pepper. Sprinkle with oregano, salt and pepper. Add water, cover and microwave on Full Power for 6 minutes. Arrange tomato wedges over vegetables and microwave, covered, for 2 – 3 minutes, or until tomatoes are heated through. Sprinkle with cheese and microwave for 1 minute more to melt cheese.
Serves 4

Stuffed peppers

Full Power
16 minutes

½ onion, finely chopped
1 garlic clove, finely chopped
15 mℓ (1 tablespoon) oil
350 g (12 oz) minced beef
salt and black pepper
75 g (2½ oz) cooked rice*
100 g (3½ oz) mushrooms, sliced
2.5 mℓ (½ teaspoon) mixed herbs
45 mℓ (3 tablespoons) soft breadcrumbs
60 g (2 oz) Cheddar cheese, grated
4 large green peppers

Place onion, garlic and oil in a casserole and microwave on Full Power for 2 minutes. Add beef and season with salt and pepper, mixing well. Microwave for 4 minutes. Stir in rice, mushrooms, herbs, breadcrumbs and cheese.

Cut stem ends off peppers and reserve. Scoop out seeds and pith, rinse well. Spoon in meat mixture and stand peppers in a dish. Replace tops, cover with vented plastic wrap and microwave for 10 minutes. Stand for 5 minutes before serving.
Serves 4

PESTO
One of Italy's famous sauces used to top steaming hot pasta. This 'pounded', fragrant, green sauce, made with fresh basil leaves and garlic cloves, may also be stirred into hearty vegetable soups or be used as a topping for baked potatoes. Use the microwave to heat the oil slightly when making the sauce, or to reheat the pasta and sauce perfectly.

Italian pesto

Full Power, Medium (50%)
7 minutes

1 bunch of fresh basil (about 60 g (2 oz))
2 garlic cloves
30 g (1 oz) parsley sprigs
30 mℓ (2 tablespoons) pine nuts or walnuts
salt and pepper
125 mℓ (4 fl oz) Italian olive oil
60 g (2 oz) grated Parmesan cheese

To serve
300 g (11 oz) pasta, cooked*

Place basil, garlic, parsley, nuts and seasonings in the bowl of a food processor. Process until smooth. Pour oil into a jug, microwave on Full Power for 1 minute. Slowly pour oil through the top of the food processor on to the moving blade and process until smooth and thick. Add cheese, process to combine. To serve, combine pasta and pesto in a shallow serving dish, cover with vented plastic wrap. Microwave on Medium (50%) for 6   9 minutes, until piping hot. Serve immediately. *Serves 4*

PICCALILLI
A mixture of pickled vegetables, especially onions, cauliflower and cucumber, in a piquant mustard sauce which is served as a relish with cold meats and cheese.

Piccalilli

Full Power
21 minutes

1 cucumber
250 g (9 oz) small onions, peeled
10 – 15-cm (4 – 6-inch) long piece of vegetable marrow, peeled
1 cauliflower
4 courgettes
100 g (3½ oz) green beans
20 mℓ (4 teaspoons) salt

Sauce
600 mℓ (19 fl oz) white vinegar
15 mℓ (1 tablespoon) pickling spice
200 g (7 oz) soft brown sugar
30 g (1 oz) plain flour
10 mℓ (2 teaspoons) turmeric
10 mℓ (2 teaspoons) dry mustard
7.5 mℓ (1½ teaspoons) ground ginger

Cut the vegetables into small, even-sized pieces. Place in a bowl, sprinkle with salt and stand for 12 hours. Rinse and drain. To make the sauce, pour the vinegar into a large jug and add the pickling spice. Microwave on Full Power for 5 minutes. Strain. Meanwhile,

combine all the remaining ingredients in a large bowl. Pour on the hot vinegar and stir well. Microwave for 8 minutes, stirring every 2 minutes. Add vegetables. Microwave on Full Power for a further 8 minutes, stirring from time to time. Cool, pack into clean, dry jars, cover and store. This pickle may be eaten immediately.
Makes about 2 kg (4¼ lb)

PICKLED FISH *See* Fish

PICKLING

The microwave makes pickling simple. Chutneys and relishes microwave to setting point in a fraction of the time they usually take and the strong smell of vinegar, which normally fills the kitchen when pickles are being made, is contained in the microwave. Use the largest bowl available, for example, the pottery bowl from a slow cooker is an excellent choice. Like all preserves made in the microwave, all the natural flavours and colours of the pickled fruit and vegetables are retained.

Cucumber pickle

Full Power
16 minutes

This pickle is delicious served sliced or chopped in salads, on sandwiches or with cheese.

2 very large cucumbers
30 mℓ (2 tablespoons) salt
300 mℓ (½ pint) white vinegar
5 mℓ (1 teaspoon) dill
5 mℓ (1 teaspoon) mustard seed
75 g (2½ oz) caster sugar
1 large onion, sliced

Peel cucumbers. Slice thickly down length of cucumber and discard fleshy centre portion. Place cucumber strips in a flat, non-metallic basin and sprinkle with salt. Stand for 8 hours. Drain off liquid and pat dry with kitchen paper.

Place vinegar, dill, mustard seed and sugar in a large bowl. Cover with vented plastic wrap. Microwave on Full Power for 7 minutes. Divide cucumber strips into three batches. Microwave each batch, uncovered, in the vinegar for 3 minutes on Full Power. Add a little onion to each batch after it is cooked, then place cucumbers in a clean, dry jar. Cover with pickling liquid. Cover jar and refrigerate. Keep for a few days before using. This pickle lasts for up to six months.
Makes about 900 g (2 lb)

Spicy cucumber pickle

Full Power
11 minutes

This pickle is excellent served with cheese or salads, or as a snack.

3 medium-sized cucumbers
375 mℓ (12 fl oz) water
200 mℓ (6½ fl oz) vinegar
15 mℓ (1 tablespoon) salt
10 mℓ (2 teaspoons) peppercorns
2 bay leaves
2 garlic cloves, chopped

Wash the cucumbers. Using a fork, score the cucumbers down the length. Slice thickly. Combine the remaining ingredients in a large bowl. Cover and microwave on Full Power for 7 minutes. Add cucumber slices and microwave, covered, for 4 minutes. Pour into a large bottle whilst still hot. Cool, cover and refrigerate. This pickle will keep in the refrigerator for several weeks.
Makes about 900 g (2 lb)

Pickled onions

Full Power
10 minutes

1 kg (2¼ lb) pickling onions
30 g (1 oz) salt
300 mℓ (½ pint) white vinegar
60 mℓ (4 tablespoons) caster sugar
10 mℓ (2 teaspoons) mustard seed
10 mℓ (2 teaspoons) pickling spice
2 – 3 blades of mace
2 red chillies

Carefully remove tops and roots from onions. Place in a large bowl and cover with boiling water. Stand for 30 seconds, drain and cover with cold water. Peel onions under cold running water. Place onions in a bowl, layering them with salt. Stand overnight. Rinse well in a colander.

Combine all remaining ingredients in a large bowl. Microwave on Full Power for 5 minutes. Add onions, then microwave again for 5 minutes. Pack onions into clean, dry jars. Pour the hot, strained vinegar over. Cover loosely while still hot. Tighten lid when cool and stand for at least three weeks before serving. To make pickled onions with an extra bite, add 1 – 2 additional chillies to bottled onions.
Makes about 1.5 kg (3 lb)

Mixed vegetable pickle

Full Power
8 minutes

Use a selection of the following vegetables:
½ small cauliflower
1 small cucumber
2 – 3 carrots
6 – 8 small onions
green beans
courgettes

salt

Pickling liquid
300 mℓ (½ pint) white vinegar
1 bay leaf
small piece of fresh ginger
1 green chilli
small piece of mace
6 whole allspice

First prepare vegetables. Cut cauliflower into small florets. Slice unpeeled cucumber thickly and cut into quarters. Peel carrots, then slice thickly. Peel and quarter onions. Slice beans into short lengths. Cut unpeeled courgettes thickly. Layer vegetables in a bowl with salt. Cover and stand overnight. Drain, then rinse well in a colander and allow to dry.

Combine ingredients for pickling liquid in a large bowl. Cover with vented plastic wrap. Microwave on Full Power for 4 minutes. Add vegetables, cover and microwave for another 4 minutes. Using a slotted spoon, pack vegetables into clean, dry jars. Strain pickling liquid and cool. Cover vegetables with liquid. Cover jars, label and store.
Makes about 900 g (2 lb)

Pickled red cabbage

Full Power
5 minutes

1 red cabbage, shredded
15 mℓ (1 tablespoon) salt
600 mℓ (19 fl oz) white vinegar
30 mℓ (2 tablespoons) pickling spice
8 whole allspice
5 mℓ (1 teaspoon) dry mustard

Spread cabbage out in a shallow non-metallic dish, sprinkle with salt and stand for 24 hours. Drain very well, pack into jars. In a 1-litre (1¾-pint) jug, combine remaining ingredients. Microwave on Full Power for 5 minutes, allow to cool to room temperature. Strain and pour over cabbage, cover, label and store. Do not use vinegar while hot as the cabbage discolours.
Makes about 1.5 kg (3 lb)

Peach pickle

Full Power
22 minutes

1.5 kg (3 lb) peeled and stoned cling peaches
3 onions, coarsely chopped
250 mℓ (8 fl oz) water
720 mℓ (23 fl oz) vinegar
350 g (12 oz) preserving sugar
pinch of ground cloves
5 mℓ (1 teaspoon) turmeric
5 mℓ (1 teaspoon) ground ginger
2.5 mℓ (½ teaspoon) ground coriander
15 mℓ (1 tablespoon) curry powder
1 large green chilli, chopped
15 mℓ (1 tablespoon) cornflour

Roughly chop peaches. Combine peaches, onions and water in a bowl, cover with vented plastic wrap. Microwave on Full Power for 6 minutes. Add 600 mℓ (19 fl oz) of the vinegar, microwave for 5 minutes. Stir in sugar, microwave for 6 minutes, stirring every 2 minutes to dissolve sugar. Combine the remaining vinegar with remaining ingredients, stir into peach mixture. Microwave for 5 minutes. Pour into clean, dry jars. Cover, label and store. *Makes about 900 g (2 lb)*

PIES

Most microwaved pies start with a pre-baked pastry shell. If the pastry is not baked first, it may absorb moisture from the filling and become soggy. Fruit and custard fillings tend to boil over in the microwave, so be sure to make a deep rim on the pastry shells. When a filling is too liquid it may seep through the pastry. To prevent this occurring it is advisable to seal the pricked holes in baked pastry shells with a little beaten egg yolk, then microwave for a few seconds to set the egg before you add the filling.

Most types of pastry can be thawed in the microwave. However choux, puff and flaky pastries need hot dry air to keep them crisp, so best results are achieved if these pastries are reheated conventionally. *See also* Pastry.

To reheat a single serving of an open pie such as a quiche or fruit flan, place slice on a sheet of kitchen paper on a small plate and microwave for 1 – 1½ minutes on Full Power or High (70%).
To reheat individual meat pies, remove the foil, place on a sheet of kitchen paper and microwave on Full Power for 1½ – 2 minutes, or until heated through. Carefully turn the pie over halfway through the cooking time.

PILAFF

Pilaff is a spicy rice dish of Persian origin. The rice is cooked in stock flavoured with spices and herbs until all the liquid has been absorbed. Chicken, cooked meat, fish, fruit or vegetables are also added to make it a tasty meal-in-one.

Fruited chicken pilaff

Full Power
22 minutes

200 g (7 oz) rice
500 mℓ (16 fl oz) water
1 chicken stock cube
200 g (7 oz) mixed dried fruit, coarsely chopped
30 mℓ (2 tablespoons) raisins
salt and black pepper
pinch of turmeric
generous pinch of cinnamon
generous pinch of dried thyme
½ onion, chopped
1 celery stick, thinly sliced
30 g (1 oz) butter
400 g (14 oz) cooked chicken, coarsely chopped
90 g (3 oz) fresh or canned pineapple pieces, drained
60 mℓ (4 tablespoons) coarsely chopped pecan nuts

Place rice, water, crumbled stock cube, dried fruits, raisins, salt and pepper, turmeric, cinnamon and thyme in a large casserole. Stir well, cover and microwave on Full Power for 15 minutes. Stand for 15 – 20 minutes or until liquid is absorbed. Meanwhile, place onion, celery and butter in a bowl and microwave for 2 – 3 minutes, until onion is tender. At the end of the standing time for the rice, add onion mixture, chicken, pineapple pieces and nuts. Microwave, covered, for 3 – 4 minutes or until heated through.
Serves 4 – 6

PILCHARDS

This inexpensive source of protein is often overlooked. Canned pilchards are available plain, in tomato sauce or with chilli. Substitute pilchards for other types of fish, use them to top a quick microwaved pizza or add to a pasta casserole or to a fish pie.

Cheesy tomatoes with pilchards

Full Power, High (70%)
13 minutes

6 tomatoes
45 g (1½ oz) margarine
1 onion, chopped
30 g (1 oz) soft white breadcrumbs
2.5 mℓ (½ teaspoon) dried thyme
425 g (15 oz) canned pilchards in tomato sauce
30 mℓ (2 tablespoons) chopped parsley
salt and black pepper
75 g (2½ oz) Cheddar cheese, grated
15 g (½ oz) margarine
45 mℓ (3 tablespoons) dried breadcrumbs
5 mℓ (1 teaspoon) paprika

Slice tops of tomatoes, remove flesh and set aside. Place margarine in a bowl, microwave on Full Power for 1 minute. Add onion, toss to coat with margarine. Microwave for 3 minutes, then add half the tomato. Microwave for 4 minutes.

Stir in soft breadcrumbs, thyme, pilchards, parsley, seasonings and three-quarters of the cheese. Fill tomatoes with mixture. Microwave 15 g (½ oz) margarine for 30 seconds. Add remaining cheese, dried breadcrumbs and paprika, stir to combine. Top each stuffed tomato with this mixture. Arrange in a circle on a plate, cover with waxed paper. Microwave on High (70%) for about 4 – 5 minutes. Serve hot.
Makes 6

PINEAPPLE

This popular tropical fruit is usually available year round, and if fully ripe needs very little added sugar. Simply served, it is a worldwide favourite. Pineapple can be used in salads, cooked with ham or pork and other savoury foods, or be flavoured with Kirsch, vodka, sherry or white wine and served as a dessert.

Fresh pineapple contains an enzyme called bromeline that acts on proteins. For this reason, fresh pineapple cannot be used in dishes which contain gelatine or fresh cream. Cooked or canned pineapple is safe to use, however, as the enzyme is destroyed by heat.

Pineapple dessert

Full Power
9 minutes

30 g (1 oz) desiccated coconut
5 mℓ (1 teaspoon) butter
1 large pineapple, peeled and cut into chunks
300 g (11 oz) canned mandarin oranges, drained
150 g (5 oz) seedless green grapes
75 g (2½ oz) soft brown sugar
45 mℓ (3 tablespoons) rum
30 g (1 oz) butter

Place coconut in a small bowl. Microwave butter for 10 seconds to melt, then add to the coconut, mixing well. Microwave coconut on Full Power for 2 – 2½ minutes, stirring every 15 seconds. The coconut should be lightly browned. Place pineapple, mandarins, grapes, brown sugar, rum and remaining butter in a casserole. Cover and microwave for 4 – 6 minutes, until bubbly. Sprinkle with the coconut and serve warm with cream, or chill if desired.
Serves 6

PITTA BREAD

Pitta, the unleavened, flat bread of the Middle East, is sometimes called 'pocket bread', as it is hollow inside and makes a perfect edible container for any number of sandwich or salad fillings. Pitta bread is available from delicatessens and many large supermarkets and is useful for making a quick and tasty meal.

To thaw frozen pitta bread, separate pieces and defrost three at a time. Place on kitchen paper and microwave on Defrost (30%) for 30 – 40 seconds. Stand for 1 – 2 minutes.

Mexican beef pittas

Full Power
12 minutes

500 g (18 oz) minced beef
1 small onion, chopped
1 garlic clove, finely chopped
½ green pepper, chopped
30 g (1 oz) raisins
5 mℓ (1 teaspoon) salt
30 – 45 mℓ (2 – 3 tablespoons) chilli sauce
45 mℓ (3 tablespoons) chutney
2.5 mℓ (½ teaspoon) cinnamon
125 g (4 oz) tomatoes, chopped
30 g (1 oz) almonds, toasted
45 g (1½ oz) stuffed olives, sliced
6 – 8 pitta breads, halved
½ small head of lettuce, shredded
250 mℓ (8 fl oz) soured cream

Crumble beef into a casserole, add onion and garlic. Cover with waxed paper and microwave on Full Power for 3 minutes. Break up and stir. Cover and microwave for 2 – 3 minutes longer or until very little pink remains in the meat. Drain. Add green pepper, raisins, salt, chilli sauce, chutney and cinnamon. Microwave, covered, until hot for 3 – 4 minutes. Stir in tomato, half the almonds and olives. Microwave, covered, until heated through for 1 – 2 minutes. Spoon mixture into pitta bread halves and garnish with shredded lettuce, soured cream and the remaining almonds.
Serves 6 – 8

Note: The meat mixture can be made in advance and reheated before serving in the pitta breads.

PIZZA

Pizza means 'pie' in Italian, and in its simplest form is a round of dough, spread with tomato or tomato sauce and Mozzarella cheese, then baked in a hot oven. The range of ingredients added to a pizza is almost limitless, and could include onions, salami, sausage, minced beef, olives, anchovies, herbs, mushrooms, prawns, tuna and a variety of cheeses. Microwaved pizzas are not quite as crisp as conventionally baked ones, but turn out reasonably successfully. For best results use a special pizza browning dish and follow the manufacturer's instructions.

To microwave frozen pizza
Place on kitchen paper and microwave on Full Power for 4 – 5 minutes. You may wish to cover the pizza with waxed paper to prevent spattering. Frozen pizzas can also be heated on a browning dish.

To reheat a wedge of cooked pizza
Place on kitchen paper or paper plate and microwave on Full Power for about 30 seconds if pizza is at room temperature, 45 seconds if refrigerated or 1 minute if frozen.

Easy pizza

Full Power
5 minutes

125 g (4 oz) plain flour
generous pinch of cream of tartar
pinch of bicarbonate of soda
pinch of oregano
30 g (1 oz) margarine
60 mℓ (4 tablespoons) milk

Topping
345 mℓ (11 fl oz) tomato topping*
100 g (3½ oz) Cheddar cheese, grated
30 g (1 oz) canned anchovy fillets
few stuffed olives, sliced

To make the base, sift the dry ingredients. Add the oregano and margarine, and rub in. Mix to a moist scone dough consistency with the milk. Grease a 20-cm (8-inch) plate or pizza plate and press the dough to fit. Microwave on Full Power for 2 minutes. Spread tomato mixture over the dough. Sprinkle with cheese and arrange anchovy fillets in a lattice design. Place a slice of stuffed olive in each 'diamond'. Microwave for 3 minutes. Stand for at least 2 minutes before serving.
Serves 4

Italian pizza

Full Power, Defrost (30%)
25 minutes

125 mℓ (4 fl oz) warm water
5 mℓ (1 teaspoon) dried yeast
5 mℓ (1 teaspoon) caster sugar
250 g (9 oz) plain flour
5 mℓ (1 teaspoon) salt
30 mℓ (1 tablespoon) oil
690 mℓ (22 fl oz) tomato topping*
400 g (14 oz) Mozzarella cheese, thinly sliced
60 g (2 oz) canned anchovies, sliced
    lengthwise

Combine the water, yeast and sugar in a small bowl. Sprinkle 45 mℓ (3 tablespoons) of measured flour on to the yeast mixture, but do not stir in. Cover with plastic wrap. Microwave for 30 seconds on Full Power. Leave to stand until bubbles form. Sift flour and salt into a mixing bowl. Add oil to yeast mixture, then add this liquid to the flour. Mix to a firm dough and knead until smooth. Shape into a ball and brush it with a little extra oil to prevent a skin from forming. Place in a large bowl and cover tightly with plastic wrap. Microwave on Full Power for 15 seconds. Rest for 5 minutes. Repeat this three or four times, until the dough has doubled in size.
    Divide risen dough into four portions and knead each piece lightly. Roll each portion into a 20-cm (8-inch) round. Grease four plates and dust lightly with flour. Cover plates with dough. Microwave each round of dough on Defrost (30%) for 15 seconds, then rest for 4 minutes. Repeat at least twice, or until dough has doubled in size.

Divide the tomato topping between the flour pizzas, and spread over the dough. Cover with slices of cheese, and finally with slices of anchovy. Microwave pizzas, uncovered, one at a time on Full Power for 5 minutes. Stand for at least 3 minutes before serving.
Serves 4

Variations
Seafood Pizza: 200 g (7 oz) canned shrimps, drained, 225 g (8 oz) canned mussels, drained, 15 mℓ (1 tablespoon) chopped parsley. Arrange on top of cheese.
Mushroom Pizza: 350 g (12 oz) mushrooms, sliced, 30 mℓ (1 tablespoon) oil, generous pinch of dried thyme. Combine all the ingredients. Add to pizza, on top of cheese.
Artichoke Pizza: 400 g (14 oz) canned artichokes, drained and sliced, 30 mℓ (2 tablespoons) chopped parsley, 30 mℓ (2 tablespoons) capers. Add to pizza, on top of cheese.
Salami Pizza: 20 thin slices salami. Arrange salami around the edges of pizza, on top of cheese.
Ham Pizza: 100 g (3½ oz) ham, diced, 30 mℓ (2 tablespoons) chopped parsley, paprika. Combine ham and parsley, add to pizza on top of cheese and sprinkle with paprika.
Tuna Pizza: 200 g (7 oz) canned tuna, drained and flaked, 10 mℓ (2 teaspoons) lemon juice, 2 celery sticks, chopped. Combine all the ingredients. Add to pizza on top of cheese.

Note: For a special pizza use a combination of two or more of these variations.

PLUMS
The plum is a delicious fruit that comes in a variety of colours, shapes and sizes. It has sweet, light flesh, a pleasant aroma and a flat stone. Plums can be eaten raw, or be combined with other fruits in stewed fruits and made into pies or puddings.

To stew plums, wash 500 g (18 oz) plums, remove stones and place in casserole. Sprinkle with 125 g (4 oz) caster sugar and the grated rind of ½ lemon if desired. Cover and microwave on Full Power for about 5 minutes or until plums are soft, stirring gently at least once.

Baked plum dessert

Full Power
15 minutes

1 kg (2¼ lb) ripe plums, halved and stoned
60 mℓ (4 tablespoons) honey
30 mℓ (2 tablespoons) medium sherry
225 g (8 oz) plain flour
15 mℓ (1 tablespoon) baking powder
5 mℓ (1 teaspoon) salt
30 g (1 oz) caster sugar
60 g (2 oz) butter
1 egg, beaten
90 mℓ (3 fl oz) milk
15 mℓ (1 tablespoon) soft brown sugar
5 mℓ (1 teaspoon) cinnamon

Place plums in a shallow baking dish. Mix honey and sherry and add to plums. Cover with vented plastic wrap and microwave on Full Power for 5 minutes, stirring once. Meanwhile, combine flour, baking powder, salt and sugar. Rub in butter until the mixture resembles fine crumbs. Mix the egg and milk and add to the dry ingredients to form a soft dough. Reserve enough of the milk mixture to brush top of dough. Pat dough out on a floured surface and stamp out 8 – 10 rounds. Place rounds of dough in an overlapping circle on top of plums and brush with remaining milk mixture. Mix brown sugar and cinnamon together and sprinkle over dough. Microwave for 8 – 10 minutes, or until dough is nicely risen. Serve warm. *Serves 6*

Plum ice cream

Full Power, Defrost (30%)
10 minutes

500 g (18 oz) red plums
100 g (3½ oz) caster sugar
250 mℓ (8 fl oz) single cream
100 mℓ (3½ fl oz) milk
3 egg yolks
caster sugar

Cut plums in half, remove stones. Place in a shallow casserole, sprinkle with sugar. Cover, microwave on Full Power for 5 – 6 minutes. Allow to cool, then purée until smooth. In a large jug, combine cream and milk, microwave for 2 minutes. Beat yolks well, add cream and stir to combine. Microwave on Defrost (30%) for 3 minutes, stirring every minute. Cool and combine with puréed fruit. Add sugar to taste. Freeze until solid. Cut into 3-cm (1¼-inch) blocks. Fit a food processor with bowl and metal blade, process blocks in two batches until pale in colour and smooth. Freeze until firm. Serve in scoops.
Serves 6

POACHING
Poaching refers to foods cooked in a flavoured or seasoned liquid or stock. It is a method of cooking suited to the microwave, especially for eggs, fish, poultry and some fruits.
See also Eggs and Fish

POPCORN
Popcorn is a special type of maize with small, hard kernels. When exposed to dry heat, the kernels burst open and turn inside out, resulting in a white starchy mass, more than twice the size of the original kernel. Popcorn is generally eaten with a dusting of salt and melted butter, but it may also be coated with caramel (see page 45) or flavoured with seasoning salt, finely grated cheese, garlic butter or even sugar.

Read the instructions for your microwave before attempting to pop corn in it, as many manufacturers do not recommend it. The syrup or savoury coating, however, can easily be prepared in a microwave.

Popcorn Seasonings
Curried popcorn: Place 45 g (1½ oz) butter in a jug and microwave on Full Power for 30 seconds. Pour over 225 g (8 oz) of popped corn and toss to mix well. Combine 2.5 mℓ (½ teaspoon) curry powder, a generous pinch of turmeric, a generous pinch of ground ginger and a pinch of cayenne. Sprinkle over popcorn and toss well.
Herbed popcorn: Place 45 g (1½ oz) butter in a jug and microwave on Full Power for 30 seconds. Pour over 225 g (8 oz) popped corn. Combine ½ chicken stock cube, crumbled, 5 mℓ (1 teaspoon) dried parsley, 2.5 mℓ (½ teaspoon) dried sage, 2.5 mℓ (½ teaspoon) celery salt and 5 mℓ (1 teaspoon) dried marjoram. Sprinkle over corn, tossing well to mix.
Savoury popcorn: Combine 90 g (3 oz) pretzel rings with 450 g (1 lb) popped corn in a large casserole dish. Place 60 g (2 oz) butter in a jug and microwave on Full Power for 45 seconds or until melted. Add 30 ml (2 tablespoons) onion soup powder and stir well. Pour over popcorn and toss well. Microwave on Full Power for 2 minutes, stirring once. Cool, then store in an airtight container.

PORK
Pork is a versatile meat that lends itself easily to microwave cooking and can always be counted upon to provide a nutritious and satisfying meat. It can be seasoned with savoury, spicy or sweet ingredients.

Fresh pork should have pale pink flesh with firm, creamy-coloured fat. Most pork now comes from young animals, and if properly prepared and cooked, will give tender results. Many cookbooks used to recommend that pork be well cooked to minimize the danger of parasites, but with new developments in breeding, and improved care during feeding, it is now safe to cook pork to the internal temperature of 75°C (167°F). At this temperature, the flesh should stay moist and tender.

Kasseler rib is the German way of making smoked pork rib or loin. It can be left in one piece or divided into chops. If cooked whole, it is best placed in a roasting bag with desired liquid to keep moisture and flavour in. Chops can be marinated and baked or boiled with seasonings.

Serving suggestion
☐ For a delicious mustard topping, cover baked kasseler chops with a mixture of 30 ml (2 tablespoons) prepared mustard, 15 ml (1 tablespoon) wine vinegar and 5 ml (1 teaspoon) brown sugar. Microwave on Full Power for 1 minute.

Pork and ginger casserole

Full Power
25 minutes

1 kg kasseler chops
15 mℓ (1 tablespoon) oil
1 onion, chopped
1 large carrot, sliced
2 celery sticks, sliced
salt and black pepper
15 mℓ (1 tablespoon) cornflour
30 mℓ (2 tablespoons) water
generous pinch of ground ginger

Marinade
30 mℓ (2 tablespoons) honey
60 mℓ (4 tablespoons) brown vinegar
30 mℓ (2 tablespoons) tomato sauce
generous pinch of sage
5 mℓ (1 teaspoon) Worcestershire sauce
150 mℓ (5 fl oz) ginger ale
15 mℓ (1 tablespoon) dry mustard
1 garlic clove, crushed

Place chops in a shallow dish. Combine all the ingredients for the marinade, pour over chops and stand for at least 1 hour. Drain chops, place in a shallow casserole and cover. Microwave on Full Power for 10 minutes, keep warm. In another dish, microwave oil for 1 minute, add onion, carrot and celery. Toss to coat with oil. Microwave for 4 minutes, stirring once during cooking time. Season lightly. Combine cornflour, water and ginger and add to vegetables, with the marinade. Microwave for 7 minutes, stirring at least once during cooking time. Pour over meat, microwave for 2 – 3 minutes until piping hot.
Serves 4

Italian pork chops

Full Power
18 minutes

4 pork chops, about 2.5-cm (1-inch) thick
1 onion, chopped
5 mℓ (1 teaspoon) dried basil
2.5 mℓ (½ teaspoon) dried oregano
30 g (1 oz) butter
30 mℓ (2 tablespoons) cornflour
400 g (14 oz) canned whole tomatoes, chopped
15 mℓ (1 tablespoon) tomato paste
45 mℓ (3 tablespoons) dry white wine
5 mℓ (1 teaspoon) lemon juice
15 mℓ (1 tablespoon) chopped parsley
150 mℓ (5 fl oz) chicken stock
salt and black pepper

Place chops in a casserole with the thin ends towards the centre and microwave on Full Power for 6 minutes. Remove from the microwave and keep warm. Combine onion, basil and oregano in a jug and microwave for 4 minutes, stirring once. Add butter and stir to melt. Mix in cornflour, undrained tomatoes, tomato paste, wine, lemon juice, parsley and stock. Microwave, covered, for 3 – 4 minutes,

stirring every minute. Adjust seasoning if necessary. Pour sauce over drained chops and microwave 3 – 4 minutes. Serve with hot buttered noodles or rice.
Serves 4

Glazed pork spare-ribs

Full Power, Medium (50%)
2 hours

1.5 kg (3 lb) pork spare-ribs, cut in portions
500 mℓ (16 fl oz) hot water
1 onion, sliced
1 lemon, sliced
salt and black pepper

Glaze
125 mℓ (4 fl oz) tomato sauce (as served with pasta)
30 mℓ (2 tablespoons) chilli sauce
200g (7 oz) red currant jelly
30 mℓ (2 tablespoons) soy sauce

Place spare-ribs, bone side up, in a large casserole. Add the water, cover and microwave on Medium (50%) for 40 minutes. Turn spare-ribs over, cover with onion and lemon slices and sprinkle with salt and pepper. Cover and microwave for another 40 minutes. Drain spare-ribs and discard onion and lemon.

To make the glaze, mix tomato sauce, chilli sauce, red currant jelly and soy sauce in a large jug and microwave, covered, on Full Power for 3 minutes. Stir and pour over spare-ribs. At this point the spare-ribs can be refrigerated, covered, for 24 hours. To reheat, cover spare-ribs and microwave on Medium (50%) for about 30 minutes, rearranging every 10 minutes. The spare-ribs should be hot and very tender.

The spare-ribs can also be finished off over a barbecue. Place over hot coals and brush several times with the glaze until nicely browned and heated through.
Serves 4 – 6

Pork fillets in apple and wine sauce

Full Power
26 minutes

4 pork fillets
1 onion, chopped
100 g (3½ oz) mushrooms, sliced
1 celery stick, sliced
1 small apple, peeled and sliced
10 mℓ (2 teaspoons) lemon juice
5 mℓ (1 teaspoon) grated lemon rind
5 mℓ (1 teaspoon) chopped parsley
5 mℓ (1 teaspoon) chopped sage
5 mℓ (1 teaspoon) chopped tarragon
30 g (1 oz) butter
45 g (1½ oz) plain flour
60 mℓ (4 tablespoons) chicken stock
90 mℓ (3 fl oz) apple juice
125 mℓ (4 fl oz) white wine
salt and pepper

To garnish
apple slices

PORK CHART

	DEFROSTING TIME Per 500 g (18 oz) On Defrost (30%)	COOKING TIME Per 500 g (18 oz) On Full Power	METHOD
Leg	8 – 9 minutes, stand 1 – 1½ hours	11 – 14 minutes, stand 20 minutes	Select a joint with a uniform shape. Tie into shape if necessary.
Loin	6 – 8 minutes, stand 30 minutes	8 – 11 minutes, stand 10 minutes	Shield bone-end during defrosting and half-way through cooking time.
Chops	3 – 5 minutes, stand 10 – 15 minutes	10 – 12 minutes, stand 2 minutes	Separate chops during defrosting. Microwave in browning dish. Turn after 3 minutes.

Place fillets in a shallow dish and microwave, covered, on Full Power for 11 – 13 minutes. Turn fillets over and rearrange halfway through cooking time. Remove from the microwave and keep warm.

Combine onion, mushrooms, celery, apple slices, lemon juice, lemon rind, parsley, sage and tarragon in a bowl. Cover and microwave for 5 minutes. Stir in butter, then flour. Drain meat juices and add to stock, along with the apple juice and wine. Stir into flour mixture and microwave for 3 – 4 minutes, stirring every minute.

Pour sauce over fillets, turn to coat with sauce and microwave, covered, for 3 – 4 minutes. Stand for 5 minutes before serving. To serve, slice fillets, arrange on a platter and spoon sauce over. Garnish with apple slices.
Serves 6

Stuffed roast loin of pork

Full Power, Medium (50%)
50 minutes

1 loin of pork, boned (about 1.5 kg (3 lb))
30 mℓ (2 tablespoons) oil
5 mℓ (1 teaspoon) salt

Stuffing
1 onion, chopped
30 g (1 oz) butter
125 g (4 oz) soft white breadcrumbs
5 mℓ (1 teaspoon) dried sage
salt and pepper
45 mℓ (3 tablespoons) finely chopped dried apricots
45 mℓ (3 tablespoons) peach chutney
generous pinch of curry powder
beaten egg to bind

To make the stuffing, place onion and butter in a small bowl and microwave on Full Power for 4 minutes. Add breadcrumbs, sage and seasoning, apricots, chutney and curry powder. Bind ingredients together with a little beaten egg.

Lay pork on a board and make a deep slit in the meaty part. Fill with stuffing, then bring edges together and tie or sew to form a good shape. Score the skin with a sharp knife and brush with oil. Sprinkle with salt and place on a roasting rack in a casserole.

Cover with a tent of waxed paper and microwave on Medium (50%) for 13 – 15

minutes per 500 g (18 oz). If crackling is not crisp, place pork under a hot grill for a few minutes, then stand, covered, for 10 – 15 minutes before serving.
Serves 6 – 8

Note: If a temperature probe or microwave meat thermometer is used, the reading should be 75°C (167°F).

Pork fillet with spinach stuffing

Full Power
21 minutes

750 g (1¾ lb) pork fillets, about 4
30 g (1 oz) butter
30 mℓ (2 tablespoons) French mustard
300 g (11 oz) spinach
30 mℓ (2 tablespoons) oil
1 small onion, chopped
30 mℓ (2 tablespoons) chopped parsley
30 mℓ finely chopped chives
salt and black pepper
300 g (11 oz) streaky bacon, rinds removed
30 mℓ (2 tablespoons) plain flour
75 mℓ (2½ fl oz) red wine
100 mℓ (3½ fl oz) chicken stock
100 mℓ (3½ fl oz) single cream

To garnish
pear slices
parsley sprigs

Make a lengthwise slit in the meat, without cutting it into two. Open out flat, place meat between two layers of plastic wrap, pound gently with a meat mallet or the side of a cleaver until about 5-mm (¼-inch) thick. Spread meat with butter and French mustard. Wash spinach well, place in a large bowl with water that clings to the leaves. Cover with vented plastic wrap, microwave for 4 minutes. Drain, chop coarsely, set aside.

Microwave oil in a bowl for 30 seconds. Add onion, toss to coat with oil and microwave for 2 minutes. Add spinach, parsley, chives and seasonings. Divide filling between fillets, roll up lengthwise. Wrap bacon around meat to secure. Arrange meat in a casserole, cover with waxed paper. Microwave on Full Power for 9 – 10 minutes, turning meat over halfway through cooking time. Remove meat and drain off excess fat. Add flour to fat residue, microwave for 30 seconds. Stir in wine and stock,

microwave for 4 minutes. Add meat, cover and microwave for 4 – 6 minutes. Stir in cream, microwave for 1 – 3 minutes more until piping hot. To serve, cut meat in 2.5-cm (1-inch) thick slices, spoon a little sauce over meat. Garnish with pear slices and parsley sprigs.
Serves 6

Pork goulash

Full Power, High (70%), Medium (50%)
1 hour

60 mℓ (4 tablespoons) oil
1 onion, chopped
1 garlic clove, crushed
2 bacon rashers, rinds removed, chopped
750 g (1¾ lb) stewing pork, cubed
45 g (1½ oz) plain flour
10 mℓ (2 teaspoons) paprika
salt and black pepper
2.5 mℓ (½ teaspoon) dried sage
400 mℓ (13 fl oz) chicken stock
60 mℓ (4 tablespoons) tomato paste
2 carrots, sliced
2 potatoes, diced
1 bay leaf

Place oil in a large casserole, microwave on Full Power for 2 minutes. Add onion, garlic and bacon, microwave for 3 minutes. Toss cubes of pork in flour, paprika, seasonings and sage. Add to onion mixture, stir to combine. Microwave for 2 minutes. Stir in remaining ingredients and cover. Microwave on High (70%) for 15 minutes, stand for 10 minutes. Uncover, microwave on Medium (50%) for 35 minutes, stirring from time to time. Remove bay leaf. Stand for at least 5 minutes before serving.
Serves 4 – 6

PORRIDGE

All types of porridge oats are easily and quickly cooked in the microwave. Porridge can be microwaved in one large container or in individual serving dishes. Washing-up is simplified as the porridge does not stick to the cooking dish.

To microwave porridge

Mix dry porridge oats with hot tap water in a container large enough to prevent mixture from boiling over. Microwave, uncovered, on Full Power, stirring mixture halfway through cooking time. Add raisins, sultanas or nuts for variety, or try adding fresh fruit, honey, butter, jam or marmalade.

POT ROAST *See* Beef Pot Roasts

POTATOES

The baked potato is truly a wonder of microwave cooking. One potato can be baked in 4 – 6 minutes and six potatoes take just 20 – 25 minutes. Not only are microwaved potatoes baked quickly, they taste great too, and left-over potatoes can be saved for another use. The microwave is also useful for cooking new potatoes

PORRIDGE MICROWAVE CHART

	SERVINGS	WATER	SALT	CEREAL	CONTAINER	COOKING TIME on Full Power
Oatmeal, quick	1	185 mℓ (6 fl oz)	generous pinch	60 g (2 oz)	large cereal bowl	1 – 2 minutes
	2	375 mℓ (12 fl oz)	2.5 mℓ (½ teaspoon)	125 g (4 oz)	1-litre (1¾-pint) bowl	2 – 3 minutes
	4	750 mℓ (1¼ pints)	2.5 mℓ (½ teaspoon)	250 g (9 oz)	2-litre (3½-pint) bowl	5 – 6 minutes
Cream of wheat	1	250 mℓ (8 fl oz) (or half milk)	generous pinch	45 g (1½ oz)	large cereal bowl	2½ – 3 minutes
	2	450 mℓ (14½ fl oz) (or half milk)	2.5 mℓ (½ teaspoon)	60 g (2 oz)	1-litre (1¾-pint) bowl	4½ – 5½ minutes
	4	815 mℓ (26 fl oz) (or half milk)	2.5 mℓ (½ teaspoon)	125 g (4 oz)	2-litre (3½-pint) bowl	6½ – 8 minutes

quickly and boiling potatoes for mashed potatoes. Potato casseroles can also be cooked quickly and easily in the microwave.

Potato chips, oven chips and roast potatoes depend on oil and hot dry air to become golden brown and crisp, so cook them conventionally.

Baked potatoes

Wash potatoes and pat dry. Prick with a fork or skewer in several places. Place potatoes on kitchen paper at least 2.5 cm (1 inch) apart. If microwaving several potatoes, arrange them in a circle as shown. Turn potatoes over after half the cooking time. Microwave on Full Power. Potatoes may still feel firm when done, but will soften while standing. If you wrap them in aluminium foil, shiny side in, after they have been microwaved, they will keep warm for up to 30 minutes.

QUANTITY	TIMING
1	4 – 6 minutes
2	6 – 8 minutes
3	8 – 12 minutes
4	12 – 16 minutes
5	16 – 20 minutes
6	20 – 25 minutes

Potato toppings

These toppings add interest and flavour to microwave baked potatoes. Make up two or three and let everyone help themselves. Each makes enough for four baked potatoes.

Chive topping: Mix 30 ml (2 tablespoons) finely chopped chives and a generous grinding of freshly ground black pepper into 250 ml (8 fl oz) soured cream.

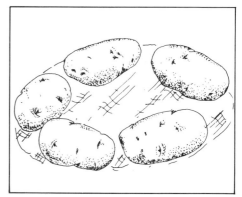

Baked potatoes are ideal for cooking in a microwave. Arrange the potatoes at least 2.5 cm (1 inch) apart in a circle on kitchen paper.

Tangy topping: Mix 90 ml (3 fl oz) mayonnaise into 125 ml (4 fl oz) single cream. Add 10 ml (2 teaspoons) lemon juice, 15 ml (1 tablespoon) finely chopped onion, and 3 anchovy fillets, chopped. Season with pepper to taste.

Blue cheese topping: Grate or finely chop 100 g (3½ oz) blue-veined cheese and mix into 250 ml (8 fl oz) soured cream. Add black pepper to taste and stir in 10 ml (2 teaspoons) chopped parsley.

Bacon cheese topping: Mix 15 ml (1 tablespoon) finely chopped onion, 60 ml (4 tablespoons) grated Cheddar cheese and 3 cooked, chopped bacon rashers into 250 ml (8 fl oz) soured cream and season well with pepper.

Bangers and mash stuffed potatoes

Full Power
6 minutes

4 baked potatoes*
60 g (2 oz) butter
milk
125 g (4 oz) pork sausage-meat
2.5 mℓ (½ teaspoon) dried sage
30 mℓ (2 tablespoons) chopped parsley
30 mℓ (2 tablespoons) chopped onion
90 g (3 oz) Cheddar cheese, grated
salt and black pepper

Cut tops off the baked potatoes and carefully scoop out flesh. Mash the flesh with the butter and add a little milk to moisten. Place crumbled sausage-meat in a casserole with the sage, parsley and onion. Microwave on Full Power for 3 – 4 minutes or until no pink remains in the meat, stirring twice. Drain mixture and stir into the potato mixture with half the grated cheese. Season with salt and pepper. Add a little more milk if the mixture is too stiff. Spoon into potato shells, place potatoes on kitchen paper, sprinkle with remaining cheese and microwave for about 2 minutes to heat through.
Serves 4

Mashed potatoes

Full Power, High (70%)
20 minutes

4 medium-sized potatoes
45 mℓ (3 tablespoons) water
salt and pepper
45 g (1½ oz) margarine
30 – 45 mℓ (3 – 4 tablespoons) milk
pinch of baking powder

Peel and quarter potatoes. Place in a 1-litre (1¾-pint) bowl. Add water and a little salt and pepper. Cover and microwave on Full Power for 16 – 18 minutes or until potatoes are soft. Drain well and stand for 2 – 3 minutes. Add margarine and milk to potatoes, then beat until smooth. Add baking powder and seasoning to taste. Beat once again until fluffy. Reheat for 2 minutes on High (70%).
Serves 4

New potatoes

Full Power
13 minutes

500 g (18 oz) new potatoes
30 mℓ (2 tablespoons) water
salt and black pepper
30 g (1 oz) butter
15 mℓ (1 tablespoon) chopped parsley

Scrub potatoes well and prick skins. Place in a large bowl with water, cover and microwave on Full Power for 12 – 13 minutes. Stand for 5 minutes before serving. Season with salt and pepper, melted butter, and parsley if desired.
Serves 4 – 6

Note: Dried mint or thyme also tastes good with new potatoes.

Crunchy topped potatoes

Full Power
15 minutes

3 large potatoes, peeled and halved lengthwise
45 g (1½ oz) butter

Topping
30 g (1 oz) pecan nuts, chopped
45 g (1½ oz) celery, chopped
30 mℓ (2 tablespoons) brown onion soup mix
15 mℓ (1 tablespoon) chopped parsley
5 mℓ (1 teaspoon) chopped dill
30 g (1 oz) Cheddar cheese, grated

To make the topping, combine pecans, celery, soup mix, parsley and dill. Place grated cheese in a separate small bowl.

Make a criss-cross pattern in the cut-side of each potato half with a sharp knife. Place butter in a casserole and microwave on Full Power for about 1 minute. Toss potatoes in butter, then place cut-side down in the dish. Cover and microwave for 11 - 12 minutes, or until potatoes are tender. Turn potatoes over and rearrange half-way through cooking time.

Sprinkle each potato half with some of the topping mixture and a little of the grated cheese. Microwave for 1½ – 2 minutes to heat through and melt cheese.
Serves 6

Potatoes au gratin

Full Power
42 minutes

60 g (2 oz) butter
750 g (1¾ lb) onions, thinly sliced
750 g (1¾ lb) potatoes, thinly sliced
5 mℓ (1 teaspoon) freshly grated nutmeg
salt and black pepper
30 mℓ (2 tablespoons) chopped parsley
200 g Emmenthal or Gruyère cheese, grated
375 mℓ (12 fl oz) milk

Microwave butter in a large casserole on Full Power for 1 minute. Add onion, stir well. Cover and microwave for about 20 minutes or until onions are tender. Combine potatoes, nutmeg, salt, pepper and parsley, tossing to coat. Place half the potatoes in a large casserole. Add half the onions, then half the cheese. Repeat layers. Microwave milk for 1 minute, then pour over cheese. Microwave, covered, for 18 – 20 minutes, or until potatoes are tender. Stand for 5 minutes before serving.
Serves 8

Potato and onion slices

Full Power
18 minutes

15 g (½ oz) butter
1 onion, sliced
4 potatoes, sliced
salt and black pepper
150 mℓ (5 fl oz) milk
45 g (1½ oz) butter
15 mℓ (1 tablespoon) chopped parsley

Place butter in a bowl, microwave on Full Power for 45 seconds. Add onion, toss to coat with butter, microwave for 2 minutes. Grease a flat casserole, arrange a layer of potatoes in the dish. Add a layer of onion and cover with remaining potato. Place seasonings, milk and butter in a jug. Microwave for 1 minute on Full Power, pour over potatoes. Cover and microwave for 16 – 18 minutes, until potatoes are tender. Sprinkle with chopped parsley.
Serves 4 – 6

POULTRY *See* individual names

PRALINE *See* Almonds

PRAWNS
Prawns, one of the world's most popular seafoods, are small, clawless crustaceans with a sweet, delicate flavour. They are available fresh in some areas, but are usually sold frozen. When thawed they should be firm and unbroken, with a translucent, greyish shell.

Prawns turn bright pink and become opaque when cooked. For best results, they should be simmered gently, not violently boiled. Prawns that are slightly undercooked are soft; overcooking will only toughen them. The exact cooking time depends on the size of the prawns, so they should be watched carefully.

To clean prawns, thaw and rinse. Slit the back of the shell with a pair of scissors or a sharp knife and remove the black vein which may be gritty, especially in larger prawns. The head, shell and tail may be removed or left on, depending on the recipe.
To thaw prawns, place 500 g (18 oz) large, unshelled prawns in a microwave container. Cover with waxed paper and microwave on Defrost (30%) for 7 – 8 minutes. Stand for 5 minutes. For small, peeled prawns, microwave for 2 – 4 minutes, stand 5 minutes.

Mussel and Leek Starter (page 157), an impressive starter

To microwave prawns

Devein 500 g (18 oz) prawns and set aside. Microwave 500 ml (16 fl oz) salted water in a large container for 4 – 5 minutes, or until boiling. Add prawns and microwave on High (70%) for 4 – 5 minutes, or until they turn opaque and pink. Drain and serve hot or chilled. For small peeled prawns, microwave for 2 – 4 minutes.

How to clean a prawn

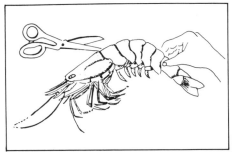

With a pair of scissors or a sharp knife slit open the back of the shell starting at the head end.

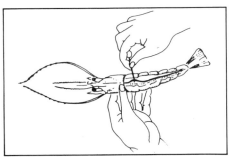

Insert a wooden cocktail stick beneath the vein until you have dislodged it.

Prawns flambéed with whisky

Full Power, Medium (50%)
12 minutes

1 kg (2¼ lb) prawns, unpeeled
30 mℓ (2 tablespoons) chopped thyme
15 mℓ (1 tablespoon) chopped parsley
30 mℓ (2 tablespoons) dry white wine
30 mℓ (2 tablespoons) lemon juice
5 mℓ (1 teaspoon) grated lemon rind
30 mℓ (2 tablespoons) oil
black pepper
30 g (1 oz) butter
pinch of salt
60 mℓ (4 tablespoons) whisky

Peel prawns and devein, leaving tails intact. Mix together the thyme, parsley, wine, lemon juice, lemon rind, oil and pepper. Pour over prawns and marinate for 8 hours or overnight in the refrigerator.

To cook, drain prawns, reserving the liquid. Microwave butter in a casserole dish on Full Power for 1 minute. Add liquid from the prawns and salt. Microwave for 2 – 3 minutes or until boiling. Add prawns, cover and microwave on Medium (50%) for 8 – 10 minutes or until

prawns turn pink. Remove dish from microwave. Microwave whisky in a jug for 15 seconds, pour over prawns and ignite. When flames subside, spoon prawns into small dishes, add juices and serve immediately.
Serves 4

Seafood roll with lemon sauce

High (70%), Full Power, Defrost (30%)
20 minutes

500 g (18 oz) cod or haddock
3 eggs
125 mℓ (4 fl oz) single cream
salt and black pepper
250 g (9 oz) peeled and deveined prawns
225 g (8 oz) canned pink salmon, bones and skin removed
45 mℓ (3 tablespoons) chopped parsley

Sauce
250 mℓ (8 fl oz) dry white wine
30 mℓ (2 tablespoons) lemon juice
250 g (9 oz) butter
salt
cayenne
2.5 mℓ (½ teaspoon) grated lemon rind
6 spring onions, chopped

To garnish
8 prawns, unpeeled
shredded spring onion tops, soaked in iced water for 1 hour

To make seafood roll, place cubes of cod or haddock in bowl of a food processor, process until smooth. Pour in eggs, cream and seasonings, process until smooth. Chill for at least 1 hour. Coarsely chop prawns, add flaked salmon and parsley, chill well. Fold prawn mixture into cod or haddock mixture.

Cut two pieces of parchment paper 40 x 25-cm (16 x 10-inch), spray or grease lightly. Divide mixture between the two sheets, form into two rolls. Wrap each roll carefully, tie the ends with string, place on a microwave baking sheet. Microwave on High (70%) for 12 – 14 minutes, do not overcook. Carefully remove rolls and place on a board, stand for 5 minutes. Slice thickly with a serrated knife, arrange two slices on each plate. Spoon a little sauce over each portion, garnish with a whole prawn and shreds of spring onion. Serve immediately.

To make sauce, combine wine and lemon juice in a bowl, microwave on Full Power for about 4 minutes, until the mixture has reduced by half. Whisk in butter a little at a time. Microwave on Defrost (30%) for 2 minutes, whisking every 30 seconds. Whisk in seasonings, grated lemon rind and spring onions.

To cook prawn garnish, remove vein from the back of the prawn. Place prawns on a plate, cover with vented plastic wrap. Microwave on High (70%) for 2 – 3 minutes, until just pink in colour. Remove prawn shell, leaving tail intact.
Serves 6 as a starter

Prawn cocktail

Full Power, High (70%)
16 minutes

750 mℓ (1¼ pints) beer
1 bay leaf
10 mℓ (2 teaspoons) pickling spice
10 mℓ (2 teaspoons) grated lemon rind
1 kg (2¼ lb) prawns, peeled and deveined
lettuce leaves

Cocktail sauce
45 mℓ (3 tablespoons) chilli sauce
90 mℓ (3 fl oz) tomato sauce
60 mℓ (4 tablespoons) mayonnaise
15 mℓ (1 tablespoon) grated horseradish
30 mℓ (2 tablespoons) finely chopped onion
5 mℓ (1 teaspoon) dried dill
15 mℓ (1 tablespoon) lemon juice
15 mℓ (1 tablespoon) Worcestershire sauce
few drops of Tabasco

To make the sauce, combine all ingredients, mixing well. Cover and chill until needed.

Combine beer, bay leaf, spices and lemon rind in a deep casserole. Microwave on Full Power for 8 minutes or until mixture boils. Add prawns and microwave on High (70%) for 7 – 8 minutes, or until prawns turn pink, stirring occasionally. Drain well, remove shells, leaving tails intact, and chill.

To serve, arrange prawns on lettuce leaves on small plates and top with cocktail sauce.
Serves 4 – 6

PRESERVES *See* Chutney, Jams, Pickling, etc.

PRUNES

Prunes are plums which are picked and dried when fully ripe so as to capture all the sweetness and flavour. Stewed prunes are sometimes eaten as dessert or are served at breakfast, but they are also stewed with other fruits and used in puddings, cakes or stuffings.
To plump prunes, heat 250 ml (8 fl oz) water on Full Power for 2 – 3 minutes, pour over dried prunes and stand for a few minutes.

Stewed prunes

Full Power, Defrost (30%)
15 minutes

350 g (12 oz) dried prunes
500 mℓ (16 fl oz) hot water
60 g (2 oz) caster sugar

Place prunes in a casserole and add hot water. Cover and microwave on Full Power for 4 – 6 minutes or until boiling. Stir, cover and microwave on Defrost (30%) for 5 – 7 minutes or until prunes are tender. Add sugar, cover and microwave for 2 minutes more to dissolve sugar.
Makes about 400 g (14 oz)

Prunes with brandy or sherry

Full Power
3 minutes

350 g (12 oz) dried prunes
30 g (1 oz) raisins
½ lemon, thinly sliced
200 mℓ (6½ fl oz) brandy or medium sherry
200 mℓ (6½ fl oz) apple juice

Place prunes, raisins and lemon in a 1-litre (1¾-pint) jar. Combine brandy or sherry and apple juice in a large jug and microwave on Full Power for 3 minutes. Pour over fruit and stand overnight. Store in the refrigerator and serve with meat or in fruit salad.
Makes about 400 g (14 oz)

PUDDING

This culinary term sometimes describes the dessert course of a meal, the content of which can be anything from a light soufflé to a rich Christmas pudding. In general, however, the term refers to baked desserts such as sponge or steamed pudding, bread puddings and Christmas puddings. The microwave is a great help in preparing these types of puddings.
See also Christmas pudding.

Vanilla pudding

Full Power
8 minutes

150 g (5 oz) caster sugar
30 mℓ (2 tablespoons) cornflour
500 mℓ (16 fl oz) milk
2 egg yolks, lightly beaten
30 g (1 oz) butter
few drops of vanilla extract

Combine sugar and cornflour. Beat in milk and microwave on Full Power for 6 – 7 minutes, stirring well every 2 minutes. The mixture should be thick and bubbly. Stir a small amount of the hot mixture into the egg yolks, then return to the bowl. Mix well and microwave for 1 minute. Mix in butter and vanilla extract. Cover surface of pudding with waxed paper and cool, then chill. Spoon into individual dishes to serve.
Serves 4

Variation
Chocolate Pudding: Add 100 g (3½ oz) plain chocolate broken in small pieces to the hot mixture before adding the egg yolks.

Apricot sponge pudding

Defrost (30%)
9 minutes

400 g (14 oz) canned apricot halves, drained
30 mℓ (2 tablespoons) golden syrup
60 g (2 oz) margarine
60 g (2 oz) caster sugar
1 egg, beaten
125 g (4 oz) plain flour
5 mℓ (1 teaspoon) baking powder
generous pinch of salt
60 mℓ (4 tablespoons) milk

Place apricot halves in a well-greased 750 mℓ (1¼-pint) deep baking dish. Drizzle golden syrup over the apricots. Mix margarine, sugar and egg with dry ingredients until smooth. Then gradually add milk to give a soft consistency. Spoon mixture over apricots and smooth the surface. Microwave on Defrost (30%) for 7 – 9 minutes, or until the top of the mixture is only slightly moist. Stand for 5 minutes. Turn out on a serving dish and serve with cream or custard*.
Serves 4

Spicy steamed pudding

Full Power, High (70%)
19 minutes

220 mℓ (7 fl oz) water
30 mℓ (2 tablespoons) brandy
150 g (5 oz) sultanas
30 g (1 oz) butter
100 g (3½ oz) caster sugar
150 g (5 oz) molasses
1 egg
175 g (6 oz) plain flour
5 mℓ (1 teaspoon) bicarbonate of soda
5 mℓ (1 teaspoon) salt
2.5 mℓ (½ teaspoon) cinnamon
pinch of nutmeg

Microwave water on Full Power for 3 minutes, add brandy and pour over sultanas and stand until cool. Beat the butter with sugar, molasses and the egg. Sift dry ingredients together and add to butter mixture along with the sultanas and water. Mix well and pour into a greased 2-litre (3½-pint) ring dish. Cover with vented plastic wrap and microwave on High (70%) for 14 – 16 minutes or until pudding appears set but still glossy. Remove from the oven, stand for 15 – 20 minutes, then turn out on a wire rack to cool. When cool, wrap well and age in the refrigerator for about one week before serving.
Serves 10

Hot sponge pudding mixes

Full Power
6 minutes

300 g (11 oz) packet sponge pudding mix

Follow packet instructions for mixing. Place in a deep, 1-litre (1¾-pint) casserole and

microwave on Full Power for 5½ – 6½ minutes. Serve warm.
Serves 4

PUMPKIN

Pumpkins are firm-fleshed vegetables of the gourd family. They come in many shapes and sizes and are at their best in autumn and early winter. The sweetish orange flesh is rich in vitamins and is used for soups, as a vegetable dish and as an ingredient in breads or muffins and in American pumpkin pie.
See also Butternut and Squash.

To microwave pumpkin

Peel and dice 450 g (1 lb) pumpkin, place in a casserole. Add 45 ml (3 tablespoons) water, cover and microwave on Full Power for 8 – 10 minutes or until tender.

Curried pumpkin soup

Full Power, Medium (50%)
23 minutes

1 large onion, sliced
2 young leeks, white part only, sliced
60 g (2 oz) butter
250 g (9 oz) cooked pumpkin*
1 litre (1¾ pints) chicken stock
1 bay leaf
2.5 mℓ (½ teaspoon) sugar
2.5 mℓ (½ teaspoon) curry powder
pinch of nutmeg
30 mℓ (2 tablespoons) chopped parsley
500 mℓ (16 fl oz) single cream
salt and black pepper
single cream
parsley sprigs

Place onions and leeks in a casserole with the butter and microwave on Full Power until tender, about 4 minutes. Add pumpkin, stock, bay leaf, sugar, curry powder, nutmeg and chopped parsley. Microwave, covered, for 4 minutes, then reduce power to Medium (50%) and microwave for 10 minutes more, stirring occasionally. Purée in a food processor or blender and return to the pan. Add cream and season to taste with salt and pepper. Microwave on Medium (50%) for 4 – 5 minutes to heat through. Serve garnished with swirls of cream and parsley sprigs.
Serves 6

Overleaf left: clockwise, Cheese Ramekins (page 52), Prawn and Tomato Timbales (page 212), Orange Crème Caramel (page 71), Crème Brûlée (page 71), Smoked Salmon with Smoked Trout Mousse (page 216)
Overleaf right: from top to bottom, Trout (page 216): fried, poached and devilled

QUENELLES

Quenelle is a French term for a finely textured, souffléed dumpling that is gently poached in stock or water. Chicken, fish, veal and potato may all be used for quenelles. The ingredients are pounded or blended to a paste, which is well chilled, then gently shaped into ovals and placed in a buttered dish. Hot liquid is carefully added and the quenelles are simmered until done. Quenelles may be served as an entrée, in soups or used as a garnish for other foods.

Salmon quenelles with dill sauce

Full Power, Medium (50%)
11 minutes

170 mℓ (5½ fl oz) dry white wine
15 mℓ (1 tablespoon) water
30 g (1 oz) butter
30 g (1 oz) wholewheat flour
salt and pepper
5 mℓ (1 teaspoon) chopped fresh dill
25 mℓ (5 teaspoons) grated onion
1 egg
1 egg white
225 g (8 oz) canned red salmon, drained and
   flaked
375 mℓ (12 fl oz) hot water
5 mℓ (1 teaspoon) salt

Dill sauce
125 mℓ (4 fl oz) plain yoghurt
30 g (1 oz) cream cheese or low-fat soft cheese
10 mℓ (2 teaspoons) finely chopped dill

To garnish
fresh dill
radish slices
spring onions

Place 45 mℓ (1½ fl oz) of the wine and the water in a 1-litre (1¾-pint) glass bowl and microwave on Full Power for 45 seconds. Add butter and stir to melt . Add flour, salt and pepper and mix well to form a ball. Leave to cool for a few minutes, then add dill, onion and egg and beat well. Beat egg white to stiff peaks and fold into flour mixture. Fold in salmon and chill very well.

To cook, lightly grease a large, deep casserole. Using two spoons, mould the fish mixture into eight ovals and place in casserole dish. Combine hot water, remaining wine and salt. Gently pour down side of dish. Cover and microwave on Medium (50%) for 7 – 9 minutes until quenelles are set. Remove quenelles with a slotted spoon, draining well. Arrange two on each of four individual serving plates.

To make the sauce, place yoghurt, cheese and dill in a measuring jug and microwave on Medium (50%) for 30 – 45 seconds. Stir well. Pour a little of the sauce over each quenelle and garnish with dill, radish slices and spring onions.
Serves 4

QUICHE

A quiche is an open savoury flan with an egg custard filling and a shortcrust base. A variety of other ingredients, such as cooked bacon, ham, onion, cheese, spinach or seafoods, can be added to the basic egg mixture, and often several ingredients are combined to produce delicious results. When microwaving quiche, it is important to partially bake the pastry crust before adding the filling to prevent the crust from becoming soggy.

Basic quiche

Full Power, Medium (50%)
17 minutes

1 x 22.5-cm (9-inch) shortcrust pastry shell*
5 mℓ (1 teaspoon) Worcestershire sauce
1 egg yolk

Filling
15 g (½ oz) butter
1 onion, chopped
5 mℓ (1 teaspoon) mixed herbs
125 g (4 oz) Cheddar cheese, grated
4 eggs
125 mℓ (4 fl oz) single cream
125 mℓ (4 fl oz) milk
dash of Tabasco
salt and pepper

Brush pastry with mixture of Worcestershire sauce and egg yolk. Microwave on Full Power for 2 minutes, then cool. For the filling, microwave butter for 30 seconds, add onion, toss to coat and microwave 2 minutes. Add herbs. Sprinkle three-quarters of the cheese over the bottom of the pastry, top with onion mixture. Combine eggs, cream, milk, Tabasco, salt and pepper and mix well. Gently pour over onion and cheese and microwave on Medium (50%) for 11 – 13 minutes. Sprinkle with remaining cheese during last minute of cooking. Stand for 5 – 10 minutes before serving.
Serves 6 – 8

Variations
Mozzarella Quiche: Use Mozzarella cheese instead of Cheddar and basil instead of mixed herbs. During last minute of cooking, arrange sliced tomatoes on top.
Bacon Quiche: Add 100 g (3½ oz) cooked chopped bacon to quiche after adding onion.
Spinach Quiche: Mix 125 g (4 oz) cooked, well drained, chopped spinach with the onion and herbs. Stir in a pinch of nutmeg. Substitute soured cream for fresh cream.

QUICK BREADS

Quick breads are the answer for those who want to have homemade bread, but do not have much time. Quick breads are not leavened by yeast, but use baking powder or bicarbonate of soda. The basic ingredients are similar for all quick breads, but they differ according to the amounts used and how they are mixed or baked. Many quick breads react well to microwave baking, especially coffee cakes, fruit breads, American muffins and yoghurt breads which rise well and look good too. Although scones can be baked in the microwave, they do not brown and need added ingredients to give an attractive appearance. Many quick breads can be baked in a ring dish and this gives an interesting appearance and promotes even baking. Those containing brown sugar, treacle or wholewheat flour look better than plain quick breads which may need to be sprinkled with wheatgerm, cornflake crumbs or chopped nuts to give a more appetizing finish.

When converting quick bread recipes for microwave use, it may be necessary to decrease the liquid by about 30 ml (2 tablespoons) if the batter is very moist. Increasing fat by about 30 g (1 oz) will improve the texture if the batter is not very rich.
See also Muffins and Scones.

Savoury celery and onion loaf

High (70%)
6 minutes

225 g (8 oz) self-raising flour
2.5 mℓ (½ teaspoon) salt
generous pinch of baking powder
15 g (½ oz) sultanas, rinsed
1 celery stick
2 eggs
15 mℓ (1 tablespoon) finely chopped onion
125 g (4 oz) low-fat soft cheese
45 g (1½ oz) soft butter or margarine

Sift flour, salt and baking powder into a mixing bowl, and add sultanas. Cut celery into 1-cm (½-inch) lengths and place in the goblet of an electric blender. Add eggs, onion, cottage cheese and soft butter. Blend until smooth, then add to the dry ingredients and mix thoroughly, making a dough of a fairly stiff consistency. Spoon into a greased 20-cm (8-in) ring pan and microwave on High (70%) for 5½ – 6 minutes, or until well risen and a wooden cocktail stick inserted near the centre comes out clean. Stand in the pan for 10 minutes, then turn out on a wire rack and cool.
Makes 1 ring loaf

Walnut coffee bread

High (70%)
8 minutes

250 g (9 oz) plain flour
15 mℓ (1 tablespoon) baking powder
2.5 mℓ (½ teaspoon) salt
10 mℓ (2 teaspoons) instant coffee powder
150 g (5 oz) soft butter or margarine
3 eggs
150 g (5 oz) soft brown sugar
100 g (3½ oz) walnuts, coarsely chopped
45 mℓ (3 tablespoons) milk

Combine flour, baking powder, salt and instant coffee powder in a mixing bowl. Add remaining ingredients and beat well. Spoon mixture into a deep, greased 22.5-cm (9-inch) ring pan and microwave on High (70%) for 7 – 8 minutes. Stand 10 minutes in the pan, then turn out on a wire rack to cool.
Makes 1 ring loaf

Peanut butter loaf

High (70%)
8 minutes

100 g (3½ oz) self-raising flour
100 g (3½ oz) wholewheat flour
5 mℓ (1 teaspoon) salt
5 mℓ (1 teaspoon) baking powder
60 g (2 oz) soft brown sugar
90 g (3 oz) peanut butter
220 mℓ (7 fl oz) milk
30 mℓ (2 tablespoons) finely chopped nuts

Combine flours, salt and baking powder in a mixing bowl. Stir in sugar. Rub in peanut butter until the mixture is crumbly. Add milk and mix well. Spoon mixture into a greased loaf dish and sprinkle with nuts. Microwave on High (70%) for 7½ – 8½ minutes. Stand in the dish 10 minutes, then turn out on a wire rack to cool.
Makes 1 loaf

Marsala date bread

High (70%)
9 minutes

2 eggs
250 g (9 oz) plain flour
100 g (3½ oz) caster sugar
100 g (3½ oz) soft brown sugar
100 mℓ (3½ fl oz) Marsala
75 mℓ (2½ fl oz) oil
15 mℓ (1 tablespoon) baking powder
2.5 mℓ (½ teaspoon) bicarbonate of soda
2.5 mℓ (½ teaspoon) salt
150 g (5 oz) stoned dates, coarsely chopped
100 g (3½ oz) walnuts, coarsely chopped

Beat eggs until well mixed, then add remaining ingredients except dates and nuts. Mix well, then stir in dates and nuts. Spoon into a greased 22.5-cm (9-inch) ring dish and microwave on High (70%) for 8 – 9 minutes, or until a wooden cocktail stick inserted near the

centre comes out clean. Stand 10 minutes in the dish, then turn out on a wire rack to cool.
Makes 1 ring loaf

Wholewheat quick bread

High (70%)
12 minutes

250 g (9 oz) wholewheat flour
60 mℓ (4 tablespoons) crushed wheat
30 mℓ (1 tablespoon) wheatgerm
5 mℓ (1 teaspoon) salt
5 mℓ (1 teaspoon) bicarbonate of soda
15 mℓ (1 tablespoon) molasses
350 mℓ (11 fl oz) buttermilk
crushed wheat

Combine flour, crushed wheat, wheatgerm and salt in a bowl. Mix bicarbonate of soda, molasses and buttermilk together. Add to dry ingredients, stir well. Brush a 25 x 12.5-cm (10 x 5-inch) loaf dish with oil, sprinkle dish liberally with crushed wheat. Spoon in bread mixture, sprinkle with crushed wheat. Microwave on High (70%) for 12 – 13 minutes. Stand for 10 minutes in the dish, invert on to a cooling rack. Serve warm.
Makes 1 loaf

Cornmeal bread

Medium (50%), Full Power
9 minutes

125 g (4 oz) cornmeal
125 g (4 oz) plain flour
30 g (1 oz) caster sugar
5 mℓ (1 teaspoon) salt
15 mℓ (1 tablespoon) finely chopped onion
2.5 mℓ (½ teaspoon) mixed herbs
45 g (1½ oz) Cheddar cheese, grated
1 egg
250 mℓ (8 fl oz) milk
125 mℓ (4 fl oz) oil

Combine cornmeal, flour, sugar, baking powder, salt, chopped onion, herbs and cheese, mixing well. Beat egg, milk and oil together and add to the dry ingredients, mixing well. Pour mixture into a well-greased 20-cm (8-inch) ring dish and microwave on Medium (50%) for 5 minutes, then microwave on Full Power for 2 – 4 minutes or until a wooden cocktail stick inserted near the centre comes out clean. Stand for 5 minutes, then turn out and cool on a wire rack.
Makes 1 ring loaf

QUINCE

The quince is a yellow, pear-shaped fruit with a tart, astringent flavour. It is not eaten raw, but has a high pectin content and is excellent for jams and jellies. Stewed quinces can be served hot with whipped cream or custard* or can accompany venison or lamb roasts.
See also Fruit, stewed

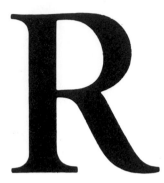

R

RABBIT

Rabbit is a very versatile meat, mild in flavour and at its best cooked in sauces containing red or white wine, herbs and spices and even mustard. Like most tender meats, rabbit cooks fairly quickly and microwaves well. The flesh tends towards dryness, so it is best cooked in a well-seasoned stock, or a mixture of stock and wine. Vegetables with distinct flavours, such as onions or tomatoes, also improve the flavour of rabbit.

Braised rabbit with brandy cream sauce

Full Power, High (70%)
28 minutes

1 rabbit, cut into 6 – 8 pieces
45 mℓ (3 tablespoons) seasoned flour
90 g (3 oz) butter
1 onion, chopped
1 garlic clove, finely chopped
75 mℓ (2½ fl oz) brandy
5 mℓ (1 teaspoon) dried tarragon
5 mℓ (1 teaspoon) dried thyme
salt and black pepper
200 mℓ (6½ fl oz) chicken stock
125 mℓ (4 fl oz) Madeira
125 mℓ (4 fl oz) single cream
300 g (11 oz) mushrooms, sliced
parsley

Rinse rabbit pieces and pat dry. Dredge with seasoned flour. Melt half the butter in a frying pan and brown pieces of rabbit conventionally. Meanwhile, microwave remaining butter in a large casserole on Full Power for 1 minute. Add chopped onion and garlic and microwave for 3 minutes. Remove casserole from oven, add

Previous page left: Upside-down Gingerbread (page 104), Pineapple Upside-down Cake (page 221)
Previous page right: Rhubarb Charlotte (page 185), Pineapple Rice Pudding with Meringue (page 188)

rabbit pieces. Warm half the brandy on Full Power for 15 seconds. Pour over rabbit and ignite. When flame subsides, add remaining brandy, tarragon, thyme and salt and pepper.

Pour in stock and Madeira, cover and microwave for 15 minutes, stirring and rearranging pieces twice. Remove rabbit pieces and keep warm. Stir cream into the liquid and microwave on High (70%) for 5 – 7 minutes, stirring frequently, until sauce is slightly thickened. Stir in mushrooms, microwave for 2 minutes more and serve sauce over the rabbit. Garnish with parsley.
Serves 4

RAMEKINS

Small, straight-sided ramekin dishes made of china, pyrex or pottery are ideal for use in the microwave. Though these dishes are commonly used for individual servings of crème caramel, crème brûlée, pâtés and so on, they can also be used in the microwave for poaching eggs, making individual baked desserts such as rum babas or even individual servings of vegetables. When microwaving food in ramekin dishes, be sure to arrange them in a circle for even cooking.

Tasty egg ramekins

Full Power, Medium (50%)
6 minutes

2 – 3 bacon rashers, rinds removed, and chopped
10 button mushrooms, chopped
15 mℓ (1 tablespoon) chopped chives or parsley
salt and black pepper
60 mℓ (4 tablespoons) single cream
4 eggs

Divide bacon between four ramekins, arrange ramekins in a circle in the microwave. Microwave on Full Power for 2 – 3 minutes. Add mushrooms, stir to combine, microwave for 1 minute. Add chives and seasonings, spoon

15 mℓ (1 tablespoon) cream into each dish. Carefully add an egg to each ramekin, prick the yolks with a needle and cover loosely with waxed paper. Microwave on Medium (50%) for 2½ – 3 minutes, stand for about 1 minute before serving.
Serves 4

Variations
☐ Use 1 – 2 skinned and chopped tomatoes in place of mushrooms or bacon.
☐ Add 15 mℓ (1 tablespoon) grated cheese to each ramekin with the cream.
☐ Spoon 30 mℓ (1 tablespoon) creamed spinach into each ramekin, top with 15 mℓ (1 tablespoon) single cream, 15 mℓ (1 tablespoon) grated cheese and an egg. Microwave as above.

RASPBERRIES

Fresh raspberries are one of the most delicious summer fruits, making only a brief appearance in most supermarkets and greengrocers. Canned and frozen raspberries are always available. Fresh raspberries freeze well. Place the punnets in small plastic bags and freeze for later use.

Frosty raspberry squares

Full Power
7 minutes

75 g (2½ oz) butter
125 g (4 oz) plain flour
45 g (1½ oz) soft brown sugar
1 litre (1¾ pints) vanilla ice cream
500 mℓ (16 fl oz) raspberry flavoured yoghurt
400 g (14 oz) canned raspberries
15 mℓ (1 tablespoon) Kirsch
15 mℓ (1 tablespoon) cornflour

Microwave the butter in a 20-cm (8-inch) square glass baking dish on Full Power for 30 seconds. Mix in flour and brown sugar and spread evenly in the dish. Microwave for 3 – 4 minutes or until lightly browned, stirring every minute. Reserve about 60 g (2 oz) of the mixture, and press remaining mixture evenly over the bottom of the dish. Cool. To make the filling, soften ice cream and lightly mix in yoghurt. Carefully spread over the base, and top with reserved crumb mixture. Freeze, covered, for 8 hours or overnight.

To make the sauce, carefully drain the raspberries. Place the juice and liqueur in a jug and add enough water to measure 250 mℓ (8 fl oz). Stir in cornflour and microwave for 2½ – 3 minutes, stirring every minute. Add raspberries. Cut frozen mixture into squares and serve with warm raspberry sauce.

Serves 9 – 12

RATATOUILLE

A versatile and colourful vegetable dish originating in Provence, ratatouille generally consists of green peppers, aubergines, tomatoes and courgettes. Try adding cheese, mint or other herbs for a fresh variation. This dish may be eaten hot or cold, as a vegetable accompaniment, cold starter or as a well-chilled salad.

Ratatouille

Full Power
17 minutes

45 mℓ (3 tablespoons) oil
1 large onion, chopped
1 green pepper, sliced
1 garlic clove, crushed
4 courgettes, sliced
1 medium-sized aubergine, diced
2 tomatoes, skinned and chopped
100 mℓ (3½ fl oz) tomato purée or pousada
salt and black pepper
100 g (3½ oz) mushrooms, sliced
15 mℓ (1 tablespoon) chopped mint
30 mℓ (1 tablespoon) Parmesan cheese

Microwave oil in a large bowl on Full Power for 1 minute. Add onion, green pepper and garlic, toss to coat with oil. Cover, microwave for 3 minutes. Stir in courgettes, aubergines, tomatoes and tomato purée, cover and microwave for 10 minutes. Stir in seasonings, mushrooms and mint, cover and microwave for 3 minutes more. Sprinkle with cheese and serve.

Serves 6 – 8

REDUCE

To reduce a liquid means to boil it down in order to concentrate the flavour and thicken to the consistency of a sauce. This is easily and speedily done in the microwave. *See* Sauces.

REHEATING FOODS

One of the microwave's most outstanding features is the excellent results achieved when foods are reheated. Dinners no longer need to be kept warm for hours on end, as food is reheated in a minute or two when it is needed. Foods may be prepared in advance and be reheated with no loss of flavour, colour or texture.

Hints for reheating foods

☐ When reheating most foods, cover with waxed paper so as to hold in the heat and at the same time allow the steam to escape.
☐ Stir stews and casseroles when reheating.
☐ Sausage rolls and pies should be heated with care as overcooking occurs quickly.
☐ When reheating a plate of food, all the foods should be at the same temperature. Arrange the plate so that the food which takes the longest to heat is on the outside.
☐ Canned foods need only be heated before serving, as they are already completely cooked.
☐ Remove frozen 'dinners' and casseroles from their foil trays before reheating.
☐ Be sure foods are properly heated before serving and are not just warmed around the edges. The food is usually heated through when the centre of the underside of the container is warm.

RHUBARB

Technically a vegetable, rhubarb is widely used in sweet dishes, pies and jams. It mixes with fruits such as apples and strawberries, and combines well with ginger, orange or even angelica. Pale pink, young stems of rhubarb have the best flavour, while the older, deep red stems tend to be very acidic and need plenty of sweetening. The leaves of rhubarb are high in acid content and should be discarded.

To microwave rhubarb

Wash and trim 450 g (1 lb) rhubarb stems and cut into 3-cm (1¼-inch) lengths. Add 100 g (3½ oz) caster sugar and a strip of lemon peel. Microwave on Full Power for 8 – 10 minutes, then stand until cool.

Rhubarb charlotte

Full Power
16 minutes

Topping
125 g (4 oz) soft white breadcrumbs
60 g (2 oz) soft brown sugar
2.5 mℓ (½ teaspoon) ground ginger
generous pinch of cinnamon
10 mℓ (2 teaspoons) finely grated orange rind
125 g (4 oz) butter
15 mℓ (1 tablespoon) orange liqueur

Filling
450 g (1 lb) rhubarb
1 apple
175 g (6 oz) caster sugar
10 mℓ (2 teaspoons) grated orange rind
15 mℓ (1 tablespoon) water
15 mℓ (1 tablespoon) orange liqueur
125 g (4 oz) fresh strawberries, halved

To make the topping, mix breadcrumbs with sugar, ginger, cinnamon and orange rind. Microwave butter on Full Power for 1 – 1½ minutes and pour over the breadcrumbs. Sprinkle with orange liqueur and microwave for 3 – 4 minutes, stirring twice.

To make the filling, wash and trim rhubarb and cut into 1-cm (½-inch) slices. Core and slice apple and add to rhubarb. Add the sugar, orange rind, water and orange liqueur. Microwave on Full Power for 8 – 11 minutes or until rhubarb is tender, stirring at least once. Add strawberries and gently mix together. Layer the fruit mixture with the breadcrumb mixture in a bowl, ending with a layer of the breadcrumb mixture. Serve warm or cold with custard* or cream.

Serves 6

RICE

This popular grain forms the staple diet of over half the world's population. Originating in Asia, it has been cultivated in India and China for over 5 000 years. Whilst there are many varieties of rice, those most frequently used are white polished rice and brown rice.

Cooking rice in the microwave has both advantages and disadvantages. Rice must be fully hydrated during the cooking process and the microwave cannot speed up this process. It may be advantageous to cook the rice conventionally, leaving the microwave free to cook sauces or toppings for the rice. On the other hand, when cooked in the microwave, the rice will not burn if neglected. Another advantage is that rice reheats far better in a microwave oven than it does conventionally.

RICE COOKING CHART

	QUANTITY	COOKING TIME (on Full Power)	PREPARATION
Rice	200 g (7 oz)	12 – 15 minutes, stand 20 minutes	Add 500 mℓ (16 fl oz) boiling water, 2.5 mℓ (½ teaspoon) salt, 5 mℓ (1 teaspoon) oil and cover. Keep sealed during standing time.
Brown rice	200 g (7 oz)	25 – 30 minutes, stand 20 minutes	Add 600 mℓ (19 fl oz) boiling water, 2.5 mℓ (½ teaspoon) salt, 5 mℓ (1 teaspoon) oil and cover. Keep sealed during standing time.

Overleaf left: top, Warm Lettuce Salad (page 192); bottom left, Main Dish Chicken Pasta Salad (page 192); bottom right, Fennel and Walnut Salad (page 93)

Overleaf right: Cream of Vegetable Soup has several variations (page 201)

To reheat rice, place rice in a suitable container, cover tightly and microwave on Full Power for 1 – 3 minutes, depending on the quantity. Stir lightly with a fork to 'fluff' up the rice. No additional liquid is necessary when reheating rice.

Spanish rice

Full Power, Medium (50%)
40 minutes

4 bacon rashers, rinds removed, cooked*
60 g (2 oz) butter
1 onion, chopped
1 green pepper, seeded and chopped
1 small garlic clove, finely chopped
1 celery stick, thinly sliced
2 x 400-g (14-oz) cans whole tomatoes, drained
    and coarsely chopped
reserved tomato liquid plus water to equal
    500 mℓ (16 fl oz)
200 g (7 oz) rice
salt and black pepper
few drops of Tabasco
60 g (2 oz) Cheddar cheese, grated

Crumble bacon and set aside. Microwave butter in a large casserole on Full Power for 1 minute. Stir in onion, green pepper, garlic and celery. Microwave for 4 – 5 minutes or until ingredients are tender. Add tomatoes and liquid. Cover and microwave about 6 minutes, or until boiling. Add the rice, season with salt, pepper and Tabasco and mix well. Microwave, covered with vented plastic wrap, on Medium (50%) for 25 – 28 minutes, or until rice is tender and liquid has been absorbed. Sprinkle bacon and cheese over before serving.
Serves 6

Pineapple rice pudding with meringue

Full Power, Medium (50%)
38 minutes
Bake 160 °C / 325 °F / gas 3
25 minutes

75 g (2½ oz) rice
45 g (1½ oz) caster sugar
600 mℓ (19 fl oz) milk
15 g (½ oz) butter
200 mℓ (6½ fl oz) single cream
400 g (14 oz) canned pineapple chunks,
    drained
10 mℓ (2 teaspoons) chopped ginger
3 eggs, separated
100 g (3½ oz) caster sugar

Place rice, sugar, milk and butter into a large bowl, microwave on Full Power for 8 minutes, stirring twice. Add cream, reduce power to Medium (50%), microwave for 25 – 30 minutes, stirring every 5 minutes, cover and stand for 10 minutes. Stir in pineapple chunks, ginger and egg yolks. Pour into a greased 20-cm (8-inch) pie plate. Cover, microwave for 5 minutes. Beat whites until stiff, gradually beat in caster sugar until stiff peaks form. Spread on top of rice mixture. Place in a conventional oven at 160 °C / 325 °F / gas 3 for 25 minutes, until meringue begins to brown. Serve hot.
Serves 6

RISOTTO
An Italian dish consisting of rice, spices and a selection of chopped vegetables cooked together and served in a variety of ways. Like all rice dishes cooked in the microwave, there is no time advantage when microwaving risotto. However, the vegetables retain both colour and shape particularly well and the rice remains fluffy and is not too dry. Risotto may be eaten either as a main dish or as a vegetable.

Risotto

Full Power
20 minutes

30 g (1 oz) butter
1 onion, chopped
1 garlic clove, crushed
1 small green pepper, or 2 celery sticks,
    chopped
200 g (7 oz) rice
500 mℓ (16 fl oz) boiling chicken stock
salt and black pepper
1 bay leaf
30 g (1 oz) Parmesan cheese, grated
30 mℓ (1 tablespoon) chopped parsley

Place butter in a casserole, microwave on Full Power for 1 minute, add onion, garlic and green pepper, toss to coat with butter. Microwave for 4 minutes, stirring once. Add rice, stock, seasonings and herbs. Cover, microwave for 15 minutes, stirring at least twice during cooking time. Stand tightly covered for 20 minutes. Remove bay leaf, add Parmesan and parsley.
Serves 6 as a side dish

Variations
☐ Add 250 g (9 oz) peeled and deveined prawns 5 minutes before the cooking time is completed.
☐ Fry 2 chopped bacon rashers with onion mixture. Stir in 200 g (7 oz) sliced mushrooms at the beginning of standing time.
☐ Add pinch of turmeric, 2 chopped tomatoes and 2 sliced courgettes before adding boiling stock.

ROASTING *See* Beef Roast and individual names

ROASTING BAGS
Roasting bags are convenient and extremely efficient containers for foods cooked in the microwave. They promote the browning of roast meats and poultry, while retaining heat and moisture. They can also be used for cooking vegetables and portions of meat or chicken in a marinade.

Do not use a metal or foil strip to seal the bag, as the metal becomes very hot and the paper covering can ignite. Fasten with string or an elastic band and make one or two slashes to prevent the bag from 'ballooning' during cooking. If a lot of liquid is being cooked in a bag, tie string loosely to allow the steam to escape and do not make slashes.

Warning: Do not use plastic bags as a substitute for roasting bags in the microwave.

Tangy chicken drumsticks

Full Power, High (70%)
23 minutes

60 mℓ (4 tablespoons) soy sauce
30 mℓ (2 tablespoons) honey
75 mℓ (2½ fl oz) tomato sauce (as served with
    pasta)
1 garlic clove, crushed
75 mℓ (2½ fl oz) dry sherry
pinch of ground ginger
10 – 12 chicken drumsticks
30 mℓ (2 tablespoons) cornflour
30 mℓ (2 tablespoons) water

Place all the ingredients, except drumsticks, cornflour and water, in a cooking bag. Microwave on Full Power for 1 minute, until honey melts. Now add drumsticks and spoon mixture over until well covered. Stand for 2 – 3 hours, turning from time to time. Tie bag loosely with string. Microwave on High (70%) for 20 minutes, stand for 5 minutes. Remove drumsticks, arrange in a shallow dish, cover and keep warm. Combine cornflour with a little water, stir into sauce. Microwave for 2 – 3 minutes until thickened, stirring once during cooking time. Spoon the sauce over the drumsticks and serve.
Serves 6

Chicken roasted in a bag

High (70%)
26 minutes

1 – 1.5 kg (2¼ – 3 lb) chicken
salt and black pepper
1 small onion
rosemary sprig
15 mℓ (1 tablespoon) oil

Season chicken with salt and pepper. Place onion and rosemary sprig in the cavity, pour oil on to chicken. Place chicken in a roasting bag. Tie the end loosely with a piece of string to allow the steam to escape. Microwave on High (70%) for 26 – 30 minutes. Stand for 10 minutes before serving.
Serves 4
For a browner appearance, brush chicken with a little soy or Worcestershire sauce and sprinkle with paprika or barbecue spice.

ROQUEFORT

Roquefort cheese is a blue French cheese made from sheep's milk. It has a creamy texture with blue veining, and a natural rind. The flavour is strong and sharp. Any blue cheese may be substituted for Roquefort in most recipes.

Roquefort rarebit

Full Power, High (70%)
9 minutes

125 mℓ (4 fl oz) light beer
30 g (1 oz) plain flour
15 mℓ (1 tablespoon) chopped parsley
pinch of dry mustard
225 g (8 oz) Cheddar cheese, grated
225 g (8 oz) Roquefort cheese, crumbled
6 slices of hot buttered toast

Place beer in a large casserole and microwave on Full Power for 3 minutes. Combine flour, parsley and dry mustard and sprinkle over cheeses, mixing well. Remove casserole from the oven and mix in cheeses, beating well. Return to oven and microwave on High (70%) for 3 minutes. Mix well, then microwave for 2 – 3 minutes more, until mixture is well heated. Mix again, then serve on hot buttered toast.
Serves 6

ROTI

This flat, round unleavened bread is made from either wholewheat or white flour. Roti is traditionally Indian and is served instead of bread with curries. In many Indian and Malay homes, rotis are still made daily. They are best eaten on the day that they are made.

Wholewheat roti

Full Power
40 minutes

125 g (4 oz) plain flour
125 g (4 oz) wholewheat flour
salt
15 mℓ (1 tablespoon) ghee* or 15 g (½ oz) butter, softened
100 mℓ (3½ fl oz) water
30 mℓ (1 tablespoon) milk
extra ghee or melted butter

Place flours and salt in the bowl of a food processor or in a mixing bowl, rub in ghee or softened butter. Add liquids to form a firm dough, knead well. Wrap dough in plastic wrap, stand for 1 hour before using. Divide dough into twelve portions, roll each one paper-thin to form a 20-cm (8-inch) circle, brush each roti with a little ghee. Heat browning dish on Full Power for 5 minutes, lay roti flat, microwave for 30 seconds, turn and microwave for 35 seconds. Reheat browning dish for 2 – 3 minutes each time before cooking additional rotis.
Makes 12

ROUX

Roux refers to equal quantities of flour and butter cooked together and used as a basis for sauces or as a thickening agent. The roux may be a white, fawn or brown colour, according to the length of cooking time.
See also Sauces.

RUM BABA

This rich yeast dessert is typically French. The dough used is identical to that for a savarin, with the addition of dried fruit (see below). Babas may be made in small ring moulds, ramekin dishes or custard cups. For directions to microwave rum babas *see* Savarin but add the following to the savarin dough: 45 g (1½ oz) currants and 45 g (1½ oz) sultanas, soaked in 60 ml (4 tablespoons) rum.

RUSKS

When making rusks in the microwave, be sure to use at least one ingredient which will add a brown colour, for instance, brown sugar, a little digestive bran, muesli or wholewheat flour.

To dry rusks, place the baked rusks on a microwave baking dish, cover with waxed paper. Microwave on Low (15%) for 25 – 30 minutes, rearranging the rusks every 5 minutes. Cool and store.

Health rusks

Full Power, High (70%)
35 minutes

200 g (7 oz) margarine
150 g (5 oz) soft brown sugar
450 g (1 lb) self-raising flour
5 mℓ (1 teaspoon) baking powder
pinch of salt
150 g (5 oz) muesli
1 egg
300 mℓ (½ pint) buttermilk

Place margarine and sugar in a bowl, microwave on Full Power for 3 minutes, stirring at least twice. Sift flour, baking powder and salt, add muesli and butter mixture and mix well. Mix egg and buttermilk, add to rusk mixture, mix well. Grease or spray a rectangular dish 30 x 20-cm (12 x 8-inch). Line base with kitchen paper or plastic wrap. Grease hands with a little margarine, roll walnut-sized pieces of dough. Arrange in rows, leaving space between each ball to allow for rising. Microwave on Full Power for 7 minutes, reduce power to High (70%) for about 25 minutes. Stand for 5 minutes, then break into rusks.
Makes about 20 rusks

SABAYON

Sabayon is a lightly whipped mixture of egg yolks, sugar and sweet wine, sherry or fruit juice. It is usually served hot as a sauce, dessert or beverage. Use the microwave oven to heat the wine before adding it to the egg yolks and sugar, and for heating the sauce to thicken it before serving.

Sultana sabayon

Full Power, Medium (50%)
5 minutes

3 egg yolks
75 g (2½ oz) caster sugar
pinch of cornflour
125 mℓ (4 fl oz) sultana dessert wine or
 muscatel

Beat egg yolks, sugar and cornflour together until pale and thick. Microwave the wine on Full Power for 1 – 1½ minutes, or until just boiling. Slowly pour the wine on to the egg mixture, beating constantly. Then microwave the mixture on Medium (50%) for 3 – 4 minutes, or until mixture thickens, beating well after every minute. Spoon mixture into small glass serving bowls and serve with wafer biscuits.
Serves 4

SAFFRON

Saffron strands are the dried stigmas of the crocus and are used in cooking to give a bright yellow colour and a very distinctive flavour to many foods. Known as the world's most expensive spice, the tiny strands have to be harvested by hand and over 75,000 are needed to produce 500 g (18 oz) of saffron. The spice is used mainly for colouring and flavouring rice dishes such as paella and risotto. It is especially good with fish and is an essential ingredient in bouillabaisse. It is also sometimes used

Prawns Flambéed with Whisky (page 176) and served with Parsley Rice (page 162)

in cakes and breads. Saffron is available as stigmas or powder and is almost always infused in liquid before it is used.

To infuse saffron

Pound 6 strands (or as many as directed in the recipe) to a powder. Microwave 45 ml (1½ fl oz) water, or liquid from the recipe, on Full Power for 45 seconds and pour over saffron. Stir, then stand until liquid is cool and is vivid bright orange or yellow. Strain the liquid before using, if desired.

Saffron cream

Full Power, High (70%)
3 minutes

6 saffron strands
45 mℓ (3 tablespoons) water
150 g (5 oz) caster sugar
15 mℓ (1 tablespoon) powdered gelatine
45 mℓ (3 tablespoons) water
250 mℓ (8 fl oz) single cream
375 mℓ (2 fl oz) soured cream
few drops of vanilla extract

Pound saffron to a powder. Microwave water on Full Power for 45 seconds and pour over saffron. Stand until water is bright yellow and cool. Mix sugar with gelatine and stir in remaining water and saffron infusion. Mix well. Microwave the mixture on High (70%) for 2 – 3 minutes, or until sugar and gelatine have dissolved, stirring after every minute. Set aside to cool.

 Place cream in a mixing bowl. Mix soured cream with vanilla. Gradually add gelatine mixture to cream, mixing well, then stir in soured cream. Turn into a lightly oiled mould or six individual moulds. Cover and chill for at least 4 hours or overnight. Turn out and serve with strawberry or kiwi fruit purée.
Serves 6

SAGO

Almost pure carbohydrate, these starchy grains are a product of the sago palm.

Long, slow cooking is necessary to soften the granules, making sago ideal for microwave cooking. Though sago is sometimes used as a thickening agent for soups and casseroles, it also makes a delicious milk pudding. Semolina or tapioca may be substituted for sago in the recipe below.

Sago pudding

Full Power, Low (15%)
22 minutes

30 g (1 oz) sago
600 mℓ (19 fl oz) milk
45 mℓ (1½ oz) caster sugar

Place ingredients in a large bowl. Microwave on Full Power for 5 minutes, stir well. Cover with vented plastic wrap, microwave on Full Power for 2 minutes. Reduce power to Low (15%) for 15 – 18 minutes until sago is soft, stirring every 5 minutes. Stand for 7 minutes before serving.
Serves 4

Variations

Fruity Sago: Serve with a tart stewed fruit, such as apricots or plums
Citrus Sago: Add 5 mℓ (1 teaspoon) finely grated lemon or orange rind to the above ingredients, before cooking.
Chocolate Sago: Add 30 g (1 oz) chopped chocolate to the pudding after cooking. Stir to melt.

SALAD

The word 'salad' comes from the Latin term for 'salt' suggesting that the earliest salads may have been fresh lettuce or other vegetables liberally seasoned with salt. Although the different types of lettuce and other vegetables still predominate in salads, almost any combination of foods may be used, including meats, fish, poultry, cheese, fruit, egg, pasta and rice.

 Salads may be served at the beginning of a meal to stimulate the appetite, they may also accompany the main course or be

served between courses to refresh the palate. A salad with fruit, nuts and a creamy dressing makes a delicious dessert. Moulded salads, with gelatine as an ingredient, can be served at the beginning of a meal or as a dessert, depending on content. A more substantial salad containing rice, pasta, meat or cheese may become the main course for a light meal.

When making salads, use your microwave oven to speed up the preparation of moulded salads by dissolving the gelatine, to blanch vegetables, to prepare cooked salad dressings, and to heat ingredients for warm salads.

Main course chicken pasta salad

Full Power
7 minutes

3 chicken breasts, boned and halved
125 mℓ (4 fl oz) chicken stock
400 g (14 oz) canned thin noodles, cooked
400 g (14 oz) canned chick peas, drained
400 g (14 oz) canned artichokes, drained and coarsely chopped
300 g (11 oz) frozen peas, thawed
300 g (11 oz) mushrooms, sliced
90 g (3 oz) stuffed olives, sliced
1 green pepper, cut into strips
1 celery stick, thinly sliced

Dressing
150 mℓ (5 fl oz) oil
45 mℓ (3 tablespoons) red wine vinegar
45 mℓ (3 tablespoons) chopped parsley
15 mℓ (1 tablespoon) Dijon mustard
2.5 mℓ (½ teaspoon) curry powder
salt and pepper
1 small garlic clove, peeled and chopped
90 g (3 oz) toasted almonds*

Place chicken portions, skin side up, in a round dish. Pour chicken stock over, cover and microwave on Full Power for 5 – 7 minutes, or until just cooked. Leave to cool in stock, then drain and remove skin. Cut into chunks, and place in a large bowl. Add noodles, chick peas, artichokes, peas, mushrooms, olives, green pepper and celery to the chicken, toss and chill well.

To make the dressing, combine oil, vinegar, parsley, mustard, curry powder, salt, pepper and garlic in a blender and blend well. Pour dressing over salad, tossing well and chill until ready to serve. Serve sprinkled with toasted almonds.
Serves 10

Moulded mixed salad

Medium (50%)
1½ minutes

30 mℓ (2 tablespoons) powdered gelatine
500 mℓ (16 fl oz) cold water
250 mℓ (8 fl oz) tomato juice
250 mℓ (8 fl oz) French dressing
100 g (3½ oz) lettuce, finely shredded
1 carrot, finely shredded
½ green pepper, finely chopped
60 g (2 oz) small cauliflower florets, blanched*
4 spring onions, sliced
1 celery stick, finely sliced
30 g (1 oz) stuffed green olives, finely sliced
60 g (2 oz) bean sprouts

Soften gelatine in 250 mℓ (8 fl oz) of the cold water. Stand for 5 minutes, then microwave on Medium (50%) for 1 – 1½ minutes, or until gelatine has dissolved. Add remaining water, tomato juice and French dressing. Chill until almost set, then fold in all the remaining ingredients. Turn the mixture into a ring mould and chill for several hours until set. To serve, unmould on a plate and garnish with herbs or vegetables. Serve with mayonnaise, if desired.
Serves 8

Hot cabbage toss

Full Power
2 minutes

½ medium cabbage, finely shredded
100 g (3½ oz) frozen peas, thawed
125 g (4 oz) mixed bean sprouts
100 g (3½ oz) mushrooms, sliced
1 small bunch of radishes, sliced
4 – 5 spring onions, sliced, including green tops
½ cauliflower, broken into florets and blanched*
1 celery stick, sliced
150 g (5 oz) fresh or canned pineapple chunks
croutons*

Dressing
90 mℓ (3 fl oz) oil
15 mℓ (1 tablespoon) white vinegar
15 mℓ (1 tablespoon) lemon juice
30 mℓ (2 tablespoons) soy sauce

To make the salad, combine cabbage, peas, bean sprouts, mushrooms, radishes, spring onions, cauliflower, celery and pineapple. Refrigerate, covered, for several hours. To make the dressing, mix oil, vinegar, lemon juice and soy sauce together and microwave on Full Power for 45 seconds. Pour over salad and toss well. Then microwave salad for 1½ minutes, or until vegetables and cabbage are just wilted. Toss with croûtons.
Serves 6

Warm lettuce salad

Full Power
5 minutes

6 bacon rashers cooked*, and dripping reserved
6 spring onions, sliced
60 mℓ (4 tablespoons) white vinegar
60 mℓ (4 tablespoons) water
15 mℓ (1 tablespoon) sugar
2.5 mℓ (½ teaspoon) salt
freshly ground black pepper
1 head lettuce
3 fresh mint leaves, finely chopped
300 g (11oz) young spinach
1 small bunch of radishes, sliced
2 hard-boiled eggs, coarsely chopped

Crumble cooked bacon and set aside. Place bacon dripping in a bowl with the spring onions and microwave on Full Power for 2 minutes. Add vinegar, water, sugar, salt and pepper and microwave for about 2 minutes, or until boiling. Stir well. Tear lettuce into bite-sized pieces and place in a large microwave bowl. Add mint. Tear spinach leaves and add to bowl, tossing well. Pour hot dressing over and toss. Microwave 1 minute, toss again and add crumbled bacon, radishes and eggs. Serve while still warm.
Serves 6

Hot chicken salad

Full Power
11 minutes

30 g (1 oz) butter
3 celery sticks, sliced
½ onion, chopped
½ green pepper, cut in thin strips
400 g (14 oz) cooked chicken, cut into bite-sized pieces
400 g (14 oz) canned cream of celery soup
250 mℓ (8 fl oz) mayonnaise
pepper
15 mℓ (1 tablespoon) dry sherry
1 small packet potato crisps, crushed

Microwave butter on Full Power for 15 seconds. Add celery, onion and green pepper and mix well. Microwave, covered, for 3 minutes or until vegetables are just tender. Add chicken, soup, mayonnaise, pepper and sherry, mixing well. Top with crushed potato crisps and microwave for 7 – 9 minutes, until well heated and bubbly. Stand 5 minutes before serving.
Serves 6 – 8

SALAD DRESSING
Salad dressings range from a simple mixture of oil and vinegar or a sprinkling of lemon juice and salt, to more elaborate combinations involving cream, cheese, herbs and other ingredients. When choosing a dressing to suit a salad, it should not overpower the ingredients and should be used sparingly.
See also Mayonnaise.

Hot French dressing

Full Power, Medium (50%)
4½ minutes

250 ml (8 fl oz) French dressing*
2 hard-boiled eggs, finely chopped
15 ml (1 tablespoon) chopped parsley
10 ml (2 teaspoons) finely chopped chives
15 ml (1 tablespoon) celery leaves
2.5 ml (½ teaspoon) dry mustard
2.5 ml (½ teaspoon) Worcestershire sauce

Microwave French dressing on Full Power for 2½ – 3 minutes. Remove from the oven and beat in eggs, parsley, chives, celery leaves, mustard and Worcestershire sauce. Microwave on Medium (50%) until heated through, about 1 – 1½ minutes. Use this dressing on spinach salad.
Makes about 375 ml (12 fl oz)

French dressing

Although this dressing and the vinaigrette dressing are not made in the microwave, they are classics and can be used on many salads.

100 ml (3½ fl oz) oil
60 ml (4 tablespoons) white vinegar
salt and black pepper
pinch of cayenne pepper
generous pinch of dry mustard
generous pinch of caster sugar

Combine all ingredients and shake well. Use as required. This dressing may be kept refrigerated for a few days.
Makes about 150 ml (5 fl oz)

Variations

Herb Dressing: Add 5 ml (1 teaspoon) freshly chopped parsley, 5 ml (1 teaspoon) finely choped chives and 5 ml (1 teaspoon) fresh tarragon to the basic mixture.
Garlic Dressing: Add 1 finely chopped garlic clove to the basic mixture.

Vinaigrette salad dressing

125 ml (4 fl oz) oil
60 ml (4 tablespoons) wine or cider vinegar
30 ml (2 tablespoons) chopped parsley
5 ml (1 teaspoon) dry mustard
5 ml (1 teaspoon) salt
5 ml (1 teaspoon) caster sugar
black pepper
generous pinch of paprika

Combine all ingredients in a jar. Cover and shake well. Store in the refrigerator.
Makes about 200 ml (6½ fl oz)

SALMON
The fine pink flesh of the North Atlantic and Pacific salmon is considered a great delicacy. Salmon is obtainable either whole or in steaks, which, if frozen, are best thawed, then baked or poached in the microwave.

Canned salmon is often used in starters and main dish casseroles, and the more expensive smoked salmon, though usually eaten plain, makes a fine addition to quiches, mousses and other starters. (*See* Smoked Salmon with Smoked Trout Mousse page 216.)

To defrost salmon steak, remove wrappings from 500 g (18 oz) salmon steaks. Place on a plate and cover with waxed paper. Microwave on Defrost (30%) for 5 minutes and stand for 5 minutes before using.

Poached salmon steaks

Full Power
9 minutes

4 salmon steaks, 2.5-cm (1-inch) thick
100 ml (3½ fl oz) water
100 ml (3½ fl oz) dry white wine
15 ml (1 tablespoon) lemon juice
1 bay leaf
1 onion slice
peppercorns
1 small carrot, sliced
generous pinch of salt
30 g (1 oz) butter

Wipe salmon steaks, pat dry and set aside. Place water, wine, lemon juice, bay leaf, onion, a few peppercorns, carrot and salt in a large shallow casserole. Cover and microwave on Full Power for 3 minutes. Add salmon with narrow ends towards the centre of the dish, dot with butter and microwave, covered, for 6 minutes, or until flesh starts to turn opaque. Serve hot with velouté* or hollandaise* sauce, or serve cold with creamy horseradish sauce or with lemon wedges and mayonnaise.
Serves 4

Salmon and cheese ring with dill

High (70%), Medium (50%)
15 minutes

3 eggs
250 ml (8 fl oz) milk
60 ml (4 tablespoons) dry white wine
10 ml (2 teaspoons) chopped dill
10 ml (2 teaspoons) chopped parsley
2.5 ml (½ teaspoon) dry mustard
10 ml (2 teaspoons) lemon juice
salt and lemon pepper
6 slices of bread, cubed
100 g (3½ oz) Cheddar cheese, grated
200 g (7 oz) canned salmon, drained and flaked

Beat eggs with milk, wine, herbs, mustard, lemon juice and seasonings. Microwave on

High (70%) for 3 – 4 minutes, stirring every minute. The mixture should be hot and beginning to thicken. Add bread cubes to the egg mixture along with the cheese and salmon. Turn mixture into a 1.5-litre (2¾-pint) ring dish and microwave, covered with waxed paper, on Medium (50%) for 8 – 11 minutes, or until centre is almost set. Leave to stand for 5 minutes, then turn out on to a serving plate. Serve cut in slices, with lemon wedges and mayonnaise.
Serves 4 – 6

Salmon steaks en papillote

Full Power, Medium (50%)
18 minutes

6 x 32.5-cm (13-inch) squares of parchment paper
7 g (¼ oz) margarine
1 large onion, thinly sliced
½ green pepper, diced
30 g (1 oz) butter
6 salmon steaks, poached*

Sauce
250 ml (8 fl oz) velouté sauce*
45 ml (1½ fl oz) dry white wine
15 ml (1 tablespoon) lemon juice
freshly ground black pepper
4 mushrooms, chopped
2.5 ml (½ teaspoon) dried dill or 5 ml (1 teaspoon) fresh dill

Grease one side of each piece of parchment paper with margarine. Place onion and green pepper in a bowl with butter. Microwave on Full Power for 2 minutes, then place a little onion and green pepper just off centre on each piece of paper, so one side can fold over the other. Top with poached salmon steaks.

For the sauce, place velouté sauce, wine, lemon juice, pepper, mushrooms and dill in a bowl. Microwave on Medium (50%) for 3 – 4 minutes, stirring every minute. Spoon some of the sauce over each salmon steak. Fold half of each parchment square over steaks to make a triangle. Fold edges to seal. Place three packets in a baking dish and microwave on Full Power for 4 – 6 minutes, or until heated through. Remove and keep warm. Repeat with the three remaining packets. To serve, let each person open his or her packet. *Serves 6*

SALTED BEEF
Because salted beef is cured in brine, it needs to be simmered in plenty of water to which a few seasonings are added. This takes almost as long in the microwave as it does on top of the stove, but you have the advantages of reduced steam and cooking smells in the kitchen. Canned salted beef is known as corned beef in England.

Corned beef pie

Full Power, High (70%)
16 minutes

1 x 22.5-cm (9-inch) savoury crumb crust*
60 mℓ (4 tablespoons) savoury crust mixture,
    reserved from above
30 mℓ (2 tablespoons) oil
1 onion, chopped
30 mℓ (2 tablespoons) chopped parsley
300 g (11 oz) canned corned beef, chopped
3 eggs
75 mℓ (2½ fl oz) single cream
75 mℓ (2½ oz) milk
60 mℓ (4 tablespoons) mayonnaise
generous pinch of mixed herbs
45 g (1½ oz) Cheddar cheese, grated
salt and black pepper
pinch of paprika
30 mℓ (2 tablespoons) dried breadcrumbs

Pour oil into a small bowl and microwave for 45
seconds. Add onion and stir to coat with oil.
Microwave for 2 minutes, stirring well. Add
parsley and corned beef, stir to combine.
Lightly beat eggs, cream, milk, mayonnaise,
herbs, 30 g (1 oz) of the grated Cheddar, salt
and black pepper. Stir in corned beef mixture
and pour into biscuit crust. Combine the
savoury crust mixture, remaining Cheddar,
paprika and breadcrumbs. Sprinkle over the
filling. Microwave on High (70%) for 13 – 15
minutes, until just firm in the middle. Stand for
3 minutes before serving.
Makes 1 x 22.5-cm (9-inch) pie

SANDWICHES

The sandwich is not a modern invention,
but dates back to medieval times in Scandi-
navian countries when hot meals were
served on slices of bread. The name, however, is attributed to the Earl of Sandwich
who, in 18th-century London, had his
meals delivered to him on slices of bread
when he refused to leave the gambling
tables. Today the term sandwich refers to
anything served on, or between, slices of
bread. The microwave can be used to heat
sandwiches or bread rolls, toast sandwiches
and in the preparation of hot open sandwiches.

Hints for microwaving sandwiches

☐ Microwave sandwiches on kitchen
paper so bread will not become soggy.
☐ Be sure not to overheat sandwiches, as
this will cause the bread to become tough
and dry.
☐ For very moist fillings, microwave
filling separately until hot, then microwave
filling and bun together only until the bun
is warm.
☐ Grilled or toasted microwave sandwiches require a browning pan (see recipe
below for toasted sandwiches).
☐ To prevent sandwiches from becoming
soggy, it is best to use firm-textured bread
and to place moist fillings, such as tomato,
between slices of meat or cheese.

Toasted cheese sandwich

Full Power
7 minutes

2 slices of wholewheat bread
mustard
2 slices of processed cheese
chopped spring onion or chives
1 slice of cooked ham or gammon
butter or margarine

Spread one side of each slice of bread with a
little mustard. Add one slice of cheese and
sprinkle with chopped spring onion or chives.
Add ham or gammon and remaining cheese.
Top with remaining bread, mustard-side down.
Spread outside of both slices with butter. Heat
a browning dish on Full Power for 5 minutes.
Place sandwich on browning dish and press
down slightly. Stand for about 25 seconds. Turn
sandwich over and stand for 25 seconds.
Microwave for 30 – 45 seconds to melt cheese.
To make more than one sandwich at a time,
increase time by 10 – 15 seconds per extra
sandwich.
Serves 1

Note: When making several sandwiches, the
browning dish will have to be reheated. Be sure
to wipe surface very clean to prevent
ingredients burning on.

Corned beef and mayonnaise sandwiches

Full Power
14 minutes

150 g (5 oz) corned beef
15 mℓ (1 tablespoon) finely chopped chives
15 mℓ (1 tablespoon) chopped parsley
pinch of dried oregano
45 g (1½ oz) Cheddar cheese, grated
60 mℓ (4 tablespoons) mayonnaise
cayenne
10 mℓ (2 teaspoons) Worcestershire sauce
salt and black pepper
1 tomato, sliced
8 slices of bread
butter

Combine all ingredients, except tomato, bread
and butter. Spread thickly on four slices of
bread. Top with slices of tomato, then bread.
Spread outside of both slices of bread with
butter. Microwave one or two sandwiches at a
time as for toasted cheese sandwiches.
Makes 4 sandwiches

Tuna and mushroom sandwiches

Full Power
14 minutes

200 g (7 oz) canned tuna, drained and flaked
15 mℓ (1 tablespoon) chopped onion
15 mℓ (1 tablespoon) chopped parsley
1 small apple, chopped
Tabasco
salt and black pepper
canned mushroom soup, to moisten
8 slices of bread
butter

Combine all filling ingredients. Spread on four
slices of bread. Top each with a slice of bread.
Spread outside of both slices with butter.
Microwave one or two sandwiches at a time as
for toasted cheese sandwiches.
Makes 4 sandwiches

Ham salad sandwiches

Full Power
4 minutes

300 g (11 oz) cooked ham, chopped
1 celery stick, finely chopped
1 dill pickle, finely chopped
15 mℓ (1 tablespoon) chopped onion
5 mℓ (1 teaspoon) prepared mustard
60 mℓ (4 tablespoons) boiled mayonnaise*
90 g (3 oz) Cheddar cheese, grated
salt and pepper
6 – 8 slices bread, rye or wholewheat

Mix all ingredients except bread together.
Lightly toast the bread and spread with ham
mixture. Microwave two slices at a time on Full
Power for about 1 minute, or until mixture is hot.
Repeat with remaining slices. *Serves 6 – 8*

SAUCES

At first it may appear that making a sauce
in the microwave takes almost as long as it
does conventionally. However, microwave
cooking offers a number of advantages as
many sauces can be measured, mixed and
microwaved in the same container and
there is no need to stir them constantly.
With no dirty saucepans, washing up is reduced to a minimum. Sauces can also be
made well in advance and reheated at the
last moment without affecting the texture
or flavour.

Sauces thickened with flour need no
changes in ingredients when converting to
microwave use, they just need less attention. Sauces using cornflour thicken more
rapidly and need even less stirring than
flour-based sauces, but sauces thickened
with egg yolk do need careful preparation.
Some of the hot sauce should always be
stirred into the beaten egg yolks until
about half the sauce has been used. The
egg yolk mixture can then be stirred into
the remaining sauce. This prevents the egg
yolk being cooked before it is properly in-
corporated into the sauce.

Microwaving sauces

☐ Use a glass measuring jug with a capacity twice that of the amount of sauce to be made. Remember that sauces containing milk will boil up and may boil over.

☐ Melt the butter or margarine in the glass measure on Full Power for 30 seconds.

☐ Stir flour or cornflour and dry seasonings into the melted butter to make a smooth paste. This mixture should be microwaved on Full Power for about 30 seconds. This essential step ensures that the sauce thickens sufficiently.

☐ Whisk liquid into the flour mixture, blending very well to prevent lumps from forming.

☐ Microwave the mixture, on Full Power unless otherwise directed, for 3 – 4 minutes per 500 ml (16 fl oz) liquid. Stir the mixture well after every minute. The sauce will begin to bubble around the edges before it is done, so continue microwaving until desired thickness is achieved.

☐ Stir in cheese or other additions after the sauce has thickened and microwave, usually on Full Power, for a few seconds to heat through.

☐ To prevent a skin from forming on a hot sauce, place plastic wrap or waxed paper directly on the surface of the sauce.

Basic white sauce

Full Power
4 minutes

30 g (1 oz) butter or margarine
30 mℓ (2 tablespoons) plain flour
salt and pepper
250 mℓ (8 fl oz) milk

Place butter in a 1-litre (1¾-pint) glass jug and microwave on Full Power for about 30 seconds to melt. Stir in flour, salt and pepper. Microwave for 45 seconds. Stir, then slowly whisk in milk, blending well. Microwave for about 2 minutes, stirring twice. Remove from oven and stir well. Serve hot.
Makes about 250 mℓ (8 fl oz)

Variations

Make up the basic sauce, then try one of the following:

Cheese Sauce: Stir in 45 – 100 g (1½–3½ oz) grated mature Cheddar cheese. Mix until cheese melts and sauce is smooth. If cheese has not completely melted, microwave on Full Power for about 30 seconds and stir again. Add 2.5 mℓ (½ teaspoon) prepared mustard if a tangy cheese sauce is desired.
Dill Sauce: Stir in 15 mℓ (1 tablespoon) freshly chopped dill or 5 mℓ (1 teaspoon) dried dill and 10 mℓ (2 teaspoons) lemon juice. Mix until smooth.
Mornay Sauce: Add 45 g (1½ oz) grated Gruyère or Parmesan cheese to the sauce, mixing until cheese has melted and sauce is smooth. Add a pinch of cayenne and mix well.

Curry Sauce: Add 2.5 – 5 mℓ (½ – 1 teaspoon) curry powder or to taste, and 5 mℓ (1 teaspoon) lemon juice. Stir until smooth.
Horseradish Sauce: Add 5 – 10 mℓ (1 – 2 teaspoons) prepared horseradish or to taste, and mix well.
Thick White Sauce: Use 45 mℓ (3 tablespoons) plain flour instead of 30 mℓ (2 tablespoons) in the basic recipe.

Béchamel sauce

High (70%), Full Power
10 minutes

300 mℓ (10 fl oz) milk
1 thick slice of onion
1 small carrot, cut up
1 parsley sprig
2 cloves
1 blade of mace
black peppercorns
1 bay leaf
45 g (1½ oz) margarine
45 mℓ (3 tablespoons) plain flour
salt

Place milk, onion, carrot, parsley, cloves, mace, peppercorns and bay leaf in a jug. Microwave, uncovered, on High (70%) for 3 minutes. Remove from oven, leave to stand for 15 minutes, then strain. Using a large jug or bowl, heat margarine on Full Power for 2 minutes. Stir in flour. Add half the infused milk and stir well. Stir in remaining milk. Microwave for about 5 minutes, stirring every minute during cooking time. Add a little salt and use as required.
Makes about 300 mℓ (10 fl oz)

Velouté sauce

Full Power, Medium (50%)
6 minutes

30 g (1 oz) butter
30 mℓ (2 tablespoons) plain flour
375 mℓ (12 fl oz) stock (chicken or fish, depending on the dish)
salt and pepper
lemon juice
1 egg yolk
15 mℓ (1 tablespoon) single cream

Microwave butter in a large jug or deep bowl on Full Power for 30 seconds. Whisk in flour and microwave 30 seconds. Stir well. Gradually stir in the stock, mixing well. Microwave 3 – 4 minutes, stirring well after every minute until sauce is thick and smooth. Season with salt, pepper and lemon juice.

Mix egg yolk and cream together, then very gradually beat a little of the hot sauce into the egg yolk. When about half the hot sauce has been used, return mixture to jug and stir well. Microwave on Medium (50%) for 2 minutes, stirring twice.
Makes about 375 mℓ (12 fl oz)

Hollandaise sauce

Full Power
3 minutes

125 g (4 oz) butter
2 egg yolks
15 mℓ (1 tablespoon) lemon juice
2.5 mℓ (½ teaspoon) dry mustard
salt and pepper

Place butter in a glass measuring jug and microwave on Full Power for 2½ – 3½ minutes until hot and bubbly. Place remaining ingredients in a blender or food processor. When butter is ready, turn blender or processor to highest speed and slowly add hot butter, mixing until sauce is creamy and thickened.
Makes about 170 mℓ (5½ fl oz)

Béarnaise sauce

Full Power
7 minutes

45 mℓ (3 tablespoons) dry white wine
15 mℓ (1 tablespoon) tarragon vinegar
2 spring onions, chopped
generous pinch of dried tarragon
black peppercorns
3 egg yolks
125 g (4 oz) butter
salt

Place white wine, tarragon vinegar, spring onion, dried tarragon and peppercorns in a flat dish. Microwave, uncovered, on Full Power for 4 minutes, until liquid has reduced to at least half. Strain and set aside. Using a food processor fitted with a metal blade, process egg yolks until light in colour. Microwave butter for 3 minutes (butter must be very hot). With machine running, pour hot butter on to yolks. Process for about 45 seconds. Add strained liquid and a little salt. Process to combine. Serve hot with beef, lamb, chicken or fish.

To reheat the sauce, microwave, covered, on Defrost (30%) for 2 – 4 minutes, depending on how cold the sauce is. Whisk well and serve.
Makes about 170 mℓ (5½ fl oz)

Variations

Avocado Béarnaise: Follow directions for making Béarnaise sauce, substituting wine vinegar for tarragon vinegar. Finally, fold in 1 puréed avocado. Serve with beef, chicken or fish.
Pineapple Béarnaise: Follow directions for making Béarnaise sauce, substituting pineapple juice for dry white wine. Finally, stir in 60 g (2 oz) crushed pineapple. Serve with beef or chicken.

Barbecue sauce

Full Power
19 minutes

45 mℓ (3 tablespoons) oil
1 large onion, chopped
1 garlic clove, crushed
400 g (14 oz) canned tomatoes, liquidized
60 mℓ (4 tablespoons) brown malt vinegar
15 mℓ (1 tablespoon) Worcestershire sauce
45 g (1½ oz) caster sugar
10 mℓ (2 teaspoons) dry mustard
salt and black pepper
pinch of cayenne
1 bay leaf
5 mℓ (1 teaspoon) soy sauce

Pour oil into a large bowl, microwave on Full
Power for 1 minute. Add onion and garlic, stir to
coat with oil, microwave 3 minutes. Add
remaining ingredients, stir well. Microwave for
15 minutes, stirring every 5 minutes. Remove
bay leaf. Serve with grilled meats, hamburgers
or hot dogs.
Makes about 500 mℓ (16 fl oz)

Brown sauce

Full Power
27 minutes

45 mℓ (3 tablespoons) oil
1 onion, chopped
1 bacon rasher, rind removed, chopped
1 celery stick, chopped
1 carrot, sliced
45 mℓ (3 tablespoons) plain flour
6 mushrooms, chopped
300 mℓ (10 fl oz) beef stock
10 mℓ (2 teaspoons) soy sauce
30 mℓ (2 tablespoons) tomato paste
1 tomato, chopped
1 bay leaf
black pepper
pinch of mixed herbs
45 mℓ (3 tablespoons) sherry

Preheat browning dish for 3 minutes on Full
Power. Pour oil into browning dish, microwave
on Full Power for 1 minute. Add onion and
bacon, microwave for 1 minute, now add celery
and carrot, stir to coat with oil. Cover,
microwave for 4 minutes, stirring twice. Add
flour, microwave for 3 – 4 minutes, stirring
every minute. Add remaining ingredients,
except for sherry. Cover, microwave for 15
minutes, stirring twice during cooking time.
Strain sauce, stir in sherry. Use as a base for
meat, game or chicken dishes.
Makes about 250 mℓ (8 fl oz)

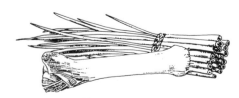

Mexican sauce

Full Power, Medium (50%)
10 minutes

2 bacon rashers, coarsely chopped
½ onion, chopped
400 g (14 oz) canned baked beans
10 mℓ (2 teaspoons) vinegar
10 mℓ (2 teaspoons) Worcestershire sauce
salt
Tabasco
60 g (2 oz) processed cheese

Place bacon in a bowl, microwave on Full
Power for 2 minutes. Add onion, toss to coat
with fat, microwave 2 minutes more. Place all
ingredients in a blender, blend until smooth.
Return to microwave, cook on Medium (50%)
for 7 minutes. Serve warm. This sauce is
excellent served with hot dogs and on tortillas*.
Makes about 500 mℓ (16 fl oz)

Extra creamy chocolate sauce

Full Power
5 minutes

This sauce is perfect for serving with
profiteroles (cream-filled choux pastry puffs
coated with a creamy chocolate sauce).

150 g (5 oz) milk chocolate, chopped
150 mℓ (5 fl oz) milk
150 mℓ (5 fl oz) single cream
30 g (1 oz) caster sugar
30 g (1 oz) butter
15 g (½ oz) plain flour
few drops of vanilla extract

Combine chocolate, milk, cream and sugar in a
jug. Microwave on Full Power for 2 – 3 minutes,
stirring at least once. Place butter in a bowl,
microwave for 1 minute, stir in flour. Pour in hot
liquid, stir until smooth. Microwave for about
2 minutes, stirring every 30 seconds, then add
vanilla. Cover surface of sauce with a piece of
greaseproof paper and allow to cool.
Makes about 500 mℓ (16 fl oz)

Butterscotch sauce

High (70%), Medium (50%)
7 minutes

150 g (5 oz) golden syrup
100 g (3½ oz) caster sugar
250 mℓ (8 fl oz) single cream
few drops of caramel flavouring
30g (1 oz) butter

Place all ingredients in a large jug. Microwave
on High (70%) for 2 minutes, stir well. Reduce
power to Medium (50%), microwave for
5 minutes, stirring every minute. Cool to room
temperature before using. Stores well for three
to four weeks in the refrigerator.
Makes about 50 mℓ (16 fl oz)

SAUERKRAUT
Sauerkraut is made from hard, white cabbage, sliced very thinly and fermented in
brine for about four weeks. It is often flavoured with juniper berries or caraway
seeds. Sauerkraut is mostly purchased
canned, but homemade sauerkraut is
sometimes available from delicatessens.

To heat sauerkraut, place contents of
1 x 400-g (14-oz) can sauerkraut in a deep
bowl, cover with vented plastic wrap and
microwave on Full Power for 4 – 5 minutes, or until heated through.

Marinated pork chops with sauerkraut

Medium (50%)
40 minutes

4 pork chops, 2.5-cm (1-inch) thick
1 small onion, chopped
400 g (14 oz) canned sauerkraut, drained
15 mℓ (1 tablespoon) soft brown sugar
generous pinch of caraway seeds
350 mℓ (11 fl oz) beer

Place chops with thin ends towards the centre
of a casserole and spread chopped onion and
sauerkraut over each. Sprinkle with sugar and
caraway seeds and gently pour beer over.
Cover dish and marinate chops in the
refrigerator for 4 hours. Microwave, covered, on
Medium (50%) for 40 minutes or until meat is
tender.
Serves 4

Pork pot roast simmered in beer

Full Power, Medium (50%)
1 hour 44 minutes

400 g (14 oz) canned sauerkraut, drained
350 mℓ (11 fl oz) beer
1 onion, chopped
15 mℓ (1 tablespoon) chopped parsley
2.5 mℓ (½ teaspoon) dried sage, or
    5 mℓ (1 teaspoon) chopped sage
2.5 mℓ (½ teaspoon) caraway seeds
pepper
2 kg (4¼ lb) loin of pork
salt
30 mℓ (2 tablespoons) brandy
30 g (1 oz) plain flour

Combine sauerkraut, beer, onion, parsley,
sage, caraway seeds and pepper in a large
casserole. Microwave, covered, on Full Power
for 7 – 9 minutes. Sprinkle pork with salt and
place in the casserole. Spoon beer mixture over
pork. Cover and microwave on Full Power for 12
minutes. Turn pork, spoon sauce over the top
and microwave, covered, on Medium (50%) for
70 – 80 minutes, or until meat is tender.

Remove pork and keep warm. Add brandy and flour to sauerkraut and beer mixture, transfer to a blender and process until the mixture is smooth. Return sauce to the microwave and heat on Full Power for 3 – 4 minutes, or until bubbly and thickened. Serve sauce with slices of pork.
Serves 8

SAUSAGES

Sausages are made from finely minced meat, usually beef or pork, mixed with cereal and seasonings and enclosed in a thin membrane. They are usually eaten grilled or fried, and are also sometimes boiled. The first sausages were plain and unspiced, and were made from scraps of coarsely chopped meat preserved in salt. Nowadays there are hundreds of varieties of sausage available, each with a distinctive flavour.
See also Hot Dogs.

To microwave pork or beef sausages
Sausages microwaved in a browning dish look good and taste good. Leave to stand for 2 – 3 minutes before serving.
For 500 g (18 oz) sausages, microwave browning dish on Full Power for 5 – 6 minutes. Brush sausages lightly with soy or Worcestershire sauce, prick them and arrange on the dish. Cover with waxed paper and microwave for 2 minutes. Turn sausages over and microwave a further 2 minutes.
For 2 sausages, heat browning dish 4 – 6 minutes on Full Power and microwave sausages 35 – 45 seconds on each side.
For 4 sausages, heat browning dish 5 – 6 minutes on Full Power and microwave 1 – 1½ minutes on each side.

Sausage and rice casserole

Full Power, Medium (50%)
20 minutes

350 g (12 oz) pork sausage-meat
½ green pepper, finely chopped
1 small onion, finely chopped
1 small garlic clove, finely chopped
400 g (14 oz) canned whole tomatoes, coarsely chopped
45 g (1½ oz) stoned black olives, chopped
60 mℓ (4 tablespoons) chilli sauce
salt and pepper
5 mℓ (1 teaspoon) caster sugar
2.5 mℓ (½ teaspoon) dried basil
2.5 mℓ (½ teaspoon) dried oregano
pinch of sage
350 g (12 oz) cooked rice*
100 g (3½ oz) Mozzarella cheese, grated

Crumble sausage-meat in a large casserole. Add green pepper, onion and garlic. Microwave on Full Power for 4 – 6 minutes or until sausage is cooked, stirring occasionally. Drain mixture well. Combine tomatoes, olives, chilli sauce, salt and pepper, sugar, basil, oregano and sage and microwave for 4 – 5 minutes, or until bubbly. Stir in sausage-meat and rice and microwave, covered, on Medium (50%) for 3 – 5 minutes, or until heated through. Stir, then sprinkle cheese over the top. Microwave for 3 – 4 minutes to melt cheese.
Serves 4

Sausage-meat loaf

Full Power
20 minutes

500 g (18 oz) minced beef
125 g (4 oz) pork sausage-meat
175 g (6 oz) soft breadcrumbs
1 onion, finely chopped
1 celery stick, finely chopped
5 mℓ (1 teaspoon) curry powder
½ green pepper, finely chopped
15 mℓ (1 tablespoon) Worcestershire sauce
45 mℓ (3 tablespoons) chutney
30 g (1 oz) sultanas
10 mℓ (2 teaspoons) mustard
30 mℓ (2 tablespoons) tomato sauce
salt and pepper
2 eggs, beaten

Combine all ingredients and mix well. Turn mixture into a microwave loaf dish or ring dish. Microwave on Full Power for 20 – 25 minutes. Stand 5 minutes then turn out and serve.
Serves 6 – 8

SAUTÉ

Sauté comes from the French *sauter* which literally means 'to jump'. When cooked by this method, the food is stirred or the pan is shaken to keep the food in motion so that it is quickly cooked. To sauté food conventionally, only a small amount is browned or fried in very hot clarified butter or a combination of butter and oil. The food should be patted dry before sautéing so that the surface can be seared and so that the food does not steam. True sautéing cannot be done in the microwave, but food can be seared and browned in a preheated browning dish with oil added.

SAVARIN

A light, airy yeast cake, invented by the renowned French chef Brillat-Savarin. When cooked, savarin is soaked with a liqueur flavoured sugar syrup and served as dessert, though it may also be eaten for tea. Savarin is ideal for microwave cooking. Prove the yeast mixture with the help of your microwave and cook it in minutes in the traditional ring-shaped mould. Even the jam can be softened in the microwave before it is brushed over the cake.

Fresh fruit savarin

Full Power
17 minutes

150 mℓ (5 fl oz) milk
15 g (½ oz) compressed yeast
30 g (1 oz) caster sugar
250 g (9 oz) plain flour
pinch of salt
100 g (3½ oz) butter or margarine
2 eggs, lightly beaten

Syrup
300 mℓ (½ pint) water
200 g (7 oz) caster sugar
60 mℓ (4 tablespoons) dark rum

To serve
60 g (2 oz) apricot jam
500 g (18 oz) fresh fruit (strawberries, grapes or orange slices)
250 mℓ (8 fl oz) whipping cream, whipped

Pour milk into a jug, microwave on Full Power for about 15 seconds, until blood heat. Add yeast and 5 mℓ (1 teaspoon) of sugar, stir to combine. Sprinkle 30 mℓ (2 tablespoons) of measured flour on top of milk, cover with plastic wrap. Microwave for 10 seconds, then stand for 5 minutes. Repeat microwaving and standing once more. Sift remaining flour and salt into a food processor bowl or mixing bowl, add remaining sugar. Microwave butter for 30 seconds to soften. The butter should not be melted. Add very soft butter to eggs, beat lightly and stir in yeast mixture. Add to flour mixture and beat very well until a smooth soft batter forms. Grease or spray a 22.5-cm (9-inch) ring mould very well, turn batter into mould and cover with plastic wrap. To prove mixture, microwave on Full Power for 10 seconds, rest for 10 minutes, repeat microwaving and resting twice more. The mixture should rise to the top of the mould. Remove plastic wrap and microwave for 4½ – 6 minutes, until just dry on top. Stand for 10 minutes before turning out on to a cooling rack.

For the syrup, combine water and sugar in a jug and microwave for 10 minutes, stirring after 5 minutes. Cool slightly and add rum. Place a plate under the warm savarin, spoon syrup over until it is completely absorbed. Transfer to a serving plate and chill. Spoon jam into a small bowl, microwave for 1 – 2 minutes until warm. Brush top and sides with jam. Arrange fruit around edge of savarin and fill centre with cream. *Serves 8*

SCALLOPS

These free-swimming shellfish have two ribbed, fan-shaped shells. Scallops are obtained by dredging or trawling and are usually opened, cleaned and frozen at sea. The firm-textured, meaty flesh has a delicate seafood flavour that goes well with herbs, cream and wine sauces. Like other shellfish, Scallops microwave well.
See also Coquilles St Jacques.

To defrost scallops

Remove wrappings from 500 g (18 oz) frozen scallops. Place scallops in a baking dish and cover with waxed paper. Microwave on Defrost (30%) for 5 minutes. Remove any scallops that are nearly defrosted. Cover remaining scallops and microwave on Low (15%) for about 2 minutes more. Stand for 5 minutes, then use as desired.

To poach scallops

Place 500 g (18 oz) thawed scallops in a casserole dish. Drizzle with melted butter or sprinkle with 60 ml (4 tablespoons) white wine or fish stock and lemon juice. Cover and microwave on Full Power for 2½ – 3½ minutes. The flesh should be opaque and tender when tested with a knife.

Scallops with herb and lemon butter

Full Power, Medium (50%)
8 minutes

90 g (3 oz) butter
2.5 mℓ (½ teaspoon) thyme
5 mℓ (1 teaspoon) dill, chopped
5 mℓ (1 teaspoon) parsley, chopped
salt and lemon pepper
500 g (18 oz) scallops, thawed
juice of 1 lemon
paprika

Microwave butter and herbs in a casserole dish on Full Power for 1½ minutes. Add salt and pepper, scallops and lemon juice. Microwave, covered, on Medium (50%) for 6 – 8 minutes, stirring twice. The flesh should be opaque. Sprinkle with paprika and stand for about 5 minutes.
Serves 4

SCAMPI *See* Prawns

SCHMALTZ

Schmaltz is melted fat used as a substitute for butter or margarine in Kosher or traditional Jewish homes. When schmaltz is made, the fat requires long cooking and as it is difficult to control the temperature of large quantities of fat, it is not recommended that this be made in the microwave.

SCHNITZEL *See* Veal

SCONES

Scones are individual quick breads made from a soft dough that is rolled or patted into a round, cut into shapes and baked. They can be baked in the microwave, but they do not brown and are easily overcooked, so they are best baked conventionally. Scone dough, however, is used in a variety of quick bread recipes, including onion savoury ring* and strawberry shortcake ring*.
See also Quick Breads.

Basic scone mix

500 g (18 oz) plain flour
30 mℓ (2 tablespoons) baking powder
10 mℓ (2 teaspoons) salt
30 g (1 oz) caster sugar (for sweet scones only)
175 g (6 oz) butter

Sift together flour, baking powder, salt and sugar if used. Rub in butter until the mixture resembles fine crumbs. Refrigerate the mixture in a covered container and use as desired or in recipes such as strawberry shortcake ring* or onion savoury ring*.

Microwave scones

Full Power
4 to 8 minutes

250 g (9 oz) basic scone mix*
1 egg
150 mℓ (5 fl oz) milk

Place scone mix in a bowl. Beat egg and milk together and add enough to the dry ingredients to make a soft but not sticky dough. Knead lightly, roll out until 2.5 cm (1-inch) thick and cut into 5-cm (2-inch) rounds. Arrange six scones on a large plate lined with double thickness of kitchen paper. Brush tops with melted butter and sprinkle with paprika, wheatgerm, cinnamon and sugar or grated Parmesan cheese and mixed herbs. Microwave on Full Power for 2 – 4 minutes, or until no longer doughy. Stand for 1 minute then remove to a wire rack and repeat with remaining scones.
Makes 10 – 12

Onion savoury ring

Full Power, High (70%)
11 minutes

60 g (2 oz) butter
45 mℓ (3 tablespoons) onion, chopped
45 mℓ (3 tablespoons) green pepper, chopped
250 g (9 oz) basic scone mix*
2.5 mℓ (½ teaspoon) mixed herbs
30 mℓ (2 tablespoons) onion, chopped
30 g (1 oz) Cheddar cheese, grated
1 egg
200 mℓ (6½ fl oz) milk

Place butter in a microwave ring dish and microwave on Full Power for about 45 seconds to melt. Tilt dish so butter coats base evenly. Add chopped onion and green pepper. Microwave for 2 minutes, then spread mixture evenly over bottom of the dish. Combine scone mix, herbs, onion and cheese. Beat egg and add milk. Add enough of the liquid to the dry ingredients to form a soft, but not sticky dough. Form dough into ten balls and place on top of onion and peppers in the dish. Rest for 5

minutes, then place dish on an inverted saucer and microwave on High (70%) for 6 – 8 minutes. Stand for about 3 minutes, then invert on to a serving plate. Leave dish to stand over ring for a few minutes. Serve warm.
Makes 1 ring

SEAFOOD *See* individual names

SEMOLINA

A coarse cereal made from milled wheat grains. Semolina is mainly used to make milk puddings, which are ideal for light diets and for young children.

To cook semolina pudding *see* Sago. Microwave for approximately half the time given for Sago Pudding.

SENSOR COOKING

Microwaves that use 'sensor cooking' contain a device that detects the vapour or steam emitted from food as it heats. The sensor adjusts the cooking times and variable power settings for various foods and quantities. This device was developed to take the guesswork out of microwave cooking. There are no sensor cooking recipes in this book, as each manufacturer of sensor microwaves gives specific instructions for use.

SESAME SEEDS

When toasted in the microwave, sesame seeds have a rich, roasted flavour. Use them to top yeast breads, muffins and to sprinkle on chicken dishes.

To toast sesame seeds

Microwave a browning dish on Full Power for 3 minutes. Sprinkle 45 ml (3 tablespoons) sesame seeds on to dish, cover with waxed paper. Stand 2 – 3 minutes, stirring every 20 seconds.

SHALLOTS

Shallots, a variety of onion, are small and firm with red-brown outer leaves. Like garlic, they grow in clusters which form a bulb. Shallots are favoured in French cooking because of their superior taste and are used and cooked like onions. They should not be confused with spring onions as these have a milder flavour.

SHEPHERD'S PIE

Shepherd's pie or cottage pie, as it is also known, is a baked dish made with minced meat and mashed potato. When it is made with leftover cooked meat, very often there is no leftover gravy. With the help of the microwave, a tasty gravy base is made in minutes.

Shepherd's pie

Full Power
7 minutes

300 g (11 oz) cooked beef, minced
4 – 5 potatoes, cooked* and mashed

Gravy

30 mℓ (2 tablespoons) oil
1 onion, chopped
2 bacon rashers, rinds removed, and chopped
1 small carrot, grated
10 mℓ (2 teaspoons) plain flour
15 mℓ (1 tablespoon) gravy granules
200 mℓ (6½ fl oz) beef stock
30 mℓ (2 tablespoons) tomato sauce (as served with pasta)
20 mℓ (4 teaspoons) Worcestershire sauce
salt and black pepper

To make gravy pour oil into a large bowl, microwave on Full Power for 1 minute. Add onion, bacon and carrot, toss to coat with oil. Microwave for 3 minutes, stir in flour, microwave for 1 minute. Combine remaining gravy ingredients, add to bowl, stir well. Microwave for 2 – 3 minutes, stirring at least twice. The gravy should be thick. Add minced meat, stir well. Turn into a casserole, cover with mashed potato. Place under a hot grill for 4 – 5 minutes.
Serves 4

Note: 400 g (14 oz) raw mince may be used instead of 300 g (11 oz) cooked meat. The mince will need to be fried with the onion, bacon and carrot. Cooking time will increase from 3 minutes to about 10 minutes. Stir frequently, then add flour and remaining ingredients.

SHERRY

A fortified wine, frequently used in cooking to add a touch of flavour to many dishes, including chicken casseroles, soups, sauces and desserts. Sherry is available in varying degrees of sweetness. Sweet sherries are added to desserts such as sabayon or zabaglione or are sprinkled over cakes or puddings, while the dry varieties are best added to sauces and soups.

Sherry cream sauce

High (70%)
6 minutes

Delicious with fruits such as baked apples, or with baked puddings.

15 g (½ oz) cornflour
60 g (2 oz) caster sugar
250 mℓ (8 fl oz) sweet sherry
500 mℓ (16 fl oz) cream
few drops of vanilla extract

Mix cornflour and sugar in a large, deep bowl. Stir in sherry and cream. Microwave on High (70%) for 5 – 6 minutes, stirring every minute, until mixture thickens and begins to bubble. Remove from heat and stir in vanilla. Serve warm or chilled.
Makes about 750 mℓ (1¼ pints)

SHIELDING

Sensitive areas of some foods should be shielded from microwaves so that they do not overcook. Use small strips of aluminium foil to shield thin parts of poultry, such as tips of wings and legs or the breastbone, and bone ends on joints of meat.

Shielding can be useful in baking too. Use small pieces of foil to shield corners of square and rectangular dishes as these areas will overcook before the centre is ready.

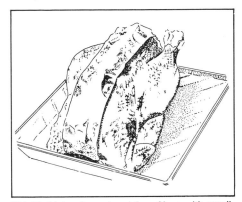

Shield chicken breast and tips of legs with small strips of aluminium foil.

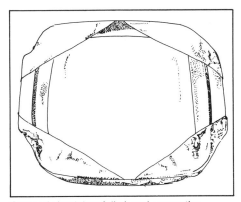

Strips of aluminium foil placed across the corners will prevent overcooking in this area.

SHORTBREAD

A rich, crumbly biscuit made from dough with a large proportion of butter. Shortbread can be made in the microwave oven, but will not be as crisp as when conventionally made and it overcooks easily. When making shortbread in the microwave, it is best baked in round dishes for even cooking. If square or rectangular dishes are used, remember to shield the corners with strips of aluminium foil.

Millionaire's shortbread

High (70%), Full Power
12 minutes

175 g (6 oz) plain flour
60 g (2 oz) cornflour
pinch of salt
60 g (2 oz) caster sugar
5 mℓ (1 teaspoon) finely grated orange rind
150 g (5 oz) butter

Topping
15 g (½ oz) butter
15 g (½ oz) soft brown sugar
125 mℓ (4 fl oz) condensed milk
100 g (3½ oz) plain chocolate, broken into pieces

Sift flour, cornflour and salt into a bowl, add sugar and orange rind. Rub in butter until mixture forms a dough. Line a 17.5-cm (7-inch) round pyrex dish with plastic wrap. Press mixture into dish, smooth with the back of a spoon and prick lightly with a fork. Microwave on High (70%) for 4 – 5 minutes. Cool slightly and cut into wedges, but do not remove from dish.

For the topping, microwave butter in a bowl on Full Power for 30 seconds. Add sugar, microwave for 1 minute. Stir in condensed milk, microwave for 2 minutes on Full Power and then 2 minutes on High (70%), stir well. Cool slightly, spread over shortbread. Place chocolate in a bowl, microwave on Full Power for 2 – 3 minutes and spread over caramel topping. Refrigerate until set. Carefully recut shortbread and lift out with the help of the plastic wrap.
Makes 1 x 17.5-cm (7-inch) round

SHORTCAKE

This dessert is usually made of layers of scone dough filled with fruit and cream. The recipe below uses a scone dough shaped into a ring and baked in the microwave. Before serving, the ring is filled with strawberries and cream.

Strawberry shortcake ring

Full Power, High (70%)
9 minutes

300 g (11 oz) strawberries, sliced
30 mℓ (2 tablespoons) orange liqueur
45 g (1½ oz) caster sugar
60 g (2 oz) butter
15 g (½ oz) Marie biscuits, crumbled
30 g (1 oz) soft brown sugar
5 mℓ (1 teaspoon) cinnamon
250 g (9 oz) basic scone mix (with sugar)*
30 g (1 oz) soft brown sugar
1 egg
200 mℓ (6½ fl oz) milk
250 mℓ (8 fl oz) whipping cream, whipped

Combine strawberries, orange liqueur and sugar and stand for at least 30 minutes. Microwave butter in a deep ring dish on Full Power for 45 seconds. Tilt dish to coat sides and bottom evenly. Mix together the biscuit crumbs, brown sugar and cinnamon and sprinkle evenly over bottom and sides of dish.

Place scone mix in a mixing bowl, add brown sugar. Combine egg and milk and add enough to the dry ingredients to make a soft, but not sticky, dough. Knead gently a few times, form into ten balls and arrange in the ring dish. Rest for 5 minutes, then place on an inverted saucer and microwave on High (70%) for 6 – 8 minutes. Stand for about 3 minutes, then invert on to a serving plate.

Just before serving, fold strawberry mixture into the whipped cream. To serve, break ring apart and cut each section in half. Spoon a little of the strawberry mixture on the bottom, replace top and spoon on a little more of the strawberry mixture. Serve with extra cream if desired.

Serves 10

SHRIMPS *See* Prawns

SIMMER

To simmer is to cook food slowly just below boiling point with only an occasional bubble showing on the surface. Simmering is a technique not often associated with microwave cooking, but the microwave can give superb results and save time, too.

Cooking foods in a covered, pre-soaked clay pot is an ideal way to simmer them and a microwave with variable power levels will make all the difference. In general, the liquid in the recipe is brought to boiling point on Full Power, then the power is reduced to Medium (50%) for the remainder of the cooking time.

SNAILS

Fresh snails or *escargots* are popular not only in France, but also in other Mediterranean countries, especially Italy, where the ancient Romans cultivated them and considered any snail dish a luxury. In most other countries, snails are purchased canned, sometimes with a bag of shells attached. Traditionally, snails are served with garlic butter, but they can also be prepared in a delicious tomato sauce, be mixed with herb butter and wrapped in lettuce leaves, or be served in such dishes as paella.

Snail-stuffed mushrooms

Full Power
9 minutes

12 mushrooms
24 canned snails, well drained
30 mℓ (2 tablespoons) lemon juice
100 g (3½ oz) butter
1 garlic clove, crushed
10 mℓ (2 teaspoons) finely chopped parsley
5 mℓ (1 teaspoon) finely chopped fresh thyme
salt and black pepper

Wipe mushrooms with a damp cloth and remove stems. Place six on a plate and microwave on Full Power for 1½ minutes. Remove and repeat with remaining mushrooms. Leave to cool, then fill each with 2 snails and sprinkle with lemon juice. Cream the butter and mix in garlic, herbs, salt and pepper. Spoon a little of the mixture into each mushroom cap. The mushrooms can now be tightly covered and refrigerated until 20 minutes before cooking. To eat, arrange six mushrooms on a plate and microwave on Full Power for 2 – 3 minutes. Remove mushrooms, keep warm and repeat with remaining

mushrooms. Serve hot with brown bread, and spoon any melted garlic butter over before serving.

Serves 4 as a starter

Sole

These flat fish microwave well and the delicate flesh remains firm and tasty. Lemon sole is not a sole at all, but belongs to the plaice family. Its flesh is softer and not of the same quality as true soles.

Sole is a versatile fish which can be prepared in a variety of ways. If you intend crumbing whole sole or baking it with a sauce, the bony frill around the outside should be removed. Sole can also be filleted, each fish providing four fillets.

To defrost fillets of sole

Place 2 large fillets of sole on a plate, cover with waxed paper and microwave on Defrost (30%) for 5 – 6 minutes. Stand for 5 minutes before using.

To microwave fillets of sole

Microwave 2 large fillets of sole on Full Power for 4 – 5 minutes. For extra flavour, add a little wine, lemon juice, herbs such as dill or fennel, or dot with a little butter.

Fillets of sole with fennel and shrimp sauce

Full Power, Medium (50%)
14 minutes

500 g (18 oz) fillet of sole, defrosted and cut into serving portions
15 mℓ (1 tablespoon) lemon juice
salt and pepper

Fennel and shrimp sauce
30 g (1 oz) butter
½ small bulb fennel, finely chopped
15 g (½ oz) flour
250 mℓ (8 fl oz) milk
1 egg yolk, lightly beaten
200 g (7 oz) canned shrimps, drained
60 mℓ (4 tablespoons) cucumber, finely chopped
pinch of chilli powder
pinch of pepper

To make the sauce, microwave butter on Full Power for 30 seconds. Stir in chopped fennel and microwave for 2 minutes. Remove from heat, stir in flour and microwave for 15 seconds. Gradually stir in milk, then microwave for about 3 minutes, stirring after every minute. Gradually stir about half the hot mixture into the egg yolk, then blend into remaining hot mixture. Add shrimps, cucumber, chilli powder and pepper and microwave on Medium (50%) for 2 minutes. Mix well.

Arrange fish in a baking dish with thickest parts to the outside. Sprinkle with lemon juice, salt and pepper. Cover with vented plastic wrap and microwave on Full Power for 5 – 6 minutes. Remove fish to platter and spoon

sauce over. Garnish with cucumber slices or fennel sprigs if desired.

Serves 4 – 6

SORBET

A sorbet is a water ice usually made of sweetened fruit juice or purée combined with a sugar syrup base and is sometimes flavoured with other ingredients, including wine, champagne or spirits. Beaten egg white or a little cream folded into the mixture gives a finer texture. Sorbets using a sugar syrup base or with cooked fruit as a flavouring can be made quickly with the help of the microwave.

Campari sorbet

High (70%)
9 minutes

750 mℓ (1¼ pints) fresh orange juice, strained
250 mℓ (8 fl oz) Campari
juice of 1 lemon
200 g (7 oz) caster sugar
2 egg whites, stiffly beaten

Combine orange juice, Campari, lemon juice and sugar in a large casserole. Microwave on High (70%) for 7 – 9 minutes, or until sugar has dissolved and the mixture is brought almost to the boil, stirring frequently. Cool mixture to room temperature, pour into a shallow freezer tray and freeze for about 2 hours. Remove from freezer, break up and beat with an electric mixer until slushy. Fold in beaten egg whites, return to freezer and freeze for 3 – 4 hours. Remove from the freezer to the refrigerator about 20 minutes before serving.

Serves 8

Creamy rhubarb sorbet

Full Power
13 minutes

350 g (12 oz) rhubarb, sliced
200 g (7 oz) caster sugar
250 mℓ (8 fl oz) water
45 mℓ (3 tablespoons) Cointreau
30 mℓ (2 tablespoons) framboise liqueur or Crème de Cassis
15 mℓ (1 tablespoon) lemon juice
45 mℓ (3 tablespoons) whipping cream, whipped to soft peaks
2 egg whites, stiffly beaten

Place rhubarb in a large bowl. Add sugar, 125 mℓ (4 fl oz) of the water, Cointreau, liqueur and lemon juice. Microwave, covered, on Full Power for 11 – 13 minutes, or until rhubarb is very soft. Place mixture in a food processor and process until smooth. Add remaining water to the rhubarb purée and pour into a freezer tray. Freeze until almost solid. Remove from the freezer, break up and place in a mixing bowl. Beat until slushy, then fold in cream and beaten egg whites. Return to the freezer and freeze for 3 – 4 hours.

Makes about 1 litre (1¾ pints)

Apple sorbet

Full Power
5 minutes

4 Granny Smith apples, peeled, cored and
chopped
125 mℓ (4 fl oz) lemon juice
150 g (5 oz) caster sugar
375 mℓ (12 fl oz) water
30 mℓ (2 tablespoons) brandy
2 egg whites, stiffly beaten

Place apples and lemon juice in a food
processor and process to a smooth purée.
Combine sugar and water and microwave on
Full Power for 2 minutes. Stir thoroughly, then
microwave for 2 – 3 minutes more, or until
sugar has dissolved. Cool, then add to apple
purée along with the brandy. Pour into a freezer
tray and freeze until slushy. Place mixture in a
bowl, beat thoroughly and fold in beaten egg
whites. Return to the freezer and freeze for
3 – 4 hours, until solid.
Makes about 1 litre

SOUFFLÉS
Light, fluffy mixtures made with egg yolks
and beaten egg whites. Baked soufflés
need hot, dry air to give them their characteristic appearance, colour and texture,
and are not suitable for microwave cooking. However, the preparation of a sweet
or savoury cold soufflé can be speeded up
by using the microwave to dissolve the gelatine.
See also Gelatine.

SOUP
There are almost as many soups as there
are ingredients from which to make them.
They also take on many forms and may be
served hot or cold. A clear, light con-
sommé stimulates the appetite, a hearty
meat and vegetable broth makes a satisfying warming winter meal in itself and a
smooth fruity soup is a delicious tongue-
tingling way to round off a meal.
   The art of soup-making begins with a
good stock made from bones, seasonings,
water and vegetables. When making stocks
and soups in the microwave, cooking times
are reduced and so is the need for constant
attention. The kitchen remains cool and
free of odours.
See also Stock.

Borscht

Full Power, Medium (50%)
35 minutes

4 medium-sized raw beetroots, peeled and
grated
2 carrots, grated
1 onion, thinly sliced
1 turnip, peeled and grated
90 mℓ (3 fl oz) dry white wine
300 mℓ (10 fl oz) water
30 mℓ (2 tablespoons) vinegar
pinch of sugar
salt
1 litre (1¾ pints) beef stock
200 g (7 oz) cooked beef, diced
½ cabbage, shredded
soured cream

Place beetroot, carrots, onion, turnip, wine,
water, vinegar, sugar and salt in a large, deep
casserole. Cover and microwave on Full Power
for 8 – 10 minutes. Reduce heat to Medium
(50%) and simmer for 10 minutes. Add beef
stock, beef and cabbage and microwave,
covered, for 10 – 15 minutes longer or until
vegetables are tender. Serve topped with
soured cream.
Serves 6

Cream of vegetable soup

Full Power
16 minutes

Using one basic recipe, you can make a variety
of delicious creamy soups.

For the basic soup
60 g (2 oz) butter
1 large onion, chopped
1 large potato, chopped
750 mℓ (1¼ pints) chicken stock
10 mℓ (2 teaspoons) cornflour
250 mℓ (8 fl oz) milk
125 mℓ (4 fl oz) single cream
salt and pepper

Place butter in a 2-litre (3½-pint) casserole and
microwave on Full Power for 30 – 45 seconds to
melt. Add onion and potato and microwave,
covered, for 3 minutes. Add stock, cover and
microwave for 10 minutes. Transfer mixture to a
blender and purée. Mix cornflour with milk and
gradually stir into the purée. Return to
casserole dish and microwave, covered, for
2 minutes, stirring after 1 minute. Stir in cream
and season to taste. Serve hot or chilled.
Serves 4 – 6

Cream of celery soup

cream of vegetable soup*
6 celery sticks, chopped
30 mℓ (2 tablespoons) chopped parsley

Add chopped celery to basic soup mixture with
the stock. Proceed as for basic soup,
increasing cooking time by 1 – 2 minutes if

necessary. Add chopped parsley with the
cream and mix well. Serve hot.
Serves 6

Cream of mushroom soup

cream of vegetable soup*
300 g (11 oz) fresh mushrooms, sliced

Add sliced mushrooms to basic soup mixture
with the stock. Proceed as for basic soup.
Serve hot.
Serves 4 – 6

Cream of carrot soup

cream of vegetable soup*
450 g (1 lb) carrots, peeled and sliced

Add carrots to basic soup mixture with the
stock. Proceed as for basic soup, increasing
cooking time by 1 – 2 minutes if necessary.
Serve hot or cold.
Serves 6

Cream of cauliflower soup

cream of vegetable soup* (excluding single
cream)
1 small cauliflower, broken into florets
10 mℓ (2 teaspoons) fresh dill or
5 mℓ (1 teaspoon) dried dill
125 mℓ (4 fl oz) soured cream

Add cauliflower to basic soup mixture with the
stock. Proceed as for basic soup, increasing
cooking time by 1 – 2 minutes if necessary.
Add the dill to the purée with the cornflour and
milk. When the soup is cooked, stir in soured
cream instead of fresh cream. Serve hot.
Serves 6

Cream of leek soup

cream of vegetable soup*
30 mℓ (1 oz) butter
300 g (11 oz) leeks, thinly sliced

Melt butter for basic soup, add an extra 30 g
(1 oz) butter, then the potato and onion from the
basic recipe. Now add the leeks. Microwave for
4 – 4½ minutes on Full Power. Add stock and
proceed as for basic soup. Serve hot or cold.
Serves 4–6

Cream of broccoli soup

cream of vegetable soup*
450 g (1 lb) fresh broccoli, or frozen and
thawed

Add broccoli to basic soup mixture with the
stock. Proceed as for basic soup, increasing
cooking time by 1 – 2 minutes if necessary.
Serve hot or cold.
Serves 6

SPAGHETTI *See* Pasta

SPARE-RIBS

Spare-ribs, usually pork, are best cut into individual pieces for microwave cooking and are most often served with a spicy or tangy sauce. Microwaved spare-ribs are fully cooked and may be glazed in a conventional oven or placed over hot coals on the barbecue for an appetizing finish. If you wish to reheat them, just place them in the microwave and microwave on Full Power for 1 – 2 minutes.

Spicy spare-ribs

Medium (50%), Full Power
1 hour 13 minutes

1.5 kg (3 lb) pork spare-ribs, cut into pieces
1 onion, chopped
250 ml (8 fl oz) beer
125 ml (4 fl oz) chilli sauce
50 g (5 oz) red currant jelly
75 ml (2½ fl oz) vinegar
45 g (1½ oz) soft brown sugar
30 ml (2 tablespoons) soy sauce
15 ml (1 tablespoon) Worcestershire sauce
Tabasco

Place spare-ribs in a shallow casserole. Add onion and beer. Cover and microwave on Medium (50%) for 30 minutes, rearranging the ribs every 10 minutes. Drain, reserving liquid.

Mix remaining ingredients together in a jug and add about 125 ml (4 fl oz) of the reserved liquid. Microwave on Full Power for 2 – 3 minutes or until boiling. Pour over the ribs and marinate for at least 3 hours, or overnight.

To cook spare-ribs, cover and microwave on Medium (50%) for 35 – 40 minutes, rearranging every 15 minutes, until meat is very tender.
Serves 4

Note: To finish ribs over a barbecue, omit second microwave cooking and place ribs over hot coals. Baste frequently, turning occasionally, for about 15 minutes.

SPICES

Spices are dried seeds, bark, roots or flower buds of aromatic plants which are used either whole or ground to give flavour and aroma to foods. The demand for spices has been known since ancient times, and the spice trade was once the most profitable in the world.

Flavouring food with spices should enhance the dish and not obscure the taste. Ground spices lose flavour more quickly than whole ones and should be added to a dish towards the end of a long cooking time if possible. However, when microwaving curries, spices should be added when preparing the ingredients. For grills or roasts, spices may be rubbed into the surface of the meat. In pies and cakes, the spices are added when mixing in dry ingredients.

The flavour of whole spices is intensified if they are placed on a baking sheet and heated conventionally at 160 °C/325 °F/gas 3 for about 5 minutes. Do not try to roast spices in the microwave, because if the spices are very dry, there will be no reaction and if spices do contain some moisture, they tend to burn.

SPINACH

This nutritious green vegetable has a pleasant, slightly acid taste and is valued for its vitamins A and C, and iron content. Spinach makes a delicious accompanying vegetable for egg and fish dishes and can be used for quiche fillings or for salads. It can also be served with pasta and poultry in savoury casseroles.

To microwave spinach

Wash 450 g (1 lb) spinach and shake leaves well but do not dry. Remove thick stalks and place leaves in a casserole with only the water clinging to them. Cover and microwave on Full Power for 5 – 8 minutes, or to desired texture. Season to taste.

Serving suggestions

☐ Crumble 2 – 3 cooked bacon rashers* over hot spinach. Toss with a little melted butter and season with salt and pepper.
☐ Microwave 45 g (1½ oz) butter with a generous pinch of nutmeg or mace until butter melts. Pour over spinach. Add about 45 ml (1½ fl oz) single cream, toss to mix and add salt and pepper to taste.
☐ Add 45 g (1½ oz) melted butter, 30 ml (2 tablespoons) fried chopped onion and 5 ml (1 teaspoon) red wine vinegar to the cooked spinach. Season with salt and pepper.

Spinach cheese casserole

Full Power, High (70%)
13 minutes

450 g (1 lb) cooked spinach*
½ small onion, chopped
30 g (1 oz) butter
1 chicken stock cube
salt and pepper
generous pinch of nutmeg or mace
3 eggs, beaten
350 g (12 oz) low-fat soft cheese
60 g (2 oz) cheddar cheese, grated
15 g (½ oz) butter
30 g (1 oz) soft brown breadcrumbs
15 g (½ oz) Parmesan cheese, grated

Chop spinach and set aside. Place onion and butter in a deep, 20-cm (8-inch) casserole and microwave on Full Power for 2 minutes. Stir in spinach, stock cube, salt, pepper and nutmeg. Mix eggs with soft and grated Cheddar cheeses, and stir into the spinach, mixing well.

Microwave butter for a few seconds to melt, then pour over breadcrumbs. Add Parmesan cheese and toss lightly to mix. Sprinkle over the spinach mixture. Microwave on High (70%) for 9 – 11 minutes, or until mixture is nearly set. Stand for 5 – 8 minutes before serving.
Serves 6

SPONGE CAKES *See* Cakes

SQUASH

Squash is the term used for a number of marrows, pumpkins and gourds, all of the same family. Species differ from each other mainly in shape and colour, and all have a similar, somewhat bland flavour. Most squash are cooked in the same way, being boiled, steamed or baked. They may be served with butter and spices or sauces, or they may be stuffed and baked.
See also Butternut and Pumpkin.

To microwave squash

Hubbard squash: Peel and dice 450 g (1 lb) hubbard squash, add 45 ml (3 tablespoons) water and microwave on Full Power, covered, for 8 – 10 minutes. Season to taste. Add butter, garlic salt and pepper, or season with herbs such as basil, marjoram or rosemary. Mash and add a little butter and cinnamon or sprinkle with grated cheese.
Serves 4

Patty pan and squash: Wash and remove stem and blossom ends from 500 g (18 oz) patty pan squash. Leave whole, but pierce the skin in several places with a skewer. Place in a casserole, add 60 ml (4 tablespoons) water and microwave, covered, on Full Power for 5 – 7 minutes, or until tender. Season to taste and stand for 3 minutes before serving.
Serves 4

Stuffed patty pan squash

Full Power
14 minutes

12 small patty pan squash
30 ml (2 tablespoons) water
30 ml (2 tablespoons) olive oil
1 small garlic clove, crushed
2 spring onions, chopped
3 small plum tomatoes, skinned, seeded and chopped
2.5 ml (½ teaspoon) lemon juice
2.5 ml (½ teaspoon) caster sugar
30 ml (2 tablespoons) chopped parsley, preferably French
10 ml (2 teaspoons) chopped lemon thyme or generous pinch of dried thyme
black pepper

Place 6 patty pan squash with water in a casserole. Cover and microwave on Full Power for 3 minutes. Rinse under cold water. Repeat with remaining patty pan squash. With a melon baller, remove core and pulp from centre of each patty pan squash, reserving pulp. Microwave oil for 45 seconds, add garlic and spring onion and microwave for 1 minute. Add patty pan pulp, tomatoes, lemon juice, sugar, half the parsley, thyme and pepper. Microwave for 2 minutes. Turn mixture into a blender or food processor and blend until smooth. Fill patty pan squash with the mixture and arrange six on a microwave baking sheet. Microwave for 2 minutes or until heated through. Repeat

with remaining patty pan squash and serve sprinkled with the remaining parsley as an accompaniment to lamb or beef.
Serves 6

SQUID

Squid, also known as calamari, is a saltwater mollusc related to the octopus and cuttlefish. The flesh is slightly chewy, with a delicate, almost sweet flavour. Squid is sold either 'au naturel' or as cleaned, frozen tubes or rings. The tubes are ideal for stuffing, and stew in minutes in the microwave. Crumbed squid rings cannot be crisped in the microwave and are best deep-fried.

To clean squid, soak in cold water for 10 minutes. Pull the head and tentacles out of the body. Carefully cut off the tentacles and set aside. Discard the innards, including the ink sac, eyes and beak. Pull the transparent quill out of the body. Remove the thin black skin from the tentacles and body with your fingers, using a little salt if necessary. Wash the squid in plenty of cold running water to remove the yellowish deposit and any sand. Dry on a piece of kitchen paper.

Braised stuffed squid

Full Power. High (70%)
33 minutes

750 g (1¾ lb) baby squid
30 mℓ (2 tablespoons) oil
1 medium-sized onion, chopped
10 button mushrooms, finely chopped
1 – 2 garlic cloves
1 thick slice of white bread, made into crumbs
30 mℓ (2 tablespoons) chopped parsley
salt and black pepper.

Sauce
30 mℓ (2 tablespoons) oil
1 medium-sized onion, chopped
1 small green chilli, chopped
5 – 6 tomatoes, skinned and chopped
2.5 mℓ (½ teaspoon) thyme
45 mℓ (3 tablespoons) water
30 mℓ (2 tablespoons) tomato paste
45 mℓ (3 tablespoons) tomato purée or pousada
salt and black pepper
5 mℓ (1 teaspoon) caster sugar

Clean the squid, set the tubes aside and chop the tentacles. Microwave the oil in a bowl on Full Power for 1 minute, add onion and stir to coat with the oil. Microwave for 1 minute. Add mushrooms and garlic, combine and microwave for 3 minutes. Add breadcrumbs, parsley, seasonings and chopped tentacles, mix well. Fill each tube with a little of this mixture but do not overfill as the stuffing swells during cooking. Set aside.
For the sauce, microwave oil for 1 minute in a large shallow casserole. Add onion and chilli, stir to coat with the oil. Microwave for 3 minutes,

add remaining ingredients and stir well. Microwave for about 14 minutes, until thickened. Add stuffed squid, spooning a little sauce over each tube, cover and microwave on High (70%) for 10 – 12 minutes. Do not overcook, as squid will become tough.
Serves 4

STANDING TIME

Food continues to cook after it has been removed from the microwave, so it is important to let it 'stand' before serving. The length of standing time varies, but in general depends on the volume and density of the food. Meat dishes such as roasts or poultry will continue to cook for 10 – 20 minutes after the microwave energy has been turned off. Other foods, such as cakes or puddings, depend on standing time to finish cooking. Because of this, it is important to take standing time into consideration when experimenting with foods or trying new recipes, so that foods will not be overcooked. It is always better to slightly undercook foods, as they can easily be heated again if they are not quite cooked. Follow recipe directions for standing times.

STEAKS

Steak refers to tender cuts of beef from the fillet, rump or sirloin or other meaty, lean parts of the animal. Thick cuts of fish, such as hake, salmon, swordfish, or tuna are also called steaks. Steaks can be fried on a browning dish or cooked with a sauce in the microwave.
See also Beef and Fish.

STEAMED PUDDINGS *See* Puddings

STEW *See* Beef and individual names

STIR-FRY

Stir-frying is an Oriental method of cooking food whereby thinly sliced foods are stirred in a little hot oil over a high heat for a short period of time. Almost any food, including vegetables, meat, fish and poultry, can be cooked this way and the constant stirring of the food ensures fast, uniform cooking and tasty, nutritious eating. A wok is usually used for stir-frying but for microwave cooking a browning dish works well.

Beef and vegetable stir-fry

Full Power
13 minutes

60 mℓ (4 tablespoons) oil
1 garlic clove, chopped
500 g (18 oz) sirloin steak, sliced paper-thin
1 onion, thinly sliced
1 green pepper, thinly sliced
1 carrot, cut in julienne
45 mℓ (3 tablespoons) water
300 g (11 oz) mushrooms, sliced
2 courgettes, sliced
125 mℓ (4 fl oz) beef stock
30 mℓ (2 tablespoons) cornflour
45 mℓ (3 tablespoons) soy sauce
30 mℓ (2 tablespoons) dry sherry
black pepper
60 g (2 oz) bean sprouts

Preheat a browning dish according to manufacturer's instructions, usually 5 – 6 minutes on Full Power. Add oil, garlic and beef and stir well, then microwave on Full Power for 1 – 1½ minutes. Stir and set aside. Place onion, green pepper and carrot in a bowl, add water and microwave, covered, for 2 minutes. Drain well and add to the beef with the mushrooms and courgettes. Combine stock, cornflour, soy sauce and sherry. Microwave for 1 minute, then pour over beef mixture, stir well and microwave for about 3 minutes, stirring every minute. Season with pepper, toss in bean sprouts and serve with rice.
Serves 4

Stir from the outside inwards.

STIRRING

In conventional stove-top cooking, food is stirred from the bottom upwards to ensure even heating. Since the outer edges of food normally cook first in microwave cooking, foods should be stirred from the outer edges inwards to promote even cooking. Foods that normally need constant stirring, such as sauces or custards, need only occasional stirring in the microwave. However, these foods may need to be stirred a little more frequently in a microwave without a turntable.

STOCK

Stock is the liquid obtained by simmering meat, chicken or fish bones and trimmings with water, vegetables and seasonings. A good stock is the basis for most soups and sauces, and is used to add body to casseroles, gravies and other dishes. The quality of the ingredients used is important and it is wise to experiment by adding various herbs and wine to flavour stocks. Microwaving stock saves time, and it does not need attention during cooking.
See also Court Bouillon and Giblets.

Beef stock

Full Power, Medium (50%)
1 hour 23 minutes

1.5 kg (3 lb) beef bones, such as shin and
  marrow
45 mℓ (3 tablespoons) oil
2 litres (3½ pints) water
4 peppercorns
3 whole cloves
1 bay leaf
3 parsley sprigs
1 carrot, thickly sliced
2 celery sticks with leaves, coarsely chopped
1 onion, quartered
thyme leaves
5 mℓ (1 teaspoon) salt

Break up bones. Preheat a browning dish for 6 minutes on Full Power. Add oil and then bones, and microwave on Full Power for 5 minutes, turning over half-way through the cooking time. Place bones in a large, deep bowl and add remaining ingredients. Microwave on Full Power for 10 – 12 minutes, or until mixture boils rapidly. Reduce heat to Medium (50%) and simmer for about 60 minutes. Strain liquid and cool. When stock has cooled, skim off fat and refrigerate. The stock will keep a few days in the refrigerator or it can be frozen. Use as desired.
Makes about 1.5 litres (2¾ pints)

Chicken stock

Full Power, Medium (50%)
1 hour 12 minutes

1 kg (2¼ lb) chicken backs, necks, wings and
  bones
2 litres (3½ pints) boiling water
2 litres (3½ pints) cold water
6 peppercorns
1 bay leaf
thyme leaves
4 whole cloves
4 parsley sprigs
1 onion, quartered
1 celery stick with leaves, thickly sliced
1 carrot, thickly sliced
2.5-cm (1-inch) strip of lemon peel

Place chicken in a large deep bowl. Pour boiling water over, stand for 5 minutes, then drain. Cover with cold water, add remaining ingredients and microwave on Full Power for about 10 – 12 minutes, or until water is rapidly boiling. Reduce power level to Medium (50%) and microwave for about 1 hour. Strain stock and cool. Remove fat and refrigerate stock. Use for soups, sauces and to flavour casseroles and gravies.
Makes about 1.5 litres (2¾ pints)

Fish stock

Full Power, Medium (50%)
26 minutes

45 mℓ (1½ oz) butter or margarine
1 small onion, chopped
1 carrot, chopped
1 celery stick, sliced
6 peppercorns
3 cloves
125 mℓ (4 fl oz) dry white wine
30 mℓ (2 tablespoons) white vinegar
750 mℓ (1¼ pints) cold water
strip of lemon rind
750 g (1¾ lb) fish bones, heads, trimmings
½ bay leaf
3 parsley sprigs
thyme leaves

Microwave butter in a large bowl for 45 seconds on Full Power. Add onion, carrot and celery. Microwave for 3 minutes. Add remaining ingredients and microwave for 8 – 10 minutes. Reduce power to Medium (50%) and microwave for 10 – 12 minutes. Strain stock, cool and use for fish soups or sauces.
Makes about 750 mℓ (1¼ pints)

STRAWBERRY

Strawberries are a unique fruit because the seeds are scattered on the outside. When ripe, they are bright red in colour and have a tangy sweetness. Strawberries can be canned or frozen, made into jam, or used in desserts and puddings, but one of the best ways to enjoy them is to eat them fresh with cream, or they can be served in bowls with champagne.
See also Jam and Shortcake.

Strawberries in peppered wine

High (70%)
2 minutes

Believe it or not pepper enhances the delicate strawberry flavour.

675 g (1½ lb) fresh strawberries
250 mℓ (8 fl oz) orange juice
2.5 mℓ (½ teaspoon) coarsely ground black
  peppercorns
500 mℓ (16 fl oz) red wine
60 mℓ (4 tablespoons) brandy
10 mℓ (2 teaspoons) grated orange peel

Wash berries, halve if they are large and place in a deep bowl. Place orange juice and pepper in a jug and microwave on High (70%) for 2 minutes. Add red wine, brandy and grated peel. Pour over berries and stand for about 2 hours before serving.
Serves 6

STREUSEL TOPPING

This delicious topping mixture is made of brown sugar, flour, butter, spices and sometimes chopped nuts. It is sprinkled on top of microwaved cakes, coffee cakes or American muffins to improve the appearance and to add flavour.

Streusel topping

Combine 100 g (3½ oz) soft brown sugar, 30 ml (1 tablespoon) plain flour, 10 ml (2 teaspoons) cinnamon, 30 g (1 oz) butter and 45 g (1½ oz) chopped nuts. Mix well, use as desired.

STUFFING

Stuffings are useful as they not only add to the flavour of food, but also help it go further and, in the case of poultry and boned meats, help them to maintain their shape. Fresh breadcrumbs form the basis of most stuffing mixtures but rice, sausage-meat and chestnuts can be used too. Do not pack the stuffing too tightly as it swells during cooking. When microwaving stuffed meats, the total weight must be calculated to make the timing accurate.

Tasty stuffing for chicken

Full Power
4 minutes

45 mℓ (3 tablespoons) oil
1 onion, chopped
liver from chicken, cleaned and chopped
100 g (3½ oz) mushrooms, chopped
125 g (4 oz) soft breadcrumbs
30 mℓ (2 tablespoons) chopped parsley
2.5 mℓ (½ teaspoon) dried mixed herbs or
  tarragon
salt and black pepper
1 egg
milk if necessary

Place in a large bowl, microwave on Full Power for 2 minutes. Add onion and chicken liver, toss to coat with oil. Cover with waxed paper, microwave for 2 minutes. Stir in remaining ingredients, soften with a little milk if mixture is too dry.
Use to stuff a 1.5 kg (3 lb) chicken

SUGAR

Microwave energy reacts to the presence of moisture, sugar and fat in foodstuffs. Dry granulated or caster sugar alone is not readily affected by microwave energy, but with the addition of moisture or fat, the reaction is speedy and dramatic. Sugar can be quickly dissolved in liquid to form a syrup and can easily be caramelized in the microwave. Take care when microwaving soft brown sugar because the high amount of molasses attracts microwave energy. *See also* Caramel and Syrup.

To soften brown sugar
When opened packets of brown sugar become hard and unusable, a few seconds in the microwave will return the sugar to a soft consistency:

Place 200 g (7 oz) sugar in a glass dish. Add a slice of white bread or a wedge of apple, cover and microwave on Full Power for about 25 seconds. Stand for several minutes before using.

SULTANAS *See* Raisins

SWEET POTATO
Sweet potatoes are not related to ordinary potatoes, although they both probably originated from Central America. This elongated tuber is either white or orange fleshed and can be baked whole or boiled and mashed. It is also used in sweet dishes such as cakes and pies or served as a vegetable, seasoned with butter, sugar, cinnamon or cloves.

To microwave sweet potatoes
Wash 4 medium-sized sweet potatoes and pierce to allow steam to escape. Arrange in a circle on kitchen paper and microwave on Full Power for 8 – 10 minutes, or until tender when pierced with a fork. Stand for 5 minutes before using. To serve, cut open, add butter and salt and pepper, or peel and mash flesh with butter, a little sweetened apple sauce and season with cinnamon, cloves or ginger.
Serves 4

Nutty orange sweet potatoes

Full Power
6 minutes

4 cooked sweet potatoes*
pinch of salt
125 g (4 oz) orange marmalade
30 g (1 oz) pecan nuts, coarsely chopped

Cut potatoes into bite-sized pieces and place in a 1-litre (1¾-pint) casserole. Sprinkle with salt and spoon marmalade over. Cover with waxed paper and microwave on Full Power for 4 minutes. Add nuts, stir gently and microwave, covered, for 1 – 2 minutes longer, or until heated through.
Serves 4

SWEETBREADS
Sweetbreads are generally the thymus glands taken from a calf. They have a similar appearance and texture to brains and are an important ingredient in several famous French dishes. Most sweetbreads have been cleaned by the butcher, but if

not, they will need to be soaked in cold water for several hours, changing the water frequently, to allow impurities to seep out. Blanching sweetbreads for a few minutes before cooking makes it easy to trim away the membranes and ducts. The sweetbreads are now ready to be cooked whole, to be sliced and sautéed, or to be cooked in a sauce.

Sweetbreads in creamy wine sauce

Full Power, High (70%)
23 minutes

350 g (12 oz) sweetbreads, thawed and well cleaned
300 mℓ (10 fl oz) water
15 mℓ (1 tablespoon) lemon juice
2.5 mℓ (½ teaspoon) salt
30 g (1 oz) butter
1 large carrot, coarsely grated
1 small onion, sliced
125 mℓ (4 fl oz) chicken stock
125 mℓ (4 fl oz) dry white wine
20 mℓ (4 teaspoons) red currant jelly
7.5 mℓ (1½ teaspoons) fresh thyme or
   2.5 mℓ (½ teaspoon) dried thyme
5 mℓ (1 teaspoon) lemon juice
8 button mushrooms, sliced
7.5 mℓ (1½ teaspoons) cornflour
30 mℓ (2 tablespoons) brandy
60 mℓ (4 tablespoons) cream
salt and black pepper

Place sweetbreads in a casserole. Add water, lemon juice and salt. Microwave, covered, on Full Power for 7 – 9 minutes, or until sweetbreads are firm and no pink remains. Stand for 10 minutes, then drain and cool. Remove membrane and any tubes from the sweetbreads. Break or cut into small clusters.
  Place butter in a casserole. Microwave for 45 seconds to melt. Add carrot and onion and microwave, covered, for 3 minutes. Add stock, wine, jelly, thyme and lemon juice. Microwave for 3 minutes more. Add mushrooms and microwave for 1 minute. Combine cornflour and brandy and stir into the vegetable mixture. Microwave for 2 – 3 minutes, stirring every minute until mixture is thick and clear. Add cream and sweetbreads and microwave, covered, for 2 – 3 minutes on High (70%) to heat through. Season to taste with salt and black pepper and serve with hot toast if desired.
Serves 4 as a starter or 2 as a main course

SWEETCORN
Fresh sweetcorn is available in supermarkets for most of the year and can be eaten either on the cob or cut off the cob. It is also available frozen or in cans, either in whole kernels or creamed. The cobs take only a few minutes to cook in the microwave and no water is added so all the flavour and goodness are retained.

To prepare corn-on-the-cob, remove the stalk, leaves and silk.

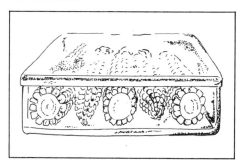

Arrange sweetcorn in a glass casserole, cover and microwave.

Corn-on-the-cob

Full Power

Remove husks and silk if necessary and place sweetcorn in a glass casserole. Cover and microwave on Full Power for the following times:

1 ear	2 – 3 minutes
2 ears	4 – 6 minutes
3 ears	6 – 7 minutes
4 ears	7 – 8 minutes
6 ears	8 – 9 minutes

Rotate ears half-way through the cooking time, and stand for 5 minutes before serving. Serve with melted butter, salt and pepper.

Sweetcorn relish

Full Power
3 minutes

Delicious served with glazed ham or gammon

100 g (3½ oz) caster sugar
75 mℓ (2½ fl oz) vinegar
2.5 mℓ (½ teaspoon) salt
2.5 mℓ (½ teaspoon) celery seeds
generous pinch of mustard seeds
several drops of Tabasco
400 g (14 oz) canned sweetcorn kernels,
    drained
30 mℓ (2 tablespoons) green pepper, chopped
30 mℓ (2 tablespoons) celery, chopped
30 mℓ (2 tablespoons) onion, chopped

Mix sugar, vinegar, salt, celery and mustard
seeds and Tabasco in a casserole. Microwave
on Full Power for 3 minutes, stirring once. Mix in
remaining ingredients. Cover and refrigerate
overnight to blend flavours.
Makes about 600 mℓ (19 fl oz)

Sweetcorn savoury

400 g (14 oz) canned creamed sweetcorn
15 mℓ (1 tablespoon) finely chopped chives
3 slices of ham or gammon, roughly chopped
pinch of dry mustard
45 mℓ (3 tablespoons) single cream
cayenne
black pepper

To serve
4 slices of buttered toast

Place sweetcorn in a bowl and microwave on
Full Power for 4 minutes, stirring at least once
during cooking time. Add remaining
ingredients, stir to combine. Microwave for
1 – 2 minutes more until piping hot. Spoon over
hot buttered toast.
Generously covers 4 slices of toast

SYRUP

A solution of sugar dissolved in water and
sometimes flavoured with fruit juice, citrus
rind or, as in the recipe below, rose petals.
Syrups are used for sweetening poached
fruits or fruit salads, as a base for sorbets
and ice creams and for pouring over baked
desserts. When microwaving syrups use a
large, heatproof bowl. It may be necessary
to brush the sides of the bowl with water to
remove any stray sugar crystals.
See also Fruit.

Syrup of rose petals

Full Power
11 minutes

Use this syrup to pour over ice cream or to add
colour and flavour to milk shakes.

petals from 12 fully opened red and pink roses
juice of 2 lemons
400 mℓ (13 fl oz) boiling water
600 g (1 lb 5 oz) caster sugar
few drops of wine red colouring

Separate petals, rinse well. Place in a large
bowl, add half the lemon juice, leave overnight.
Combine sugar and water, microwave on Full
Power for 4 minutes, stirring twice. Add
remaining lemon juice, microwave for 4 minutes
longer. Chop the rose petals in batches in a
food processor, add to syrup. Microwave for 3
minutes, cover and allow to cool. Strain through
muslin, add a few drops of colouring to give a
good colour. Pour into a jar or bottle, store in a
cool place.
Makes about 750 mℓ (1¼ pints)

From top to bottom: Mexican Sauce (page 196),
Hollandaise Sauce (page 195), Barbecue
Sauce (page 196)

TACOS

Tacos are folded or rolled cooked Mexican tortillas* filled with a spicy mixture. They are quick to prepare and make interesting meals. Heat up leftover savoury mince or chicken mixtures in a few seconds in the microwave, and add cheese, salad ingredients, chillies and canned beans for unusual fillings.

Mince and sausage taco

Full Power
11 minutes

30 mℓ (2 tablespoons) oil
1 onion, chopped
100 g (3½ oz) minced meat
100 g (3½ oz) sausage-meat
1 green pepper, chopped
125 mℓ (4 fl oz) tomato purée or pousada
Tabasco
salt and black pepper
6 tortillas*
½ lettuce, shredded
2 – 3 tomatoes, finely chopped
1 bunch of spring onions, chopped
1 avocado, mashed or diced
100 g (3½ oz) Cheddar cheese, grated

Place oil in a bowl, microwave on Full Power for 1 minute. Add onion, toss to coat with oil, microwave for 2 minutes. Add minced meat and sausage-meat, break up with a fork. Microwave for 3 – 4 minutes, stirring every minute. Add green pepper, tomato purée, Tabasco and seasonings, mix well. Microwave for about 5 minutes, stirring twice. Divide meat mixture between tortillas, add a spoonful of each salad ingredient and top generously with cheese.
Makes 6

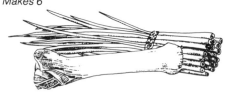

TAMALE

Tamales are served on special occasions and fiesta days in Mexico. They are made of minced meat mixed with corn meal and seasonings, wrapped in a sweetcorn husk and microwaved.

Tamale

Full Power, Medium (50%)
15 minutes

1 litre (1¼ pints) boiling water
8 – 10 large sweetcorn leaves

Filling
250 g (9 oz) finely minced beef
1 onion, chopped
1 garlic clove, crushed
1 green chilli, chopped
60 mℓ (4 tablespoons) tomato sauce (as served with pasta)
1 large tomato, skinned* and chopped
salt and black pepper
60 g (2 oz) butter or margarine
60 g (2 oz) cream cheese
30 g (1 oz) Cheddar cheese, grated
100 g (3½ oz) cornmeal
2.5 mℓ (½ teaspoon) baking powder
1 egg
pinch of caraway seeds, crushed
pinch of cinnamon

Pour boiling water over sweetcorn leaves, set aside. To make the filling, combine minced meat, onion, garlic and chilli in a bowl. Microwave on Full Power for 3 – 4 minutes, stirring twice during cooking time. Add tomato sauce, tomato and seasonings, mix well, microwave for 4 minutes. Microwave butter for 1 minute, mix in cream cheese, add remaining ingredients, mix to combine, and season lightly. Drain sweetcorn leaves, pat dry with kitchen paper, lay flat. Divide the cheese mixture between the leaves, spread down the centre of each husk, top with meat mixture. Roll sides of the leaves around meat mixture, fold ends under and tie each end with string or a strip of

leaf. Arrange in a dish, add 45 mℓ (1½ fl oz) water, cover with vented plastic wrap. Microwave on Medium (50%) for 7 – 10 minutes, until set. Stand for 3 minutes before serving.
Makes 8 – 10

TANDOORI

Tandoori chicken is the Indian cook's version of spicy barbecued chicken. Traditionally this dish is baked in a special outdoor oven called a 'tandoor'. The microwave recipe below is quick to make, and the result is tender and juicy. To finish off the dish, grill or barbecue the chicken portions just before serving.

Tandoori chicken

High (70%)
15 minutes

10 chicken portions
30 mℓ (2 tablespoons) lemon juice
salt
5 mℓ (1 teaspoon) coriander seeds, crushed
2.5 mℓ (½ teaspoon) caraway seeds, crushed
pinch of turmeric
1 small piece of fresh ginger, finely chopped
1 garlic clove, crushed
generous pinch of cayenne
45 mℓ (1½ fl oz) natural yoghurt
few drops of red food colouring
15 mℓ (1 tablespoon) oil

Make a few shallow slits in the skin of each chicken portion. Lay portions in a shallow dish, sprinkle with lemon juice and salt, and rub in. Combine all the remaining ingredients to form a thick paste. Spread over chicken portions, cover and refrigerate for at least 12 hours, turning pieces from time to time. Cover chicken with vented plastic wrap, microwave on High (70%) for 15 minutes. Grill or barbecue portions until crisp and browned. Serve immediately.
Serves 4 – 6

TAPIOCA

A starch-based product extracted from the roots of the cassava plant. Like sago, tapioca is used mainly as the base for milk puddings and it is also sometimes used as a thickener in soups, especially tomato soup, and casseroles. The large, round globules become completely transparent when cooked. Tapioca takes a long time to microwave so use the par-cooked variety where possible.

See also Sago.

TEA

Tea is a refreshing drink made from the dried leaves of the evergreen plant *Camellia sinensis*. The numerous commercial varieties available are a result of the locality and type of soil in which the plants are grown, as well as the manufacture and blending of the tea leaves and the addition of blossoms, spices and zests to the finished product. In cooking, tea is used for soaking dried fruits to make them plump and moist for use in cakes or compotes.

Single cups of tea may be made quickly and without fuss in the microwave. Boil the water in the cup, add a tea bag and allow to steep. This way the tea remains piping hot. If you wish to make a small pot of tea, use an old-fashioned earthenware pot. Most of the glass teapots available have metallic fittings and are unsuitable for use in the microwave.

Herbal teas

Teas such as camomile, peppermint and raspberry are becoming popular as more and more people are discovering their soothing, beneficial qualities. These teas are made in the same way as ordinary tea, but because they are milder and devoid of astringent tannic acid, they may be reheated with no ill effects.

Tea

Full Power
1½ minutes

185 mℓ (6 fl oz) water
1 tea bag
sugar, milk or lemon as desired

Microwave water in a cup on Full Power to boiling, about 1½ minutes. Add tea bag and steep to desired strength. Add milk, sugar or lemon as desired.
Serves 1

TEMPERATURE PROBE

Temperature probes take the guesswork out of timing, and allow you to control the internal temperature of the food. The probe is especially useful for cooking roasts or whole poultry, for reheating foods and, in some cases, for simmering and slow cooking. Follow directions for its use. The probe's flexible connection fits into a socket inside the oven and the point is inserted into the food being cooked. The placing of the probe is important, usually in the thickest part of the poultry or meat, or in the centre of a casserole or stew. Foods cook to a pre-set temperature, then the oven automatically turns off. However, food continues to cook even after the oven switches off, so you may wish to select a lower temperature. It is always easy to microwave the food for a few minutes more, but it is impossible to remedy overcooking.

Warning: Never use a conventional meat thermometer made of metal in your microwave.

TERRINE

Food baked in an earthenware dish is traditionally called a terrine, a large variety of which are always displayed in any French *charcuterie*. Meat, fish, chicken and vegetable terrines are easily cooked in the microwave and it is not necessary to stand these terrines in a water bath during cooking time. Serve terrines with crusty French bread, Melba toast or an interesting wholewheat loaf, for lunch or as a first course.

Layered vegetable terrine

Full Power, High (70%), Medium (50%)
40 minutes

300 g (11 oz) spinach
pinch of nutmeg
salt and black pepper
250 mℓ (8 fl oz) single cream
45 mℓ (3 tablespoons) grated Parmesan cheese
30 g (1 oz) butter
500 g (18 oz) mushrooms, finely chopped
½ onion, chopped
1 garlic clove, crushed
6 – 8 carrots, finely chopped
30mℓ (2 tablespoons) orange juice
2.5 mℓ (½ teaspoon) finely grated orange rind
6 eggs

Wash spinach well, place in a bowl with the water that clings to the leaves. Cover with vented plastic, microwave on Full Power for 5 minutes, stirring once during cooking time. Drain well, chop finely in a food processor or blender, add nutmeg, seasonings and 75 mℓ (2½ fl oz) cream, process to combine. Turn into a bowl, microwave on High (70%) for 4 minutes, add Parmesan, set aside.

Microwave butter in a bowl on Full Power for 45 seconds, add mushrooms, onion, garlic and 75 mℓ (2½ fl oz) cream. Microwave on High (70%) for 8 minutes, stirring at least twice, drain off excess liquid and cool.

Combine carrots, orange juice, rind and remaining cream in a bowl, microwave on Full Power for 10 minutes, stirring frequently. Lightly beat eggs, two at a time, add to each vegetable, mix well.

Grease and line the base of a loaf dish with parchment paper. Turn spinach mixture into dish, then carrot, and lastly the mushroom mixture. Cover loosely with waxed paper. Microwave on Medium (50%) for 10 – 12 minutes until firm. Stand for 5 minutes before turning out. Cut into thick slices.
Serves 8

Country terrine

Full Power, Defrost (30%)
52 minutes

2 chicken breasts, skinned and boned
15 mℓ (1 tablespoon) brandy
250 g (9 oz) streaky bacon rashers, rinds removed
250 g (9 oz) chicken livers
225 g (8 oz) boneless lean veal
500 g (18 oz) pork fillet
1 onion, chopped
1 garlic clove, finely chopped
15 g (½ oz) butter
30 mℓ (2 tablespoons) dry sherry
salt and black pepper
30 mℓ (2 tablespoons) chopped parsley
5 mℓ (1 teaspoon) tarragon
pinch of cloves
pinch of nutmeg
125 mℓ (4 fl oz) single cream
1 small carrot, grated
45 g (1½ oz) pecan nuts

Cut the chicken breasts in half lengthwise and sprinkle with brandy. Set aside. Use the bacon to line a loaf dish or terrine and set aside. Mince the chicken livers, veal and pork and place in a large bowl. Combine onion, garlic and butter and microwave on Full Power for 2 minutes, stirring after 30 seconds. Add to the meat. Add the sherry, salt, pepper, herbs and spices and mix well. Mix in the cream.

Place a third of the mixture in the prepared loaf dish. Arrange half the strips of chicken breast down the centre of the meat mixture. Top with half the grated carrot and arrange pecans on top. Add half the remaining meat mixture, and top with remaining chicken, carrot and nuts. Add remaining meat mixture and smooth the top.

Cover tightly with plastic wrap and vent by piercing two holes in the wrap. Place pan in another, larger microwave container as the mixture has a tendency to boil over. Microwave on Defrost (30%) for 50 minutes. Remove from the microwave and cool for 30 minutes. Then press a heavy weight (a brick covered in foil works well) on top of the terrine and leave to cool. Chill overnight.

To serve, turn out and cut into slices. Serve with mixed vegetable pickle*, pickled onions* and French bread if desired.
Serves 6 – 8

Overleaf left: Country Terrine (page 209)
Overleaf right: Chicken and Corn Tortillas (page 216)

French terrine

High (70%), Medium (50%)
19 minutes

6 – 8 streaky bacon rashers, rinds removed
250 g (9 oz) boneless pork, minced
125 g (4 oz) veal, minced
125 g (4 oz) ham or tongue, minced
2 slices of brown bread, crumbed
pinch of allspice
salt and black pepper
pinch of thyme
5 mℓ (1 teaspoon) coarse-grained mustard
30 mℓ (2 tablespoons) chopped parsley
2 spring onions, chopped
60 g (2 oz) pistachio nuts, shelled and roughly
  chopped
100 mℓ (3½ fl oz) single cream
1 egg

To serve
1 quantity cranberry orange sauce*
lettuce leaves
parsley or cress
gherkins

Stretch bacon rashers with the back of a knife, and use to line a loaf dish. In a bowl combine all ingredients except egg and cream, mix very well. Beat egg and cream lightly, stir into mixture. Pack into loaf dish. Cover with vented plastic wrap, microwave on High (70%) for 5 minutes. Reduce power level to Medium (50%), microwave for 12 – 15 minutes. Uncover and leave to cool. Cover with aluminium foil, weight top and chill. Turn out, slice thickly, serve each portion on a lettuce leaf with cranberry sauce. Garnish with parsley or cress and gherkins.
Serves 6 – 8

TESTING CONTAINERS

If you are unsure whether your earthenware or ceramic containers are suitable for microwave cookery, this simple test will put your mind at rest:

Testing containers for microwave safety
Measure 250 ml (8 fl oz) water in a glass measuring jug. Place the container you wish to test in the microwave and stand the jug in it. Microwave on Full Power for about 1 minute. At the end of that time, the water should be warm and the container cool. If so, the container is ideal for microwave use. If both the water and container are warm, the container can be used, but the cooking time must be increased, as it has attracted some of the microwave energy. If the container is warm but the water is cool, the container has attracted much of the microwave energy and should not be used for microwave cooking.

TIMBALES

Timbales are creamy custard mixtures made from meat, fish, poultry or vegetables set in moulds which may be large or small with straight or sloping sides. Timbales of all kinds cook quickly in the microwave and do not need to be cooked in a bain-marie. Stand for a few minutes before serving.

Prawn and tomato timbales

Full Power, Medium (50%)
14 minutes

30 g (1 oz) soft white breadcrumbs
185 mℓ (6 fl oz) single cream
30 g (1 oz) butter
½ onion, chopped
4 tomatoes, skinned, seeded and chopped
15 mℓ (1 tablespoon) tomato paste
5 mℓ (1 teaspoon) caster sugar
100 g (3½ oz) peeled and deveined prawns
75 g (2½ oz) blue cheese, crumbled
6 egg yolks
salt and black pepper

Sauce
200 mℓ (6½ fl oz) soured cream
30 mℓ (2 tablespoons) finely chopped chives
salt and pepper
10 mℓ (2 teaspoons) lemon juice

Combine breadcrumbs and cream, soak for a few minutes. Microwave butter on Full Power for 45 seconds, add onion and toss to coat. Microwave for 2 minutes, stir in tomatoes, tomato paste and sugar. Microwave for 4 – 5 minutes, until thick, stirring twice during cooking time. Chop prawns, reserving a few for decoration. Add prawns to tomato mixture together with cream mixture, cheese, egg yolks and seasonings, mix well. Spoon into six greased timbale moulds. Arrange in a circle in microwave, cover with waxed paper. Microwave on Medium (50%) for 7 – 10 minutes. The timbales are cooked when the outside is set and the middle is just firm. Stand covered for about 3 minutes before serving. Microwave remaining prawns for about 30 seconds on Full Power. Turn timbales out on to fish plates, spoon on a little sauce, garnish with thin wedges of tomato and prawns. To make sauce, combine all the ingredients.
Serves 6

TOASTED SANDWICHES
See Sandwiches

TOFFEE
Hard or soft toffees can be made successfully in your microwave. However, care should be taken not to overcook the sugar mixture as it will burn very quickly. Select a very large, heat-resistant bowl to prevent the mixture from boiling over.

Golden caramel toffee

Full Power
21 minutes

450 g (1 lb) caster sugar
150 mℓ (5 fl oz) water
200 g (7 oz) golden syrup
30 g (1 oz) butter
100 mℓ (3½ fl oz) single cream or
  evaporated milk
few drops of vanilla extract

Combine sugar, water and syrup in a large bowl. Microwave on Full Power for 5 minutes, stirring once. Stir well to dissolve sugar. Brush edges of bowl with water to remove any crystals. Microwave without stirring for 6 – 7 minutes, until the mixture reaches soft ball stage. Stir in butter. When melted, carefully add cream and vanilla. Microwave for about 10 minutes more, until hard ball stage is reached. Pour into a well-greased 15-cm (6-inch) square pan. Cool until firm, mark in squares. When set, cut into squares. Wrap each square in cellophane paper. *Makes 36 squares*

TOMATOES
Tomatoes must certainly rate as the most versatile fruit in the kitchen. They are eaten raw in salads, and may be baked, stuffed or added to soups and casseroles. The skins are loosened in seconds with the help of the microwave.

To skin tomatoes
Arrange 3 – 4 ripe tomatoes in a circle on kitchen paper in the microwave. Microwave on Full Power for 10 to 15 seconds. Stand for 5 minutes, then skin.

Stuffed tomatoes
Cut tops off tomatoes, scoop out some of the pulp and fill with one of the following:
Chicken and sweetcorn filling: Combine 150 g (5 oz) cooked, shredded chicken with 400 g (14 oz) canned creamed sweetcorn. Divide between 6 – 8 tomatoes. Top with a mixture of grated cheese, chopped parsley and 2 – 3 cooked, crumbled bacon rashers*. Arrange in a circle on a plate, microwave on Full Power for 5 – 7 minutes.
Mixed vegetable filling: Combine 125 g (4 oz) leftover, cooked vegetables such as peas, carrots, mushrooms and cauliflower. Heat 15 ml (1 tablespoon) oil on Full Power for 30 seconds, add 1 chopped onion. Stir and microwave for 1 minute. Add half of the tomato pulp, season and microwave for 3 minutes. Add vegetables and 100 ml (3½ fl oz) cheese sauce*. Spoon into 6 tomatoes, top with a little extra cheese. Microwave for 5 – 7 minutes, until piping hot.
Bolognese filling: To use up a bolognese sauce, combine 250 ml (8 fl oz) with 45 ml (3 tablespoons) soft breadcrumbs and spoon into tomatoes. Top with extra crumbs and dot with butter. Microwave on Full Power for 5 – 7 minutes.

Baked tomatoes

Full Power
3 minutes

2 – 3 tomatoes, thickly sliced
salt and black pepper
2.5 mℓ (½ teaspoon) caster sugar
generous pinch of oregano or basil
15 g (½ oz) margarine

Arrange slices of tomato in a circle on a plate, sprinkle with salt, pepper, sugar and oregano or basil. Dot with margarine and cover with waxed paper. Microwave on Full Power for about 3 minutes.
Serves 6

Tomato topping

Full Power
20 minutes

Use to top spaghetti, pizza or cabbage.

2 x 400-g (14-oz) tomatoes
15 mℓ (1 tablespoon) oil
salt and black pepper
5 mℓ (1 teaspoon) sugar
1 – 2 garlic cloves, crushed
15 mℓ (1 tablespoon) chopped fresh basil or
  5 mℓ (1 teaspoon) dried basil

Drain tomato liquid into a large bowl, cut tomatoes up roughly and add to juice. Add oil, salt, pepper and sugar. Microwave on Full Power for 20 – 25 minutes, stirring every 5 minutes. When thickened, add garlic and basil. Use as required.
Makes about 500 mℓ (16 fl oz)

TONGUE
Ox, calf's or lamb's tongues are delicious served hot or cold. Select tongues that weigh less than 1.5 kg (3 lb) and are soft to the touch. Tongue may be purchased either fresh or pickled. If pickled, it will need to be soaked in cold water for a few hours before cooking. Tongue takes almost as long to cook in the microwave as it does conventionally, but the kichen remains cool and free of cooking odours.

Ox tongue

Full Power, Medium (50%)
2 hours 15 minutes

1.25 – 1.5 kg (2¾ – 3 lb) tongue, fresh or
  pickled
6 whole allspice
6 peppercorns
1 bay leaf
pinch of thyme
1 parsley sprig
1 onion, coarsely chopped
1 carrot, coarsely chopped
1 celery stick, coarsely chopped
2.5 mℓ (½ teaspoon) salt (for fresh tongue only)
water

Soak pickled tongue for a few hours, drain. Place tongue in a large casserole or soaked clay pot, add remaining ingredients and cover with water. Cover casserole and microwave on Full Power for 10 minutes, reduce power to Medium (50%) for 2 – 2½ hours, until tongue is tender. Leave to cool slightly in the liquid. Remove skin, root and small bones. Slice and use as required.
Serves 4 – 6

Pickled tongue with cucumber sauce

1.5 kg (3 lb) pickled tongue, cooked*
125 mℓ (4 fl oz) oil
100 mℓ (3½ fl oz) wine vinegar
1 egg yolk
15 mℓ (1 tablespoon) lemon juice
2.5 mℓ (½ teaspoon) caster sugar
2.5 mℓ (½ teaspoon) dry mustard
cayenne
salt and black pepper
45 mℓ (3 tablespoons) chopped pickled
  cucumbers
15 mℓ (1 tablespoon) capers, chopped
1 hard-boiled egg, chopped

To garnish
parsley
tomato wedges

Slice cold tongue, arrange on a platter. In a blender or food processor combine oil, vinegar, yolk, lemon juice, sugar, mustard and seasonings. Stir in remaining ingredients. Spoon over tongue. Garnish with parsley and tomato wedges.
Serves 4 to 6

Tongue with sweet and sour sauce

Full Power, High (70%)
10 minutes

1.5 kg (3 lb) fresh tongue, cooked*

Sauce
45 mℓ (3 tablespoons) oil
1 onion, chopped
30 mℓ (2 tablespoons) plain flour
350 mℓ (11 fl oz) reserved tongue liquid
15 mℓ (1 tablespoon) wine vinegar
100 mℓ (3½ fl oz) tomato sauce (as served with
  pasta)
5 mℓ (1 teaspoon) dry mustard
Tabasco
15 mℓ (1 tablespoon) soft brown sugar

Slice tongue, arrange in a shallow casserole. Microwave oil in a bowl on Full Power for 2 minutes, add onion, toss to coat. Stir in flour, microwave for 30 seconds. Pour in tongue liquid, stir well, add remaining ingredients. Microwave for 3 – 4 minutes, stirring at least twice. Pour sauce over tongue, cover, microwave on High (70%) for 4 – 5 minutes, until piping hot.
Serves 4 - 6

TORTILLAS
Tortillas, plain or crisply fried, are served flat, folded or wrapped around a variety of spicy fillings. Mexican tortillas are made from cornmeal, but a combination of flour and cornmeal will also produce a good result. These may be made in the microwave in a browning dish.
See also Tacos.

To reheat tortillas, arrange 4 tortillas on a plate and cover with a damp sheet of kitchen paper. Microwave on Medium (50%) for about 3 minutes or until warm. Repeat with remaining tortillas.

Tortillas

Full Power
28 minutes

150 g (5 oz) plain flour
90 g (3 oz) cornmeal
generous pinch of salt
5 mℓ (1 teaspoon) baking powder
45 g (1½ oz) lard
125 mℓ (4 fl oz) water
oil

Place dry ingredients in the bowl of a food processor, pulse to aerate. Add lard and pulse four or five times to rub in. With the machine running, add water until a stiff dough forms. Continue to process for about 45 seconds, until dough is smooth and pliable. Stand, covered, at room temperature for about 30 minutes.

Divide dough into eight, roll out each piece on a lightly floured board until paper-thin and about 15 cm (6 inch) in diameter. Microwave a browning dish on Full Power for 5 minutes, wipe dish with a little oil. Place one tortilla in dish, microwave for 30 seconds, turn and microwave for 30 – 45 seconds. Reheat browning dish for 2 minutes, then repeat cooking and reheating times for remaining tortillas.
Makes 8

Note: Either pile cooked tortillas one on top of another or carefully fold in half in a U-shape taking care not to crease the base. Stand U-shaped tortillas upright against each other until cool.

Overleaf left: Stuffed Patty Pan Squash (page 202)
Overleaf right: Quick Paella (page 162)

Chicken and corn tortillas

High (70%)
4 minutes

8 tortillas*
1 cooked chicken*
1 small onion, chopped
1 green pepper, chopped
2 – 3 tomatoes, diced
400 g (14 oz) canned whole kernel sweetcorn,
   drained
salt and black pepper
1 – 2 avocados, diced
1 small chilli, finely chopped (optional)
1 butter lettuce

Sauce
250 mℓ (8 fl oz) soured cream
5 – 10 mℓ (1 – 2 teaspoons) chilli sauce
60 mℓ (4 tablespoons) tomato sauce (as served
   with pasta)
15 mℓ (1 tablespoon) lemon juice
1 bunch of spring onions, chopped
salt and black pepper

To make the sauce, combine all the
ingredients, season well and set aside. Place
chicken, onion, green pepper, tomatoes and
sweetcorn in a bowl and cover. Microwave on
High (70%) for 4 – 5 minutes, stirring once.
Season, add avocado and chilli and toss lightly.
Line 8 warm tortillas with lettuce leaves. Divide
filling betwen tortillas and generously top each
one with sauce. Serve immediately.
Serves 8

TRIFLE *See* Desserts

TRIPE

Tripe is the stomach lining from beef or
lamb, which should be thoroughly cleaned
before being cooked. Tripe requires long,
slow cooking to become tender. When
microwaved it becomes tough and rubbery,
so it is best cooked conventionally.

TROUT

Rainbow trout are farmed commercially
and are readily available fresh, frozen or
smoked. The delicate and distinctive flavour of freshwater trout is retained when it
is cooked in the microwave, and the fish remains succulent.

To prepare trout for microwave cooking,
rinse and pat dry carefully. Leave the head
and tail intact but remove the gills if you
wish. After cooking, the skin is easily removed in one piece. The fish may also be
skinned and filleted before cooking. Trout
is at its best poached in a court bouillon* or
cooked in butter.
See also Fish.

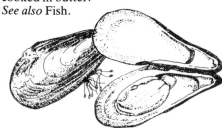

Poached trout

Full Power
7 minutes

2 trout
salt and black pepper
75 mℓ (2½ fl oz) white wine
30 mℓ (2 tablespoons) water
1 onion slice
1 lemon slice
parsley sprigs
tarragon or dill sprigs

Rinse trout and pat dry with kitchen paper,
season. Place in a shallow rectangular dish,
add remaining ingredients. Cover with vented
plastic, microwave on Full Power for 7 – 9
minutes. Drain fish and serve.
Serves 2

Serving suggestions
☐ Coat with hollandaise sauce*.
☐ Coat with béchamel sauce* to which prawns
or mussels have been added.
☐ Serve on a bed of cooked spinach.
☐ Serve with a mushroom sauce or a creamy
horseradish sauce.

Smoked salmon with smoked trout mousse

Full Power
2 minutes

300 – 400 g (11 – 14 oz) smoked salmon slices
2 smoked trout, skin and bones removed
150 g (5 oz) cream cheese
60 g (2 oz) butter
3 spring onions, chopped
15 mℓ (1 tablespoon) brandy
15 mℓ (1 tablespoon) Cinzano
salt and black pepper
125 mℓ (4 fl oz) single cream
15 mℓ (1 tablespoon) lemon juice
5 mℓ (1 teaspoon) chopped dill

To garnish
6 butter head lettuce leaves
6 lemon twists
dill
capers

Line the sides of six lightly greased ramekins
with smoked salmon. Place smoked trout and
cream cheese in the bowl of a food processor,
process until smooth. Place butter in a small
bowl, microwave on Full Power for 1 minute.
Add spring onion and microwave for 1 minute.
Add butter mixture, brandy, Cinzano,
seasonings, cream, lemon juice and dill to
smoked trout, process to combine. Divide
mousse between the lined ramekins. Fold
salmon edges over top of mousse. Refrigerate
until set.
   To serve, place a lettuce leaf on a fish plate.
Carefully run a spatula around the edge of each
ramekin and turn out on to lettuce leaves. Add a
lemon twist, a dill sprig and a few capers.
Serves 6

Devilled trout

Full Power
9 minutes

2 trout
10 mℓ (2 teaspoons) dry mustard
salt and black pepper
pinch of caster sugar
2.5 mℓ (½ teaspoon) horseradish sauce
5 mℓ (1 teaspoon) Worcestershire sauce
water
15 g (½ oz) butter

Rinse trout and pat dry with kitchen paper. In a
small bowl, combine mustard, seasonings,
sugar, horseradish and Worcestershire sauce.
Add enough water to form a stiff paste. Using a
sharp knife, slash trout skin a few times on both
sides. Spread mustard mixture on trout, dot
with butter and place trout in a shallow dish.
Cover with waxed paper and microwave on Full
Power for 9 – 10 minutes. Baste with sauce
half-way through cooking time. Stand for a few
minutes before serving.
Serves 2

TRUFFLES, CHOCOLATE

These mouthwatering bite-sized chocolates
make perfect after-dinner treats. The
truffle mixture may be flavoured with liqueur, spirits, grated citrus rind, coffee,
fruit or nuts. For the final touch, roll the
chocolate balls in grated chocolate, chocolate vermicelli, cocoa or drinking chocolate
powder, or dip in melted chocolate.

Rich chocolate truffles

Full Power
4 minutes

200 g (7 oz) plain chocolate, broken into pieces
2 egg yolks
125 g (4 oz) butter
100 g (3½ oz) icing sugar, sifted
45 mℓ (3 tablespoons) single cream
30 g (1 oz) digestive biscuit crumbs
30 mℓ (2 tablespoons) whisky
cocoa powder

Place chocolate in a bowl, microwave on Full
Power for 3 – 4 minutes, stirring at least once.
Add yolks and butter, stir until butter has
melted. Add icing sugar, cream, biscuit crumbs
and whisky. Refrigerate until firm. Form
chocolate mixture into balls, roll in cocoa
powder. Place in paper cases.
Makes about 40

Variations
☐ Substitute white chocolate for plain
chocolate
☐ Flavour with rum, brandy, Grand Marnier or
strong coffee.
☐ Add chopped nuts or glacé fruit to the
mixture.

TRUFFLES, FRESH

Fresh or canned truffles are extremely expensive and are associated with haute cuisine. It is not possible to cultivate truffles commercially as the fungi usually grow in the soil at the base of oak trees. There are many varieties of truffle, the most expensive being a black truffle from Perigord in France which is harvested with the help of trained dogs or pigs. Stuffings, pâtés or sauces to which truffles have been added may be cooked in the microwave.

TUNA

Tuna may be bought in cans, packed in either oil or brine, or as fresh, dark-fleshed tunny steaks which may be baked or poached in the microwave. Tuna is perhaps best known in its canned form, and with the help of the microwave, may be transformed into a piping hot, tasty meal in just a few minutes.

Mexican tuna casserole

Full Power, High (70%)
12 minutes

30 g (1 oz) margarine
1 onion, chopped
1 green pepper, chopped
1 – 3 long, green chillies, bottled and
    preserved in vinegar
200 g (7 oz) canned tuna
3 eggs
250 g (9 oz) cottage cheese
salt and black pepper
generous pinch of mixed herbs
5 mℓ (1 teaspoon) chilli powder
pinch of crushed caraway seeds
200 g (7 oz) tortilla chips, crushed
125 g (4 oz) Cheddar cheese, grated
100 g (3½ oz) Edam cheese, grated
250 mℓ (8 fl oz) soured cream

Microwave margarine in a bowl on Full Power for 45 seconds. Add onion and green pepper. Toss to coat with margarine, microwave for 4 minutes. Stir in chillies and tuna, set aside. Beat eggs, cottage cheese, seasonings, mixed herbs, chilli powder and caraway seeds. Grease a large shallow casserole, spread about one-quarter of the crushed chips on the base, cover with half the egg mixture and then half the tuna mixture. Combine the cheeses, sprinkle three-quarters over tuna layer, add remaining cheese to soured cream, set aside. Top cheese with most of the remaining chips, then remaining egg mixture and tuna mixture. Pour soured cream and cheese over the top and sprinkle with remaining chips. Microwave on High (70%) for 7 – 9 minutes until piping hot. Stand for a few minutes before serving.
Serves 6 – 8

TURKEY

Crisp, evenly browned turkey is traditional Christmas fare. Use your microwave in conjunction with either a combination microwave convection oven or a conventional one to accomplish this in about half the time normally required.

Turkey is normally purchased frozen, and depending on the room temperature, it will take between one and three days to defrost. It is extremely important that a turkey is completely defrosted before being stuffed and cooked. While it is best to thaw turkey at room temperature, the microwave will be a great help if time runs out.

To defrost turkey in the microwave

Place turkey in a roasting bag, tie with string or an elastic band. Place turkey breast side downwards, microwave on Defrost (30%) for about half of the calculated time below. Turn the bird over and continue on Defrost (30%). A turkey is sufficiently thawed when the giblets can be removed easily and the inside feels very cold.

MASS	TIME ON DEFROST (30%)
3.5 kg (8lb)	1 hour 15 minutes – 1 hour 30 minutes
4.5 kg (10 lb)	1 hour 20 minutes – 2 hours
5.5 kg (12 lb)	2 hours – 2 hours 30 minutes
6.5 kg (14 lb)	2 hours 20 minutes – 3 hours

To cook turkey

Turkey may be cooked with or without stuffing. If unstuffed, add extra moisture and flavour by adding an onion, carrot, potato and a selection of fresh herbs or 30 ml (2 tablespoons) orange liqueur to the main cavity. When using stuffing, calculate microwave time by weighing the bird after filling the cavity.

Shield wing tips, drumstick ends and the top of the breast with strips of foil and place turkey in a roasting bag before microwaving. Microwave turkey on High (70%) for 10 minutes per 500 g (18 oz). Remove turkey from roasting bag and remove foil. Cook conventionally for the following times:

TURKEY MASS	MICROWAVE TIME ON HIGH (70%)	CONVENTIONAL OVEN 180 °C/350 °F/gas 4
3.5 kg (8 lb)	1 hour 10 minutes	45 minutes – 1 hour
4.5 kg (10 lb)	1 hour 30 minutes	45 minutes – 1 hour
5.5 kg (12 lb)	2 hours	1 hour – 1 hour 15 minutes
6.5 kg (14 lb)	2 hours 15 minutes	1 hour 15 minutes – 1 hour 30 minutes

For combination microwave convection cooking refer to instruction book supplied with the microwave.

Stuffed roast turkey

Full Power, High (70%)
1 hour 36 minutes

Bake 180 °C/350 °F/gas 4
45 minutes to 1 hour

4.5 kg (10 lb) turkey
60 g (2 oz) butter
salt and black pepper
pinch of paprika
10 mℓ (2 teaspoons) Worcestershire sauce
10 mℓ (2 teaspoons) lemon juice
10 mℓ (2 teaspoons) brown sugar

Stuffing
100 mℓ (3½ fl oz) oil
2 onions, chopped
liver from turkey, finely chopped
175 g (6 oz) soft white breadcrumbs
250 g (9 oz) pork sausage-meat
salt and black pepper
45 mℓ (3 tablespoons) chopped parsley
100 mℓ (3½ fl oz) unsweetened chestnut purée
1 apple, peeled and diced
2 eggs
2 celery sticks, chopped

First make the stuffing. Microwave oil in a large bowl on Full Power for 2 minutes. Add onion and liver, stir to coat with oil. Microwave for 4 minutes, stirring twice. Add remaining ingredients and mix well. Either fill both cavities with stuffing, or just the neck cavity. The remaining stuffing may be cooked separately in a casserole dish. Secure the neck skin with wooden cocktail sticks.

Spread turkey with butter, season well. Truss with string, shield wing tips, drumstick ends and top of the breast with foil. Place in a large roasting bag, tie bag end loosely with string. Weigh turkey and calculate microwaving time, allowing 10 minutes per 500 g (18 oz) on High (70%). Place turkey in microwave, breast-side down, microwave for about one-third of the calculated time, then turn turkey over. Baste with butter, microwave for one-third longer, turn and baste again. Microwave for remaining time.

Remove turkey from bag, and remove foil shields. Place turkey in a roasting pan. Combine Worcestershire sauce, lemon juice, brown sugar and 30 mℓ (2 tablespoons) of the pan juices, pour over turkey. Roast at 180 °C/350 °F/gas 4 for 45 – 60 minutes, basting at least twice. Stand turkey for 10 minutes before carving. To test if the turkey is cooked, press drumstick between fingers; it should be soft and move up and down easily.
Serves 10
Note: To cook stuffing separately, spoon it into a shallow casserole, cover. Microwave on High (70%) for about 10 minutes, stand for 5 minutes.

Overleaf left: Yeast Breads (pages 228 – 229) from top to bottom, Savoury Brown Loaf, Microwave Muffin Loaf
Overleaf right: Quick Breads (page 181) clockwise, Walnut Coffee Bread, Peanut Butter Loaf, Marsala Date Bread

Turkey Tetrazzini

Full Power, High (70%)
17 minutes

45 g (1½ oz) butter or margarine
1 onion, sliced
2 celery sticks, sliced
100 g (3½ oz) mushrooms, sliced
10 mℓ (2 teaspoons) lemon juice
30 mℓ (2 tablespoons) plain flour
2.5 mℓ (½ teaspoon) paprika
400 mℓ (13 fl oz) chicken stock
30 mℓ (2 tablespoons) sherry
salt and black pepper
125 mℓ (4 fl oz) single cream
300 g (11 oz) cooked turkey*, coarsely
   chopped
175 g (6 oz) spaghetti or macaroni, cooked*
30 g (1 oz) flaked almonds
30 g (1 oz) Parmesan cheese, grated
generous pinch of paprika

Place butter in a bowl, microwave on Full Power for 1 minute. Add onion, toss to coat with butter, microwave for 2 minutes, stir in celery, mushrooms, lemon juice, flour and paprika. Add stock, stir well. Microwave for 4 minutes, stirring every minute. Add sherry, seasonings, cream and turkey. Place cooked spaghetti in a shallow casserole, pour turkey sauce over and sprinkle with almonds, Parmesan and paprika. Microwave on High (70%) for 10 – 12 minutes.
Serves 4

TURKISH DELIGHT

This typically Middle Eastern sweetmeat provides a fragrant, soothing contrast to round off a rich spicy meal. Turkish delight may be flavoured with rose water, lemon juice or peppermint essence and coloured sparingly with pink, yellow or green food colouring according to the flavouring. When cooked in the microwave, the mixture will not 'catch' as it is inclined to do when boiled on top of the stove. Turkish delight keeps well and makes an unusual gift wrapped in cellophane or packed in a pretty container.

Turkish delight

Full Power, Medium (50%)
16 minutes

375 mℓ (12 fl oz) water
45 g (1½ oz) powdered gelatine
60 g (2 oz) cornflour
750 g (1¾ lb) caster sugar
generous pinch of tartaric acid
30 mℓ (2 tablespoons) rosewater or lemon juice
cornflour
icing sugar, sifted

Place 100 mℓ (3½ fl oz) of the water in a jug, add gelatine and set aside. Blend cornflour to a paste with a little water, set aside. Microwave remaining water on Full Power for about 2 minutes until boiling. Pour boiling water over soaked gelatine, stir well. Microwave on Medium (50%) for 2 minutes to dissolve. Combine hot mixture and cornflour paste in a very large bowl, add sugar and tartaric acid. Cover with vented plastic, microwave on Full Power for 5 minutes, stir well. Microwave uncovered for 7 minutes, stir in rosewater and colour as desired. Pour into a well-greased 25-cm (10-inch) square pan, cool and chill well. Turn out on to a board sprinkled with cornflour and icing sugar. Cut into squares with a knife dipped into hot water. Roll each piece in cornflour and icing sugar.
Makes about 90 squares

TURNING FOODS

Foods that cannot be stirred during cooking need to be repositioned to heat evenly or to brown each side.
☐ Roasts, poultry and large pieces of vegetables or meat should be turned during the cooking time to ensure even heating.
☐ Foods such as hamburgers, steaks or chops microwaved in a browning dish, will need turning to ensure even browning.
☐ In microwaves without a turntable it is advisable to rotate the container a quarter- or half-turn during the cooking time if the food appears to be cooking unevenly.
☐ Foods defrost more evenly if turned during the defrosting time.

TURNIP

A strong-tasting vegetable which is not always popular served on its own. However, as a winter root vegetable, it is a useful addition to soups and casseroles. Choose young turnips and peel thickly before cooking.

To microwave turnips
Peel and dice 4 – 5 medium-sized turnips. Place in a bowl, add 45 ml (3 tablespoons) water and a little salt. Cover with vented plastic wrap, microwave on Full Power for 14 – 16 minutes. Stir at least twice during cooking.

Serving suggestions
☐ Microwave 30 ml (1 oz) butter and 15 ml (1 tablespoon) caster sugar for 1 minute on Full Power, add cooked turnips, toss to coat with butter mixture.
☐ Pour 150 ml (5 fl oz) white sauce, cheese or parsley sauce over cooked turnips.
☐ Stir 10 ml (2 teaspoons) finely chopped chives into 150 ml (5 fl oz) soured cream, pour over cooked turnips.
☐ Toss cooked turnips in 30 ml (2 tablespoons) melted butter, sprinkle with chopped parsley or dust with paprika.
☐ Cut turnips in julienne and combine with carrots and courgettes.

TURNTABLE

Many microwaves are likely to have hot and cold spots, so it is important that food be turned occasionally during defrosting, heating or cooking. Some microwaves have a turntable or rotating platform that automatically rotates the food during the cooking time, eliminating the need to turn or rotate containers and promoting even cooking. Follow the manufacturer's directions for using the turntable. In some models, the microwave should not be used without the turntable in position. In place of a turntable, some makes of microwave have a stirrer fan system to distribute microwaves for even cooking.

U

V

UPSIDE-DOWN CAKE

A cake baked with an arrangement of fruit and nuts on a sugar-coated base so that when the cake is turned out on to a plate, the decorative arrangement is on top. An upside-down cake is particularly successful baked in the microwave and it looks attractive too. Serve for dessert with whipped cream. *See also* Lemon and Cherry Upside-down Cake (page 44) and Upside-Down Gingerbread (page 104).

Pineapple upside-down cake

Full Power
12 minutes

150 g (5 oz) plain flour
150 g (5 oz) caster sugar
10 mℓ (2 teaspoons) baking powder
2.5 mℓ (½ teaspoon) salt
1 egg
60 g (2 oz) butter, softened
pineapple liquid and milk to make 125 mℓ
   (4 fl oz)
few drops of vanilla extract

Topping
60 g (2 oz) butter
75 g ((2½ oz) soft brown sugar
400 g (14 oz) canned pineapple slices
6 maraschino cherries, halved

To make the topping, place butter in a 20-cm (8-inch) round glass baking dish and microwave on Full Power for 1 minute. Tilt dish to coat bottom evenly. Sprinkle brown sugar evenly over the bottom. Arrange pineapple slices and cherries in the dish. Place all the cake ingredients in a food processor or mixer bowl and beat on low speed until mixture is smooth, about 3 minutes. Spread mixture over pineapple. Place dish on inverted saucer and microwave on Full Power for 9 – 11 minutes, or until a wooden cocktail stick inserted near the centre comes out clean. Invert cake on to a serving plate and let dish stand over cake for a few minutes. Serve warm or cool. *Serves 8 – 10*

VANILLA

A vanilla pod is the fruit of a climbing orchid native to the tropical forests of Central America. Its strong, pleasant taste has long been used in cooking to flavour chocolate dishes, custards, ice creams, biscuits and cakes. The dried pods are expensive, but last a long time as they can be used more than once. A less expensive synthetic vanilla flavouring, made from clove oil, is often used in baking. Vanilla needs to be used with discretion as it is a powerful flavouring agent.

To infuse vanilla

A vanilla-flavoured custard or cream is made by heating the milk on High (70%) until hot, but not boiling. Add a piece of vanilla pod and let mixture cool. The vanilla pod can then be rinsed and dried so that it can be used again. Vanilla-flavoured sugar syrup is made in the same way.

To flavour sugar

Place a piece of vanilla pod in a jar of sugar and leave it for several days. Use the sugar in milk puddings, milk tarts and custards, including crème caramel and crème brûlée.

VEAL

Veal is meat from a young calf and is usually tender with a delicate flavour, which marries well with tomato, wine, cream or fruit sauces. The flesh is pale in colour and there is little fat so large cuts should be larded with pork or bacon fat and basted frequently during cooking to prevent them from becoming dry. Veal does not keep for as long as beef, and should be frozen if you wish to keep it for more than a few days.

Different cuts of veal make interesting and varied meals. For example, escalopes and schnitzels can be fried and sautéed in portions, and chops can be grilled and fried. For braising or roasts, the leg, shoulder, loin or nut of veal can be used.

Hints for microwaving veal

☐ When microwaving veal dishes microwave on High (70%) to prevent the flesh from drying out.
☐ Whenever possible cover meat during cooking time, or alternatively use a roasting bag.
☐ When using joints select evenly shaped pieces of meat.

Baked veal with tomato

High (70%)
40 minutes

1 – 1.5 kg (2¼ – 3 lb) nut of veal
salt and pepper
400 g (14 oz) canned tomato purée
1 bay leaf
1 garlic clove, crushed
4 bacon rashers, rinds removed
10 mℓ (2 teaspoons) green peppercorns
15 mℓ (1 tablespoon) chopped parsley
2.5 mℓ (½ teaspoon) caster sugar

Season meat very lightly, place in bag. Pour tomato purée over meat, add bay leaf and garlic, close bag loosely with string. Microwave on High (70%) for 12 – 14 minutes per 500 g (18 oz). Half-way through cooking time, open bag, turn bag over and baste with sauce, lay bacon on top of meat, close bag and complete cooking. Remove meat from roasting bag and cover with a tent of aluminium foil, shiny side in. To complete sauce, chop bacon roughly and add to tomato mixture in the roasting bag. Add peppercorns, parsley and sugar. Microwave for 3 minutes, remove bay leaf and serve with meat.
Serves 6

Note: Veal may be microwaved on Full Power for 8 – 11 minutes per 500g (18 oz), but is inclined to dry out.

Wiener schnitzel

Full Power
15 minutes

125 g (4 oz) dry breadcrumbs
salt and pepper
generous pinch of paprika
6 veal schnitzels, flattened slightly
30 g (1 oz) plain flour
1 egg, beaten
30 mℓ (2 tablespoons) oil
30 g (1 oz) butter
lemon slices
capers (optional)
anchovy fillets (optional)

Season breadcrumbs with salt, pepper and paprika. Coat schnitzels with flour, dip in beaten egg, then in seasoned crumbs, coating well. Preheat a microwave browning dish on Full Power for 6 minutes. Add half the oil and butter and stir to melt. Place three schnitzels in the browning dish and press down for about 30 seconds to sear. Microwave for 30 seconds, turn meat over, press down and microwave for 1 – 2 minutes. Remove from pan and keep warm. Wipe dish clean, reheat on Full Power for 3 minutes and repeat process. Serve schnitzels garnished with lemon slices and add capers and anchovy fillets if desired.
Serves 6

Escalopes of veal with artichokes

High (70%), Full Power
25 minutes

4 veal escalopes
30 g (1 oz) plain flour
salt and black pepper
15 g (½ oz) butter
15 mℓ (1 tablespoon) oil
1 onion slice
100 mℓ (3½ fl oz) stock
100 mℓ (3½ fl oz) white wine
1 garlic clove, crushed
1 bouquet garni
100 g (3½ oz) button mushrooms, quartered
400 g (14 oz) canned artichoke hearts, quartered
10 baby onions
15 mℓ (1 tablespoon) water
salt
2.5 mℓ (½ teaspoon) caster sugar
15 mℓ (1 tablespoon) brandy
45 mℓ (3 tablespoons) single cream
15 g (½ oz) butter
15 g (½ oz) plain flour
thyme sprigs

Sprinkle veal lightly with flour and seasonings. Place butter and oil in a large shallow casserole. Microwave on Full Power for 2 minutes. Add veal, cover lightly and microwave

Mouthwatering Watermelon Preserve (page 226)

on High (70%) for 1 minute on each side. Add slice of onion, stock, white wine, garlic and bouquet garni. Microwave on High (70%) for 4 minutes, remove meat and set aside. Microwave liquids on Full Power for 3 minutes, stir in mushrooms and artichokes, cover and set aside. Combine onions, water, salt and sugar in a bowl. Cover with vented plastic wrap and microwave for 4 – 5 minutes, until just tender, drain. Add onions, brandy and cream to casserole, microwave for 4 minutes, stirring once. Mix butter and flour together, add to casserole 5 mℓ (1 teaspoon) at a time, stirring until sufficient has been added to thicken the liquid. Microwave for 2 minutes. Add escalopes, spoon sauce over, cover and microwave on High (70%) for 4 minutes, or until heated through. Garnish with thyme sprigs.
Serves 4

Tropical veal chops

Full Power
16 minutes

4 veal chops
black pepper
45 mℓ (3 tablespoons) soy sauce
pinch of mace
45 mℓ (3 tablespoons) dry sherry
45 mℓ (3 tablespoons) finely chopped spring onion
pinch of ground coriander
plain flour
30 mℓ (2 tablespoons) oil
15 g (½ oz) butter
180 mℓ (6 fl oz) apricot juice
60 mℓ (4 tablespoons) dry white wine
5 mℓ (1 teaspoon) cornflour
2 kiwi fruit
toasted coconut*

Sprinkle veal chops lightly with pepper, patting into the surface of the meat. Place chops in a glass dish. Combine soy sauce, mace, sherry, onion and coriander. Gently pour over chops. Marinate for 3 hours in the refrigerator, turning chops at least once. When ready to cook, remove chops from marinade, reserving the liquid.
   Pat chops dry and dredge lightly with flour. Heat a browning dish on Full Power for 6 minutes, add oil and butter and add chops. Microwave for 1 minute, turn chops and microwave for 2 – 3 minutes more, or until chops are cooked. Remove chops and keep warm. Wipe pan clean, then microwave apricot juice and reserved marinade on Full Power for 3 minutes, or until boiling. Mix wine with cornflour and add to the pan. Microwave for 2 – 3 minutes, or until sauce has thickened, stirring twice. Add sliced kiwi fruit and heat through. Serve chops with sauce spooned over and sprinkled with toasted coconut.
Serves 4

VEGETABLES
Vegetables taste superb when cooked in the microwave. They need little added water and steam quickly in their own mois-

ture, retaining colour, flavour and texture, as well as vitamins and minerals. For these reasons, cooking in the microwave is the most nutritious way of preparing vegetables.
See also individual names and Blanching.

Hints for microwaving vegetables
☐ Cut vegetables into even-sized slices or pieces for even cooking.
☐ If using a cooking liquid, add salt to the liquid. If not, add a little salt to the vegetable after it as been microwaved. Remember when vegetables are cooked in the microwave, far less salt is needed.
☐ Cooking time will vary depending on size, thickness and age of the vegetable. Always check vegetables after the minimum time stated on the chart.
☐ Allow 2 – 4 minutes standing time before serving vegetables as they continue to cook for some time after being removed from the microwave. Vegetables should still be firm or crisp when cooking time is up. If they overcook, they dehydrate.
☐ Arrange vegetables in a circle if they are being cooked whole, for example potatoes. Also arrange vegetables with fibrous stems, such as broccoli, with the stem end towards the outside. Vegetables which have an irregular shape, such as whole courgettes, should be arranged with the thin end towards the middle of the dish. Rearrange or stir vegetables half-way through cooking time to ensure even cooking.
☐ When possible, cook vegetables with their skins on. Simply pierce the skin to allow steam to escape.
☐ Cover vegetables before cooking. Use a lid or vented plastic wrap. When uncovering cooked vegetables, uncover from the edge farthest away from you because the escaping steam may cause a bad burn. Vegetables may also be cooked in a roasting bag or be individually wrapped in plastic wrap.
☐ All vegetables are microwaved on Full Power, unless otherwise stated.
☐ Microwave time increases with the amount of food cooked. If the quantity of vegetables given on the chart above is altered in a recipe, the cooking time must be adjusted accordingly. Allow one-third to one-half extra time if the amount is doubled.

To microwave frozen vegetables
There is no need to thaw frozen vegetables before microwaving, nor to add any extra water. Just place them in a suitable container, even a boilable plastic container or a roasting bag. Before microwaving, frozen vegetables should always be covered and roasting bags or plastic wrap must be pierced to prevent steam from building up. Microwave frozen vegetables for approximately two-thirds of the time required for fresh vegetables.

FRESH VEGETABLE COOKING CHART

VEGETABLE	QUANTITY	WATER ADDED	COOKING TIME (On Full Power)	PREPARATION
Artichokes, globe	4	150 mℓ (5 fl oz)	15 – 20 minutes	Wash and trim lower leaves
Asparagus, green	250 g (9 oz)	45 mℓ (3 tablespoons)	6 – 8 minutes	Trim ends, leave whole
Asparagus, white	250 g (9 oz)	45 mℓ (3 tablespoons)	8 – 10 minutes	Trim ends, leave whole
Aubergine	2 medium-sized	45 mℓ (3 tablespoons)	8 – 10 minutes	Slice, sprinkle with salt Stand for 30 minutes, rinse and dry
Beans, broad	450 g (1 lb)	45 mℓ (3 tablespoons)	9 – 11 minutes	Remove from pods
Beans, green	450 g (1 lb)	45 mℓ (3 tablespoons)	8 – 10 minutes	String and slice, or cut
Beetroot	6 medium-sized	150 mℓ (5 fl oz)	28 – 32 minutes	Trim tops, prick
Broccoli	450 g (1 lb)	45 mℓ (3 tablespoons)	8 – 12 minutes	Trim ends, cut into even-sized lengths
Brussels sprouts	450 g (1 lb)	45 mℓ (3 tablespoons)	12 – 15 minutes	Remove outer leaves, trim
Butternut	1 medium-sized	45 mℓ (3 tablespoons)	12 – 15 minutes	Cut in half, remove membranes and seeds. Cook cut side down. Turn half-way through cooking time
Cabbage	450 g (1 lb)	15 mℓ (1 tablespoon)	7 – 9 minutes	Shred or chop
Carrots, whole new	450 g (1 lb)	45 mℓ (3 tablespoons)	7 – 9 minutes	Scrape
Carrots, sliced large	450 g (1 lb)	45 mℓ (3 tablespoons)	8 – 10 minutes	Peel, slice in rings or long strips
Cauliflower, whole	1 medium-sized	45 mℓ (3 tablespoons)	9 – 11 minutes	Trim outside leaves and stem
Cauliflower, cut into florets	1 medium-sized	45 mℓ (3 tablespoons)	7 – 9 minutes	Cut into medium-sized florets
Celery	450 g (1 lb)	45 mℓ (3 tablespoons)	10 – 12 minutes	Trim and slice
Courgettes	450 g (1 lb)	30 mℓ (2 tablespoons) water or stock	6 – 8 minutes	Trim ends and slice
Leeks	4 medium-sized	45 mℓ (3 tablespoons)	7 – 11 minutes	Trim and slice or cook whole if small
Marrow	450 g (1 lb)	15 mℓ (1 tablespoon)	8 – 10 minutes	Cut into slices and quarter Add 30 g (1 oz) butter with water
Mushrooms	250 g (9 oz)	30 mℓ (2 tablespoons) water or stock, or 30 g (1 oz) butter	4 – 6 minutes	Wipe and slice or cook whole
Onions, whole	4 – 6	30 g (1 oz) butter or 30 mℓ (2 tablespoons) oil	8 – 10 minutes	Peel
Onions, sliced	4 – 6	30 g (1 oz) butter or 30 mℓ (2 tablespoons) oil	7 – 9 minutes	Peel and slice
Parsnips	450 g (1 lb)	45 mℓ (3 tablespoons)	9 – 11 minutes	Peel and slice
Peas, shelled	250 g (9 oz)	30 mℓ (2 tablespoons)	8 – 10 minutes	Add a mint sprig
Potatoes, new	450 g (1 lb)	30 mℓ (2 tablespoons)	12 – 13 minutes	Scrub well and prick
Potatoes, baked	4 medium-sized	–	12 – 16 minutes	Scrub well and prick
Potatoes, mashed	4 medium-sized	45 mℓ (3 tablespoons)	16 – 18 minutes	Peel and cut into cubes
Pumpkin	450 g (1 lb)	45 mℓ (3 tablespoons)	8 – 10 minutes	Peel and dice
Spinach	450 g (1 lb)	–	6 – 9 minutes	Cook with water that clings to the leaves Remove thick stalks
Squash, hubbard	450 g (1 lb)	45 mℓ (3 tablespoons)	8 – 10 minutes	Peel and dice
Squash, patty pan	4 medium-sized	45 mℓ (3 tablespoons)	5 – 7 minutes	Wash well and prick
Sweet potatoes	4 medium-sized	45 mℓ (3 tablespoons)	12 – 15 minutes	Peel and slice
Sweetcorn	4 ears	–	7 – 8 minutes	Rotate half-way through cooking time
Tomatoes, sliced	4 medium-sized	–	4 – 5 minutes	Slice, dot with butter
Tomatoes, stewed	4 medium-sized	15 mℓ (1 tablespoon)	6 – 8 minutes	Peel and chop roughly
Turnips	3 medium-sized	30 mℓ (2 tablespoons)	10 – 12 minutes	Peel and dice

VENISON

Venison is the name given to meat from any deer or antelope. It is dry meat, with very little fat, so it should be well barded with pork or bacon fat before being roasted or braised. All cuts are improved by being marinated either in a wine-based marinade or buttermilk. Venison has a strong flavour which combines well with sweet jellies such as red currant, apple and cranberry, as well as chestnut purée. One of these is often added to the accompanying sauce or casserole liquid. Venison requires long, slow cooking to become tender so time is not really saved when it is cooked in the microwave, but the kitchen and house remain cool and free of the normal strong venison smell.

Braised venison

Full Power, High (70%), Medium (50%)
1 hour 40 minutes

1 – 1.5 kg (2¼ – 3 lb) venison, cubed
3 bacon rashers, rinds removed, coarsely chopped
1 quantity brown sauce*
45 mℓ (3 tablespoons) apple jelly
100 mℓ (3½ fl oz) single cream
12 small onions
pinch of nutmeg
45 mℓ (3 tablespoons) ruby port
salt (optional)

Marinade
500 mℓ (16 fl oz) buttermilk
1 small onion, quartered
1 carrot, coarsely chopped
1 celery stick, coarsely chopped
black peppercorns
1 bay leaf
6 allspice berries

Place meat in a large earthenware bowl and add all marinade ingredients. Cover and refrigerate for 24 hours, turning meat at least three times. Drain meat from marinade and reserve. Place meat and bacon in a casserole, add brown sauce and stir to coat. Cover, microwave on Full Power for 5 minutes. Reduce power to High (70%) for 30 minutes, stir well. Cover and microwave on Medium (50%) for

about 1 hour or until tender, stirring from time to time. Add a little marinade if the sauce becomes too thick. Stir in remaining ingredients and microwave for 5 minutes more to heat through.
Serves 6

VICHYSSOISE

A soup with simple beginnings. It is made with leeks and potatoes and is usually served cold. American-based French chef, Louis Diat, created this smooth creamy soup and named it after Vichy, as a tribute to the wonderful cooking in this area. Like all soups, this one microwaves perfectly.

Vichyssoise

Full Power
20 minutes

6 potatoes, diced
6 leeks, thinly sliced
45 mℓ (3 tablespoons) finely chopped celery
generous pinch of dried tarragon
45 g (1½ oz) butter or margarine
750 mℓ (1¼ pints) chicken stock
125 mℓ (4 fl oz) dry white wine
salt and pepper
250 mℓ (8 fl oz) single cream
chopped chives

Combine potatoes, leeks, celery, tarragon, butter and 60 mℓ (4 tablespoons) of the chicken stock in a casserole. Cover and microwave on Full Power for 10 minutes, stirring twice. Add remaining stock and microwave, covered, for 8 – 10 minutes or until vegetables are very tender. Add wine and season with salt and pepper. Purée the mixture in a blender or food processor and chill until needed. To serve, stir in cream. Garnish with chopped chives.
Serves 6

VINE LEAVES *See* Dolmades

VINEGAR

Vinegar comes from the French 'vin aigre' which means 'sour wine'. The discovery that fermented wine could be used as a condiment led to the development of a great variety of vinegars. Because of its acetic acid content, vinegar is widely used as a preservative for pickles and chutneys. Salad dressings and certain sauces also contain vinegar for piquancy.

There are many vinegars to choose from. Cider vinegar, made from apple pulp, is widely used in cooking. It also makes good salad dressings and can be substituted for rice vinegar in oriental cooking. Distilled vinegar is colourless, very strong, and is often used for pickling. Wine vinegar, made from red or white wine or from sherry, is used for sauces and for mayonnaise. Malt vinegar is also very strong and is mainly used for pickling. Flavoured vinegars are made from herbs, raspberries or other fruits soaked in wine vinegar. These vinegars add subtle flavour to sauces and salad dressings.

Herb vinegar

Medium (50%)
2 minutes

1 litre (1¾ pints) wine vinegar
60 g (2 oz) fresh herbs, such as tarragon, thyme, rosemary or basil

Place vinegar in a glass jug and microwave on Medium (50%) for about 2 minutes, or until just warm. Place herbs in a jar and pour vinegar over. Seal and stand for about two weeks, then strain into a clean jar and seal.
Makes 1 litre (1¾ pints)

Spiced vinegar

High (70%)
4 minutes

1 litre (1¾ pints) cider vinegar
75 g (2½ oz) caster sugar
10 mℓ (2 teaspoons) whole cloves
5 mℓ (1 teaspoon) whole allspice
3 mace blades
10 mℓ (2 teaspoons) celery seeds
10 mℓ (2 teaspoons) mustard seed
10 mℓ (2 teaspoons) whole black peppercorns
10 mℓ (2 teaspoons) turmeric
10 mℓ (2 teaspoons) sliced ginger root
1 garlic clove, peeled

Place all ingredients, except garlic, in a large glass bowl and microwave on High (70%) for 3 – 4 minutes, or until hot but not boiling. Pour mixture into a sterilized jar and add garlic. Seal and stand in a cool place for three weeks before using. If desired, strain spiced vinegar into a clean jar. Combine with oil for a delicious French dressing.
Makes 1 litre (1¾ pints)

Raspberry vinegar

Medium (50%)
2 minutes

1 litre (1¾ pints) wine vinegar
75 g (2½ oz) fresh raspberries
30 mℓ (2 tablespoons) caster sugar

Place vinegar in a jug and microwave on Medium (50%) for 2 minutes until warm. Place raspberries in a large bowl and sprinkle with sugar. Pour the warm vinegar over, cover and stand for 24 hours. Gently pour mixture into a jar, seal and stand for two weeks. Then, when the vinegar has a rosy colour, strain into a clean jar and seal.
Makes 1 litre (1¾ pints)

W

WALNUTS

The two-lobed seed of the walnut tree is much used in cooking for confectionery, baking, salads and with chicken or meat dishes. Walnuts are high in oil content and pressed walnut oil is prized for use in salad dressings. Young green walnuts are pickled in vinegar and are generally served with cold roast meats.

Glazed walnuts

Full Power
5 minutes

60 g (2 oz) butter
100 g (3½ oz) soft brown sugar
generous pinch of cinnamon
pinch of allspice
pinch of ground cloves
300 g (11 oz) walnut halves

Place butter in a casserole and microwave on Full Power for 45 seconds or until melted. Stir in brown sugar and spices, mixing well. Microwave for 1½ minutes. Stir in walnuts, coating well, then microwave for 2 – 3 minutes more. Turn nuts out on a large piece of waxed paper and spread out to cool. Store in an airtight container.
Makes 300 g (11 oz)

Pickled walnuts

Full Power
15 minutes

2 kg (4¼ lb) green walnuts
1 litre (1¾ pints) water
200 g (7 oz) salt
1 litre (1¾ pints) white vinegar
30 mℓ (2 tablespoons) pickling spice
15 mℓ (1 tablespoon) mustard seed

Prick the skins of the walnuts very well with a fork, place nuts in a non-metallic dish. Microwave water and salt on Full Power for 5 minutes, pour over nuts. Stand for five days. Drain, turn nuts on to a large piece of muslin, allow to dry in the sun for about four days until the nuts have turned black. Turn nuts from time to time. Pack black nuts into jars. Combine remaining ingredients, microwave for 10 minutes, strain and pour over nuts. Cover, label and store for at least three weeks before using.
Makes about 2 kg (4 lb)

WATERMELON PRESERVE

A crisp preserve made from thick watermelon rinds steeped in a honey-like syrup. It can be spread on bread or toast and may also be served as part of a dessert course after a Chinese meal. Like all preserves, it may be made in a fraction of the time taken conventionally by using the microwave.

Watermelon preserve

Full Power
50 minutes

500 g (18 oz) watermelon rind, skin removed
1 litre (1¾ pints) cold water
2.5 mℓ (½ teaspoon) slaked lime
1 litre (1¾ pints) boiling water
600 g (1 lb 5 oz) preserving sugar
700 mℓ (22 fl oz) water
pinch of cream of tartar
15 mℓ (1 tablespoon) lemon juice
2.5-cm (1-inch) piece of cinnamon stick
small piece of root ginger

Remove all traces of pink flesh from the white rind, prick well on both sides. Cut into 2.5-cm (1-inch) pieces, place in an earthenware bowl. Add cold water and slaked lime, cover and soak overnight. Drain, rinse well and soak in clean water for 2 hours. Place boiling water in a large bowl, add pieces of rind, cover and microwave on Full Power for 15 minutes until the rinds start to become transparent, drain.

Combine sugar and water, microwave for 10 minutes. Add cream of tartar, lemon juice, cinnamon stick and ginger. Add peel, microwave for 25 – 30 minutes until the rinds have a pale golden colour and a syrupy taste. Pack rinds into hot sterilized jars. Remove cinnamon and ginger, fill jars with syrup. Cover and seal immediately, leave for one week before using.
Makes about 900 g (2 lb)

Note: To sterilize jars *see* Jams and Jellies.

WAX

Candle or paraffin wax will not melt in the microwave as the wax is electrically neutral and microwaves pass straight through without affecting it in any way.

Sealing wax does melt in the microwave, but takes a long time. Microwave half a stick of red sealing wax on High (70%) for 4 – 5 minutes to soften.

WELSH RAREBIT

This dish dates back to the 18th century when it was often served as the 'savoury' course in a meal. Today, however, it usually makes a quick and tasty snack. The cheese melts very easily in the microwave and will not 'catch' on the base of the bowl. Take care not to overcook or the cheese will become stringy.

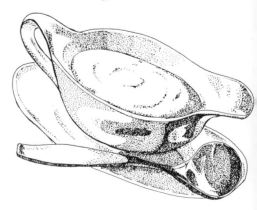

Welsh rarebit

High (70%), Medium (50%)
8 minutes

200 g (7 oz) Cheddar cheese, grated
10 mℓ (2 teaspoons) plain flour
5 mℓ (1 teaspoon) dry mustard
5 mℓ (1 teaspoon) Worcestershire sauce
pinch of cayenne
60 mℓ (4 tablespoons) beer
60 mℓ (4 tablespoons) milk
1 egg yolk
2 slices of processed cheese
4 – 6 slices of bread, toasted and buttered

Place cheese in a bowl, sprinkle with flour and mustard, stir to combine. Add all ingredients except egg yolk, processed cheese and toast, stir to combine. Microwave on High (70%) for about 4 minutes, until cheese has melted, stir frequently. Whisk egg yolk lightly, and add together with the processed cheese to mixture in bowl, stir well. Microwave on Medium (50%) for 4 – 5 minutes, whisking frequently, until piping hot. Spoon over slices of toast.
Serves 4

WHISKY
Whisky is distilled from malted barley which gives it a distinct flavour. The waters of Scotland and the superior quality of the barley grown there produce some of the finest whisky in the world. Use whisky in place of brandy for flavouring rich fruit cakes, desserts and hot drinks.
See also Alcohol.

Hot toddy

Full Power
2 minutes

30 mℓ (2 tablespoons) whisky
30 mℓ (2 tablespoons) honey
lemon juice
water

Combine whisky and honey in a cup or mug. Stir in a little lemon juice, add water to almost fill the cup. Microwave on Full Power for 2 minutes. Serve hot.
Serves 1

WHITE SAUCE *See* Sauces

WINE *See* Beverages and Jelly

YEAST COOKERY

Yeast breads baked in the microwave do not brown, nor do they develop a crisp crust as they do when baked conventionally. Hot, dry air is needed to dry the outer surfaces, giving the crust its characteristic brown colour and crispy texture. However, toppings of cheese, sesame or poppy seeds, or crushed wheat will help to give the necessary colour and texture to microwaved breads. Soft yeast breads that do not have the traditional crust are probably the most successful breads to bake in the microwave.

Dough for yeast breads can be proved in the microwave in about half the normal time by using short bursts of microwave energy with resting periods of about 10 minutes. For those recipes requiring scalded milk, or heated milk and butter mixtures, the microwave will be a great help.' Once the dough has risen, it can be shaped and baked conventionally.

See also Beesting Cake, Rum Baba and Savarin.

To prove yeast dough

Mix and knead dough according to recipe directions. Place dough in a large, greased bowl and cover. Microwave on Full Power for 15 seconds, then rest in the microwave oven for 8 – 10 minutes. Repeat the process two or three times until the dough has doubled in bulk. It can then be knocked back and shaped as desired. If a glass or ceramic ovenproof container is used, the dough may be proved a second time in the microwave before baking conventionally.

To defrost compressed yeast

Place 30 g (1 oz) frozen compressed yeast in a small bowl and cover. Microwave on Medium (50%) for 15 seconds, rest for 1 minute. Microwave on Defrost (30%) for 5 seconds, rest for 1 minute. Repeat microwaving on Defrost (30%) and resting two or three times more until yeast softens.

Savoury brown loaf

Full Power, Medium (50%)
15 minutes

250 g (9 oz) plain flour
250 g (9 oz) wholewheat flour
15 mℓ (1 tablespoon) dried yeast
5 mℓ (1 teaspoon) salt
5 mℓ (1 teaspoon) mixed herbs
60 g (2 oz) butter
250 mℓ (8 fl oz) milk
15 g (½ oz) butter
30 mℓ (2 tablespoons) finely chopped onion
90 g (3 oz) Cheddar cheese, grated
15 mℓ (1 tablespoon) wheatgerm
15 mℓ (1 tablespoon) sesame seeds

Combine plain flour, wholemeal flour, yeast, salt and mixed herbs in a mixing bowl. Cut butter into cubes and rub into dry ingredients. Microwave milk in a jug on Full Power for 1½ minutes and add to dry ingredients. Mix to form a soft, but not sticky, dough. Place butter in a small jug, microwave for 15 seconds, add onion and microwave for 1 minute. Drain onion, saving butter. Knead dough until smooth and elastic, working in the chopped onions and two-thirds of the cheese. Shape dough into a smooth ball and place in a well-greased, deep, 17.5-cm (7-inch) soufflé dish.

Cover with kitchen paper and prove in the microwave by microwaving on Full Power for 15 seconds, then standing for 10 minutes. Repeat process at least once more or until dough has doubled in bulk. Brush with reserved melted butter and sprinkle with wheatgerm, sesame seeds and remaining cheese. Microwave on Medium (50%) for 6 minutes, then on Full Power for 3 – 4 minutes. Gently remove loaf from the dish, place on kitchen paper on base of microwave or turntable and microwave for 1 minute. Stand for 5 minutes, then cool on a wire rack. This bread is best eaten within two days of baking.
Makes 1 round loaf

Note: To bake bread in a loaf dish, shape into loaf after kneading, place in well-greased microwave loaf dish and proceed as above.

Variations
Ham and Cheese Loaf: Proceed as above, working in 60 mℓ (4 tablespoons) finely chopped cooked ham with the cheese during kneading.
Garlic Herb Loaf: Add 10 mℓ (2 teaspoons) freshly chopped parsley to the dry ingredients, and 1 finely chopped garlic clove to the onion. Proceed as above.
Brown Bread: Omit the herbs, cheese and onion from the mixture and add 10 mℓ (2 teaspoons) soft brown sugar to the dry ingredients. Proceed with method as above.

Microwave muffin loaf

Full Power
8 minutes

500 mℓ (16 fl oz) milk
125 mℓ (4 fl oz) water
15 mℓ (1 tablespoon) caster sugar
30 g (1 oz) fresh yeast
600 g (1 lb 5 oz) plain flour
5 mℓ (1 teaspoon) salt
2.5 mℓ (½ teaspoon) bicarbonate of soda
cornmeal

Place milk and water in a jug, microwave on Full Power for 1 – 1½ minutes until warm. Add yeast and sugar, and stir until yeast is well combined. Sprinkle mixture with 30 mℓ (2 tablespoons) of the measured plain flour and cover with vented plastic wrap. Microwave for 10 seconds on Full Power, stand for 3 minutes and repeat once more. The top will begin to foam. Meanwhile sift remaining flour, salt and bicarbonate of soda into a large bowl. Pour in the yeast mixture and mix with an electric mixer for about 4 minutes. Grease two 25 x 12.5-cm (10 x 5-inch) microwave loaf dishes and sprinkle a little cornmeal over the base and sides. Spoon in the bread mixture, dust tops with a little more cornmeal. Cover with plastic

wrap, microwave for 15 seconds, then rest for 10 minutes. Repeat two or three times until the bread has doubled in size. Microwave each loaf separately for 5½ – 6½ minutes. The surface of the cooked loaves will be pale in colour. Stand for 10 minutes before removing from the pan. To serve, slice and toast, serve with butter and honey or syrup.
Makes 2 loaves

Rye round

Full Power
8 minutes

5 mℓ (1 teaspoon) dried yeast
10 mℓ (2 teaspoons) molasses
425 mℓ (14 fl oz) warm water
350 g (12 oz) plain flour
150 g (5 oz) rye flour
generous pinch of salt
oil
caraway seeds

In a bowl, combine yeast, molasses and half the water, sprinkle with 30 mℓ (2 tablespoons) of measured flour, cover with plastic wrap. Microwave on Full Power for 10 seconds, stand for 5 minutes until foam appears on the surface. Sift flours, salt and 5 mℓ (1 teaspoon) caraway seeds into a large mixing bowl. Add yeast mixture and enough of the remaining liquid to form a workable dough, knead with an electric mixer for about 4 minutes. Cover bowl with plastic wrap, microwave for 15 seconds, rest dough for 10 minutes. Repeat process at least three times, until dough has doubled in size. Knock back and knead dough until smooth, shape into a round. Place into a greased round 22.5-cm (9-inch) casserole. Brush top with oil, sprinkle with rye flour and a few caraway seeds and cover with plastic wrap. Prove by microwaving for 15 seconds, rest for 5 minutes and repeat at least twice more until bread has doubled in size. Microwave for 5 – 6 minutes, stand for 15 minutes before turning out on to a wire rack to cool.
Makes 1 x 22.5-cm (9-inch) loaf

YOGHURT
As far back as 500 BC, Indian yogis believed that yoghurt was food for the gods and it is still an essential ingredient in the diets of many people who live in India and the Middle East.

Yoghurt is fermented milk. Both cow's milk and goat's milk are used and the milk may be full cream or skimmed. For a successful yoghurt culture, commercial natural yoghurt should be added to the warm milk mixture. Yoghurt cultures grow at a temperature between 40 °C (104 °F) and 43 °C (109 °F). This is very easily achieved in the microwave, but do not stir or move the culture while it is incubating as it will separate. Refrigerate for a few hours before serving.

The uses for yoghurt are numerous. It may be eaten plain or with fruit and nuts, used for salad dressings and baked potato toppings. It may also be used as a marinade to ensure tenderness. Substitute low-fat yoghurt for creaming soups, sauces and desserts for healthier eating. When using yoghurt for cooking, especially when it is to be added to soups and starters, it is necessary to stabilize it to prevent it from separating. Combine 5 ml (1 teaspoon) cornflour with 15 ml (1 tablespoon) water. Add this mixture to 375 ml (12 fl oz) yoghurt and stir to combine.

Creamy yoghurt

Low (15%)
1½ hours

90 g (3 oz) skimmed milk powder
690 mℓ (22 fl oz) warm water
170 mℓ (5½ fl oz) evaporated milk
10 mℓ (2 teaspoons) soft brown sugar
45 mℓ (3 tablespoons) natural yoghurt

Combine skimmed milk powder and warm water in a large bowl. Add remaining ingredients and mix well. Cover with vented plastic wrap. Microwave on Low (15%) for 1½ hours. Cool, then refrigerate.
Makes 900 mℓ (28 fl oz)

Homemade yoghurt

Full power, Low (15%)
1¼ hours

500 mℓ (16 fl oz) milk
15 mℓ (1 tablespoon) natural yoghurt
30 mℓ (2 tablespoons) dried full-cream milk powder

Pour the milk into a large bowl. Cover with vented plastic wrap. Microwave for 6 minutes on Full Power. Uncover and cool over a basin of cold water until warm to the touch, about 45 °C (113 °F). Add the yoghurt and the milk powder, and whisk to combine. Cover once more. Microwave on Low (15%) for 70 minutes. Cool and refrigerate.
Makes 500 mℓ (16 fl oz)

Chicken in yoghurt

High (70%)
11 minutes

5 – 6 chicken breast fillets
15 mℓ (1 tablespoon) water
pinch of turmeric
salt and black pepper
pinch of cayenne
150 mℓ (5 fl oz) yoghurt
100 mℓ (3½ fl oz) single cream
5 mℓ (1 teaspoon) cornflour
paprika or chopped parsley

Slice chicken into long shreds, 1-cm (½-inch) wide, place in a small casserole. Combine water, turmeric, salt, pepper and cayenne. Sprinkle over chicken, cover and stand for 20 minutes. Microwave on High (70%) for 6 minutes, stir. Combine remaining ingredients, pour over chicken, stir to coat chicken. Cover, microwave for 5 minutes, stirring once during cooking time. Sprinkle with paprika or parsley before serving.
Serves 4

ZABAGLIONE
This light, foamy dessert is an Italian dish made with egg yolks, sugar and Marsala all whipped together and served hot with wafer biscuits.

Zabaglione cream

Full Power, Medium (50%)
5 minutes

125 mℓ (4 fl oz) whipping cream
75 g (2½ oz) caster sugar
8 egg yolks
125 mℓ (4 fl oz) Marsala
15 mℓ (1 tablespoon) finely grated orange rind

Whip the cream with 15 mℓ (1 tablespoon) of the sugar. Spoon into six serving bowls and chill. Add remaining sugar to the egg yolks and beat with an electric mixer until very light and fluffy. Place marsala in a jug and microwave on Full Power for 1½ minutes. Gradually add hot marsala to the egg yolks, beating constantly until well mixed. Microwave on Medium (50%) for 3 minutes, beating very well after each minute. The mixture should be thickened and smooth. Beat in orange rind and spoon over whipped cream. Serve immediately.
Serves 6

ZUCCHINI *See* Courgette